FROM BOTH SIDES NOW

Paratrooper, Green Beret, Fighter Pilot

Colonel Harry C. Stevenson
USAF (Ret.)

NewFawn Press
Bulverde, Texas

FIRST EDITION

Library of Congress Control Number: 2017949591

NewFawn Press, Bulverde, TX

Print Book ISBN: 978-0-692-71989-3

eBook ISBN: 978-0-692-71990-9

1. Stevenson, Harry C. (Steve), 1944 -, 2. Vietnam War, 1961-1975 – Infantry, Special Forces, 3. Vietnam War, 1961-1975 – Tactical Fighters - 4. Vietnam War, 1961-1975 – Personal Narrative, American, 5. Fighter Pilots A-10 – United States – Biography, 6. Biography and Autobiography – Military.

2

DEDICATION

To my wonderful wife, Claire, who stuck with me and supported me through all the moves, tough tours and foreign countries. Some places were my best assignments while being the toughest for her. Through it all, she raised two good boys to become good grown men and encouraged me to put pen to paper.

INTRODUCTION

In 1967, Ms. Joni Mitchell composed a song entitled *"Both Sides Now."* My career reflected much of that song as I had the opportunity to look at war and peace from multiple perspectives.

"I've looked at life from both sides now
From up and down, and still somehow
It's life's illusions I recall
I really don't know life at all"

CONTENTS

Grunt

GRUNT: *An infantryman. The term is associated with frequent utterances made by said infantryman as he carries 80-90 pound tactical loads including weapon, ammunition, food, clothes, water, grenades, claymore mines, batteries, first aid kits, insect repellant, ponchos, poncho liners, ruck sacks, load bearing equipment and various knives, entrenching tools and other special equipment as he moves into remote areas in search of the enemy. His job is to locate and destroy the enemy, often up close and personal. The title "Grunt" was and is a source of considerable pride for those who earn it.*

South Vietnam 1967 - 1969

1

One Minute!

Over the sounds of howling wind and pounding rotor blades, the Huey crew chief raised one finger and yelled "One minute!"

I inched across the floor of the Huey helicopter toward the open door. My CAR-15 rifle hung across my chest as I pulled the pin from a red smoke grenade and stuffed the pin into my left breast pocket. I slowly stepped out onto the right skid of the chopper, gripped the forward door edge with my left hand, and balanced on the skid.

Flying low at 90 knots, the Huey rounded a green forested ridgeline toward a series of small, brown, dry rice paddies. As the helo would bank or skid, my sixty-pound rucksack tried to sling me into or off the helicopter.

Final approach into the landing zone (LZ): the leading choppers began to flare to a split-second hover, red smoke billowed next to them, and, from the right tree-line - multi-colored tracers laced the air.

A "hot" LZ.

"Sheee-itt! How did you get your young ass in this situation, Lieutenant Stevenson?"

I arrived as an Infantry platoon leader in my company of the 101st Airborne Division in Vietnam's Quang Ngai Provence in early 1967. My first helicopter ride from the 1st Brigade base camp at Duc Pho was a clue that war is different from training: no passenger seats, no cabin doors, just loads of ammunition and supplies on the floor, and three passengers seated on the floor. At Ft. Benning, when we conducted our one and only airmobile training exercise, everyone had canvas web seats and seat belts. In Vietnam: none.

I climbed in, moved to the center, leaned my huge rucksack against the rear cabin wall and faced forward to look between the two pilots, Our Warrant Officer pilots cranked up the engine which emitted a clicking of the engine igniters before it gave a slight "whump" of ignition, whined to life and slowly began to move the rotor blades. The rotor blades sped up and soon with increased "whup, whup" rotor sound, a lot of flying dust and finally cool air, the bird lifted to a low hover; then from mere inches off the ground, the nose of the chopper dipped so that I was looking at the horizon line almost up to the top of the front windscreen. Momentary panic told me "Helicopters are not supposed to fly this way!" We accelerated forward with the rotor blades just missing the ground and then a barb wire fence. Passing through translational lift, the chopper's nose came up, climbing, and the aircraft assumed a more normal level flying attitude.

We turned westward, away from the coastline of the South China Sea, and I watched the terrain passing underneath, feeling the wind and aircraft vibrations. This would be fun if I wasn't going to war. I noticed that the experienced troops sat sideways with their legs out the left side of the cabin and their feet almost touching the skid. I carefully leaned out the right door to see more countryside, my heart in my throat, afraid of falling. I thought: "Well, this is it. You have been training for years and now you are about to become a platoon leader in combat. Damn, I hope I am ready."

I was not impressed by a few of the veteran Infantry lieutenants I met. Was survival a function of training and leadership or purely the luck of the draw? I sat in that Huey and felt the cold physical fear. It was the fear of failing as a Platoon Leader: I never feared for my own safety. OK, stop that kind of thinking and get ready to lead and learn.

My helicopter bypassed our battalion Tactical Operations Center (TOC), which shared a hilltop with an artillery battery, and we flew directly to Cobra Company, set up on the east side of the Song Ve river. We flew at an altitude of 3000 feet to stay well clear of the heavily forested ridgeline before entering the Song Ve valley, where the river flowed from south to north, then turned northeast across the coastal plain and out to the South China Sea. I leaned out the right side of the chopper: again, no doors, as they were removed to reduce aircraft weight, and I tried to keep up with our position on my map. Soon, the chopper began a rapid right-hand spiral. For the first two revolutions, I couldn't determine where we were going to land. Then, descending through 1000 feet altitude, I saw a smoke grenade ignite and send bright yellow smoke streaming downwind across a large clearing. The chopper continued the rapid descent, slowed, turned into the wind and I could now make out dozens of bodies on or moving around the LZ.

This was the second time I was assuming a position for which I didn't feel ready. Interestingly, years later, General Colin Powell said if you did not feel uncomfortable, you were not being challenged enough as a leader. Obviously, I was being challenged enough. Serving as a mortar platoon leader at Ft Campbell was one leadership experience, albeit mostly personnel issues, training and maintenance. There was no way of knowing the answer to the questions: Are you ready? How can I remember everything that I have been taught? How will I do when the real shooting starts? Where do I get more information? How will I stack up against the other platoon leaders? I prayed I would learn company and platoon procedures fast enough to avoid doing anything dumb. The men of the second platoon expected me to make good decisions quickly and take actions to protect them from unnecessary risks. I didn't have to be the best at land navigation, although I was soon one of the best. I sure as hell was not expected to be a "shooter" or to walk point on patrols. My job was to be a filter and a conduit between my troopers and the company commander, implementing his plans and looking out for my men. I was there to get support: air, artillery, gunships, whatever was necessary for my platoon.

I recalled an expression from Jump School that stayed with me: "I don't mind dying; but I don't want to embarrass myself doing it." This is not to say I wasn't terrified when bullets started to prune trees or cut grass around me. That fear is almost paralyzing when you get caught in a relatively exposed position as the fight starts. But I fell back on another Infantry School standard: "What are you going to do now, Lieutenant?" The answer was almost always "Move!" Find a place that's a bit safer and then take the fight to the enemy.

Longevity was an unheard-of concept for infantry platoon leaders. You *were* going to be wounded; the question was when and how badly. As I joined the Cobras via that resupply helicopter, there were three other platoon leaders with combat experience in the field. Six days later I was the sole officer platoon leader because the others became casualties. Lt Benjamin Wells mentored me for three days, but was killed in an ambush. The 4th platoon leader, who was once wounded and returned to the line, came down with acute malaria on my fifth day and the other platoon leader set off a booby trap and was wounded on my sixth day. The sun came up on day seven and I was the only officer platoon leader left in Cobra Company. The other three platoons were now led by great NCOs until more officers arrived "in country" or were transferred from battalion staff. I found that my platoon was led, pending my arrival, by my Platoon Sergeant.

My helicopter landed in a clearing near the Song Ve River. Dark green forested hills overlooked the company resupply area on three sides and from the far side of the river. From the air, I discerned the large, 200-meter diameter, defensive circle that the company had established in an area of knee-high grass. From above, I could make out the connecting paths between the two or three-man fighting positions on the perimeter and the trails leading to a central location that was obviously the company command post (CP). The central position presented eight or ten rucksacks arranged in three clusters, at least two tall radio antennas erected to 10 – 12 feet (called 292s), and several smaller "whip" antennas sticking up from the rucksacks.

The helicopter landed about 20 meters from the CP and I saw troopers carrying off the supplies that were being distributed next to our landing site. With the chopper still twenty feet in the air, the three veteran troopers were outside standing on the skids. One trooper held only a light grip on a door edge and the guy behind him balanced on the skid by leaning back against the floor of the slick. I swung my legs over the floor edge and slowly inched my butt and rucksack forward with a death grip on the door frame behind the pilot. There was no blowing sand or dirt as we approached the ground, just some stray grass blown away from the chopper. The troopers on the opposite side hopped off while the chopper was still about a foot off the ground, and, after the chopper touched down, I finally put my full weight on the skid and stepped onto the ground, a lot less spryly than the veterans. By the time I alighted, two shirtless, troopers started unloading supplies from each side of the chopper so it could get back in the air as rapidly as possible. There was no use offering "Charlie" a good target.

One of the company commander's Radio Operators (RTOs) approached me; and asked, "You Lieutenant Stevenson?"

"Yes."

At least I was expected and I'm sure I was easy to pick out with new, clean jungle fatigues, looking healthy and well-fed. I wore 2LT rank insignia, a 101st shoulder patch and a nametag on my jungies. As I approached the CP, I noticed none of the paratroopers wore any insignia or patches. Even the Company Commander (the "CO") wore no rank or name tag. The RTO led me to the company CP area, the collection of rucksacks and radios, where I met my company commanding officer: CPT Bill Northquest.

Northquest was a veteran with over ten months "in country" and had been the CO for the past four months. He showed the weight loss and tired appearance that I soon associated with the paratroopers who spent hours each day carrying a 40–70-pound rucksack up and down hills in staggering heat and humidity, and then suddenly engaging in firefights. A 9-year Army veteran with previous company command jobs, Northquest observed and trained his platoon leaders to be good in all aspects of combat leadership in the forests and valleys of Vietnam. He demanded excellence in everything: if a platoon leader could not precisely state his location, Cobra 6 would chew his butt in person or over the radio; or if your platoon was not well set up at night or made noise while moving. All Northquest's lieutenants became excellent combat leaders - if they stayed alive that long.

I received his welcome, a briefing on standard procedures, and his expectations of me as a platoon leader. He said my platoon would travel with the company CP for a few days to let me get the routine down. CPT Northquest ended with the best advice for a new LT: listen to and communicate with your NCOs; learn from your platoon sergeant. Then he called "2-6 Bravo" over, platoon sergeant, SSGT Amos T. Griffey, Jr.

Following CPT Northquest's introduction of SSGT Griffey, "Griff" and I walked from the company CP over to the quadrant of the perimeter defended by the 2nd platoon. Like an individual's radio call sign, the second platoon as a unit was referred to phonetically as "two-zero" (2-0). Everyone in the company was accustomed to similar titles, even the company CO. Captain Northquest, and later COs, used the call sign "Cobra 6." Cobra 6's instruction in the morning briefing might sound like: "2-0 leads out up that western ridge, followed by 3-0. 1-0, 4-0 and the CP will move up the eastern ridge."

Each platoon leader added a numeric "6" to the 2-0 call sign, so I was known as "Cobra 2-6"; the first platoon leader was "Cobra 1-6", etc. The senior NCO in a unit added a "Bravo" to the leader's call sign; so,

13

my platoon sergeant, SSGT Griffey, was "2-6 Bravo"; the company first sergeant was "Cobra 6 Bravo" and the company XO was "Cobra 5." He had to be different!

Call signs on external radio nets randomly rotated and replaced the "Cobra" portion of the call sign, while on the internal frequencies the numeric stayed the same. By mid-1968, we received secure, encoded radio equipment in the PRC-77; and we did not change call signs as frequently on external comm Nets. The task of carrying the radio fell to one of the platoon soldiers, who most often volunteered for the job. The role of the RTO was never appreciated in units that did not hump a heavy rucksack. The RTO carried all his personal gear plus the PRC-25 radio and extra batteries. The RTO's position in life was to be within arm's reach of his leader, be that a platoon leader, company commander, platoon sergeant, artillery Forward Observer (FO) or another leader. At night, I always required one of my RTOs to sleep within three feet of me, with the radio between us.

Second Platoon, Cobra Company, 1st Battalion (Airborne) 327th Infantry - When I joined the 2nd platoon, my platoon sergeant, SSGT Amos T. Griffey, Jr., was a career NCO with 11 years in the Army, all it with the 101st Abn Div. He was a short, stout man. A broad face with a roll of skin across the back of his neck added to his stocky appearance. He kept his curly black hair closely cropped like a good paratrooper - although, whenever we were in the field for 30 plus days, I noticed a bit of gray beginning to show in the "longer" hair. SSGT Griffey had a quiet demeanor, and, although he demanded attention to detail from the platoon NCOs and troopers, I never heard him raise his voice.

SSGT Griffey - Photo by Fox Ford

He was all business with the platoon and his business was to keep them alive. He was in the field for his entire tour and was capable of leading the platoon before I arrived and in my absence.

Every new platoon leader needs a SSGT Griffey when they arrive in combat. Each evening when we were in the field, I held a discussion with SSGT Griffey that became a part of my professional development as an officer and certainly as a combat platoon leader. We covered the day's actions, personnel issues, the "big picture" from battalion level to the Vietnam War and then the situation back in the States. These evening conversations with my NCOs continued over years, particularly with my own 1st Sergeant, 1SG Alton Barker, when I became a Company Commander.

On paper, my infantry platoon was four squads with eleven troopers in each squad. On the ground in Vietnam that squad trooper number varied from five to eight men. I was fat as a platoon when we totaled 30 men and I remember being down to 17 troopers for a few days. I started my tour with three squads and about 25 troopers.

My first squad was led by Sergeant (SGT) Dennis Ruth from New Jersey. He was an average size African-American E-5 who had been in country four months and showed good skill at directing his squad and ensuring they did it right, be it setting up for the night defensive perimeter, patrolling or cleaning weapons. SGT Ruth was a "Shake and Bake" E-5, meaning an instant NCO who attended the NCO course right after Basic and Airborne training.

Outstanding enlisted soldiers went to OCS to be trained as 2LTs. Other soldiers who showed potential were selected for E-5 school and upon graduation were promoted to E-5. It probably took SSGT Griffey six years to make E-5 because he was a professional NCO before the Vietnam War force buildup. The derogatory and yet complimentary term for a soldier like Sergeant Griffey was "Lifer." He was in the Army for a career, for "life", not two or three years and out like our youngest troopers whether draftees or volunteers. A Lifer was also the enforcer of Army rules and regulations.

The Shake & Bakes were new soldiers trained to be infantry team and squad leaders. As the war escalated, more and more units received instant E-5s in small-unit leadership positions. My experience with "Shake and Bake" NCOs at Ft Campbell was not all positive, but I soon realized that, while the NCO course produced good combat infantry sergeants, they lacked professional development in the skills of maintenance, training and administration needed in the "garrison life" of a stateside unit.

The second squad leader was SGT Anthony J. Tinsley, a rangy athletic troop from Louisville, Kentucky, and a career NCO with six years Army time. "SGT T" was exceptionally well read, despite having only a high school education. He understood the big picture of company

15

and battalion operations and was excellent at adjusting artillery fires and map reading.

The third squad was led by SGT Patrick Lacy, from Granbury, Texas, who truly led his men from the front and by example in every task. SGT Lacy and I developed a friendly rivalry as to who could best navigate along the forested ridges, draws and exposed river bottoms. It gave me immense pleasure to be more accurate on our location. The challenge made us both better map readers, a skill that came in very handy when I later became the senior platoon leader in C Company. SGT Lacy's squad had a young black trooper from Roxbury, Massachusetts: Willie C. Hooker. The "Hook", as he referred to himself, had a real back-on-the-block personality and proved himself a great field soldier. He was responsible for my introduction to Motown music and for becoming a lifelong fan of music by Gladys Knight and Tina Turner.

I soon earned the title of "Boonie Rat." The term evolved from working out in the "boondocks" and the term was applied in a derogatory manner by the soldiers that worked in the rear areas or large base camps. Boonie Rats were dirty, stinky, unshaven troops who were in the rear area only to resupply, drink, and raise hell. The term was one of respect when used by the troops that humped a heavy rucksack and searched for a fight with "Charlie." These were the infantry, artillery, medic and engineer troopers who carried all their possessions in a rucksack and everyday took the fight to the bad guys. While troops at battalion and higher were combatants, they enjoyed many comforts that Boonie Rats did not - days without clothing resupply, clean water, and/or adequate rations. Often our idea of cleaning up was wading a fast running creek. We avoided still water ponds because they were populated by water leeches up to ten inches in length. A Vietnam Boonie Rat earned my immediate respect. Any person not familiar with the term can never understand the effort, sacrifice and tragedy that made up the life of a "Boonie Rat." I am proud to have been one.

Most days for Boonie Rats followed the same pattern. Before dawn, we held a "stand to" when every trooper manned his fighting position; the VC often attacked at dawn to catch units sleepy and disorganized. Nice try, Charlie, but it wasn't going to happen to any of the 101st troopers. After dawn, the platoon leaders met with the company commander, physically or by radio, and received the plans for that day. We took time for a fast breakfast and then began our daily hump to a new objective or a new location. Enroute to or at the objective, our standing platoon plan was to find the enemy, engage them, call in supporting firepower if necessary, fix him in a position and then coordinate the arrival of the rest of the company to engage the enemy force. At the end of each day or at the end of any fight that ended late in the day, we set up a night defensive position, placing night patrols or listening posts out from the company or platoon area.

The rucksack we carried became both best friend and evil enemy that weighed you down. The size and weight of the rucksack varied depending upon the job held in the platoon and when your last resupply was made. After a resupply, the rucksack could weigh 70 pounds and was packed with five days of rations, four to six quarts of water, extra ammo, radio batteries, explosives, smoke grenades or flares, new equipment, a small container of personal items and whatever else you were assigned to carry, i.e. claymore mines, a LAW, or machine gun ammo. These hard-core paratroopers resembled stranded turtles once they dropped to the ground with this huge rucksack. If seated or reclining on his rucksack, a Grunt often found it impossible to simply get up due to the rucksack's weight. The paratrooper had to roll over onto his hands and knees and then slowly work his way up. Often it was a two-man job just to stand up.

We reduced rucksack weight by eating the heavy food first. Appropriate meals or taste were not an issue. Our basic issue of food was a case of "C Rations" containing twelve individual meals, some great, some OK and some we hoped Charlie ate. The passable meals were cans of meat loaf or beef and potatoes, referred to as "beef and shrapnel." The pecan roll was OK, but universally acclaimed by the grunts as best was a meal containing a can of peaches and a smaller can of pound cake. These two items were hoarded for a special occasion meal or to barter. When a case of Cs was divided among troopers, the meal boxes were placed label-down on the ground, usually by the senior NCO in the unit and you got what you picked up. Luck of the draw and let the whining and trading begin. There was no rooting through the boxes for the peaches and pound cake. Same rules applied for platoon leaders and the company commander!

Except for a thin coastal plain, the terrain in northern portions of South Vietnam was mountainous with forested hillsides. A double or triple canopy was formed when the first growth of trees established a single canopy approximately 30 to 40 feet off the ground; the next generation of trees penetrated that level and grew up above for another 40 or 50 feet and then branched out and grew leaves forming a second canopy. In some cases, there was even a third layer of leaves to form a third canopy. It produced a very solid green overcast through which little sunshine reached the floor; therefore, there was very little undergrowth in many areas. Think hiking through the redwood forests of California. They were huge trees in girth and height, often dense teakwood. Normally, we were moving through a forest of trunks without any of the Hollywood version vines and undergrowth, and very few weeds.

On my second day as a Cobra platoon leader we were airlifted to an open area on a ridgeline about five kilometers, or "klicks," south. As my platoon departed the sunny, open LZ and moved under the forest canopy, I thought, "Jesus, it is dark in here." The humidity rose dramatically once we were out of the sun. Within moments, we were soaked in sweat and our dark green jungle fatigues became almost black in color. I felt my rucksack sliding back and forth on my shirt. I was continually wiping sweat from my face. This was why many of the troopers wore the GI-issue forest green towel around their shoulders, a habit I soon adopted. An occasional afternoon thunderstorm shower brought some relief. We were still wet, but cooler.

The Infantry School at Ft Benning forgot to tell us some things. On my second day in the field, the second platoon engaged in its first firefight with 2LT Stevenson as its platoon leader. We were moving along the left side of a crop field that filled the center of the valley. Charlie must have been waiting for us to cross the field, but we foiled them by skirting it. One NVA troop couldn't wait and fired a short burst at 2-0. We turned on line and returned fire. Immediately, a dozen NVA soldiers opened fire. I hit the ground, crawled behind a tree, and on my platoon radio started to call for supporting artillery fire. The AK-47 rounds made a sharp "crack" sound as they went by and I could hear the rounds slapping the branches and leaves above me. I directed a squad around to the left and one squad around to the right, reminding them we didn't know the actual size of the enemy force. The NVA stayed in the fight for about twenty minutes with lots of AK-47 fire clipping through the trees above me. When I got the first artillery spotting round to within one hundred yards of their location, the NVA decided to withdraw to fight another day. Moments later, I was sitting with my RTO, briefing Cobra 6 by radio on the action, when SSGT Griffey approached. Griff pulled out his bayonet, leaned over and with one swift slash he felled the 12-inch thick tree that I used for cover in the firefight. He smiled and said, "L.T., I would pick something other than a banana tree for protection in a firefight." That says it all!

2

Air Assaults Into Trouble

An Air Assault is the insertion of an infantry unit into an open area landing zone ("LZ"), usually with enough helicopters to insert a platoon or company at one time. If the bad guys were around, then firepower on the ground was a critical factor for us: the more paratroopers, the better. Depending on the air temperature, age of the Hueys, altitude of the Pickup Zone or "PZ" and LZ, we could load from four to six troopers in a copter. Circumstances dictated whether I rode in the first, second or third chopper. If we could land everyone from the platoon at one time, I rode in the second or third chopper. When we used a small LZ where only one or two choppers could land at a time, then I went in the first load to be there when my platoon began to arrive. If 2-0 was the lead element for a company air assault, I rode in the lead "lift" and did my "John Wayne" act of standing on the skid as we approached the LZ. Instead of holding my CAR-15 in a shooting position, I pulled the pin on a red smoke grenade and held it firmly with the handle still attached, as I stood outside the helicopter. If we received enemy fire I tossed the smoke grenade so following lifts knew by the red smoke it was a "hot" LZ. I, like the other platoon leaders, believed if I was hit by enemy fire, I would drop the smoke grenade and the signal was sent. I didn't have to make a radio call or even be alive to send that message. There was nothing macho or cowboy about that practice, just the way things were done.

Fortunately, I never dropped a red smoke grenade, but I tossed several on "hot" LZs. I think my first opportunity to toss red smoke came about ten days into my time as a platoon leader when Bill Northquest tasked 2-0 to be the lead element in an air assault. I was out on the skid with a primed smoke grenade when a door gunner in the second helicopter opened fire with his M60 machine gun on the tree line of the LZ. Before I could finish the thought "What is that all about?" WHACK! An AK-47 round hit the door frame some six inches above my hand. Smoke away! We un-assed the chopper while two feet in the air and our escorting gunships worked over the tree line with rockets and machine guns. No more AK fire after that.

The approach to LZs presented another problem as you were unsure what the landing surface would be. Sometimes it was sand, sometimes a cut in the teak forest, or a bomb crater from a B-52 strike, or a rice paddy (dry or wet). The air could be clear or full of blowing dirt/sand, kicked up by the choppers' rotor wash. In early June, the second platoon was lead element for Cobra Company and we were lifted to an LZ on a beautiful grassy finger of a high ridge. On this assault, I was riding in the lead aircraft, standing on the left skid. The chopper slowed to a flare just off the grass, which waved under the rotor wash and reminded me of the fields of "buffalo grass" I loved in Texas.

The chopper was still about two feet above the grass as my RTO, PFC James Weaver, hopped off the skid. I was a half second behind him in departing the chopper. I watched Weaver disappear into the grass, and, instead of landing on the grassy surface, we continued to drop. Just before I impacted the ground, carrying 70 pounds of rucksack and gear, I realized "Crap, this is six or seven feet of razor-sharp elephant grass." Thud, I hit the ground and Weaver's rucksack at the same time. Weaver was pissed, either at me or the elephant grass. When I stood up, I found the grass had sliced fine bloody lines across my forearms and hands. Lesson to Lieutenant Stevenson: If you are making *any* air assault, roll your friggin' sleeves down. 2-0 hacked and crashed our way through the elephant grass to the tree line 60 meters to the north and regrouped. There, I made a warning radio call to the battalion Command and Control chopper advising of the LZ conditions and hoped that the follow-on troopers could avoid looking like they lost a fight with a big cat.

May 25th started off rough and got worse. Cobra Company was moved from a large clearing along the Song Ve river to a nearby valley. The aviation guys were already short on choppers and lifting only one platoon at a time; then they lost a helicopter due to a maintenance problem and they could not move a whole platoon as a unit. That strung out the company airlift over an hour. We were fortunate that Charlie wasn't around and in a mood to pick a fight. But, he was watching and planning.

Following that air assault, Cobra Company moved in four roughly parallel columns up four fingers of a mountain ridge. 2-0 moved on the left finger, 3-0 on a finger about 800 meters to our right, 1-0 with the CP behind them, on a finger about 500 meters to the right and 4-0 on the right flank 600 meters farther out. Each finger was narrow, steep sided and forested with 100 – 200-foot-tall trees. LT Wells' 3-0 discovered a small trail that led up the ridge and his platoon pulled slightly ahead of the other platoons. My platoon did not have a trail but there was little undergrowth on the forested ridge, so movement was easy except for the incline and our heavy rucksacks. Suddenly there was a sustained level of automatic weapons fire off on our right side. The rounds were not aimed at us but many cracked through the trees on our ridge sending us to the ground. Convinced that we were not engaged, 2-0 again moved forward. From the sound of M-16s, AK-47s, grenades and M79 rounds exploding we knew it was a serious firefight for 3-0. The distinct sound of a Soviet-made RPD machine gun then told us the bad guys were, most likely, a platoon of NVA. 3-0's fight began at about 11:45 a.m. and here is when time plays tricks on you. The whole fight and follow-up seemed to take just a few minutes when it took almost four hours. I experienced similar "temporal distortion" several times in combat.

My platoon soon reached the top of the ridge and we found a trail that ran left to right along the hilltop, from our ridge finger toward the finger where 3-0 was engaged. The firing slowed to sporadic shots and bursts and my RTO relayed the information he heard over the company radio net. 3-0 walked into a well-prepared ambush while moving up the ridge finger. There were numerous casualties in 3-0, and 3-6 (LT Wells), was hit in the first moment. LT Wells' status was unknown as well as that of several men from the point squad. The rest of 3-0 dropped back out of the ambush area but they left casualties behind. Cobra 6 and 1-0 began to move laterally toward the ambush site; the travel was extremely tough, down the side of a steep ridge and then up the ridge where 3-0 was located.

If my map reading was correct, my location was on the main ridge top and the trail running from my left to right along the ridge top would take us over to the next finger where we could maneuver down the finger on which 3-0 was fighting. We should arrive behind the NVA in the ambush area. I was explaining what I wanted to do to Cobra 6 when the Battalion Commander, flying overhead in a helicopter, came on the radio and said helicopter gunships were on the way and to have all units hold their position. It took the Battalion CO and the gunships a hell of a long time to locate the target area and other friendlies. This was all wasted time in my mind. My plan was to get over there and assist 3-0, but I was being told to sit on my ass and wait while the battalion commander got involved.

21

The tree canopy was so thick and towering that the colored smoke from a smoke grenade dissipated before it could rise through the canopy and mark our position. SSGT Griffey finally sent a young trooper climbing up a tree with a smoke grenade attached to the end of a 30-foot-long cut branch. The trooper set off the smoke grenade and raised it high enough in the tree that the colored smoke escaped and could be identified by the helicopters. With all the units located, the gunships pounded the finger just above the ambush site with rockets and machine gun fire. After waiting 30 minutes or more from the initial contact, 6 said I could proceed across the ridge top and warned me to watch for NVA backside security.

Sure enough, as we advanced along the ridge top, my platoon's lead element surprised and engaged three NVA watching the trail on which we were traveling. SGT Tinsley's troops killed two of the NVA, but the third soldier got away. We now moved more cautiously. About 250 meters along the trail, we came to an intersection with a crossing trail which I believed led downhill to the ambush site. I informed Cobra 6 that we were approaching 3-0's location from the ridge top and we started down the ridge finger. It was amazing how quietly paratroopers carrying massive rucksacks and equipment could move through the forest. There was no scratching of branches, no metallic clinking and no talking. Our point man was checking every sign and sound, using eyes, ears, and even smell. Soon we could smell the burned cordite of explosions and small arms fire. We heard no NVA weapons for some time but we didn't know if the NVA retreated or were waiting. The fact that we killed two of the NVA trail watchers surely alerted the bad guys that there was an American unit on the ridge top above the ambush site.

My platoon entered the ambush site at the same time Cobra 1-0 and 6 linked up with the rear elements of 3-0 farther down the ridge. I set security out to our rear and two sides and then I walked the ambush site. The NVA bunkers were dug in, well-constructed and camouflaged. They held no NVA soldiers but I saw blood in two abandoned bunkers. As I moved into the ambush "kill zone" I saw two, then three American bodies and the scout dog's body. The final count was eight Americans dead. I had seen only five or so dead NVA since arriving in Vietnam, but had never encountered dead Americans until now.

The medics from 2-0 and 1-0 moved up to treat wounded troopers and I found LT Wells' body. Up near the front of his ambushed troopers, Lt Wells received at least two wounds in the initial ambush, but what killed him was a small caliber pistol shot square in the middle of the forehead. The NVA executed him during their sweep of the ambush site. To say I was stunned by LT Wells' death is an understatement. I was paralyzed. Cobra 6 came up the trail and found me staring at the body. He sent me back to my platoon and I went through the motions of leading my platoon for the remainder of the day and setting in for the night on an adjacent ridge top.

That night I confirmed with SSGT Griffey what I saw. There were already rumors rattling through the company about LT Wells' death. As I checked the perimeter after dark, I made a mental note: *Now I understand their rules of the game!* Months later, when CPT Northquest relinquished command of Cobra Company, he told me he did not know at that time if I would recover from the shock of Well's death. Thanks to Captain Northquest's leadership and SSGT Griffey's counsel, I did recover and worked diligently to become a good Platoon Leader.

The morning of May 29th started out well, meaning gently downhill for an infantryman. The afternoon before, the company air assaulted onto the top of a small mountain and today we were working our way down the mountain's western side. I didn't care about the date or what day it was; just another day of humping the hills and looking for NVA. As had become a company practice, 2-0 was assigned the duty of clearing a creek bottom that ran down the hill. We travelled so many rocky creek beds in the past week, we were beginning to refer to ourselves as "the creek bottom kids." The creek beds were usually clear of the overhanging, multiple canopy forest, so we saw sunlight as we bounded from large boulders to the creek bank and back, working our way down the creek bed. There was a valid reason to travel the boulder-strewn creek bottoms, as water collection points and even aqueducts off the mountain stream were often the first indicator of an NVA camp or bunker complex. Some of the aqueducts were well constructed and carried fresh water hundreds of meters on a downhill angle to a camouflaged camp. Over the past week, we detected four or five company-size NVA bunker complexes, but the bad guys were not home. We destroyed the bunkers and wrecked the split bamboo water troughs that serviced the complex. Now, as we bounded from boulder to boulder, the biggest threat to my platoon seemed to be twisted ankles and knees.

Today, we were on the right flank of Cobra Company with the 1st platoon on our left side. We moved almost 900 meters down the mountain and found no sign of NVA camps. My trusty RTO, Weaver, moved up to tell me that he heard 1-6 (LT John Carey) radio 6, informing him that 1-0 was traveling along a small path that ran down the ridge finger on our left side. At almost the same instant, slightly above and behind 2-0, the first platoon was engaged by multiple weapons, including at least one NVA machine gun. Again, the sound of an RPD machine gun alerted us that 1-0 had engaged a moderate sized NVA unit. The firing continued at a furious rate for at least three minutes and thereafter sporadically, but in heavy bursts. 1-0 was engaged in a hell of a firefight and I later discovered their cost. I told 6 where my platoon was in relation to the fight and then turned my platoon to the left, moving on line, and started up the hill. This was a forested ridge with lots of 24-inch diameter trees and decaying leaves but not much ground cover. Charlie obviously did not know that we were in the creek bed and we were now abreast their position and not coming down the trail into their ambush. But the NVA prepared camouflaged bunkers around the small hilltop and my squads were soon slowed and halted as the NVA opened fire from the concealed bunkers.

On my left side, Sgt Tinsley's squad found the trail on which the First Platoon was descending. Creeping toward the sound of NVA machine gun fire, Tinsley's men spotted a three-man NVA machine gun crew in the middle of the trail and quickly dispatched them with M79 grenades and M16 fire. As soon as Sgt Tinsley's men engaged the NVA machine gunners, NVA bunkers farther up the hill opened up and Sgt T's men were pinned down. My other squads also received fire from NVA bunkers and the troopers began to shoot and move on two sides of the small hill. Fire and maneuver just like the classes at Ft. Benning were my thoughts, "Get people moving!" I was on the left edge of my center squad and when Tinsley yelled that he was stymied, I began to crawl on all fours in that direction. Suddenly, an NVA soldier popped up from a well camouflaged bunker about 15 yards away. The NVA soldier pointed his AK-47 at me and ripped off a burst of six rounds. I dove to my left and rolled over twice. Sumbeech; he missed me. Weaver, moving right behind me, returned fire and didn't miss, popping the guy with three rounds before the AK stopped firing.

The loss of that bunker convinced the NVA there were Americans now advancing on two other sides of their hill and the initial contact with 1-0 blocked a third side. They began to disengage SGT Tinsley's squad and fall back to secondary bunkers farther up the hill. Now amid all the firing, I could make out the distinctive sounds of my two M-60 gunners, Privates Perry and Curry, engaging the bad guys with alternating five round bursts. Damn, that was well-disciplined fire. Noises everywhere! The crack of bullets passing overhead. Bullets slapping leaves and trees. My squad leaders yelling directions. I heard somebody on the right side of our platoon yell "LAW!" That signaled they were going to fire a Light Anti-Tank Weapon (LAW) at the bunkers. I heard the bang of a launch and the loud explosion that followed. The LAW caught the NVA by surprise, was very effective, and for a moment the hilltop was silent.

I could tell that the left and right flanks were now making progress and I crawled up behind my center squad leader, SGT Ruth. I tapped him on the leg and yelled, "Keep moving! Get your squad to move!" Sergeant Ruth was silent and did not move. I crawled around his right side. Ruth had taken a bullet in his head just above his right eye. He was lying face down, his helmet still on, and blood covering his M16. I yelled for our medic, PFC Larry Orosco, and told the rest of the squad that SGT Ruth was down, but to press on. We crawled forward another 10 yards, hiding behind and shooting around the huge teak trees. I paused and hugged the ground as the squad members engaged an NVA bunker about 12 yards to our front. I rolled onto my back to get the radio handset from my RTO, and saw tree limbs being chopped off and splintered as the teak trees were ripped by enemy fire, all about two feet over our heads. I could hear the bullets thudding into the trees just behind me. They were shooting at *me*! That less-than-brilliant observation was further reinforced when I yelled a command to one of my squads, and, as I got the first words out, the trees over me were again ripped by AK or RPD fire. Charlie wasn't stupid; they were firing at any voice location because commands were coming from leaders and leaders were prime targets.

One of the troopers on my right side called, "Grenade up", pulled the pin and tossed a grenade which exploded about three feet short of the nearest NVA bunker. My RTO, "sure-shot" PFC Weaver, shed his radio to toss a grenade at the bunker. Weaver gave it a strong throw, but that was followed by a sound of "bonk" as the grenade hit a limb. Weaver muttered "Oops", and the grenade bounced back into the midst of my paratroopers. We dove in different directions just before it exploded and we were fortunate there were no casualties from Weaver's mighty throw. Not to be discouraged, Weaver pulled the pin on another grenade and raised to a kneeling position to throw again. Before he could throw the grenade, Weaver was spun 360 degrees around to his left, landing face down with his right arm pinned under his body. Terror on his face, Weaver yelled, "Somebody help me, I've got a live grenade."

25

He was shot in his left upper arm, the bone was broken, but his right side was intact. Weaver held the handle of the grenade in place with his good right hand until another trooper, PFC James Alvis, rolled him over, rapidly grabbed the grenade and tossed it up the hill.

After Weaver was wounded, I began to move laterally to my right. Seeing what I thought was a bunker, I raised my CAR-15 rifle to mark it with a tracer round. "Blam!" There was an explosion just to my right side and I rolled off to the left. I did a rapid self-examination and found no wounds, but my right hand was numb and tingling. I could slowly wiggle my fingers. Where the hell was my CAR-15? I scrambled around for a minute but could not find it. I crawled down the hill to where Doc Orosco was behind a huge teak tree, working on Weaver's arm.

"Doc, do you have your 45 pistol?"

"Yes, sir"

"Give the 45 to Weaver. Weaver, your right arm and hand work, so you are now rear security. I need your M-16."

Weapons swaps completed, I crawled up the hill towards my center squad with Weaver's M-16 to continue the assault. Meanwhile, over on my platoon's right flank, SSGT Griffey was urging the troops to shoot and move. Specialist Willie C. Hooker and Lacy's squad (aided by a second LAW firing) routed the NVA. Hooker was awarded a Silver Star for gallantry when, despite heavy enemy fire, he killed the occupants of an NVA machinegun (RPD) bunker and then, low on his M-16 ammo, Hooker picked up the RPD and used it to continue the assault. The Second Platoon soon swept over the top of the hill, clearing bunkers and ensuring no live NVA remained. The bad guys left six dead soldiers behind and blood trails indicated more had been badly wounded.

After the fight, one of my troopers located my CAR-15 buried in leaves, about five yards down the hill from where I lost it. The magazine and magazine housing were destroyed and the bolt was twisted half out of the weapon. An NVA round hit the magazine and several of the bullets exploded in the magazine, destroying the weapon. I was glad to still have a right hand.

That seemingly short fire fight, in fact, took hours, and it was rapidly becoming dark when the entire company closed onto the hilltop. We set up a night defensive position, were resupplied by chopper and evacuated our wounded and KIAs. James Alvis became my new RTO and we ordered a replacement PRC-25 radio because Weaver's radio was hit by both small arms fire and fragmentation. Better to hit the radio than Weaver. The good news coming with Alvis' new job was getting to hang around the platoon CP, hearing discussions with the CO and other platoons, and thus, becoming the conduit for informal information to the platoon. The bad news was humping an extra 20+ pounds of radio and batteries.

During his exam, Doc Orosco found SGT Ruth unresponsive but with a pulse, so, Doc treated his head wound as best he could. I thought SGT Ruth was dead when I looked at him; nobody could survive that type of head wound. We found out much later that SGT Ruth was evacuated to a hospital in the States but died on 21 June 1967, almost a month after he was wounded. The battle cost Cobra Company a total of ten KIAs; First Platoon lost nine troopers killed with three more wounded. My SGT Ruth later died from his head wound and 2-0's only seriously wounded was my RTO, PFC Weaver - the last trooper to be lifted out by chopper and who actually apologized for getting wounded. I could have used about 25 more troopers like James Weaver.

Early the next morning, May 30th, the battalion logistics chopper flew in replacements for the First Platoon. Then we saddled up to continue our sweep down the ridges, with no significant findings. Reaching the valley floor in mid-afternoon, all Cobra units set up in a company defensive position, a rare occurrence. The next morning, we were told to prepare for an extraction for a standdown back at Duc Pho. Hooah! The nearby field and dry rice paddy was only large enough to airlift one platoon at a time, so dear old 2-0 drew the duty to be the last platoon off the PZ. That could be touchy with multiple lifts and flight time turn-around because it gave Charlie time to figure out where you were and what was going on.

Murphy's Law was alive and well that morning because when the Cobra CP and other platoons were extracted, the aviation unit lost one chopper due to mechanical problems, so somebody from 2-0 was going to stay on the PZ for an extra flight turnaround. I discussed it with Griff and then I got two volunteers to stay behind with me. SSGT Griffey was not keen on the idea of me staying behind.

"L.T. somebody else should stay. You're the Platoon Leader."

27

"Griff, you can run the platoon as well as I can. I'll see you in Duc Pho."

We gathered extra ammo, two radios and then hunkered down in the field as my platoon lifted off, waving cheerfully, for the short flight to the "civilized" rear area. They left me with visions of battalions of NVA descending on the PZ and three lonely paratroopers. So, we moved to a slight depression near the field's eastern edge for more cover, where we waited and sweated in the sun. Just before our pickup chopper called inbound, a couple of snipers started popping shots at us from a ridge across the field.

"Cobra 2-6, Minuteman 3-7 is four minutes out for pickup." our radio squawked.

As our Huey ride approached the valley, so did our Brigade Forward Air Controller (FAC) in his tiny O-1 spotter aircraft, calling on our company radio frequency. Cobra 6 sent him to see if we needed any air cover.

"Cobra 2-6, this is Bilk 2-2 on station with two F-4s. I have your field but not your position. Over."

"Bilk 2-2, this is Cobra 2-6. We are in a depression on the far eastern edge of this field and the bad guys are firing from the ridge on the far western side. Over."

"Copy. Bilk 2-2 has the target and the fighters have me in sight. Stand by for a mark."

From 3000 feet altitude, the little Cessna rolled almost onto its back, reversed direction, rolled wings level in a dive. "Bang!" A white phosphorous rocket hit in the middle of the ridge.

"Minuteman 3-7 has the smoke. We are clear to the east side for pickup."

"Cobra 2-6 confirms target. Bilk is cleared hot. Over."

"Bilk 2-2 copies cleared hot. Stand by, fighters inbound."

I stood up, arms raised in the air, and quickly stepped several yards into the field to show Minuteman our new location. As

Minuteman 3-7 moved toward our position and flared to a hover, the F-4s covered the far ridge with thousands of exploding bomblets from CBU-24s (cluster bombs), a sparkling fireworks show. It was a great demonstration of American firepower and I am sure it ruined Charlie's morning. Our small team ran and jumped into the Huey. Minuteman lifted, made a pedal turn in place and headed out of the valley.

"Great work 2-2, Cobra 2-6 is airborne and headed home. Thanks for the cover."

Thinking, "That must be a great way to fight this war," I watched Bilk 2-2 and the pair of F-4s depart the area.

We were finally enroute to Duc Pho.

3

New Lieutenants – Finally!

Cobra Company was extracted from that PZ to the 1st Brigade base camp at Duc Pho where we began a four-day standdown to refit, train on reaction drills, and conduct more weapons qualifications. I soon found out that my M-79 guys were phenomenal. Troopers like James Gormley could drop an M-79 grenade through a door or hit a tree stump from 40 meters and were still deadly accurate out well past 100 meters. More importantly, I soon met our three new Platoon Leaders: 2LTs Tom Kinane, Steve Davis, and Ty Herrington. Cobra was again up to four lieutenant platoon leaders in the field.

3 June – Cobra Company headed back to the woods with the three new platoon leaders. With several firefights behind me, it was hard to believe that I was the veteran platoon leader in less than two months' time. CPT Northquest told the new platoon leaders to learn from their NCOs and me. I traveled mostly with 3-0 (2LT Stephen Davis).

We started the day with a hot breakfast at the Duc Pho base camp before we air assaulted onto some hill top or into the next valley. As we ate breakfast, the ground began to shake and a low rumble filled the air. Beyond the first set of western ridges the USAF flew an "Arc Light" mission of B-52s to saturate bomb an area suspected of heavy NVA traffic. We stepped out of the mess tent to watch and we could see the brown haze of dust raised by the six B-52 loads of 750-pound bombs. Over the next few days I learned to hate moving through the Arc Light areas.

Our next mission was to see if the bombing effectively destroyed NVA units, equipment or facilities. Most of the time, we were just climbing over massive splintered logs, falling into craters and breathing explosive tainted dust, all exhausting. Cobra Company decided that Arc Light bomb damage assessment (BDA) went way down on our list of preferred missions.

Ty Herrington, the new Cobra 1-6, was too good looking to be true. A tall OCS grad, he served time as a platoon leader and then moved to 5th Special Forces in November of '67. We crossed paths again in January 1968 in Saigon. More on that later. Ty later courted and married a beautiful Hollywood starlet, Chris Noel, who was doing USO stage shows and an Armed Forces Radio program for the GIs. She was the best thing that ever happened to a miniskirt and go-go boots. Their engagement and wedding were plastered all over the *Stars and Stripes* newspaper and Hollywood. But, unfortunately, the fairy tale wedding of a starlet and a handsome Green Beret did not have a storybook ending. Ty succumbed to severe PTSD after his return to the States and in the 1970s began abusing Chris and finally committed suicide.

The leader of our "4-0", Tom Kinane, was our only West Pointer, class of '66. He was a rugby player with broad shoulders and in excellent physical shape. Tom had red hair and beard, which we rarely saw because they were usually a dirty brown. Tom was an excellent platoon leader and later returned from duty as the Brigade's Long Range Reconnaissance Patrol (LRRP) unit leader to command Cobra Company in 1968. The Army sent Tom to Medical School after his Vietnam tour and then he served a full career as a doctor and hospital commander. Tom retired as a Colonel in the 1990s and entered private practice in the state of Washington.

Stephen W. Davis, the leader of "3-0", was a Citadel graduate, class of '66, and the son of Brigadier General Franklin M. Davis, the MACV G-1. Steve was an average platoon leader and Captain Northquest asked me to help in his training as a platoon leader.

Lt Davis took a long time to master navigation in the forest-covered mountains of western Thua Thien Provence. In the second week of June, my 2-0 was trailing behind LT Davis' 3-0 up a heavily forested ridge to occupy a knoll assigned to us by Cobra 6. The hump was tough with no sunlight piercing the double canopy and some of the draws were so dark I checked my watch to see if the sun had set. Davis' platoon reached a knoll and he set out security on the far side of the hilltop. I gave my platoon a break in place on the trail and went up the hill to talk with 3-6.

"Steve, why have we stopped?"

"This is the hill top where 6 wanted us to set up for the evening."

"I don't think so. We still have another 600 meters to go and it's on the next knoll."

Davis' platoon sergeant wandered over, and, after hearing our exchange, agreed with LT Davis. SSGT Griffey remained "neutral", enjoying the disagreement among two young lieutenants. Map reading and navigation in the forest and mountains required an ability to convert map contour lines into terrain features that you could mentally "see" and then match it up with the ground you humped across. I had closely watched the terrain, even though 3-0 was the lead on this trek. To me, the slight bulge of two map contour lines with a narrowing waist of the lines meant there were two knolls separated by a small draw. We were on the first of two knolls on that ridgeline.

I challenged Davis' platoon sergeant, a tall trooper and former Ranger instructor, using the call sign 'Devil.'

"Devil, check it out and see if there is another knoll just ahead on a compass heading of 210 degrees. You will go downhill for 250 – 300 meters, cross a small draw and then start back up hill. Press on for another 300 or so meters and you will find a knoll much like this one, only a bit larger. And be careful because there might be a trail crossing in the draw. Since Charlie does not like to climb hills, he would rather go between them."

"A can of peaches says you are wrong." said Devil, as he gathered up a squad and they moved off down the hill on the 210-degree heading.

About 35 minutes later the radio announced, "Friendlies coming in from the south." Devil walked through the perimeter and up to the CP area for the two platoons.

"Round them up, Sir. We have one more hill to hump."

SSGT Griffey saddled up 2-0 and we followed 3-0 downhill, across a trail and then up to the next knoll. Griff looked over at me as we moved out.

"Stop grinning like a Cheshire cat; it looks like you are gloating."

"I'm just anticipating my next can of peaches."

Navigation out in the open, even with sky overhead, often seemed as difficult as navigation under tree canopy because you saw few references on the forested ridges; everything was green trees. A week after the above adventure, I was again following LT Davis and 3-0 as we entered an open area that held a tributary of the Song Ve River. We moved along the south side of the valley and 3-6 found a large rectangular stone-walled area, probably a former or future graveyard, which made a good night defensive position for the two platoons. The rectangular stone walls stood about four feet tall and measured 30 yards on each side. Open grass lands spread for 500 yards in every direction, offering excellent observation and fields of fire. The river branch was 800 yards away and flowed east toward the low green hills. We split the sides of the stone quadrangle with 3-0 taking the west and south and 2-0 taking the north and east sides for our night defensive positions. As was our custom in an open area, we would fire an artillery registration mission nearby so we could quickly call for artillery support if the bad guys showed up during the night and we needed more firepower.

Since Davis led into the night position, he prepared to call for the artillery 105-mm smoke round that was first in the registration process. As 3-6 discussed the fire mission with "Devil", I came over to check our navigation. When 3-6 started to call in the target coordinates by radio, I commented,

"Steve, those coordinates are our present location, not the target you want to hit."

"No, there is that ridge point and the bend in the river." Davis said, pointing at the two terrain features on his map and then across the field.

"I think the ridge peak you are referencing on the map is farther down the valley and that river bend does not exactly match the map."

"I'll shoot these coordinates and see where the smoke round lands."

Thinking "Shit, he is going to get me killed," I turned and directed:

"2-0, helmets on and up against the east wall!" The 105-mm smoke round came from an easterly direction since our battalion firebase was some eight kilometers east.

34

The artillery radio operator called "Shot, Over," and 20 seconds later "Splash, Over." The members of 2-0 pressed against the stone wall. The incoming round made a slight rumbling sound and then a very distinct "pop" as the smoke canister separated from the 105-mm casing. The projectile slammed into the field short of our quadrangle. The lighter smoke canister carried on and impacted just outside the wall and bounced over the heads of 2-0, into the midst of the 3-0 troopers. The smoke canister then ricocheted off the ground, hit the west stone wall right next to a 3-0 sergeant and flipped over the wall, all the while billowing thick white smoke. The 2-0 troops whooped and hollered like they won a football game. LT Davis got to his feet, collected himself, and radioed a correction of "Add 500" to move the registration point down closer to the river and away from our night position. Map Reading Class 201 completed, I started setting in my night defensive positions with Griff.

Two days later, while working the flat lands along the same branch of the Song Ve, I came down with a gastro virus and couldn't keep anything in my stomach. Every twenty minutes, I went outside the platoon's perimeter and puked until there was nothing left. Then I dry heaved for a minute or so and returned to the platoon CP. The heat was kicking my butt and I knew I was dehydrating, so I tried to drink and eat the blandest food from the C Rations, crackers, even peaches and pound cake. Nothing stayed down! By morning I looked like hell and felt too weak to do anything. Our orders were to move farther up the Song Ve, so Griff divided my rucksack among several troops in the platoon and left me burdened with only my LBE and CAR-15. Griff ran the platoon and I tagged along like a mascot through most of the day. After swallowing all the pills that "Doc" Orosco provided during the day and managing to keep water down, I carefully ate some dinner. Amazingly, it stayed down. As I sat there munching on crackers, Hooker shuffled up to return some of my dispersed gear and observed:

"L.T., you look like you been run over by the shit wagon." That was a keen observation by "The Hook."

"Hook, it don't mean nothing."

Hook, Griff and my two RTOs howled with laughter. It was the first time they heard one of the lieutenants use that tried and true expression.

Working with another platoon or the company CP gave us more firepower, but I felt the larger group was noisier and practiced less light discipline than 2-0. I also did not like to set up for the night while it was still light. Most days, 2-0 selected a good position for the night and then moved a couple hundred meters away to eat dinner and appear to establish our night defensive position. Then, after dusk, we moved back to the previously selected location and set in for the night. Twice, Charlie probed the "false" position, set off a trip flare and we called artillery in on the bad guys at the "wrong address." One evening, we left the company position to relocate and later watched as Charlie lobbed five mortar rounds at the company position and the sector that 2-0 no longer occupied. You presumed that Charlie watched all movement during daylight hours. Our night movements didn't always fool Charlie, as one night I was checking our perimeter after moving when two tracer rounds snapped just over our position. The bad guys knew where we were that evening. I returned the favor by calling two 105 mm artillery rounds onto the shooter's suspected location.

Proving it is a small world, in early June the Cobras were receiving resupplies on a ridgeline with heavy teak tree canopy. Because of the small LZ for the resupply Hueys, each platoon went to get their resupply and then returned to a defensive position before the next platoon moved to resupply. I was watching a returning first platoon pass through 2-0, when I saw a familiar face from the University of Texas! Humping an M-60 machinegun up the trail was a friend, Ken Pfeiffer! Almost together, we exclaimed, "Hey, I know you!" Ken was in Cobra Company for almost a complete tour, but, somehow, due to the dispersed nature of our operations, we did not encounter each other before now. We played the name and assignment history game for a few moments and then Ken was on his way to his platoon.

Ken was drafted by Uncle Sam, but volunteered to be a paratrooper. For the next few weeks whenever Cobra Company set up together, or at least our two platoons, Ken came over and had supper with me as we talked about the past and future. He soon DEROSed back to the States and I did not see him again for years.

On a late June evening, I reached one of the high points as a platoon leader. 2-0 led the company up onto a hilltop in the forest for a night defensive position. Cobra 6 and his CP were following us onto the hilltop and as Captain Northquest arrived he received a radio call from the Battalion Commander. Knowing the call might take a while, 6 called me over and said, "Steve, set in the company for the night as they come in." That meant he trusted *me* to assign defensive positions to the other platoons as they arrived on the hilltop. *I was in charge of the entire company's night defensive position.* I tried to remember everything I'd learned at Ft. Benning or in the last months from Captain Northquest: boundaries, fields of observation, likely approaches and overlapping fields of fire, outpost positions. It may seem like a little detail now, but it was a big deal to Lieutenant Stevenson at the time.

Actual combat in June remained light with few contacts involving more than five VC or NVA. The bad guys moved on or were doing a good job of avoiding the 101ˢᵗ troopers. On the evening of 29 June, CPT Northquest called me over to the Company CP and read me the Performance Report that he was submitting on me. I was absolutely floored when he said I was a great infantry platoon leader and to keep learning. Despite a very shaky start after LT Wells' death, when he wondered if I would make it, I became his most dependable and experienced platoon leader. I almost floated back to the 2-0 section of the company perimeter. The next morning, a helicopter brought in the new company commander, CPT Roger M. John (Texas A&M '64) and the battalion commander. After a brief ceremony and an exchange of handshakes in a jungle clearing, Captain Northquest departed and we were now working for a new Cobra Company Commander.

4ᵗʰ OF JULY 1967
On July 2, we secured a PZ and were extracted back to Duc Pho for a four-day standdown. We cleaned troops, weapons and equipment as soon as we arrived, trained the next day (July 3ʳᵈ) and then threw a major party to celebrate the 4ᵗʰ of July. Cobra Company began celebrating after noon chow, and, with tubs of cold beer for the troops, Cobra's platoon leaders tried to keep up with the troopers' intake of alcohol. By late afternoon everyone was mellow, including platoon leaders, and it was time for officers to gather at the O'Club.

LT Walt Hill, being a battalion staff rat, obtained a jeep and we headed to the O'Club with six lieutenants trying to sit in or hang onto the jeep. Walt managed to hit the largest road bump in the Duc Pho base camp, and Tom Kinane ("TK"), sitting on the back edge flipped out the back of the jeep: splat, in the dusty dirt road. You can't hurt a great paratrooper like TK just by tossing him out of a jeep. But, as the inebriated LT Hill put the jeep in reverse and gunned it, he nearly ran over TK and two other lieutenants who were checking Tom's condition. We loaded the staggering officers back into the jeep, and again set off for the O'Club tent.

The O'Club was a dedicated GP medium tent with a wooden floor, a bar, and "sounds." The officers party was a tradition at standdowns and provided an opportunity for the "seasoned" lieutenants to offer a "New Lieutenant's Drink" to any lieutenant who arrived in the battalion since the last standdown and officers party. The drink was half a canteen cup containing some of every beverage at the bar. The new lieutenant was supposed to chug the drink without stopping and then place the empty canteen cup on his head. That accomplished, the smarter new lieutenants had about 10 minutes to go outside and throw up the drink. Otherwise, the drinker soon become very intoxicated and unable to logically process inputs.

After three hours of frivolity and "New Lieutenant's Drinks," we were well lubricated as we staggered back to the company area. Most of the battalion turned in for the night, so TK and I decided that to celebrate the 4th of July, we needed to fire some illumination rounds from the company's 81mm mortar. Navigating to the 81mm mortar pit behind the officers' tent, Tom opened a case of illumination rounds.

"What charge should we use to propel the flares?"

"Just leave it at max charge."

Since I was a mortar platoon leader at Ft Campbell, I knew that ensured the flares would clear the 101st perimeter. Rather clumsily, Tom and I pulled the safety pins and dropped three successive flare rounds into the 81mm mortar tube. Each fired with a very loud "thunnngg" sound and soon lit up the Vietnamese night. We scrambled off toward the officers tent giggling like fools and hoping we were not going to be caught and tossed in the brig. To our amazement, nobody came to investigate, nor even seemed to notice the three 81 mm flares fired across the perimeter. It was just another night in Vietnam! We retreated to the company officers tent and tried to go to sleep. Early the next morning, our First Sergeant found me asleep slumped across the sandbag wall outside our officers' tent. I'd staggered out of the tent last night because I could not stop the bed from spinning at ever increasing RPM whenever I tried to lie down and close my eyes. B Company's XO, Lt Gooch, was found face down in the soft sand in front of the outdoor movie screen. Our 1SG shook him awake with the warning that a work detail was coming to clean the movie area and it did not look good for an officer to be passed out in the sand.

EMERGENCY LEAVE

On July 6th, First Sergeant Hodge called me into the orderly tent and handed me a Red Cross message from my brother Donald stating our Dad had died. I remember looking at the message in the Cobra Orderly Room tent and wondering what to do. The last part of the message was garbled but the basic facts were there. The First Sergeant directed the company clerk to cut emergency leave orders so I could go home. I took the message out the back of the orderly room, sat on the sandbag wall and I cried. I began to understand all the issues and sacrifices that Dad made for the three of us. I also wanted to show him that I was a good infantry officer, just as he had been.

Then things happened in a hurry. Brigade called that a C-7 aircraft was unloading supplies and it was departing for Cam Ranh Bay in forty minutes. I could make it to Cam Ranh if I hurried. I hurriedly briefed SSGT Griffey, promised him I'd be back soon, packed one khaki uniform, and Lt Hill drove me to the airstrip for leg one of the trip home. At Cam Ranh Bay, I signed in with the 101st Liaison NCO at the 22nd Repo Depot and headed for a shower. I managed to remove one layer of Duc Pho dirt when the 101st Liaison NCO stuck his head in the shower building and yelled,

"Is Lieutenant Stevenson in here?"

"Here, sergeant."

"I'm holding a C-141 with its engines running on the cargo ramp, waiting for you."

I rapidly dressed in my crumpled set of khakis and jump boots while he drove to the terminal. As I hopped out of his jeep, the 101st NCO handed me a set of metal paratrooper wings and a Combat Infantryman Badge for my uniform. He gave me a slight smile and said, "Just so the rest of the world will know": my first recognition that I was a combat veteran. I was hustled out to the C-141 by an Air Force MAC airman and then the C-141 crew chief led me up the rear ramp. He checked my name, service number, unit, and destination, then closed the ramp. Before I could find a seat, the aircraft started to roll.

Inbound to Charleston, South Carolina, the crew checked with their squadron operations and found another C-141 which was departing for Kelly AFB, Texas, in less than an hour. I never entered the Charleston passenger terminal as my first Crew Chief walked me from his aircraft directly to the C-141 going to Kelly, and handed 2LT Stevenson off to that plane's Crew Chief. I asked the next crew chief to manifest me to Kelly. Hell, I was almost home in San Antonio; and there were lots of commercial flights from the San Antonio International Airport to Dallas. Once at Kelly, the Air Force drove me to the San Antonio airport and American Airlines gave preference to military emergency leave, so I found myself on the next American Airlines flight to Dallas Love Field. I was met at the deplaning gate by Donald and our longtime friend George "Bev" Garrett. Walking outside the terminal, I was struck by the difference between Texas heat and the heat of Vietnam. In the "dry" Texas 100-degree temperatures, if you stepped into the shade, you cooled off. Back in Vietnam you were hot in the sun or in the shade. Looking to the southeast, at the Dallas skyline from the entrance to Love Field, I could hardly believe that less than 36 hours from my company orderly room, I was standing in Dallas, Texas.

I was too late to attend my Dad's funeral. Though Don included the date and time in the garbled part of the Red Cross message that made it to Cobra Company, I would not have been in time. Don's message stated that there was no need to return for the funeral, but I never saw that part of the message. My sister, Joy, was finishing her time as an exchange student in Denmark and could not come.

Within days, I had attended to any details that I could handle. I began to have major pangs of guilt about being away from my platoon in Vietnam. Don, with the assistance of our Uncle Charlie, half-brother Bill (from Dad's first marriage) and numerous friends, seemed to have a grasp on all the tasks to be accomplished. All that being considered, I bid farewell and made reservations for a flight to Seattle, Washington, and then to McCord AFB for transportation back to Cam Ranh Bay and from there north to Duc Pho and Cobra Company.

Completing the long haul across the Pacific, I returned to Cobra Company's rear area on 16 July, having been gone only a quick ten days. The next morning, I caught a chopper ride to join the Cobras in the field. The entire company was set up on a hilltop awaiting resupply so it was easy to catch a ride into their position. I checked in with the field first sergeant and Captain John and then found my way to the 2-0 portion of the perimeter. SSGT Griffey said he was glad to have me back so I could be Platoon Leader and he could return to being my Platoon Sergeant. Soon the word spread that I was back and the other Platoon Leaders and my own 2-0 troopers welcomed me, asking what it was like back in "the World", and if the beers were still cold. I was glad to be back with my

101st Band of Brothers. The next morning as 2-0 saddled up for another day of humping hills, it felt like I was in a fast-paced dream and I'd never left my platoon.

22 July, I received a radio call to report to 6's location as soon as possible. The company was searching huts in several small villages in a side valley and it was a quiet two days, so I didn't have an idea why the "Old Man" wanted me. As I arrived at the company CP, the battalion Command & Control (CC) helicopter landed next to the village and the Battalion CO, LTC Austin, hopped out to join CPT John. They walked toward the CP and then LTC Austin stuck out his hand to me and said, "Congratulations, First Lieutenant Stevenson." He took out a single silver 1LT bar and pinned it on the right collar of my jungle fatigues. I saluted him, thanked him and he once again shook my hand before turning and walking off with Cobra 6. Captain John looked back.

"Congratulations, Steve. That was it. You can go back to 2-0."

I forgot what my date of rank was and when I was scheduled to be promoted. Every day was one more day of humping with my platoon and learning to be a good platoon leader. By the time I walked the 500 meters back to my platoon, everyone there knew about the promotion and there were more congratulations all around. Later that evening, I again reflected on the fact that my Dad was a 1LT during his combat time in France. I missed telling him I was now a 1LT and I wondered if he would have been proud of me.

SSGT Griffey left the boonies for home after only two days' notice. Griff never mentioned his DEROS date or kept a "short-timers" calendar as other troopers did; and it was a real shock when Griff said "Sir, I DEROS on the next resupply chopper!" On August 1, we were being resupplied in a very small clearing, blown by the attached engineers, on a razor-back ridge high in the hills southwest of Chu Lai. Griff's DEROS chopper could barely fly at this high elevation and 100-degree heat. Instead of lifting cleanly into the air, the loaded Huey chopper hopped forward, skipped off the ground twice, arrived at the edge of the precipice and lurched over the edge, diving to get flying airspeed. SSGT Griffey was seated on the floor, but hanging onto the door edge of the chopper, his eyes wide, staring at the forest that swept toward and then finally went below him as the Huey gained flying airspeed and climbed. In two days, Griff would climb into his Boeing 707 "Freedom Bird" at Cam Ranh Bay for the flight home. I wished God Speed for a great infantry sergeant.

Amos T. Griffey, Jr. retired from the US Army as a Sergeant First Class (SFC), having served almost his entire career with the 101st Airborne Division. He returned to Clarksville, Tennessee, where he later became a minister, Senior Pastor and finally a Bishop in the Baptist Church. Griffey was followed into the ministry by his son, Amos T. Griffey III, who is now a Bishop. "Griff" died in 2010, but he left behind a great legacy for his family, his community, his church and particularly for one Infantry First Lieutenant.

August started slowly for the Cobras, 2-0, and for my replacement platoon sergeant, SSGT Fred Mitchell, another professional NCO. Despite intelligence reports of major NVA units moving into our AO (Area of Operations), we contacted no more than five NVA troops at one time. In the big picture, the head shed in southern I Corps area wanted to increase artillery support in our area, so a 155-mm battery was moved into a Special Forces Camp just west of the 1/327 AO. To provide increased perimeter security for the artillery guys, LT Steve Davis' third platoon, "3-0", was detached from Cobra Company and airlifted to SF camp A-108 at Minh Long. Steve's platoon saw no action at the camp, but they were present for a tragic accident, when an arriving C-7 Caribou was hit in mid-air by a friendly artillery round fired from Minh Long. The incident was captured on film by United  Press International photographer, Hiromichi Mine, who was later killed in a land mine explosion near Hue in March 1968.

DONALD ARRIVES IN COUNTRY

On 8 August 1967, twin brother Donald arrived in country and was sent to SERTS (Screaming Eagle Replacement Training School) at Phan Rang. The course was supposed to be a week to ten days in duration; however, after only three days, on 11 August 67, Donald was pulled out of SERTS and sent to replace a wounded Forward Observer in 2nd Bn / 502nd, one of our sister battalions in the 101st. Commonly called the "Oh Deuce," this battalion had been in serious contact and suffered losses to their Forward Observers. Timing was awful as there were no replacements in the pipeline. So, the artillery folks snatched Don from

SERTS and he came north to begin his tour as an FO. Donald's entry into combat was so rapid that he was jokingly accused of "still pissing stateside water."

15 August 1967, Cobra Company was extracted from the boonies by choppers, without incident, and flown to a road overlooking the sandy beach at Chu Lai. Secure within the Marine base perimeter for the next three days, we pitched our tents, cleaned weapons and paratroopers, replaced faulty equipment, and brought our supplies up to speed. All our troops endured some level of "jungle rot," an infection of any open wound or scratch caused by bacteria and the constantly wet uniforms of the guys out humping the jungle. A great cure for jungle rot was salt water and sunshine, so we called mandatory platoon formations standing chest deep in the surf. After the first such formation, there was no problem getting the troopers into the water. That may have been a result of a beach party with free beer, courtesy of our First Sergeant.

On the second afternoon, we were visited on the beach by three young ladies from the American Red Cross, stationed at the Chu Lai hospital complex. Egged on by dozens of cheering paratroopers, one attractive brunette shed her ARC blue uniform, and, wearing her bra and panties, joined the troops in the surf. Cobra 6 and the platoon leaders ensured that this was a look but don't touch activity. The young lady had a wonderful time and then returned to her jeep and the shocked REMF Army lieutenant who drove the girls to visit the 101st troops. If there was ever a reminder of what the paratroopers were fighting for, that pretty, young lady in soaked bra and panties was it.

Mail caught up with the Cobra troopers on the 16th, and I opened a package from Don's girlfriend, Ellen Clampitt, to find a five-inch plastic Snoopy figure. I met Ellen just before I left for Vietnam and she became Mrs. Donald Stevenson some four years down the line. Anyway, Snoop became my adult supervision and traveled with me through all the subsequent adventures of my military career. I attached Snoopy to my rucksack frame and that became the visual signal for anybody seeking the second platoon leader.

On the evening of 16 August, all the battalion officers went over to Chu Lai Airfield and the Marine Air Group 12 (MAG 12) Officers Club, where, after numerous rounds of drinks, we were introduced to "carrier landings." The Marines created a first-class representation of a carrier deck, approximately 15 feet long, made from polished teak wood and embedded into the floor of the O'Club bar. The Marines sloshed booze on

43

the area of the floor marked as a carrier deck and two pilots held a towel about eight inches above the floor at the "stern" of the carrier outline. Pilots followed the arm signals of a Landing Signal Officer, "LSO", while running around the bar area with outstretched arms making jet noises. When signaled, you lined up on the carrier deck and dove belly-first, hands folded on your back, onto the soaked floor/carrier deck, sliding under the towel and catching it with your raised heels. This simulated a "trap", engaging the arresting wires across a carrier deck as Marine aircraft returned to a carrier for landing.

After several drinks, my flying about the bar became less inhibited, and on my third try, I slid under the towel and hooked it with my heels. I was the first infantry officer to make a good carrier landing that night and thus became the senior "carrier-qualified ground aviator" in our unit. Oh, there was a wall located two feet beyond the carrier outline, and, if you got up too much speed and missed the cable/towel, you could arrive at the wall head first. More drinks for the headaches! After enough drinks, I did not feel the impact on the floor, but two days later surgeons wondered about the numerous bruises to my upper body.

4

Tough Times at Chu Lai

On August 18, 1967, the 2nd platoon of "C" Company, 1st Battalion (Airborne), 327th Infantry, 1st Brigade (Separate) of the 101st Airborne Division finished their three-day "stand-down" on the beach at Chu Lai, Vietnam. We ate a late morning, full, hot breakfast in the battalion mess tents, then loaded up our heavy infantry rucksacks (up to 85 pounds as this was a major resupply event) and moved to a helicopter assault pickup zone on a straight stretch of dirt road near our encampment area.

Sometimes our air assaults used only six Hueys and some days we utilized more. The size of the PZ or LZ often determined the number of choppers that could be used. Worst case was using a razorback ridge as the LZ, where we could insert only one chopper load of paratroopers at a time. That could get real ugly if the NVA recovered from the pre-assault barrage by artillery, gunships and Air Force fighters. I was lucky that I never landed on a single ship LZ that was "hot," but other companies were not that lucky. If you were on a single ship LZ taking fire from the bad guys, it took helicopter crews with big brass *cajones* to bring succeeding lifts into that tiny LZ.

Cobra Company was part of a truly large air assault this day, as the 101st aviation units gathered over twenty Hueys for the air assault, along with four or more pairs of gunships. Most were piloted by young Warrant Officers, who were not old enough to vote. It was unusual to have enough air assets to transport an infantry company at one time, but here we were. "Abu" Company was the first company to lift out and, after their insertion, the choppers returned to pick up and insert Cobra Company. The Hueys then refueled and flew the "Barbarians," followed by the "Demons." CPT John briefed the standard load plan: five or six troopers to a chopper with leadership and key weapons distributed among the loads, so loss of a single chopper would not disable a platoon or the company.

45

My second platoon was not the lead platoon on that day, but I thought, since we were all landing at one time, it didn't matter who was first! Tom Kinane's 4-0 platoon won the honor of leading onto the LZ. Looking down the dusty road PZ, I saw the familiar pattern of five-man groups spread along the road at 100-foot intervals, one group on each side of the road every 100 feet. Right on time we heard the "whup, whup, whup" of rotor blades. The single sound multiplied until it was thunder, and we saw a long trail of pairs of choppers flying low over the brush toward our PZ. The flight reminded me how pelicans will troll the beach on Padre Island, strung out in a line, but each keeping perfect formation with the same interval.

The lead Huey passed my platoon to reach TK's platoon and flared, nose coming up to slow the aircraft and then settling in front of the first group of troopers who huddled with their backs to the dust storm created by rotor wash, protecting their weapons from the dust, rather than themselves. As the pilot lowered the pitch of the rotor blades and the dust abated, troopers rapidly loaded from both sides of each copter, some running around the aircraft nose to the opposite side. It took only seconds to load the 100+ paratroopers and then the lead chopper lifted off and the followers lifted in pairs, trailing like the pelicans upon arrival. All the troopers and I sat on the floor of our chopper with our lower legs and feet hanging out into the breeze, no seats, nor seat belts. The large flight carrying Cobra Company rose out of the red dust into clear, cool air, and snaked around to west.

My RTO PFC Buckridge, one other trooper, and I were standing on the left skid as our helo flared to a two-foot hover with a rice paddy wall on our side of the aircraft. I thought it would be great to just step off onto the dike, but, in that thought's two second delay, troopers on the right side jumped off the chopper, and, because of the weight imbalance, the Huey rolled to the left and rotor blades began slapping the water of the upper rice paddy. I hopped off the skid and hugged the ground of the lower rice paddy, afraid that the chopper was going to crash on us, right then and there. After the three of us on the left skid departed, the chopper, once again balanced and lightened, leveled, rose slightly, then lowered its nose to gain airspeed and departed. I hoped the pilots were not as frightened as this paratrooper lieutenant, but I was sure it was an exciting few seconds in the cockpit. Suddenly, the valley seemed quiet as the helicopter formation climbed and disappeared toward the coast.

Within five minutes of arriving, Cobra Company, moving southward, was engaged by enemy forces in bunkers across a small stream and rice paddies. My 2nd platoon and the 4th platoon moved on line, and returned fire. My RTO could hear the Company Commander call for fire support and our Air Force FAC who was circling high overhead, called down a flight of two Air Force F-4s, with 500 pound high-drag bombs and napalm. The FAC and the Phantoms were scheduled to "be on station" at the place and time of the air assault in case resistance was encountered. Some of the 4-0 paratroopers were caught behind dikes within 100 meters of the bunkers, and could not move back without being exposed to raking enemy fire in open rice paddies. After a radioed target discussion between Tom Kinane and the FAC, the small O-1 Cessna aircraft made a rapid reversal to a dive and fired a white phosphorus rocket into the tree line.

Within seconds, the FAC called "Fighters inbound" over our FM radios, indicating that the F-4s had the target in sight and were starting a bomb run. From my position behind a dike, I watched the first F-4, on my right side, tighten up his turn and roll into a shallow dive. He was not pointed at me, but he wasn't far off that line. Almost on top of us, the F-4 released a pair of 500 pound "Snake-eye" bombs. I saw the four fins extend to slow each bomb as the Phantom howled over the bunkers at less than 500 feet altitude. Both bombs exploded along the tree line and I felt the blast before I heard it. As the sound reached us, the ground bounced, the air pressure forced us to yawn to protect our ears, and the loud blast felt like an ocean wave pounding us into the soil. Less than ten seconds later, the FAC again radioed "Fighters inbound", as F-4 number two began his attack run.

This time, the F-4 released silver cylinders of napalm which slowly tumbled end over end toward the trees. The nape canisters impacted short of the tree line, were ignited by a white phosphorous fuse, creating a rolling wall of fire engulfing a hundred yards of the tree line. Once more the F-4s were cleared by the FAC and returned to drop ordnance along the tree line. While the F-4s' weapons were accurate and the bunkers were neutralized, one trooper from the 4th platoon received minor napalm burns due to his proximity to the targets. If you have never been 150 yards across an open field when a 500-pound bomb detonated, you have missed a true shock...wave. By now, we could tell from the sounds and the radio chatter, that all four infantry companies of the 1st Battalion, 327th Infantry were in the valley and all were in contact with the enemy. We'd "found" the North Vietnamese Army's 2nd

Division. We searched the bunkers and found only blood trails and one severed foot, still in its sandal.

Cobra 6 directed our four platoons to move in parallel lines up four fingers extending from two low ridges at the south end of the valley. My platoon was on the company's left flank and the 3rd platoon was on my right as we advanced up the gently rising ridge fingers toward cultivated fields that covered the first plateau of the ridge, about twenty meters higher than the valley floor but set back some 600 meters. The ridge fingers were covered with small trees and shoulder-high grass which made movement difficult except for small trails worn down by the former occupants. The 3rd platoon reported being fired upon by an NVA soldier and arrived at the open field before my platoon. Well after the fact, there were some allegations that 3-0 pursued a lone shooter. That was against 101st policy because it often led to an ambush. It was never proven that Lt Davis' platoon pursued a lone shooter onto the ridge top. We dropped our heavy rucksacks and started up our ridge finger.

The east-west field was 300 meters wide, 100 meters deep, with some unknown crop that grew about four inches high in furrows that ran left to right as we approached the open area. The far south side and left edge of the field were surrounded by thicker vegetation that quickly turned to forest. In the field stood a stone wall four feet in height, about 15 meters from our near north edge and ran east from the field's right edge for 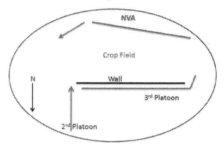 some 150 meters across the field. When the 3rd platoon entered the field and rounded the right edge of the stone wall, they were engaged by an enemy force from the far side of the field. The 3rd platoon rapidly deployed along part of the wall, around the right end of the wall and returned fire. The enemy force turned out to be a full company of NVA who had spent the previous night in the forested area just south of the field.

As 2-0 point elements emerged from the brush at the edge of the field, the 3rd platoon was involved in a very heavy firefight. Radio transmissions indicated that the 3rd platoon lost their Platoon Sergeant and their medic. My Platoon Sergeant, SSGT Fred Mitchell, asked if he and "Doc" Orosco could move down the wall to assist the 3rd platoon. I told Mitch to take an RTO as well. Crouching behind the wall, off they moved. That turned out to be a decision I have lived with for decades. From my viewpoint, it was the worst move I ever made. Although other troopers have told me it was logical to help 3-0 at the time, it is an unsettled and unsettling issue for me. I moved to the front of my platoon and entered the field at the east end of the stone wall. A small squad from the 3rd platoon was fighting from behind the wall near that point, so I moved forward to evaluate the situation and communicate with the 3rd platoon leader. Lieutenant Davis, "3-6", moved along the wall toward my position and we discussed how to best attack the NVA position.

At that moment, one of the troopers at the left end of the stone wall called out, and upon turning, we saw at least a dozen NVA in camouflaged uniforms with rucksacks and weapons moving right to left along the tree line not 70 meters away. Simultaneously, two NVA platoons assaulted the right center of the stone wall and the left flank where my platoon linked up with the 3rd platoon. Everyone became a rifleman at that time, platoon leaders, radio operators, and NCOs. A platoon leader very seldom fired his weapon, but I went through five magazines of ammunition in about one minute. The answer to repelling an attack or ambush is superior accurate firepower, and we were trying hard to achieve that. The NVA plan was to turn the left flank and catch the 3rd platoon in a cross fire: but they did not expect my 2nd platoon to be on that flank. The assaulting NVA closed to within grenade throwing range of the wall and soon we were exchanging grenades with the enemy and firing at anything that moved or produced a muzzle flash.

I started to move forward to yell at the 3rd platoon leader when I was suddenly spun around to the left and pulled backwards onto the ground. I looked at my Radio Operator and asked "What?" thinking he pulled me down. He shook his head and pointed at my left leg where I discovered a baseball size hole. I crawled to and leaned against the stone wall, pulled out a combat bandage from my shoulder package to cover the wound. Amazingly, there was no pain, little blood and I also discovered several other shrapnel holes. After applying two bandages, I thought to wiggle the toes on my left foot. They seemed to move, so that was good. At that time, I saw another 20 NVA moving farther to the left and for the first time I considered the option that this might not end well. I turned and emptied a magazine at the NVA, taking two down. GRENADE! An enemy grenade flew over the wall and landed next to our position. For an instant, I looked at the smoke of the fuse coming from the handle and then we dove away as it exploded.

In retaliation, one of the 3rd platoon troops pulled the pin on a grenade and tossed it over the wall. Wham! It exploded and I could hear voices from behind the wall or across the field. Then, the same trooper "spooned" a grenade and tossed it into the air over the wall. "Spooning" a grenade was a risky procedure to ensure that the grenade could not be picked up and thrown back. Plus, you often got the added benefit of an airburst, increasing the lethality of the explosion. The soldier pulled the pin and intentionally released the spoon safety handle on the grenade. With the handle gone, the 4.5 second fuse started. The trooper counted to two seconds (three seconds if he was insane or gutsy) and then tossed it. This grenade exploded about head high on the other side of the wall as an airburst. I heard screams. I considered our current position too exposed, so I told the 3rd platoon soldiers to move back to the far-right end of the wall with the rest of their platoon and I moved back ten meters to the edge of the brush with my troopers. The brush offered no protection from enemy fire, but it offered partial concealment that made us more difficult to target by the NVA.

Two things then went right. The remainder of my platoon, trailing behind me, deployed on line perpendicular to the end of the wall and extending a hundred meters down the hill. When the NVA moved around the left flank and started toward the fight, they came into an open area in front of my platoon on line. It was a short firefight; score one major win for the paratroopers. Up at the edge of the field, I crawled past three of my troopers, down the small brushy trail, and reached my secondary radio. As I picked up the handset, I heard somebody from the third platoon, tell 6,

"3-6 and 2-6 have been killed."

That was a shock to me! I keyed the handset and countered:

"2-6 is up. I'm still here, on the edge of the field, but I need fire support. We have people dying up here."

I was asking for fire support, preferably artillery, but I was informed no artillery was available because all four companies of the 327th were in similar contact and the other three companies were using the ongoing fire missions from the artillery. Also, the battalion's artillery firebase was taking NVA mortar and recoilless rifle fire. Crap! There was, however, a trio of Army helicopter gunships approaching and they were briefed by Cobra 6, then diverted for my use.

"Cobra 2-6, this Musket Lead. Mark position of friendlies. Over"

"Musket Lead, Cobra 2-6, stand by for mark."

I crawled half way out to the corner of the wall and tossed a yellow smoke grenade into the field. Crawling back to my radio, I called Musket Lead.

"Cobra 2-6 has smoke out, identify."

Musket Lead has banana smoke."

"Good ID. That is our position. Anybody, south or east of the smoke, is bad guys and try to concentrate on the tree line."

For the next five minutes, the gunships pounded the field and tree line with rockets and machinegun fire. As the gunships expended their last rockets, our company artillery forward observer finally received supporting fires from the artillery and in two very long minutes the first artillery spotting round landed in the trees some 100 meters beyond the field. The NVA and I knew that more artillery rounds would soon follow and be adjusted onto their positions.

The NVA fire began to diminish, which meant they were trying to break contact and withdraw. The two other platoons and the command section of Cobra Company soon arrived to help secure the area. Cobra did not pursue the NVA because 3-0 had suffered numerous casualties and we needed to evacuate the dead and wounded. Unknown to me at the time, SSGT Mitchell, Doc Orosco and my lead RTO Buckridge were among the dead.

I again noticed that time plays tricks on you in a firefight and what seemed like just minutes was a much longer battle. This fight took most of an afternoon. The fight started after a lunch break and now the sun was setting. With a 1st platoon paratrooper supporting me down the hill, it was dark by the time I arrived at the helicopter landing zone in a dry rice paddy. As the only officer at the extraction site, I crawled up onto the muddy edge of a rice patty dike and supervised the extraction of our company's wounded and dead. I assigned loads for the helicopters, talked on the FM radio to the choppers inbound, often vectoring them toward our location by sound until they were close enough to see our Landing Zone lights. We ran out of marking lights (low power flares) after the third pick up and successfully resorted to placing torn note paper in a metal helmet, dousing it with insect repellent and lighting the mixture. It produced a small blue flame (without illuminating a large area for the NVA to target with mortars) which our helicopters could see and guide on for a night landing without their landing or position lights illuminated.

The helicopters extracting our paratrooper casualties were not medical evacuation helicopters (the "Dustoff" copters) but regular assault helicopters, "slicks" pressed into duty to make night, blacked-out extraction of the 101st casualties. They did a magnificent job. Finally, we were down to the last aircraft for the night and I was helped on board along with two other wounded troopers and one KIA. When the helicopter lifted off the dry rice paddy, the aircraft, passengers and the infantrymen on the ground were again pelted with dust and flying dirt. "This can't be great for my three open wounds and I'm sure it's not helping the other guys onboard." As our helo turned away from the engagement hill and climbed enroute to the coastline, I began to realize that I had survived the day's fight. Every infantryman believed that if you made it to the evacuation helicopter, you would survive. I made it onto the chopper. While the crew was not a Medevac crew, they were my guardian angel flight crew that would get me and the other troops to the hospital.

"Hospital! Oh, crap, I really have been wounded!"

5

2nd Surgical Hospital

The helicopter exterior and interior were blacked out with only a dull glow of the instrument panel shedding light inside. No use giving the NVA a bright target. As the chopper climbed through 1500 feet the pilot turned up the interior lights and I examined my fellow wounded troopers. The wounded trooper next to me was unconscious but I found a pulse. I repeatedly checked his breathing and twice assisted his breathing by giving him CPR breaths. The door gunner watched all this activity but could be of no assistance. There were no doors on the cargo section of our helo and the cool breeze blowing through the helicopter felt great as the helicopter sped us directly to the Army's 2nd Surgical Hospital at Chu Lai. There was no blowing dust or dirt as we touched down on the asphalt Medevac pad of the 2nd Surg and a team of four soldiers scrambled toward our aircraft. Two troops hustled under the rotor blade to my side of the Huey.

"The paratrooper lying on the floor is having trouble breathing, so take him first. I can make it from here."

The medical team quickly, but gently, lifted him onto a gurney and started pushing the gurney uphill into the Emergency Room (ER) about 20 yards away. I lifted my bandaged leg over the side of the chopper floor to touch the ground and started to hobble from the chopper to the ER when a huge Specialist wrapped an arm around me and all but carried me up to the ER. Just outside the ER, the Specialist easily lifted me onto a waiting gurney, pushed me into a supine position with "Good luck, man."

Inside, I was wheeled to an open space on the left side of the room. I was one of at least eight patients on gurneys the medical teams were treating. Two medics came over and swiftly cut off my uniform to expose my wounds. Normally, in an ER, the patient's clothes are cut off by the staff, rather than make the patient move about to take off items. In two swift strokes of the trauma shears, my trousers were cut off and then my boots. It may seem funny, but as they cut off my boots I thought: "Damn, those boots are only five days old!" Next went my jungie jacket. A nurse and then a doctor came to inspect my wounds and asked the same questions:

"Can you move your toes? Can you feel this?" They touched parts of my left leg and foot.

"Yes, Ma'am. Yes, Sir"

They seemed satisfied. Then, together, they rolled me over onto my right side to check my back for wounds. Sure enough, there was a fragment wound to my left butt, but it was only flesh deep and not bleeding much. I took grief for decades from fellow paratroopers about being shot in the ass, although that was not totally accurate. Convinced that my wounds were not life-threatening, the doc and nurse rolled me onto my back and moved on. So, I lay naked on an elevated stretcher for almost an hour while the medical teams worked on the more seriously wounded. I could not complain about the prioritization because I still felt no significant pain, nor found significant bleeding. Finally, a three-person medical team came to me and, after giving me two shots, they washed my wounds, covered them with gauze bandages and gave me a hospital gown. The ER began to fade from sight and sometime in the middle of the night, I awoke in a recovery bed in a ward with about 15 other wounded troopers.

The next morning, I drifted in and out of sleep, obviously, a result of my medications. Slightly after midday, I awoke to find a Purple Heart Medal pinned on my pillow and a short hand-written note wishing me a rapid recovery. It was signed by Brigadier General S. H. Matheson, our 1st Brigade Commanding General. A short "P.S." was added saying "Good Luck, Steve" and signed by 1LT Johnny McKnight, a friend and former 101st platoon leader, now serving as General Matheson's aide. I was pissed that they elected not to wake sleeping patients, at least me. I would have traded sleep to tell BG Matheson I was disappointed to have been wounded and some of his great paratroopers were killed.

That second day brought a surprising and wonderful gift. A nurse came in and announced, "Lieutenant Stevenson, you have a visitor."

She then handed me the Snoopy figure that was attached to my rucksack. The guys in 2-0 attached a Wounded In Action casualty tag to Snoopy with my name, unit and 2nd Surg Hospital listed. They gave

Snoopy to a helicopter crew member who dutifully ensured Snoop made it to the 2nd Surg. The nurses thought Snoop was cute, probably meant a lot to me, and sent him over to my ward.

It took me two days to realize I didn't know if Donald knew I was wounded. My 1st Battalion made an inquiry and found out that Don was notified by radio the morning after I was hospitalized. However, his unit in the 2nd Bn, 502nd Infantry was out in the forests and was not able to extract Don for a couple of days. Donald missed seeing me by hours as he was pulled out of the field on the afternoon that I was evacuated to Qui Nhon in the morning. We did not get back together for almost three months and repeated this miss, only in reverse.

CHAPLAINS

The First Brigade was "blessed" to have some of the Army's best chaplains, all brother paratroopers, a fact not known by most or appreciated. Chaplain Father Torres, a short balding Jesuit priest was a floater within the First Brigade. All the battalions knew and loved him. Captain (Chaplain) Tommy Thompson, a tall lanky officer, was a good Southern Baptist and assigned to the 1/327. Either chaplain provided a religious service, and often Communion, during company resupply missions when space and time allowed. Other times, they were living on the battalion's fire base, available for counseling and services. I don't believe God favors one denomination over another, particularly in combat, and, as a life-long Episcopalian, I felt comfortable with Father Torres and with Captain Tommy Thompson. Both were there to aid my paratroopers and all comers of any denomination.

Father Torres, "El Toro," was famous throughout the First Brigade as being fearless and absolutely dedicated to the troops. He stood in awe of no rank or position. He could work personal problems for all and was a true ombudsman for the grunts in dealing with superiors or the Army bureaucracy. Tommy Thompson accepted the Army title for chaplains as "Padre" and was comfortable with all faiths, not a common trait for many Baptists. Tommy wore a large button stuck in his helmet band which proclaimed, "Kill A Commie For Christ." After Tommy was cajoled into posing for a picture with his button and a Thompson submachine gun, a *Stars and Stripes* reporter sent the picture to the Chief of Chaplains and Tommy was threatened with everything up to losing his chaplaincy and a court martial.

Tommy was there in the 2nd Surgical Hospital two days after I was wounded when I lost my self-control and broke down sobbing. I could not comprehend why my platoon sergeant, RTO and medic were killed and I was still alive. Tommy and I spent three hours leaning on a fence railing between hospital wards and discussing "why?" In tears, I asked Tommy,

"Why am I still alive while others in my platoon command element were killed?

"God must have other plans for you."

That was of small comfort. Decades later, I still feel the guilt of losing those three great troopers, my close battlefield friends. Was my career enough to offset what Fred Mitchell, Marvin Buckridge and "Doc" Larry Orosco might have done in their lives? Was Chaplain Thompson correct?

The Army's hospital system was designed to rapidly move patients to different hospitals based on the wounds and patient status. Unit Combat Medics and Medevac helicopter medics treated major trauma and did their best to deliver you alive to the Surgical Hospital. The Surgical Hospitals acted much like a civilian Emergency Room by accepting the patients, analyzing the wounds and taking necessary lifesaving steps and procedures.

The patients were treated at a Surg Hospital until they were stable enough to travel to an appropriate Evacuation Hospital. The Evac Hospitals performed the real clean up, patch up and sew up work for the patients. Think of the Evac Hospital as a civilian Operating Room. From the Evac Hospital, patients were sent to hospitals in Vietnam for rehabilitation or to hospitals out of Vietnam for more advanced treatment. The first stop out of country was usually Japan and then on to military hospitals in the United States, selected for their medical specialties or proximity to the soldier's home.

By August 21st, the doctors deemed me strong enough to be transferred. I was strapped onto a stretcher and, along with eleven other troops, travelled by ambulance bus to the Chu Lai airfield and loaded onto vertical racks in a C-130. The short flight to Qui Nhon's 67th Evacuation Hospital seemed an insult, traveling flat on my back on a stretcher. Paratroopers were supposed to jump out of C-130s, not lie on a stretcher.

The 67th Evac Hospital at Quy Nhon turned out to be a five-star hotel compared to the 2nd Surg at Chu Lai. The wards were not wood and screen "hooches" but modern, clean Quonset huts with air conditioning and real hospital beds, not cots and thin mattresses. The luxuries of clean wards with air conditioning were to reduce infection of open wounds before surgery and closed wounds afterwards, a significant medical concern. When I arrived at my bed, the ward nurse informed me I was going to surgery in four hours. The 67th Evac ran multiple operating rooms and did not waste any time before doing repairs on shot up bodies. I freely admit I was scared before going into surgery, mostly fear of the unknown. I was not in control of what was about to happen!

When my turn came, I was hooked up to a new IV, transferred onto a gurney and wheeled from my ward toward the OR. I remember watching the overhead neon lights track by, and as I was being wheeled into the Operating Room, I asked the nurse,

"You don't mind if I talk a lot because I am scared to death."

She stuck a needle into my IV line and said:

"You have nothing to worry about, Lieutenant. Now, count backwards from 100."

"OK, 100, 99, 98, 97", blackness.

I awoke back in my bed. My left leg was wrapped from hip to ankle with gauze and I could not feel the leg or foot at all. Momentary panic! No sooner did I begin to stir in my bed than a nurse Major came over saying,

"Welcome back, Lieutenant. The doctors anesthetized your entire leg and you will get your feeling back soon, but expect some pain from the closure procedure."

The surgeons cleaned out the largest wound, removed foreign objects and dead flesh, pulled the skin together over the five-inch hole on my thigh and sealed the closure with six stainless steel sutures that entered above and below the wound, were tightened and then twisted in a pig-tail closing. My sutures looked like the top strands of a chain link fence. It was not pretty, but effective. A narrow plastic tube was left in the wound and stuck out about a half inch from the lower side of the wound as I lay in bed. The tube was inserted to let the wound drain as it healed from the inside. My four lesser fragmentation wounds were closed with conventional stitches.

Day two at the 67th, the nurse Major came back with a pair of crutches and said, "Your doctor wants you to get up and walk four times a day; just don't fall onto anything or any patients."

My normal path of exercise went through the long Quonset hut that was our ward, out onto the covered sidewalk to loop the ward and then back inside to my bed. The total length of the trip was probably about 50 yards. That route initially took almost 30 minutes as I became accustomed to the crutches, discovering if I put any pressure on my left leg, it pulled on the steel sutures and hurt like hell.

I found I was not the only First Lieutenant in the ward. In my crutch travels, I noticed at the end of my ward there was a patient with a large red-bordered sign at the foot of his bed: "POW." He was a wounded NVA officer and the label on his charts said he was a 1st Lieutenant. He obviously was wounded and then captured, but the chart provided no further tactical information or intelligence. How the hospital knew this patient was an NVA lieutenant was an Intelligence question since the North Vietnamese, like the 101st Airborne, very seldom wore rank insignia on field uniforms. He was not restrained in any manner and sat silently, propped up on his bed, watching everything around him. He suffered leg and abdominal wounds and one arm in a sling.

On my second day of travels I began to glance at him each passing and offer a greeting in Vietnamese, "Chao, Trung Uy" meaning "Hello, Lieutenant." He never replied or changed expression. The NVA patient was located about 10 beds down the ward from my bed and I never heard

58

anyone speak to the soldier in Vietnamese, nor heard him speak. On the third day's exercise trip, I greeted the NVA officer as usual and he replied perfectly

"Good morning, Lieutenant."

I almost lost my balance on the crutches and the ward nurse dropped a patient chart. The Trung Uy allowed the slightest smile to creep across his face and then it instantly vanished. I was so taken aback by his very good English that all I could do was stumble out of the ward and continue my exercise route. The next morning, he was gone, and I learned I was being shipped to the Cam Ranh Bay hospital for convalescence. I mentally wished the Trung Uy a thorough and speedy recovery, knowing his future would probably be in a miserable prison, not as pleasant as my future hospital.

6TH CONVALESCENT CENTER

Another C-130 ride on a stretcher and I arrived at my initial entry port into Vietnam: Cam Ranh Bay Air Base. The patients were loaded into an ambulance bus that backed up to the tail ramp of the C-130, and we were driven toward the northwest end of the base, to the Army's 6th Convalescent Center (6th CC). It must have been a weekend or holiday as the Army medics and doctors who met our aircraft were dressed in shorts and tee shirts or Hawaiian beach attire. Five years later, I understood where the TV series "M.A.S.H" found some of its material. At the hospital, after a quick exam, I was finally allowed off the stretcher to hobble on my crutches, and shown to my new home for the coming weeks. My home was a recovery bed in a fair-weather ward, like Chu Lai, with concrete floor, half wood / half screen sides, and no air-conditioning. Located 200 yards off the beach, a nice breeze usually kept the hooch cool.

The hooch was much like the buildings that welcomed me to Vietnam, down the road in the Repo Depot, except these were all single story and longer. This ward was one of 16 to 20 wards that each could hold up to 60 wounded soldiers, with latrine, showers and administrative areas in the center of the hooch. I thought this was just another hospital until I found out the mission of the 6th CC was to treat those soldiers whose wounds were evaluated as allowing them to be returned to duty within eight weeks, providing limited surgery and lots of physical therapy to those patients. In this war, troops were the key assets. The best approach for the Army was to keep recuperating patients in country and then send them back to their units.

The 6th CC possessed over 1000 beds, several Operating Rooms, but more relevant to my recovery, more than a dozen physical therapy centers. I also found a small BX and a smaller building that was a Red Cross Recreation center with games, books, TV tuned to Armed Forces Radio and Television Service and staffed by Red Cross workers.

My ward master was a combat medic with a previous tour in the 1st Cavalry Division, SSGT Cummings. He was charged with taking care of our medical needs, ensuring we made our Physical Therapy sessions and that we kept the ward in clean condition. My recovery ward was on the north half of a building with 32 wounded patients in Army issue beds. I was the only officer. A notable ward mate was a 24-year-old E-7 Sergeant First Class from the 1st Cavalry, in for his 3rd Purple Heart trip. This guy must have been a hell of a soldier and leader to be promoted that rapidly, with time out for wound recovery.

Day two: This day was all fuzzy due to medications. Evidently all the new arrivals received massive doses of meds to ward off everything from malaria to infections. Plus, I was still on the back side of the pain meds I was given at the 67th Evac Hospital.

Day three: I was off major pain medicine and my leg hurt like hell. I was sitting on my bed while a doctor checked the drainage of my leg wounds. My big wound had become infected and turned red under the wire sutures. The doctor could tap on it and the surface was as stiff as wood. His solution: "Let's change antibiotics for a few days before we have to open it up again." Fine by me; I was not fond of going back into surgery if it could be avoided. While this exam and discussion was ongoing, in through the screen door walked one of the 6th CC Red Cross girls. Susan talked to several of the troopers, and, as she approached my bed, glanced at the wire staples in my red swollen leg, smiled saying "I'll check back later." She talked to more of my fellow patients and then went out the opposite end of the hooch. Sergeant Cummings was sitting on the side of the adjacent bed, helping the doctor. After she left, Cummings glanced up at me, grinning: "L.T. you do realize that you have no bottoms on your pajamas?" He tossed me a pair of pajama bottoms.

The doctor did not replace the gauze wrapping for the whole leg, but wrapped only the bandaged areas and the drain. The next day, SSGT Cummings said I was cleared to take a shower and clean up. I realized that I had not cleaned my funky paratrooper body since I was wounded and only body areas near my leg wounds were cleaned by the surgical staffs. SSGT Cummings wrapped my left leg in a plastic sheet and carefully taped it closed at the top, just above the bandage high on the inside of my thigh. I then hobbled on crutches to one of the shower stalls in the center of the hooch, and, standing with my right leg in and the left leg outside the curtain, attempted a shower. Damn, it felt good. I cleaned a lot of dirt off my body and then shaved with hot water from the sinks. At least I smelled a lot better than before and I felt clean for the first time since the day before our air assault on the 18th.

At the 6th Convalescent Center, physical therapy was a primary function, and, even before my wound infection was cured, I started my PT program. I needed to develop new thigh muscles to replace the quadriceps muscles that were torn or cut out. My PT consisted of three main exercises: leg lifts, curls and presses with increasing weight sand bags for weight resistance on each leg. My PT clinic sergeant drove me like he was a Marine "Gunny" Sergeant, always pressing for more weight and more reps. After three weeks, I reached a point where I complained,

"I can't lift that much weight with my good leg."

"OK, we'll increase weight on both legs."

I did leg curls while lying face down on a training table. This wasn't too tough, except when the stitches just above my knee and my metal wire stitches snagged on the sheets. Damn, that hurt, and the physical therapist showed no mercy at all. After the leg infection healed and the stitches came out, particularly those massive steel sutures, physical therapy became a lot less painful. By mid-September I was moving well enough for my physical therapist to allow me to quit using the crutches.

In mid-September, SSGT Cummings announced that all ambulatory patients could wear a jungle fatigue jacket in place of the blue pajama top we wore. The unit patches, rank and name were at our expense. The next day each patient received a new jungle fatigue jacket, still in a plastic wrapper. I pulled mine out, feeling embarrassed to wear a nice new dark green jacket when my guys in the boonies lived in faded and torn jungies with no insignia at all. I hobbled to the BX Tailor Shop and asked the Korean tailor:

"Can you sew on First Lieutenant, Infantry branch, Combat Infantryman Badge, jump wings, Stevenson name tag and a left shoulder patch of the 101st Airborne."

He gave me the standard reply "No problem, G.I. You come back, two hours."

He went straight at it and in two hours the jacket was ready. I gladly paid for the insignias to look like a paratrooper again and not just another blue pajama-clad patient.

There was one unintended consequence to wearing my jungies jacket around the hospital area. I regularly stopped by the Red Cross Recreation Center to relax with a coke (and visit a certain Red Cross young lady named Susan). I always saw South Korean soldiers and Marines (ROKs) in the Red Cross Center, not unusual since the 6th CC treated our allies as well as the US service branches. Since there was no rank on my pajamas, there was no reaction from the GIs or ROKs whenever I entered. The first day I wore my jungies jacket with officer insignia, into the Recreation Center all the Koreans jumped up and stood at attention until I told them to carry on with their activities.

The second time this occurred, I asked one of the hospital's NCOs what that was about, we were all patients. The sergeant said such respect was part of their training and if their unit heard that the Korean soldiers did not honor the American officers just as their Korean officers, the Korean troops would be beaten upon return to their units. From then on, I would sneak in the back door of the Recreation Center or check to see if there were Korean troops present. If I entered when the Koreans were present, I quickly told them to carry on and thanked them.

I knew that as soon as I was strong and mobile enough, I wanted to go back to the 327th and my platoon. That day of departure was closer with each lap I walked around the compound and on September 29th, I was officially discharged from the 6th CC with orders back to the 1st Brigade at Chu Lai. In addition to signing in at the Cam Ranh Bay Passenger Terminal for any flights northward, I checked in with the 101st Liaison NCO to see what he had moving toward the 101st: nothing until tomorrow at the earliest. So, I got a bunk for one night in the Repo Depot, not a problem. On September 30th, the 101st Liaison NCO manifested me on a C-130 flight to Chu Lai, and, strange as it will seem to anyone who has flown on a C-130 and its web seats, I enjoyed the trip. It was great to ride sitting upright after my last two C-130 rides when I was strapped onto a stretcher and felt like cargo. This was a major improvement and I felt almost like a paratrooper again.

I was picked up at the Chu Lai passenger terminal by Cobra Company 1SG Archie Hodge. I considered it a great compliment that the 1SG transported a lowly 1st Lieutenant from the terminal to the company area. While I was on my hospital vacation, the 1st Brigade rear area moved from Duc Pho to an area northwest of the Chu Lai airfield. Upon arriving in the Cobra area, I took one of the bunks in the back half of the orderly room tent. As I drew a new weapon and web gear and ruck from the company supply sergeant, even the hot canvas smell of the tent was a welcome sign for my return. Now it was back to work.

67th Evac Hospital - Qui Nhon

6th Convalescent Center - Cam Ranh Bay

6

Back With The Cobras

Chu Lai – Captain Roger John was still Cobra 6, although the new Battalion Commander changed the company's callsign to "Cutthroats". I was a very happy trooper when I returned to my 1/327 family. On October 1st, my first task was to go see CPT John. I caught the resupply Huey to the battalion firebase to see Cutthroat 6 and my 2-0 troopers. The Cutthroats were pulling security duty on the firebase so it was easy to see everyone. I did not know it at the time, but 1SG Hodge radioed CPT John the evening before with the news that I was back from the hospital.

As in the past, I sat in the open doorway of the Huey with my map on my lap, tracing our flight and evaluating the terrain below. I sighted the firebase on a small hilltop and soon the Huey flared to a landing on the logistics pad. Poncho liners, ponchos and tarps that provided sun screen for the defensive bunkers flapped in the dusty rotor wash as I hopped off the helicopter. Cutthroat field first sergeant, SSGT Coakley, shook my hand and hugged me as a greeting. Instead of going directly to the company CP, I walked the perimeter of the firebase and everyone seemed happy to see me, especially SSGT Gautney, Willy Hooker, and James Alvis. I made the rounds of every 2-0 position on the hill, but the temperature soon began to kick my butt. I walked (almost crawled) up to the battalion area on the hill top, and, as I was sitting in the shade of the Battalion Briefing Tent, Captain John came up the hill, shook my hand and heartily welcomed me back. He looked me over and said,

"You don't look like you are quite up to humping as a platoon leader, so how would you like to be my Cutthroat XO?"

"Yes, sir, I would love to be the Executive Officer."

I harbored a real fear of being shanghaied by the battalion staff upon my return and this move let me remain in Cobra/Cutthroat Company. It turned out Captain John had already approached the Battalion Commander about such a move.

The duties of XO were to run the company's admin and logistical support for the guys in the field. Oh, plus short spells as a platoon leader, when a lieutenant went on R&R or there was an underlap for replacement after a platoon leader was hit. A good XO is proactive; getting what was needed by the troops and then a few things extra and much appreciated. My staff in the rear area was initially 1Sgt Archie Hodge, Sgt Ballew in supply, Sgt Cohen and PFC Harland Stoffregen in company administration. Later we added a full-time armorer and an assistant supply trooper. We used the troopers passing through the company rear as workers on endless projects to improve facilities for the company whenever it came in from the field. The First Sergeant even used a math formula for how much beer and soda to order for a standdown based on number of troopers and how long the company was in the rear. We tracked the new guys coming in, the veterans leaving for home, the R&Rs and the medical evacuations.

8 OCTOBER 1967
At Chu Lai, Typhoon Xangsane came ashore. Per the First Sergeant's instructions, we made the tents triple secure with ropes and sand bagged along the bottom flaps. As the storm intensified, we locked down one door to the tents and nobody left the tents on the windward side. As the wind and rain increased, the XO's smaller tent blew over but stayed in place due to all the stakes & sandbags. Bravo Company lost one tent and Headquarters Company lost two tents (one blown into the perimeter barb wire a half mile away). After the storm passed, as SGT Ballew surveyed his soggy supplies, he was the first to use that fashionable infantry saying: *"It don't mean nothing!"*

One evening, the B Company 1st Shirt, nicknamed the "Mad Russian", got rip roaring drunk at the NCO Club, took a wrong turn walking home and fell into the barb wire surrounding our battalion area. He was first reported as VC in the wire so our reaction team and I went to find the intruder. We found the inebriated First Sergeant with his jungies caught in the razor wire, thrashing about, making loud references about the parentage of whoever put this wire "in the road" and not feeling the numerous small cuts that he was inflicting on himself. First Sergeant Hodge and I sat and laughed as several of the

"Barbarians" extracted their First Shirt and helped him to the Battalion Aid Station.

All the tent communities used half-barrel cans for human waste in latrines, or "heads" for our Marine friends. The Marines did not want to burn the "shit cans" in their area so they trucked the barrels to a perimeter spot below our battalion area, unloaded them and burned the waste with diesel fuel. One day, a Marine genius decided to burn the eight barrels in the bed of his 2 ½ ton. He poured diesel fuel into his barrels, ignited the diesel and departed for a coffee or leak break. The "jarhead" must have sloshed fuel or somehow the fuel spread because when he returned his "deuce and a half" truck was consumed by fire from the bed to the ground. We could do nothing as the truck was across yards of barb wire, so we watched fire consume the entire vehicle.

LOW POINT
The lowest point of my tour with the 327th was the afternoon of October 23, 1967. I'd been back with the battalion for just over three weeks and was settling into my job as Executive Officer (XO) and learning all the administrative support needed for our company in the field. 1SG Hodge took a phone call from Brigade Personnel shop stating I was needed to positively identify two paratrooper bodies at the 2nd Surgical Hospital's morgue. The two troopers were brought in the night before, after a major engagement by Cutthroat Company. Sgt Ballew drove me over to the 2nd Surg in my XO's jeep and we soon found the graves registration / morgue in an air-conditioned Quonset hut with a huge freezer attached.

A little background: My first platoon sergeant, SSGT Griffey, DEROSed and was replaced by SSGT Fred Mitchell, who was killed in our firefight on August 18th. SSGT Earl Gautney was promoted from squad leader and became the Platoon Sergeant after August 18th. SSGT Gautney was one of the two bodies that I was to identify at the morgue. The other soldier, PFC Robert Cain, was also in my Second Platoon while I was the Platoon Leader. I saw PFC Cain was killed by small arms fire, but SSGT Gautney showed only one major right arm wound. I asked one of the medics how he died and was told it was loss of blood. I thought "Why the hell didn't somebody put a tourniquet on his arm?" I was irate that Gautney bled to death, but I was not at the firefight so I couldn't throw stones. Two days later, on a resupply mission to the company, I expressed my feelings to CPT John. That very afternoon, Cutthroat 6 ensured every NCO reviewed combat first aid and blood loss control with their troopers.

October 27, 1967, was my brother Don's night to stop flying metal. MAJ Manfred "Fritz" Kelman, our Battalion XO and a great leader, called me late at night to notify me that Don was wounded seriously and was coming to my favorite place, the 2nd Surgical Hospital, just over a small hill from our battalion area. I grabbed my helmet and weapon and MAJ Kelman drove me to the hospital. On this, the scariest night of my tour in Vietnam, my imagination ran amok and all I knew was the word "seriously." We did not use that word lightly when describing casualties. MAJ Kelman dropped me at the entrance to the 2nd Surg ER and I asked the first nurse I encountered:

"Has a Lieutenant Stevenson from the 101st been admitted?"

The nurse looked at her roster and then looked at me, reading my nametag. She suddenly blinked when my name registered.

"Yes, he just arrived and is in the ER."

When I entered the ER, I found Don lying on a gurney along the left wall with a bunch of tubes sticking out of him. I was surprised that the chief surgeon let me into the ER to see Don with no fuss. The surgeon said Don had suffered a lot of damage done by shrapnel through his back and they would have to cut from the front to patch up the organ damage. I was so relieved to see him alive and conscious that I greeted him with a disrespectful "It's just like a Redleg to ruin my night's sleep." I don't know if Don remembers talking to me as he lay in the ER with docs, nurses and medics working on his injuries. He did ask me how his Recon Sergeant, SGT Grant, was doing, and all I could tell him was the surgeons were working on him. Across the ER, a team of four or more doctors were working on Don's NCO. SGT Grant did not make it, but I didn't know that until the next day. I left the ER as their crew began to prep Don for surgery. With Don being wheeled out to an OR, Major Kelman came over to me and said,

"There is nothing more you can do here. I'll drive you to the battalion area and you can drive your company jeep back after breakfast."

I was back the next morning. Don was in a ward and looked like hell. He was dirty, tubed up and bandaged from the shoulders to his waist. I spent hours talking to him as he drifted in and out of sleep. I finally went back to Cobra Company for the night and returned on day three to find that the docs wanted him to get out of bed and walk. That seemed a tough job for somebody with sliced stomach muscles and a lot of holes in his back, but I nagged him as best I could because I went through a somewhat similar process. When Don could make it out of bed, we shuffled down to the east end of the ward and looked at the beach below the hospital. I pushed the IV pole and bag connected to Don, and he slowly trudged along. Each trip was slow and painful, but necessary.

Either day four or five, I returned to the 2nd Surg Hospital and found that Don was transferred to the 67th Evacuation Hospital and would be sent back to Japan and most likely all the way to the States. I was pissed that I did not get to see him again before he was evacuated, but I knew he was out of Vietnam and on his way to recovery. Having made the evacuation trip three months before, I understood the process. His trip was long and passed through several hospitals in Vietnam and Japan but Don finally arrived at Brooke Army Medical Center (BAMC), Fort Sam Houston, Texas, on 3 December 1967, just over five weeks from the day he was wounded.

In late March 1968, MAJ Kelman was promoted to LTC and was transferred to the recently arrived Third Brigade (505th Airborne Infantry Regiment) of the 82nd Airborne Division. The Third Brigade of the 82nd was deployed to Vietnam in response to the magnitude of the Tet Offensive, arriving in late February and moving to the Hue – Phu Bai area in March 1968. LTC Kelman soon became a battalion commander, 1st Bn 505th Airborne Infantry, and offered to swap eight 82nd Division second lieutenants for the four 1/327 Company Executive Officers to become Company Commanders if they extended their tours. I said "Hell, yes." I would serve with Kelman anyplace, any time; but the swap was squashed by the 1st Brigade. The 101st did not want to release their combat experienced lieutenants. Colonel (Retired) Manfred Kelman had been a young survivor of the Nazi Concentration Camp at Theresienstadt, Czechoslovakia in WWII. He died in 2004. He was a great leader and true paratrooper.

On a three-day standdown in the first week of November, I survived an incident that could have put a damper on my position as Company XO. The battalion was in from the field and on the first evening, most of my company was consuming alcohol. One of my former troopers from the second platoon, a good troop from Arkansas nicknamed "Hill Billy Jones" got into a drunken knife fight at the Enlisted Club (tent) and was taken by MPs to the ER, at the 2nd Surg Hospital. Somehow, I got the call as company XO to go persuade the ER doctors to release him to me, not to the MPs. I was drinking at the

Officers Club party almost as much as Hill Billy Jones, but I got in my XO jeep and headed for the hospital. It was a major effort to act sober as I finally located Hill Billy. Jones was blabbering and repeatedly apologized to me, his former Platoon Leader, while a surgeon stitched up his cuts. I am certain Jones needed no anesthesia for the procedure. Somehow, I got the doctor to release Jones to my custody, probably just an act of mercy, and I found that the First Shirt sent another jeep and two troops over to the hospital so Jones and I each had a sober jeep driver to take us back to the company area. 1SG Hodge handled the disciplinary actions for Jones, and Captain John never knew a thing. This was a great lesson for a new XO: let the senior NCOs handle the "minor" enlisted problems. That's why you have NCOs! That approach made me a more effective commander with my enlisted folks for the next 20+ years.

Working mostly in the rear area gave me the opportunity to fly with our Air Force FACs. I often saw our battalion FAC, call sign "Bilk 1-7", in our Officers Mess, and whenever he appeared, I asked to fly as a passenger. Flying was fun for me and it was an opportunity to see our AO from above. Our 101st FACs recently upgraded from the tiny O-1 Birddog aircraft to the O-2 Skymaster, more commonly called a "Duck" because the landing gear retracted rearwards after takeoff, reminding viewers of a duck folding its legs. So, I rode along in the right seat of the O-2 as we watched over our Brigade's area of operation, looking for bad guys and putting in fighter strikes: mostly F-4s, F-100s and an occasional A-1, A-6 or F-105. On a couple of occasions, we expended all our white phosphorus (WP) marking rockets and resorted to tossing WP hand grenades out the window. That was my job since the only large window that could be opened was on my side of the aircraft. I also learned that an O-2 became a bomber when we placed fragmentation grenades in glass jars, pulled the pin and I tossed it out on the FAC's call. The glass jar kept the grenade handle in place so the five second fuse did not start. Upon impacting the ground or tree tops, the glass broke; the handle flew off, and, five seconds later BOOM! It did not replace F-4s, but it did serve as harassment for the bad guys. Such "bombing" was not permitted by the Air Force types in Saigon, but in the field, you do what you have to do.

I would have to worry about Air Force "Be-no's" later.

7

Phan Rang and Phan Thiet

All the 1st Brigade base camp elements began a move to Phan Rang on 18 November 1967. Not as paratroopers moving by airlift but as "swabbies." In Chu Lai harbor, we loaded the 1st/327 rear elements onto a large Navy ship, a Landing Ship Tank or LST. The sequenced loading of large trucks, trailers, jeeps, and pallets of gear was very interesting. Additionally, we loaded approximately 100 troops who were working in the battalion rear.

Adjacent to us was an LST that carried Republic of Korea (ROK) troops and we observed a different form of discipline over there. One of the ROK troops earned the wrath of a senior NCO, who commanded the troop to stand at attention while the ROK NCO, using an entrenching tool, smacked him with a blow to the helmet. This confirmed my opinion on how tough the ROKs were.

We enjoyed a two-day vacation sailing down the South China Sea to Phan Rang, fortunately in beautiful, calm weather. To test fire our weapons, we began a program to toss objects into the water and use them as targets. Everything went well until a couple of troopers engaged a target that was floating aft, almost along the ship's hull. In no time, the Skipper called down, upset by ricochets that were striking the bridge of the LST. 1SG Hodge established an aft firing limit, stating that anybody firing aft of that line was going to be the next floating object. We took him at his word and there were no more problems with ricochets or the LST's Skipper.

The two nights afloat were mental down-time for us because, no matter how far you were in the "Rear Area", you were in range of Charlie's rocket or mortar attacks. Out on the ocean, we were a moving target over the horizon and out of sight of the shore. I slept at night not worrying where my weapon and shelter were. We landed at Phan Rang Beach and were trucked to the 101st Base Camp. The First Brigade was gone for nine months and our return was the final visit of the First Brigade to Phan Rang. After the Tet Offensive of January 1968, the First Brigade Rear moved to Bien Hoa to join the Division Rear and the 1st Brigade Forward consolidated with the Division at Camp Eagle near Hue-Phu Bai.

Once in the 101st Brigade Rear facilities, we set up in the wooden-sided buildings that were built for each of the companies and headquarter units of the 1st Brigade. I did not notice when I went through the Screaming Eagle Replacement Training eight months earlier, but the C Company hooches and headquarters building were located across the street from the Brigade Officers Club. That was very convenient for a hard charging paratrooper 1LT. Our next three days were filled with preparation for a major re-supply, training and re-fitting for the Company when they arrived from Chu Lai.

The troops of C Company flew in two days before Turkey Day and they spent four days in the luxury of wooden buildings and eating at a real chow hall. After re-equipping, cleaning gear, rearming, and training a few new replacements, the battalion loaded out in C-130s from Phan Rang AB and flew south down the coast to Phan Thiet. From the Phan Thiet airfield, Cobra Company immediately conducted an air assault to the northwest, hoping to make contact with a main force of NVA moving toward Bao Loc. Bao Loc was a major agricultural center, producing foodstuffs for all Vietnam. The company rear followed by air the next day and we set up the battalion and company rear areas just off the west end of the Phan Thiet runway cargo ramp.

PERRY MASON NEVER WORE JUNGLE FATIGUES

I never thought I would have to defend a soldier at a Special Court Martial in a combat zone. In our second week at Phan Thiet, the Battalion Personnel Officer (S-1) notified me I was to be the Defense Counsel (DC) for a Special Court Martial to be held in the Battalion area. In a couple of days, a separate tent was erected and furniture arranged to create a courtroom. The five officers making up the court sat at the table on the sand floor. The Trial Counsel (TC) and DC occupied small folding tables and chairs in front of the Court Martial panel. The sides of the tents were rolled up to let light and a breeze into the tent.

The accused was an E-5 Sergeant from Alfa Company. To avoid prejudice, nobody from Alfa Company was a member of the court, and, if the Defendant had been from Cobra Company, I could not have participated in any manner. The Trial Counsel was the Platoon Leader from the Medical Platoon attached to the battalion, Lt Pritty.

Sgt Adams was charged with failure to follow an order. I found out later from some of the troopers, he had raped a Vietnamese woman, but, either the Battalion did not want to send the case to a General Court Martial, or they could not locate the Vietnamese victim. During testimony, I noticed and brought forth a discrepancy between the platoon leader's testimony and the times stated by the Sgt and his squad members. The discrepancy was enough to find him not guilty of failure to follow an order on a specific patrol.

"What now?" the sergeant turned to me and asked.

"Nothing, you are not guilty and free to go. See your First Sergeant."

He walked out of the tent in a daze and headed off to his company area. CPT Curcio, who was on the Court Martial board, walked by and said,

"Well argued, Steve." Then Major Kelman came over and said,

"Nice job as the Defense, Steve." I looked down, ashamed and said,

"Sir, he was not guilty of the technical specifications, but that guy is scum. I am sorry we could not get him for something worse.

"You now know accurate specifications must go with the charges, so it was good for you. Besides, everybody in his company knows what a scumbag he is."

After three weeks in Phan Thiet, the XO of Alpha Company, Lt Bishop, and I were sent to the evacuation hospital at Vung Tau to pay four of our battalion troopers at the hospital. The army pay system often forgot to pay troops away from their real units, and it was easier to fly the two of us to Vung Tau with a satchel of money (actually Military Payment Certificates (MPC)) to pay our troops than it was for them to fight the pay system. We caught a C-7 Caribou flight direct to Vung Tau, but we had to hitchhike our way back to Phan Thiet. Lt Bishop and I went first to the hospital and paid our 101st troopers. They were happy to see brother 101st troops, get paid, and brag to the other patients that the 101st takes care of their own.

After checking at the passenger terminal, we found there was not even a helo moving for the rest of the evening, forcing us to stay the night at the R&R hotel in Vung Tau. Darn the luck! The R&R center was in an old French hotel, now named the MACV Army – Navy Hotel, with clean beds, a great dining room, and a huge bar area. The luxury bar showed movies and a replay of a USO show by Petula Clark. I became a life-long Pet Clark fan after that evening at the Vung Tau bar. Lt Bishop and I tried to increase their annual sales of Scottish Highland Dew and crashed late in the night. Next morning, we hitch hiked a helo ride north to Phan Thiet.

On Dec 21, 1967, I rode the resupply chopper to the company in the field along with two replacements and Sergeant Bill Bazar, our Cobra Company armorer. We distributed the mail and resupplies, took orders for the next resupply and saddled up in the Huey for the return trip. Airborne and on a steady course for Phan Thiet, the chopper either took a round in the engine or the aircraft just decided to lose power. The Aircraft Commander (AC) told us to brace for a crash landing as he began an autorotation toward the most thinly forested hilltop he could reach. I remember as we were almost to the ground I saw the rotor blades hit small trees out the right door, slinging tree branches and rotor tip material everywhere. Wham! We impacted the ground in an almost level attitude. The next thing I knew I was on my back on the radio console between Pilot and AC. Sgt Bazar asked me, "Steve, are you OK?" Mumbling "Yes", I crawled out of the bent Huey fuselage. I was more amazed Bill called me Steve than I was at surviving the crash.

The Huey skids were bent up to the frame, the tail rotor broken, and the last two feet of main rotor blade shredded. I checked on our three infantry passengers while the co-pilot checked the crew. The AC suffered a rather serious back injury, but the others escaped with nothing worse than scrapes and bruises. I didn't know it then, but I would ache for the next three days from bouncing around inside the Huey on impact. I set up 360-degree security, drafting the door gunner, the crew chief and confiscating both M-60 machine guns. If things got interesting, the machine guns would do us more good on the perimeter than hanging on a busted chopper. With no precise idea where we were or what the threat was, I prepared for bad news. The copilot's radio still worked on battery power and he was able to contact our battalion Command and Control (C&C) helo, giving them our status and rough location. We treated our cuts and scratches and tried to make the AC as comfortable as possible. Only next day did I realize how lucky we were. The C&C chopper flew over our location but was too low on fuel to land. We waited 35 minutes while the C&C chopper refueled and returned to insert the first of two lifts of infantry for security and pick us up. Cutthroat 6 called the C&C helo to ask if Cutthroat 5 was OK. The Operations Officer (S-3) told him I was in the C&C, shooting pictures like a tourist. We flew back to the 1/327 firebase and then later back to Phan Thiet in another resupply chopper. Just another day in the 'Nam!

Holidays always bring back memories of my second Christmas in the US of Army: Christmas, 1967. I was still the Cobra Company XO and we were in the forests northwest of Phan Thiet. There was no Christmas standdown but we did set up for a re-supply (ammo, hot food and mail). After spending Christmas day working the Landing Zone for resupply, I returned to the CP to discover the RTOs and Artillery Recon NCO had created a "Christmas Tree" by spraying a small tree with white shaving cream and hanging Christmas cards on the limbs as decorations. We were grubby and probably smelled more like Santa's reindeer than like real people, but it was "Christmas" for a while. I can still picture that Christmas tree and remember the pride and spirit of my paratroopers.

Time does not lessen combat insanity because I was still looking for an excuse to fly with any and all aviation units. The only aviation unit stationed at Phan Thiet was a company of helicopters assigned to the 1st Battalion, 9th Cavalry of the 1st Cavalry Division. Why they were left behind in III Corps when the rest of the 1st Cav moved to I Corps was a mystery to us. The 1st of the 9th Cav aviation unit at Phan Thiet provided airlift and gunship support for the 101st and the US Army Advisor units in that region of III Corps. Just to prove that I was completely insane (according to First Sergeant Hodge), when I met a couple of gunship pilots in our little Brigade O'Club, I asked if I could fly as a door gunner on a mission. One moderately insane Cav captain thought he could let me ride as a door gunner on a day's missions. So, on my next day off as XO, I reported to 1/9th Cav, across the runway. I saddled up for a day with the gunships where I checked out the M-60 with my crew chief. He reminded me of the lead techniques to hit a ground target and helped me strap in properly. About 9:30 AM we started engines, and, with Infantry Lieutenant Stevenson as the right door gunner, the gunships lifted off from Phan Thiet airfield.

The first landing zone, not predicted to be hot, was an open area along the coast about 12 miles northeast of Phan Thiet. Our section of gunships flew east to the South China Sea, then along the coast as the door gunners checked their weapons, firing a short burst into the water. We turned inland and linked up with the assault helicopters just as they picked up the infantry troops off a large open field and then we flanked the assault helicopters and flew at 1000 feet along the coast for three or four miles. The gunships, like slicks, removed the doors from the helicopters to save weight. The 100-mph breeze felt good but it was a bit loud. The helicopter helmets kept out most of the sound and I learned a trick from our crew chief that I used for the next 40 plus years: wear ear plugs underneath the flight helmet, turn the radio or intercom volume up, and let that override any white noise that managed to get through the helmet and earplugs.

As we approached the LZ, the gunships parted left and right to make a rocket run down the tree line on each side of the hills guarding the LZ which was in a large dry rice paddy. My gun bird banked to the left leaving me with a view of the sky and not much else. As we rolled out of the left-hand turn, we went level for just a second and then the aircraft nose dropped and the copilot/gunner in the left front seat of our Huey fired off 16 rockets, 8 from each side. We made one orbit and came back over the LZ as the lift birds touched down to discharge their infantry. I did not hear the radio call that the lift birds reported ground fire from their right 2 o'clock off the LZ. This time we made a tight right-hand turn and I was staring straight down at the ground and then we rolled out; the nose went down and we launched eight more rockets along the tree line just to the right front of the LZ. As we started off in a right-hand turn, I opened fire with my M- 60, attempting to rake the tree line. I knew I needed practice since the first 20 or 40 rounds were 15 yards deep behind the leading edge of the trees. I adjusted my fire and managed to get my next burst on the edge of the tree line as we turned away from the LZ.

The first 2.75-inch rocket that our gun bird launched was from the rocket tubes on my side of the chopper and it departed, not with a "Whoosh" but with a tremendous "Bang! Even with ear plugs in and a flight helmet on, the sound startled me, and I am glad I was not on a "live" or "hot" intercom microphone because I yelled "Jesus Christ! That was loud!" The remainder of my door gunner day passed rather uneventfully.

Our time at Phan Thiet marked the end of Captain John's tour. Captain Joseph Westbrook became the Commanding Officer of Cutthroat Company. I was leery of working for a new boss who had just arrived in the battalion and whom I had not met before the change of command ceremony at our battalion firebase. Not to worry though, Captain Westbrook was a pleasure to work for. Sometime later I found out that Captain John praised my work as platoon leader and XO to Captain Westbrook. "Westy" respected my opinions on every issue and he let me run the Company rear as I saw fit. We worked well as a team. This was also the last official act of the Battalion Commander, LTC Gerald E. Morse, who days later turned the battalion over to LTC Elliot P. Sydnor. Colonel Sydnor was also a great commander to work for and a little over two years later he gained fame as the ground force commander for the Special Forces raid on the North Vietnamese Son Tay POW camp. By the end of our short stay at Phan Thiet, the Cobra platoon leaders completed a changeover as Tom Kinane went to command the 1st Brigade Long Range Reconnaissance Patrol (LRRPs) and Ty Herrington was transferred to 5th Special Forces. Steve Davis was dead and I was the company XO. The Cobra platoon leaders were now Lieutenants Moe, Iwanski and Brunson. The old guard was changed!

WILD LIFE IN THE BOONIES

I couldn't leave my story of the boonies in I Corps without commenting on the wildlife that made the life of a Boonie Rat more interesting. In the "Wizard of Oz, Dorothy exclaimed: "Lions, and tigers, and bears! Oh, my!" For this Texas boy, it was "Tigers, and elephants, and snakes! Oh, my!" Forget about jungle scenes, as almost everywhere we operated, we were in forest or out on a flat plain. The forest gave us critters that were just loud, such as howling monkeys, and, on one occasion a sister company swears that they encountered a gorilla. Monkeys raised a fuss when we entered their domain. Sometimes a whole pack of monkeys threw sticks down from the heights at intruders. Eventually they figured we were no threat and settled down, becoming our early warning system for any bad guys approaching. The VC and NVA could not figure out how to make the monkeys shut up any better than we could. Snakes were an issue with some of the troops. The bamboo viper was a brilliant, fluorescent green color and lived peacefully in the bamboo thickets. The snakes that we held a deep respect for were the smallest: brown or banded kraits. These were snakes with neurotoxin venom that was almost a "two-stepper." But like the American coral snake, the krait's mouth was very small and if you were dumb enough to handle one, you could to be bitten. So, don't do that!

Another item of concern out in the boonies was ant bushes. These bushes grew leaves about the size of southern magnolia tree leaves, but because of their shape and sap content, the leaves harbored hundreds of ants on the underside of each leaf. Brush against one of these bushes and you could have a fight on your hands. Good point men recognized these bushes and passed back a warning: "Ant bush on the left." Any water source, such as slow-moving creeks or rivers, could bring large, flat, ribbon leeches, some over 12 inches in length, which were to be avoided. Any decomposing vegetation was a source of small 2" – 3" ground leeches that made an infantryman's life uncomfortable. The forests provided "dead man" flies that showed up with their iridescent blue bodies only when there were corpses after a firefight.

We saw small Asian tigers that could scare the hell out of you, but we never heard of tigers attacking GIs. There was one tiger who stalked our battalion firebase west of Duc Pho because the big cat was attracted by food in our waste sumps. This cat could leap over all our barbwire and be inside a perimeter designed to stop major NVA assaults. The cat was scary; a lot of guys didn't sleep at night on the firebase, but the cat ultimately did no harm. We encountered small elephants that we considered to be NVA transport vehicles. They were often seen from the air by our 101st FACs but I never engaged one in a firefight. In late 1968, a platoon from Bravo Company was overrun by a startled herd of elephants, sending GIs up trees and injuring four troopers. Sorry, no Purple Hearts for wildlife injuries. One of the wildlife things I missed was song birds. In Texas, we enjoyed lots of song birds and doves to greet you in the morning, mockingbirds to harass you any time and assorted jays, cardinals, and others. I cannot recall any birds in the forests of Vietnam. Why would song birds not desire to hang around and compete with helicopters, small arms fire, artillery and jets?

8

Short Stay at Song Be

Early January 1968, the First Brigade, 101st, packed up everything at Phan Thiet and moved closer to the Cambodian border in the Phuoc Long area and the small town of Song Be. Military Engineers constructed a long SW-NE runway capable of handling C-130 aircraft, two miles southwest of Song Be. Song Be was a former French colonial center amid miles of rubber tree farms (OK, colonial plantations) and light forests. Built in a bend of the Be River, the town's terrain rose slowly, from south to north, to the former colonial government office and military compound. The main office building was a rather handsome two story white stone creation with balconies looking south over the town. The north or back side of the government compound was built to the edge of moderate cliffs with the Song Be River below, looping around the north side of town. The main road in town was a divided boulevard running true north to south for almost a mile from the front gate of the compound. The center median of the boulevard was clear of vegetation except grass and was used as a runway for light liaison and Forward Air Control aircraft.

The Vietnamese Army had a local headquarters in the government compound, along with a group of American Army Advisors and a section of USAF O-1 "Bird dog" FACs. So, there was an American presence in Song Be before the arrival of the 101st, just no conventional ground forces of any strength. Song Be's prominent terrain feature was Nui Ba Ra mountain, 723 meters (2361 feet), rising abruptly from the lowlands. Only Nui Ba Dinh, 80 miles to the SW, at 3000 feet in height, is taller in that part of Vietnam. Nui Ba Dinh was the scene of significant fighting after Tet, along with the nearby town of Tay Ninh City.

Located between our airfield and the town was a US Special Forces (SF) "B" Team compound, B-34. The SF units had worked in that area for several years, primarily with the indigenous Montagnard tribe.

One of the surprises was the presence in town of the "Yard" women whose customary dress was topless. I read about the Montagnard women's attire but never encountered any Yards in our travels of I Corps or Phan Thiet. Yes, they were topless, but a mouth discolored by years of beetle nut ensured our troopers showed no interest in the diminutive Montagnard women.

The Yards were comprised of some 30 different tribes with as many dialects. A simplistic comparison was Native American tribes: Apache, Utes, Comanches, all different but still Native Americans. The various Montagnard tribes had resided in the mountainous backbone of forests in North and South Vietnam for almost 1000 years before the white man arrived. Vietnamese history reflected a long and not so friendly relationship with the Yards. Racism and the desire for independence by these mountain villagers set the stage for numerous conflicts and occasional open rebellion against the Communist North and despotic South Vietnamese governments. The Yards were promised independence by the Communist and South Vietnamese governments, but both broke those promises. I came to believe that without American Special Forces in Vietnam in the early 1960s, the government would have actively or passively seen to the eradication of the Montagnards. As it was, the official South Vietnamese policy was to move the Montagnards from their mountain homes into resettlement villages near towns to civilize them. This sounds a lot like the US Government treatment of Native American tribes. The SF-trained Yard soldiers often referred to as Civilian Irregular Defense Group or CIDG, proved dependable and loyal allies of the US Special Forces troops. After the fall of South Vietnam in 1975, the NVA committed numerous horrific attacks on Montagnard tribes who had supported the Americans and South Vietnamese.

Song Be was our company's first experience in "outsourcing" labor to fill sandbags for the defensive walls around our tents and supplies. The brigade civil affairs troops went into Song Be each day and hired Vietnamese women to fill sandbags in the various areas for a pittance per day. By hiring six laborers to do nothing but fill bags, we finished constructing revetments in record time. First Sergeant Hodge and Sgt Ballew took turns watching the laborers while they were in our area. The clay soil allowed us to make one change in our sleeping cot arrangements. We dug a rectangular hole slightly larger than and as deep as the cot and placed the cot in the hole, so the cot edge was at ground level. If we took incoming mortars or rockets, we could roll over into the protective hole. We still had a wall of sandbags, three-feet high, around the tents, but more protection is better.

A mile east of the 101st base, Nui Ba Ra mountain rose over 2300 feet. It resembled a huge green monster watching over us with a microwave and radio relay station atop the mountain. The radio site was protected by a perimeter of bunkers and fighting positions. Our amusement was the occasions when the radio site defenders conducted a "Mad Minute" in which the defenders fired all their weapons for one minute at anything of suspicion around the perimeter. From a mile away, we saw the explosions and tracers as a fun fireworks show. I know the GIs up on the mountain thought that they were keeping the VC at bay, but we saw it as entertainment and a waste of ammunition.

The soil in the Song Be area was a red clay base that was ground talc-fine along roads. The soil was either glue-like when wet or fine red talcum powder when dry. All our clothes and equipment took on a red tinge. Even though we washed our uniforms, the seams acquired a red lining. The talc was so fine that when a vehicle drove along an unpaved surface, the red dust parted and flowed like water away from the tires. When a helicopter landed in our battalion rear, the resulting red cloud caused profanity for 30 minutes, even if it was for the Battalion Commander. I always carried a Texas flag with me after I became the XO and Song Be was my chance to  fly it. In front of our Cobra Company orderly room, the First Sergeant erected a flag pole and we declared the site as the local Consulate of The Great State of Texas.

The brigade and battalion mission was to interdict large groups of NVA that were supposedly heading for the Saigon area. Little did we know that most the NVA and Viet Cong forces were already in the Saigon area and only a small force remained in the Song Be area. When the Tet offensive started, this small force attacked the town of Song Be and was accidentally drawn into a firefight on the edge of the 101st cantonment area. While the NVA forces were advancing toward the town of Song Be, they encountered a group of Montagnards from a

81

resettlement area located across an east-west ravine and about 800 meters from our perimeter. As the fight progressed, the local forces asked for assistance from the 101st. The Brigade sent a response unit from our side of the perimeter and they were immediately engaged by the NVA. The 101st unit withdrew inside the perimeter and our defensive bunkers along the perimeter provided covering fire. The NVA decided to engage the perimeter immediately behind Company C and our three bunkers were soon trading fire at long range with NVA forces across the ravine.

I was listening to the battalion rear radio net when rounds began to crack overhead and slap through the bamboo grove that separated the company area from the perimeter. I immediately began preparations to provide mortar support for the perimeter, but the Brigade Rear command post instructed me to stand by, as there were helicopters and Vietnamese Air Force (VNAF) fighters inbound to be used against the NVA positions. Since I could not use my mortars, I grabbed my CAR-15, several bandoleers of ammo and started out toward our bunkers on the other side of the bamboo trees. Incoming small arms fire was cutting the bamboo shoots and impacting the ground as Specialist Stoffregen, our company clerk, and Sgt Ballou our supply sergeant, and I sprinted from the concealment of the bamboo thicket to the real shelter of a big sandbagged bunker.

The ground between our defensive bunkers was cleared, from five yards behind the bunkers to some 400 meters down the slope into the ravine. This gave us great fields of fire for defense against ground attacks inside that range, but it left anyone between the bunkers exposed to the NVA fire from across the ravine. I leaned around the right edge of the bunker and found I could see muzzle flashes from across the ravine. I carefully took aim and fired three or four rounds of tracers at the muzzle flashes that I could pinpoint. Nobody fired at my spotting rounds and I then saw the crew from the next bunker, 50 yards or so to our right, waving an ammo can at us. They were running low on ammunition and could not move back through the thick bamboo to get ammo from our tent area. The only trail through the bamboo came out behind our bunker; poor planning. Stoffregen immediately understood and said he would return to our company to get more ammunition. He disappeared into the bamboo and in three minutes returned carrying six ammo cans of M-16 ammo and two cans of M-60 ammo. I could not have carried that many ammo cans, but Stoffregen was a very tall, lanky kid and he stuffed two cans under each arm and hand-carried four more. Saying he would take three ammo cans to the other bunker, Stoffregen set off at a crouched run along the path to the adjacent bunker. To this day, I carry the image of the tall rangy kid carrying ammo cans, with bullets impacting the red dirt around him and cracking through the bamboo behind him. Stoffregen delivered the ammo and then retraced his route, seemingly oblivious to the enemy fire.

Stoffregen stayed as the company clerk through our moves to Hue/Phu Bai for the battle of Tet and then to Camp Eagle in mid-1968. After serving the infantrymen of Cobra Company, Stoffregen wanted to serve as an infantryman and the company commander made that happen. The clerk-turned-infantryman joined the company in the field as we moved the battalion towards the A Shau valley in mid-1968. Out in the A Shau, he took an AK-47 round in his hand, shattering several bones, and was Medevac'd to the States for treatment and ultimate discharge with his Combat Infantryman Badge and a Purple Heart. A hell of a company clerk!

One quiet evening at Song Be, Lt Tom Kinane stopped by for a social visit. Tom left the company earlier and took command of the 101st Long Range Reconnaissance Patrol (LRRP) unit. We opened a bottle of scotch and talked as long-time friends and survivors of life as platoon leaders. I enjoyed just sitting with Tom, even when not talking, because we shared a common bond. Nine months later our paths crossed again as company commanders.

R&R TIME

In mid-January, Cobra Company was well established at Song Be, so I figured it was time to take my R&R. Most troops took their R&R at midpoint in their 12-month tour, but I put mine off until after month nine. For eight days, Cobra Company had to survive without me. I was off to Hong Kong, the shopping center of the world. I stayed at the Hong Kong Hilton, built in 1961, so still relatively new. The hotel was 26 stories tall with a magnificent view of the Starr Ferry and across the harbor to Kowloon. In a slightly damp and cool Hong Kong, I spent money on tailor-made clothes, stereo gear, and great restaurants. This was a place of unbelievable deals on everything from cameras to pearls. I heard a description of Hong Kong that proved true: "This is a place to save yourself broke." Everything was an excellent deal, even compared to the BX in Vietnam. The China Fleet Club was run by the US Navy Exchange System and was four floors of unbelievable savings and rare items. Travelling both directions to Hong Kong, I again passed through the beautiful base at Cam Ranh Bay, envying the 22nd Repo Depot guys for their "big city" accommodation and white beach.

SAIGON WITH 5ᵀᴴ SPECIAL FORCES

Back at Song Be, on January 28, I was asked to go pay four 101ˢᵗ troops in the 3ʳᵈ Field Hospital in Saigon. I went to the airfield and was manifested on an Air America Volpar 18 aircraft to Saigon, courtesy of a reservation arranged by 1LT Ty Harrington who transferred to 5ᵗʰ Special Forces the previous month. Ty came out to Bien Hoa airbase from the SF Camp Goodman, met me, and, enroute home, we drove around Saigon with $200,000 in Vietnamese Piastre for the local Special Forces-trained Mike Force (mercenaries). After paying the Mike Force units, we made it to Camp Goodman and Ty announced we were invited to a going away party that evening for the actress Martha (Maggie) Ray to be held on top of Presidential Hotel. I was covered with the Song Be red clay powder and said, "No way." Ty opened a wall-length closet in the SF officers' quarters and showed me 200 plus suits with ties, shirts, shoes and accessories. "Get a shower and we will be on our way." instructed Ty.

The party was a dream-come-true for a grunt, five hours from the boonies. Maggie shook my hand and then hugged me when Ty told her I was not from Saigon, but I was a real boonie rat. I met beautiful starlets traveling with Maggie's tour, generals up to General Westmoreland, and a few US and Vietnamese civilian dignitaries. With cold drinks in hand, we watched a "Puff, The Magic Dragon" gunship working outside Bien Hoa AF. The deadly bursts from Puff's guns formed a colored neon light that stretched from black space to the earth's surface. It was hard to believe, from this rooftop, that the gunfire could be for grunts in trouble.

The following morning, I went to the 3ʳᵈ Field Hospital and paid the four 101ˢᵗ troopers. They were pleased the battalion remembered them and were elated to get a partial payment with which to cover incidental expenses during their medical stay. Just before evening meal, I met up with Ty, who was escorting James MacArthur, "Danno" of TV's "Hawaii Five-O." After a light meal, we proceeded to run the bars of Tu Do Street with Ty in the lead. James was a "real" person and not the pain that I expected from a TV star. He was amazed at the functions of the Special Forces and listened in awe to the tales that Ty and I told of being fellow platoon leaders in the 101ˢᵗ. James was recognized by a few Americans and fewer Vietnamese in the dives and bars that we entered. Of course, if the Vietnamese hookers did not recognize James, Ty would state, "He number one TV star from Hollywood." That started the frenzied competition among the bar girls for James' attention. A couple of the girls offered "free sample for Number 1 TV star." MacArthur showed the good sense to pass on those offers as we moved on. It was a tough job but somebody was needed to do the tour with James McArthur. We rolled back into Camp Goodman about 2 AM and "Hawaii Five-O" remained at the top of my favorite TV show list for many years. Next morning, Ty dropped me at the Bien Hoa Passenger Terminal and I caught the Air America aircraft back to Song Be. Little did we know that I escaped Saigon just hours before all hell broke loose: Tet Offensive 1968!

On my return to Song Be, Sgt Ballew said the battalion mortar team came to inspect our mortar and then, re-laid the mortar tube. That is a process where the tube and sights are aligned with a prime direction so the mortar can be accurately fired at targets. Since I was the only Company XO that knew anything about mortars, the Cobra troopers fired illumination and H&I fires for the Brigade rear area at night.

Two nights later, Sergeant Ballew tripped over the legs of the mortar as we fired a flare round, causing the round to go almost vertical and ignite high over the company area. The flare was no problem since it would blow away and burn out before landing. But the 81mm metal casing for the flare fell straight down with a whistling "whoo-whoo-whoo" sound and made like a cookie cutter, slicing a perfectly round hole through the top of Ballew's supply tent.

30 January 1968 - After lots of therapy and a hell of an exercise program my Redleg brother Donald passed his physical exam and fitness tests and, taking convalescent leave, caught a flight from San Antonio to Washington DC and the Department of the Army. Donald appealed to Army Officer Assignments in DC and talked his way into an immediate assignment back to the 101st in Vietnam. Don departed CONUS on 30 January 1968, for his second combat tour, just as things got tense in Vietnam.

5 February 1968 – Brother Donald finally arrived in Vietnam. He was delayed for almost a week at Clark Air Base in the Philippines because escalated Tet fighting around major cities and military posts in Vietnam closed all airfields to non-military flights, meaning contract airline flights with replacements. By the time his plane landed in Vietnam, Donald's long one-day trip turned into six days.

9

Tet Offensive – 1968

In the first week of February 1968, the true size of the Tet Offensive became obvious and the 101st was needed in I Corp to augment the Marines and 1st Cav Division, both fighting lots of well trained and equipped NVA. "The Nomads of Vietnam", the 1st Brigade, 101st Airborne, was on the move again. We packed up the battalion rear and somehow, I was volunteered as part of the Advance Party to be on the first C-130 to fly into the Hue-Phu Bai airfield.

It was hot, dusty and dry when we loaded onto the C-130 at Song Be. When we landed at Phu Bai it was cold, blowing rain and low overcast with thick clouds -- great weather for the NVA as it limited our use of airpower. That was one of the most miserable nights of my tour. Nobody at the airfield knew we were coming and we were shown to an empty soggy field where we could gather the rest of the 1/327 when they arrived. I spent the night crouched under a poncho up against the sandbag wall of a power generator. With two rocket attacks and steady rain, I got little sleep up against the loud generator, but at least it protected me from the wind. Just another night in the "Nam! The only bright spot that evening was the arrival in Phu Bai of 1LT Johnny McKnight as an envoy for BG Matheson, now at the Marine III MAF headquarters at Da Nang. BG Matheson was the MACV liaison to the Third Marine Amphibious Force (III MAF), which at that time "owned" all the American forces in I Corps. Johnny, as previously told, was BG Matheson's aide when Mat commanded the 1st Brigade and I was delighted to see Johnny, not only as a friend and former brother platoon leader, but also as an indicator that the 1st of the 327th was not forgotten by the US Army.

The next morning, I reported to the Commanding Officer of the 5th Marine Regiment as the Liaison Officer between the 1st/327 Airborne Infantry and the US Marines. *We were going to fight the remainder of the Tet offensive as part of the 5th Marines! Hoorah!* Our battalion was to relieve a Marine battalion at a base camp near the village of Phu Loc, located southwest of Hue. Our battalion's mission was to stop North Vietnamese infiltration into the Hue area and to seek out and destroy any NVA units and facilities in the nearby hills. We soon found plenty of NVA in the area. The Marines made lots of vehicles available, so our supplies at the airfield were loaded onto trucks and we were driven down QL-1 to the village of Phu Loc, our home for the next two months. Our operations from Phu Loc were quite different from the Marine Corps operations. Rather than having a base camp in a secure rear area and a forward Tactical Command Post with an artillery unit on a firebase, the battalion operated the Command Post on the Phu Loc base, along with all the supporting company and battalion rear functions. Our rifle companies fanned out from the base camp into the forested hills to the south and west, seeking NVA units.

Phu Loc in February was best described as wet, cold, miserable and it sucked. The 1/327 battalion firebase was located on a small rise south of the village and had been hardened by the Marines for more than six months. Everything was underground! The battalion TOC, unit orderly rooms, supply storage and sleeping facilities were all underground. The positions were dug out by bulldozers, roofs

constructed of steel planking, and multiple layers of sand bags placed overhead. The steady rains and vehicular traffic in the base camp turned the streets into muddy ponds. The weather was cold with frequent rain and constant low ceilings.

1LT Stevenson at Phu Loc

Most mornings brought a cloud ceiling so low that the clouds obscured the hill tops less than a mile from the base camp. I was not a great believer in wearing an armored vest or "flak jacket", but, at Phu Loc, I began to wear one just for the warmth and rain protection. It did no good to complain, as any whining about the weather or mud was greeted with the paratroopers' reply: "It don't mean nothing!"

The evening we moved into Phu Loc base camp, the Marines were cleaning out and burning old equipment and trash. First Sergeant

Hodge stuck his head into our Orderly Room and announced the Marines were burning C-4 in the area behind our company. C4 is a multipurpose, moldable explosive detonated by a blasting cap. If a small portion of C4 is ignited with a flame, it will not explode but instead burn brightly and produce intense heat. Our grunts rolled a marble size piece of C4, pinched a small tab to be lit with a match and in seconds, they had a boiling cup of water for coffee, hot chocolate or a dehydrated meal. First Sergeant Hodge and I jogged over to the burn area and found Marines breaking open old claymore mines, removing and burning the C4. We rapidly explained that we wanted all the C4 they were planning to destroy and SGT Ballew would pick up the C4. The Marine sergeant in charge agreed and began stacking the C4 extracted from the claymores. We soon collected enough C4 to provide every trooper in our company with a baseball size chunk of C4. This episode illustrated the different mentality and approaches Marines and paratroopers took to fighting this war. The Marines fought "heavy" with frequent re-supplies and food from their base camp. The paratroopers fought "light," carrying in their rucksacks everything needed for up to a week between re-supplies.

On our third day, the Barbarians made contact with bad guys about five kilometers south down a forested ridgeline from Phu Loc, a ridge we could see from the company area. The company requested tactical air support and within minutes a pair of Marine F-4s arrived to help. The clouds were down to about 1500 feet and the only way the F-4s could get into the target area was to go "feet wet" out over the water of the South China Sea and then Cau Ai bay and come in under the clouds. Under some unbelievably low ceilings and in marginal visibility, the F-4s dropped 500-pound bombs and strafed the bad guys in front of the Barbarians. I took back all the unkind things I'd ever said about Marine aviators; that was some super flying to support an Army unit, although we were part of the 5th Marine Regiment for now. The requested Air Force F-4s couldn't figure out how to get down to the target area and went back to the O'Club, but the Marines figured it out and put "steel on target." Another amazing sight for me was watching a Marine 155-millimeter artillery unit firing from a position about 800 meters to the north. The big 155 mm projectile came out of the barrel at a slow enough velocity for me to see the rounds leave the guns and arc over Phu Loc enroute to its target.

The days wore on at Phu Loc with no sun or real break in the weather. All our companies made contact with the 2nd NVA Regiment, but, due to the heavy fighting in Hue between the Marines and the NVA, most of the bad guys were trying to get away from the city rather than to get into Hue. The press in the United States published trash for status of war reports. The battle for Hue was never a disaster for US or even South Vietnamese troops. The North Vietnamese suffered a major defeat at Hue and lost almost an entire division of troops in the battles. The real tragedy fell on the civilians in the area when Tet began as the North Vietnamese executed over a thousand intellectuals and government officials.

I was getting "short" with under 100 days left on my tour, but I felt no desire to abandon my 327th brothers and go home to the US, as any assignment would be dull compared to combat. My only friends were "in country." I discussed the possibility of extending to be a Company Commander with Captain Westbrook, but he explained there was no way the battalion would make me a 1LT commander when there were plenty of captains around, although admittedly with less combat experience. So, if I wanted a command, I needed to extend for six months. During that time, I would be promoted to captain in July. Westy talked with the Battalion CO and S-3 and they said I was welcome to serve an extension as the Battalion Assistant S-3 (Air) on the firebase. No promises were made about a company command, but I would be in place as a captain with lots of time in the battalion when one of the line companies needed a new commander. I submitted my six-month extension paperwork, which was immediately approved. I knew then the 327th would be home when I completed my first year "in the Nam." It may sound strange to think of Vietnam as "home", but home is where your family is. At that time, my immediate family was my "band of brothers" in the 101st and they were in Vietnam. I could not leave them.

February 24th, 1968, was another damp, dreary afternoon and we were standing by the company orderly room bunker when I heard the distinctive "Thunggg" sound of a mortar being fired and simultaneous shouts of "Incoming" sent every trooper diving for a bunker. I was standing on the top step to the orderly room, so I wheeled and scrambled down and into the rear end of the bunker. The First Sergeant and several troopers piled down the steps and then the first incoming mortar landed with a tremendous explosion. Specialist James Gormley tumbled down the stairs, bleeding from multiple fragmentation wounds. As the First Sergeant and SGT Ballew examined Gormley, I attempted to ring the battalion aid station on our field phone. The phone was dead, so I grabbed my helmet and climbed the stairs amid the sounds of mortar rounds exploding nearby. One glance at a loose wire sticking up in the mud showed that our telephone line to the battalion switchboard was severed by one of the explosions. The incoming explosions moved away from our bunker, so I yelled down to the First Shirt "I'm going to the aid station to get help." As two more mortar rounds landed, I sprinted 200 yards across the muddy roads to the Battalion medics' bunker. A quick response by the medics with an ambulance beat me back to the company area. Spec 4 James Gormley was dead. He was killed while running for our bunker when the first round hit one foot to the right of the bunker entrance. I don't know where Gormley was when the "Incoming" was called or why he was the last man to the bunker, but one second more and he would have been safe. The impact point of the first round was pure bad luck, but the explosion could not have been more accurately placed with a laser.

I radioed Cutthroat 6 and informed him of the loss. He took the news calmly. I felt sick. A short red headed trooper with freckles and only 20 years old, Gormley was one of my M-79 gunners in the 2nd Platoon. He put in his six-month extension papers to become the company armorer when his 12-month tour was completed on March 30th. The First Sergeant recently transferred Gormley from my old 2nd Platoon to the company headquarters when we moved from Song Be up to Phu Loc. James Gormley completed 10 months on the line without a scratch and then he was killed in the rear area by a humbug mortar round.

Damn, I just extended for six more months of losing friends. I departed on my extension leave with a heavy heart.

10

Extension Leave

To start my 30-day extension leave, I hopped one of our logistics helicopters from Phu Loc to Camp Eagle. I learned that Donald was up at LZ Sally on a standdown with his unit, so I hitched a ride to LZ Sally on a 101st Aviation helo and enjoyed a two-hour reunion with Don and our friend Bev Garrett. Then it was back to the 1st Brigade rear area for the night and next morning by C-7 to Da Nang where I caught a C-130 hop to Cam Ranh Bay for my flight to the States.

My Leave airplane took off at 9:00 AM and landed at Travis AFB in the early morning on the same day (we gained a day crossing the International Date Line). In little time, I changed clothes and was on a bus to San Francisco International airport. I was lucky to catch the next American Airlines flight to Dallas Love Field and with a taxi ride I was at Bev Garrett's home before dinner.

Because our mother died when I was 13 years old and our Dad died in 1967, Donald, Joy and I were realistically "homeless." Joy was living in the dorm at The University of Texas and with Dallas classmates and friends when on school breaks. Donald and Bev Garrett were the best of friends and the Garrett family unofficially "adopted" us both when our Dad died. The Garrett house was the only place I could go when on leave. I even changed my Army home of record to the Garrett's Arlington, Texas, address. Upon my arrival, Momma Garrett gave me a tremendous pasta dinner and then I decided to go to bed early. I sat on the edge of my bed and started to giggle like an idiot. I was overwhelmed by the thought "Ha, Ha, Charlie can't get me here." With that settled, I slept for almost three days. Mama Garrett asked if there was anything I wanted to do, but I was content to unwind and sleep. "Crash" was the best description for the next two days. For the next two weeks, I planned a trip to Ft Campbell and then on to Washington, DC.

I made a trip to Ft Campbell and Clarksville, Tennessee, to see my first platoon sergeant, SFC Ernie Holmes, then to DC to see Major Bill Northquest, now on the Department of the Army staff. I wandered through the rough part of DC on the way to Ft McNair and Bill couldn't believe I had walked from my hotel out to his office. We discussed my extension plans and he wished me the best of luck and hoped I'd get to command a company. Even if I was a company commander in the next six months, it would be tough to be as fine a company commander as Bill Northquest. He set an extremely high standard as a commander. Now, it was another flight to Dallas Love Field and idle time in Arlington.

I was running out of ideas on how to entertain myself, with my friends gone from the Dallas area and many in Vietnam. I started to feel guilty about not being back with the 101st. My new plan was to report to McCord AFB early and cut short my 30-day leave time, get back and sign in at Cobra Company. I booked a flight to Seattle's SEATAC airport and took the short bus ride down to Ft Lewis and the aerial port at McCord AFB. As a returnee from ordinary leave, and an early report at that, I was so far down the priority list that I would have to spend two nights there before my flight. I checked into the BOQ at McCord and played tourist on Ft Lewis. As promised, the third morning I was manifested on a Seaboard Airlines flight bound for Cam Ranh Bay, and soon I was airborne in a "big iron bird" for the 16-hour trip. We made a stop for fuel on Wake Island, and that was an education in atolls and WW II in the Pacific. I could not fathom the loss of hundreds of lives just for this tiny chunk of coral, the location of one of the most publicized atrocities by the Japanese military in WW II. Wake was so small that the tail of our Boeing 707 was the tallest thing on the atoll. Then it was on to Clark AB for another gas stop and finally into Cam Ranh Bay.

In a policy change, we were authorized to wear jungies to or from Vietnam, if you owned jungies. My jungies were cool and comfortable compared to traveling in a khaki uniform. In Arlington, I had a tailor shop sew a screaming eagle patch on the right shoulder. The patch on a trooper's right shoulder symbolizes the soldier having completed a combat tour with that unit. Since I completed a full tour before extending, I was now entitled to wear the 101st patch on both shoulders, referred to as a "Buzzard Sandwich." I received numerous quizzical glances when Army folks saw a 23-year-old 1st Lieutenant with a Combat Infantryman Badge (CIB) and a 101st combat patch, flying to Vietnam.

This trip was quite different from my first trip to Vietnam.

11

My First Vietnam Trip

I travelled in civilian clothes to San Francisco International Airport (SFO), caught a military bus to Travis AFB and then put on a uniform and checked in at the passenger terminal. I was informed I had about eight hours before my flight was to be manifested. So, I headed for the O'Club to drink. With three other Infantry lieutenants, I managed to get somewhat drunk before the club announced a call for passengers on our flight. The Travis AFB O'Club and Travis Passenger Terminal had set up an efficient procedure to get intoxicated future combat leaders out of the club, onto a bus, through manifesting and onto the plane.

The first thing I remember after boarding was waking to a pretty, brunette stewardess passing out a remedy for the many headaches: four aspirins and a large glass of water. She was as demanding as she was cute, with a brisk:

"Take those and drink all the water or you don't get off my plane in Hawaii."

"Yes, ma'am!" and I took mine.

Twenty minutes later the Captain announced we were getting ready to land at Hickam AFB, Hawaii. With a two-hour ground time, the passengers could deplane and visit the terminal area. I stepped out onto the boarding stairs and experienced the wonderful fragrant Hawaiian weather, but also the high humidity of a tropical location. I was going to live with it for the next twelve months (which would turn out to be two and a half years).

We left Hickam AFB, refueled at Clark AB in the Philippines, and made the final two-hour flight to Cam Ranh Bay. Following a short speech by a Master Sergeant in jungle fatigues, we started down the aisle of the plane toward the stairs. I stepped out on the staircase and was hit with the tremendous heat, humidity and glare of Vietnam. "Jesus, it's hot, and bright!" There was not a cloud in the sky and mirages wiggled across the runways and cargo ramps. The sand, even around the passenger ramp, was white, multiplying the reflection and glare. The charter passenger terminal was approximately 2/3 the way up the vast west ramp, alongside the left of two long parallel runways, marked 02Left and 02Right. From the top of the boarding stairs I saw the bright blue waters of the South China Sea stretching up to the north, toward the city of Nha Trang just over the horizon. We filed down the stairs and by the time I had crossed the 50 yards of sun-bleached concrete ramp to the passenger terminal, my wrinkled khakis were seriously damp with sweat. I'm a good Texas boy who can handle heat, but the 100 plus degrees and high humidity came as a real shocker.

22ND REPO DEPOT

We loaded onto buses with heavy wire screens over the open windows to discourage Viet Cong grenades, and were delivered to the 22nd Replacement Battalion (known in-country as the Repo Depot) just off the north end of the left runway. The only other major unit on that corner of Cam Ranh was the 6th Convalescent Center. In five months, I would be back at the 6th CC as an honored guest and patient, thanks to the North Vietnamese Army (NVA). The beach and Repo Depot area were covered with the most brilliant white sand I had ever seen. Inside the dining hall, our 200 new troops did not receive the expected "Welcome to Vietnam" speech; the first item was a briefing on shelter procedures in the event of a rocket or mortar attack. Then came the welcome speech and briefings on the facilities, chow, the "be-no's" of life at Cam Ranh and Vietnam in general. The 22nd Repo Depot would be our home for approximately four days as we began our Vietnam tour, turned in our paperwork and were issued our first sets of jungle fatigues and jungle boots.

The billets were two story wood frame buildings with screens on all four sides from four feet to seven feet in height from the floor. Each building, or "hooch" was about 100 feet long, room for 48 to 60 bunk beds. The officers were treated a bit differently as our building had only 24 bunks instead of the enlisted soldiers having 60 bunks. There must have been 40 hooches in separate sections, so the number of transients could have reached 4000 troops over three or four days. Three different Army processing companies handled new replacements, troops going to / from R&R, and outbound troops headed home for DEROS or leave. That meant there were a lot of folks coming into and departing Vietnam. Cam

Ranh was but one of three major personnel transit centers, along with Bien Hoa near Saigon and Da Nang in the northern Military's First Corps area known as I Corps and pronounced "Eye Corps."

There was an informal but well defined "class system" at the Repo Depot. Each group: New Guys, R&R troops or homeward bound troops had separate areas in the Repo Depot. The R&R guys were more than happy to greet the "Fucking New Guys" or FNG's with catcalls of "How many days do you have left on your tour?" and "If I had a year to go, I'd shoot myself." They sounded full of bravado, but they would have to come back and finish their tour. The few troops that I met on return from their R&R had already made the mental shift to being combat troops again. Although many hours were spent telling tales of their drinking and sexual activities on R&R, they mostly left the FNGs alone. The troops going home for good usually greeted the "cherries" with a "Good luck, man" or "Say Hi to Charlie for me."

In the FNG area you could tell how long soldiers had been at Cam Ranh by what they wore: on day one, they were still in khaki uniforms, crumpled from the long trip from the States. On day two, they had changed into the stateside type fatigues. Late day two or early day three, everyone was issued at least one set of jungle fatigues, and, for a dollar or two, you could have the Korean tailor shop sew on your rank, branch and unit patches. After the briefings and processing on day two, it was a waiting game for transportation to your new unit's home base. Some of my infantry friends shipped out late on day three, but I had another day in the sunny 22nd Repo Depot.

1ST BRIGADE (SEPARATE), 101ST AIRBORNE DIVISION

Although I sweated a change of units, my in-country orders still sent me to the 1st Brigade (Separate) of the 101st Airborne Division. Hooah! The 101st Airborne's Screaming Eagle Replacement Training School (SERTS) was 35 miles south of Cam Ranh Bay, adjacent to Phan Rang AB. On day four at Cam Ranh, I caught a C-123 for the short flight to Phan Rang, and, finally, I was back in the 101st. I considered myself very fortunate going to a sister unit in the 101st Airborne. Most other FNG's in the 22nd Repo Depot were bound for completely strange units with no prior connection. We were just cattle being processed for movement – but hopefully not to a slaughter house.

The SERTS and 1st Brigade rear base camp was made up of dozens of single-story wood frame hooches, much like the 22nd Repo Depot, but the area was spread over a square mile and had the feel of a ghost town because all the combat troops were deployed to a forward base camp in I Corps near Duc Pho. The only activity at this large, dusty, deserted city was the SERTS on the east side. This was another Repo Depot where over 10 days, new guys were exposed to the basic procedures of the 101st line units, weapons re-familiarization, patrolling and suggested loads for the troopers' rucksacks and web gear. The only contact with Charlie was a VC sniper who had been harassing the 101st base camp for over a year and had yet to hit anyone. The instructors said catching the VC sniper was a very low priority because he might be replaced by somebody who was a better shot. About sunset we were playing basketball for physical conditioning when we heard a sharp "crack" sound and then a "thwack" as a bullet hit one of the basketball backstops. We were all eating dust on the ground, but nothing followed so we resumed our basketball game.

After completing New Guy School, twenty-one of us were herded onto a C-123 at Phan Rang AB and flown to the Duc Pho airstrip in southern I Corps. About 20 miles south of Quang Ngai city, Duc Pho was located on the 20-mile-wide Vietnam coastal plain between the rocky hills and the sandy beach line. The entire 1st Brigade Forward was located among the scrub brush and sandy paths of the Duc Pho coastline. The engineers constructed a temporary pier area so the brigade could receive large supply loads by Navy LSTs or similar vessels. The airfield was covered by peneprime, a thick fluid asphalt derivative substance used to stabilize the sandy surface, keep the sand from blowing (it failed), and, I thought, to stink up the neighborhood. Shortly after our flight's arrival, a 2 ½ ton truck pulled up to the air cargo / passenger terminal (a tent) and the eight paratroopers bound for the 1st Battalion, 327th Infantry threw our gear into the truck bed and climbed aboard.

From this point forward I am going to insert my disclaimer. Everybody sees a conflict from a unique point of view and my view of the Vietnam War was no exception. I saw it first as an infantry platoon leader, then as a rifle company Executive Officer, Assistant Battalion Operations Officer for Air, Company Commander and as an Assistant Operations Officer in Special Forces. I have for years met 101st troopers who saw the same firefight from completely different viewpoints. I know one unit that referred to an engagement as an "ambush", but since my platoon was not ambushed, our supporting fight was just a common "firefight" on that day. Forty years later I discussed a firefight with a former platoon leader who never knew who "saved" (a term I dislike) his platoon until he read a report on how my platoon attacked the flank of the enemy position on a hill. A firefight or war can be many things to many folks; it all depends on where you were when.

How and who we fought changed during my tours. In early 1967, the paratroopers of the 101st Airborne Division's 1st Brigade were fighting mostly Viet Cong insurgents, rarely in more than company size. By mid-1967, the 101st moved to contact with North Vietnamese Army (NVA) troops in the I Corps area. By late 1967, the 101st battles were almost exclusively against well-armed and trained NVA forces pouring into South Vietnam.

The 1968 Tet Offensive launched by the Communists changed the complexion of the war for US ground forces. Despite the slanted presentation of the Tet Offensive by the media in the United States, the Viet Cong, the original "Charlie," had his ass kicked during the Tet Offensive. This destruction was facilitated by NVA commanders who assumed command of VC forces and were eager to use the local VC troops as lead assault elements on US and allied forces. These initial assault troops absorbed tremendous losses and the NVA troops then followed up the initial assaults.

By summer 1968, the Viet Cong ceased to exist militarily, and were reduced to political leadership, while the armed conflict shifted to the NVA. From Tet forward, ours was not a conflict against rice farmer revolutionaries with bolt action rifles but with well trained and organized troops with tanks, heavy transportation and artillery.

12

Assistant S-3 (Air)

Now I was back from Extension Leave and back "in the 'Nam" and 1/327. My assignment as Assistant S-3 increased my "Superman" syndrome, as I knew no fear of the NVA or flying with our rotor guys. To say I took unnecessary chances is putting it mildly. It never entered my mind what I was doing was risky.

Upon return from extension leave, I was transferred to Headquarters and Headquarters Company (HHC) and began my career as an Assistant S-3 (Air). I never saw the rear area of HHC. I just picked up my paperwork from the Cobra Company orderly room tent, walked a couple hundred yards up the road at Camp Eagle and signed in at the HHC tent.

Within three hours, all my worldly possessions were packed in a ruck sack, I was issued a weapon, ammo, maps, grenades, and was on a chopper headed for the battalion Fire Support Base (FSB) where most of my work would take place. Our Battalion Commander now was LTC Elliott P. "Bud" Sydnor, a great leader with whom I enjoyed serving. My immediate boss was the Battalion Operations Officer (S-3), MAJ Horace Clark. He served a previous tour with MACV as an advisor, but I soon felt he was not a deep-to-the-core paratrooper.

On April 19th, the 1/327 secured the two adjacent hilltops that became FSB Veghel. The 101st was building fire bases along Highway 547 in a line from Hue to the A Shau Valley. Firebases Birmingham, Bastogne and Veghel were our stepping stones to the assault of the A Shau. My title "Assistant S-3 (Air)" should indicate that my primary job was requesting, utilizing and integrating all forms of aircraft and airpower in support of the Battalion. But, in learning the job from the bottom up, I started out as one of two lieutenants and one captain who served in the Battalion Tactical Operations Center (TOC) supporting the Operations Officer and Battalion Commanding Officer.

The TOC was usually a deep trench dug out by the engineers' bulldozer before the battalion CP occupied the hill. The trench was eight feet wide and twenty feet long, cut deep enough for us to stand up. One end was normally sealed, as was the overhead, with steel planking, plastic weather-proofing and multiple layers of sandbags. The entrance was an "S" shaped path design of sand bags to protect us from any explosions in front. This also reduced the escape of light during darkness, although we hung a double layer of canvas tarps over the entrance for that purpose. The interior walls were dirt, sometimes stacked sand bags, and smelled of the jungle soil. Both sides of the TOC had benches covered with radios, unit information, a telephone switchboard and maps. The room constantly hissed with the sound of radios, even when no one was talking. Light was furnished by a few hanging light bulbs, powered by one or more portable generators outside. If generators were not available, we used gas lanterns that shed a more uneven, ghostly light and added to the hiss sound level.

I learned a great deal about the tracking and reporting of company and battalion activities and the logistical requirements that kept our troopers supplied and fed. In the process, I also learned how to request and coordinate TACAIR and helicopters, my real job description. As the newest assistant S-3, I worked as a Duty Officer, primarily at night; the new guy seems to get the graveyard shift. Two operations sergeants, three RTOs and I summarized the day's activities into different reports. We made hourly radio communication checks with our infantry companies and coordinated the next day's operational plans with supporting units such as airlift, artillery, engineers, adjacent battalions, and the Air Force. A lot of the work we could do directly with other units, but much also went through 1st Brigade TOC.

I usually reported for duty after evening meal and worked in the TOC until the morning summary briefing to the CO and staff at approximately 0730. On days when there was an air assault to be flown, I would climb onto the C&C helicopter with the Commander and S-3 to oversee the aviation operation. When I was flying in the C&C, I had use of my own radio or pair of radios to communicate with the air units. Otherwise, I was off duty during daytime and could catch some sleep or hang around to see how things went. If the opportunity presented itself, I hitched a ride on a scout helicopter to recon the area and see if we could locate evidence of enemy action. The S-3 very rarely took exception with my flying since that was my "real" duty.

SCOUT HELICOPTERS

The aerial scouts from the Division's 2nd/17th Cavalry flew observation or scout missions in OH-6 Cayuse helicopters, sometimes with one or two Huey gunships for cover, but often alone. Built by Hughes aircraft, the OH-6 looked like an egg with a rotor mast and tail boom. Designated as a Light Observation Helicopter (LOH) the aircraft was called a "Loach" by the GIs. When a Loach or scout team was working in our area, or from our Firebase, I always asked if I could fly in the Loach. I figured that was part of my learning process as S-3 Air. Depending on the scout mission(s), the density altitude or fuel weight, the aircraft commander let me ride as an observer, although I always went armed with my M-16 or a borrowed M-79 Grenade Launcher and lots of ammo. The fuel weight and density altitude were important because, on the mountain firebases, a heavy weight helo may not be able to climb up to the firebase or have the power available to hover for a landing. If the weather was relatively cool and / or the scout Loach was down to half fuel or so, I could hop on as a passenger and go scout out parts of the battalion AO. On rare occasions, a scout pilot would let me ride in the right rear door seat and man an M-60 machinegun while the second crewmember on the scout normally sat in the left door with an M-60 and M-79 grenade launcher. More firepower is better.

The flying was challenging and a lot of fun until the day I rode with one of the 2/17th Cavalry scouts for about an hour as we worked the areas northwest of FSB Veghel. We did not find anything worth noting and the pilot dropped me off at the fire base, saying he was returning to Camp Eagle to refuel. About an hour later, I was back on duty when we received a radio call that a Cavalry Loach was coming to Fire Base Veghel with a wounded crew member and to have the medics standing by. Our duty RTO acknowledged the call while I notified the S-3 and our battalion medical team. Within minutes we heard and then saw a Loach coming at maximum speed from the north. The pilot whipped the aircraft around to approach the helipad from the east and flared onto the dirt Ops helo pad. Before the rotor blades slowed to ground idle, the pilot was motioning frantically for the medical team to get around to the left side where the observer / gunner was riding. I jogged down the slope behind the medics to see what I needed to report. The gunner, the pilot, and inside of the LOH were covered with blood.

The NVA opened up on them from relatively close range while the Loach was scouting on a low and slow pass, and the gunner was hit twice. One bullet penetrated his flak jacket on the left side and entered his body just below his left rib cage. The second round hit his left arm and probably clipped an artery. The arm wound bled profusely and with no doors on the Loach, the blood was blown throughout the cockpit. As soon as I saw the blood, I knew the gunner was in bad shape. Fortunately, when we received the original radio call, I requested the launch of a Medevac from Camp Eagle. Now I turned and yelled at Sgt Anders, my senior radio operator, standing at the entrance of the TOC,

"Andy, Get an ETA on the Medevac and tell them to pound it. This guy is in bad shape."

Anders ducked inside and in less than a minute he popped back out.

"Medevac is four minutes out; he is up on the Logistics freq and coming hard."

Meanwhile, the pilot reached over and unlatched the gunner's seat belt and shoulder harness as the medics arrived. The blood splattered crew and helo made it obvious that priority one was to stop the gunner's bleeding. Faster than the pilot could shut down the engine, unstrap, and run around the LOH's nose, our battalion medics lifted the gunner out of his seat, secured onto a stretcher, placed a tourniquet around his arm and started an IV saline solution to replace lost fluids. The medics also patched up the gunner's abdomen wound and began to move the stretcher to the Logistics helo pad that was some 100 feet to the side of the Ops pad and down the ridge line about 30 feet. At the same time, an NCO from the artillery battery filled a bucket with water and was using rags to clean the blood off the helicopter controls, instruments and windscreen to make it more flyable for the pilot. I was impressed with the cool thinking and personal courage on the part of the artillery NCO. I reminded myself to include his actions in the event report.

By the time the wounded crewman was moved to the Logistics helipad, we heard the very distinct Huey sound "whup, whup, whup" of the inbound Medevac. I could tell by the sound that the bird was running wide open and getting every knot of airspeed available. The Medevac made a tight circle over the firebase and flared onto the Logistics pad. Our medics rapidly moved the wounded gunner onto the chopper and the Medevac crew took over. On the ground less than a minute, the pilot pulled pitch and the Medevac lifted off the ridgeline firebase into an accelerating dive and began a high-speed run to the hospital on the coastal plains at Hue - Phu Bai. I walked back up the hill to the TOC, thinking about the sequence of events and hoping – no, praying - that we helped the gunner in time and the medics pumped enough fluid back into his system. I typed the entries into the battalion duty log and was preparing to go brief the Ops Officer, when Sgt Anders said,

"Six and a half minutes from the Loach landing until the gunner was airborne in the Medevac. Not too bad."

"I hope so. However, the 17th Cavalry is a Division asset and we may not know."

I never heard whether the gunner made it.

MORTARS (OURS AND THEIRS)

I had acquired more than a basic knowledge of mortars back at Ft Campbell during my tenure as a 4.2-inch Mortar Platoon Leader and had used mortars during my time as the Cobra Company XO when we employed 81 mms in the battalion rear area. I was very thankful that we did not use the large 4.2 inch mortars in Vietnam, at least I never saw any in the 101st, but the 81 millimeters were found on all our firebases and some companies carried the smaller 60 mm mortars. The NVA quite often used 82 and 60 mm mortars, and every firebase on which I served was hit at least once with mortar attacks. Three times while I was on TOC duty, Charlie tried to mortar Firebase Veghel with little success. The firebase was on a rather narrow razorback ridge, skinny enough so an incoming round that was 10 meters wide of the ridge top impacted hundreds of feet down slope. Any miss was a miss by a mile. When Charlie tried to shell the firebase, he usually used only one tube and tried to get off three or four rounds. With about two seconds between rounds being fired and 20 seconds to impact, I had time to step outside and get an azimuth, an accurate compass direction, to the sound of the launch. I then rapidly called our mortar unit with the azimuth. With an azimuth from another location on Firebase Veghel, our section could triangulate the approximate location of the NVA tube and return fire. On one occasion, I was quick enough to get an azimuth and have it fed to our mortar section before the incoming rounds impacted.

Technology made NVA mortar attacks and night movement risky within surveillance radar range of the firebase (AN/TPS-25 Ground Surveillance Radar). For two nights, the radar team attached to our firebase detected movement along the same location across the valley, west of Veghel. There was obviously a well-used trail in that area and we set out a plan to make it a very risky trail for "Charlie." The radar crew fed precise location data to the mortar section guys who plotted the target for their two 81 mm tubes. The next night when our radar section detected movement in that area, we alerted the mortar crews and told them to set up for the fire mission, but wait for our fire command. The radar crew computed the rate of movement for the target and when the time of foot travel by Charlie matched the time of flight for the mortar rounds we turned the mortars loose. "Blang....Blang." With their very identifiable reverberating sound, four 81 mm rounds flew in a high arc to the computed target area and landed with an audible "Krump!" The evening was ruined for whoever was traversing that trail; a long string of green tracers swung through the air, probably from an NVA soldier holding down the trigger of his weapon in the midst of the explosions. I think it was three days before we could free up an infantry unit to go check that site, finding dried blood trails and drag marks but no bodies or weapons. None were expected because Charlie was an expert in cleaning up equipment and casualties.

The firebases west of Hue and east of the A Shau provided exceptional mountain top views of the weather found in the Vietnamese mountains. Some days the mountain tops stuck up above a sea of white clouds that filled the valleys in all directions. It was absolutely beautiful. Troops on the mountain's lower slopes or flat lands suffered through fog so thick that everything they carried was damp or dripping. By mid-morning the fog burned off and another hot, humid day waited for the grunts. I often walked outside as daylight slowly swept over the firebase and looked around my mountain island in a sea of white cream. Sometimes a slight breeze did not disperse the fog, but, rather, blew white waves over the lower ridges. Some days the fog did not form and rise, but dense clouds dropped down and obscured the mountain tops. Now it was the firebase's turn to stay damp with very limited visibility on the hill as we awaited stronger winds or sunshine to clear off our weather.

Fog or clouds did not stop the infantryman's war but it limited many forms of support. Resupply could not be made, nor could Air Force fighters or helicopter gunships be employed for troops in contact with the bad guys. Only our artillery was an all-weather support weapon, but that was a limited asset unless we were in range of several artillery batteries. On a few occasions, the wind howled over the firebase so strongly that it prohibited helicopter flight. Asking a Warrant Officer to land his helo on a narrow razor-back ridge in turbulent 40+ knot winds was insanity. I excluded from the grounded category our MEDEVAC or "Dust Off" helicopter missions because I saw them fly below the clouds or climb / descend right up against the slopes of mountains in this weather to extract our wounded or injured troopers. An unwritten rule in most Officers Clubs was you could bad mouth anybody but the Dust Off and Rescue pilots. You might need them on some really bad day and they had the balls to come get you or your people, regardless.

One of the little discussed issues of a tropical war is the odor created by a troop when he has been humping the forests or jungles for days without a bath or clean clothes. We often received only food, ammo and medical supplies during a resupply mission, so we wore the same jungies until the next resupply at least another three to five days, hoping to wade across a clean creek to wash our bodies and clothes. After a few days, the grunt gave off an ammonia-like smell that grew stronger by the day. That was the scientific basis for the "people sniffer" missions flown by the Division chemical unit. Their equipment could detect concentrations of human odors even during a low altitude, high speed fly-by.

When our new S-3, Major Horace Clark, joined the 1/327, he was new in country and never humped with the grunts. After a week of living on the firebase, Major Clark and I were flying in the C&C bird when we received a radio request to extract three ill paratroopers from our "Tiger Force" recon unit. The Tiger Force was in the field over ten days without a break and I thought this might be interesting when they loaded onto the C&C in front of Major Clark. We soon located the Tiger Force unit along a tree line with a small clearing covered with elephant grass. The pilot dropped down to a two-foot high hover and the outbound Tigers hopped onto the Huey skid, crawled in and slid across the floor in front of me and Major Clark. Before the pilot could pull pitch and lift from the PZ, the odor of 10-day-in-the-field grunts began to fill the chopper. The intensified smell of ammonia and dirt seemed to reach up and smack Major Clark. I tried to keep a straight face as our new S-3 scrunched up his face, looked left and right and then turned a funny pale shade of white/green. I thought he was going to barf. One of the Tigers looked up at me with an expression that asked, "What is with the Major?" I just shrugged. When the aircraft accelerated to 90 knots, the odor dispersed a bit, but when we landed at the firebase, Major Clark beat the Tigers off the chopper. Nothing was said at any of the staff meetings, but the Tigers knew. I smugly relayed the tale to my partner Assistant S-3s.

After the 101st Division's first air assault into the A Shau in mid-1968, the enemy air defenses created a crush of damaged helos on all flat spaces at Firebase Veghel as we were the nearest friendly fixed location. Some suffered hydraulic problems; some shot-up fuel systems, or damaged rotor blades. The pilots parked two birds on our Log pad (designed for one helicopter) and two on the Command Post pad (also a one-helo design). One Huey landed in the artillery battery ammunition assembly area (it was open and almost flat) and a last chopper plopped on top of the artillery Fire Direction bunker. Our hilltop looked like a used helicopter sales lot. The 101st Aviation maintenance rapidly deployed maintenance teams to Veghel and all save one chopper were made flyable for a one-time flight to Camp Eagle. The last bird, requiring more maintenance, was to be carried out by sling below a heavy-lift Chinook helicopter the next morning. So, we kept one Huey overnight on the Logistics pad, hoping the NVA were too busy in the A Shau to worry about lobbing mortar rounds at our lame chopper.

On several occasions while I was in Cobra Company, and twice while I was working on our firebases, we were warned by the Battalion of an over flight of Air Force defoliant spray aircraft working our area. The troops in the field put on rain ponchos and sought shelter under trees while the firebase troops ducked inside bunkers when the spray birds approached. The fine liquid mist descended on everything or person exposed. After the "Operation Ranch Hand", C-123s, completed their spray run the spray stunk up the area for hours. The defoliant used was Agent Orange! Little did I or anybody in the 101st know about the long-term price we were going to pay for using that herbicide. After such a defoliant pass in mid-1968, I emerged from the TOC and snapped a picture after three C-123s passed by Firebase Veghel. The Veterans Administration, 35 years later, asked if we ever worked in areas where defoliant was used. Hell, we were *under it* when the Agent Orange was sprayed and I have the picture to prove it.

My living quarters as an Assistant S-3 (Air) were not as luxurious as those of a company XO in the rear area. In fact, the tent I enjoyed as the XO of Cobra Company was mints on the pillow / five-star hotel compared to the sleeping quarters on the firebase. But the new bunk area provided more protection. Captain Wilson and I shared a bunker just down the hill from the Battalion TOC. The bunker was dug about four feet into the ground and the roof was crisscrossed logs, topped with one layer of sandbags, plastic sheet, another layer of logs and then three layers of sandbags. I was amazed at the depth of soil on top of the Veghel Fire Base ridge because many a climb up similar ridges seemed to be on rocks with little soil. Our bunker was about eight feet long and four feet wide with just enough room for two cots side by side and eight inches between them. Captain Wilson once described it as two coffins laid side by side. Good visualization, but a questionable concept. We could not stand up in the bunker and needed to crouch to get through the exit that turned 90 degrees left at the foot of our cots. We hung our LBE and M16s from nails at the head of the bunker and shoved our rucksacks, rations and personal gear under the cots. Snoopy had his own spot above the head of my cot. Right in the middle of our passageway to the "front door" was a 12-inch depression and hole in the ground that functioned as a "grenade sump." If somebody tossed a grenade into the bunker, the grenade was supposed to roll into the sump and protect the occupants from the fragmentation and most of the blast. After a short while at FSB Veghel, our clothes smelled like the dank reddish-brown earth with some mildew thrown in. Even the clean jungle fatigues brought weekly in resupply soon took on an odor of the firebase.

The 101st occupation of Fire Bases Birmingham, Bastogne and Veghel was part of a plan to conduct combat operations westward from Hue into the A Shau. The US forces were to destroy the NVA forces and logistical infrastructure that posed a threat to the Vietnamese government and population on the coastal plains. The first 101st venture near the A Shau in March and April destroyed NVA supply bases and captured unbelievable amounts of enemy equipment. Captured weapons included field artillery pieces, anti-aircraft weapons and even track vehicle components. The NVA were now operating as a conventional army, not the portrayed hit-and-run light infantry units.

In March and April 1968, the 101st Airborne attack of enemy supply bases just outside the A Shau was preparation for Operation SOMERSET PLAIN. In May, the 1st Cav Division assaulted into the A Shau for a raid lasting several days as the 101st secured the mountain tops on the east side of the A Shau and set up artillery fire bases to support operations in the Valley. The mountaintop bases claimed historical 101st names like Eagles Nest and Berchtesgaden. Our troopers found NVA armor, large trucks and bulldozers cached along the highway approach to the A Shau. Amusingly, one of the 101st FACs located a pair of bulldozers and coordinated an attack of the dozers from the air. The first fighters diverted to the FAC were Navy A-7s with only 20mm cannon ammo remaining, but they were willing to strafe the targets. When "leader" made his strafe attack, "two" told him that he was taking a lot of ground fire. The FAC moved in closer to watch the next strafe run and discovered that the ground fire was the Navy's

20mm rounds deflecting off the heavy dozer blades and back in front of the A-7. The FAC changed the attack axis and the dozers were destroyed with no ground fire received. Don't strafe straight into a bulldozer blade! The 101st and 1st Cav would be back in the A Shau in mass in August.

I saw the significance of the anti-aircraft weapons while I flew as S-3 (Air) in the C&C helo on two occasions. In early July, we flew up to the last and tallest ridge east of the A Shau. As soon as we climbed to an altitude that unmasked our chopper from the valley floor, I heard a steady buzz in my radio headset. The S-3 asked the aircraft commander what was causing the sound and was told, "That is from an NVA radar-tracking antiaircraft gun somewhere on the western edge of the valley." We stayed east of the ridge, and as soon as we dropped into a masked position below the ridge top, the buzz stopped. That was rather disturbing to the helicopter crews and became a major intelligence point for weeks to come.

Four days later, I returned to Camp Eagle for a planning meeting and then whined my way into a ride with the Air Force FAC assigned to the 1st Brigade. We departed the Phu Bai airfield in the FAC's O-2 aircraft and flew straight down highway 547 over FSBs Birmingham, Bastogne and Veghel, to the edge of the A Shau climbing to a cool altitude of 9,000 feet. When we arrived in the A Shau, we picked up that same buzz in our headsets. Another FAC was already directing two Navy A-6 Intruders against suspected enemy supply areas on the western side of the valley. The A-6s dropped their bombs and then circled at about 7500 feet altitude for the next pass. Shortly after we tuned into the FAC-to-A-6 radio frequency, I heard the A-6 Leader ask:

"Two, are you losing oil because there is dark smoke trailing behind you?"

"No."

The FAC cut in "That's anti-aircraft fire. Move it around!"

Taking fire at 7,500 feet meant radar guided 37mm guns. This was a major force indicator for the west side of the A Shau. Not only were friendly units in the northern end of the valley exposed to NVA artillery firing from Laos, but now it seemed that heavy and modern AAA weapons were being introduced into the fight.

Every firebase enjoyed its own forms of wildlife. On one firebase near Duc Pho, it was prowling tigers; on another, screeching monkeys. On FSB Veghel, it did not take long for the jungle rodents to discover that the American GIs discarded a lot of edible goodies. When dark fell and it was quiet on the firebase, the local rodents would sneak through the barbwire and claymore mines to find dinner. Normally, the rats dug through our trash dump, and, if we did not bury the trash deep enough, one could hear the rattle of C ration cans in the dump being checked out by the rats. These were not little squeaky mice from back in "the World." The Vietnamese jungle rats were very healthy critters that could grow to be six inches tall at their shoulder, more like small dogs. The rats never bothered me until one night I was awakened by a rat licking chocolate off my fingers as I slept. I finished my C rations with the candy bar and did not wash my hands before crawling into my bunker and my cot. With my hand drooped over the edge of the cot, the chocolate remains were too tempting for the rodent intruder. Scared the living hell out of the rat and me! The only thing worse was the night my shelter mate, Captain Harvey woke up to see a huge rat coming into our shelter, so he whipped out his 45 and shot it. This was the same as being in a closet and having a 45 fired next to you. I did not know if I was shot, Captain Harvey shot, or if the NVA were inside the wire.

VERY SHORT VISIT BY DON
In late May, Don was finally back at Camp Eagle working as the Artillery Liaison Officer for the 2nd Squadron of the 17th Cavalry, commanded by LTC Julius Becton. Don called me on the radio in our TOC on LZ Veghel and said he was going to hitch a ride on our logistics bird for a short get together on Veghel. Good deal! When the Log Bird radioed inbound, I walked down to the Logistics helo pad to greet Don. Upon approach, however, the Huey "ran out of left pedal" and could not hover to land. I saw Don sitting in the doorway as the bird made a go-around from its attempted landing. He waved, I waved, and the chopper dove over the edge of the ridge line, skimming the trees while trying to get flyable airspeed and aircraft control. It was months before we saw each other again.

Don's adventure wasn't over. When the Huey got back to Camp Eagle, the pilot needed to make a running landing and when the skids were almost stopped, the bird lurched/hopped/spun 90 degrees counter-clockwise. (No left pedal) It started to roll over on its side, but righted itself after a second. The crew may have dumped a thermite can or two on the asphalt, but they all walked away. Just another day in the 'Nam, flying or riding in helicopters!

111

The next week Don left the 2nd/17th Cav and returned to the 321st Artillery Battalion becoming the Executive Officer for "A" Battery at Firebase Mongoose. On November 11th Don assumed command of "Charlie" Battery (Happy Veterans Day!) and travels with his battery found him on FSB Veghel in December for two months.

PROMOTION TO CAPTAIN

July 21, 1968 was the night that the NVA wanted to seriously test the defenses of Veghel and initiated an assault on the hill about 2200 hours. They started with a mortar attack which was only mildly accurate and followed up with rocket and recoilless rocket fire. Under the cover of those fires and darkness, an estimated two platoons of NVA attempted to sneak through the defenses on the north and west sides. The obvious objective of the attack was the artillery battery on that end of the hill. The hill reverberated with the sounds of explosive charges, grenades, AK-47, M-16 and M-60 weapons. Within minutes the infantry company that was on perimeter defense began to employ flares and protective artillery fire from FSB Bastogne. The night was an eerie scene of various colored tracers, aerial flares, and explosions. The artillery battery reported NVA inside the barb wire, but they were quickly eliminated by the infantry's reaction squad and the artillerymen themselves. The First Sergeant of the artillery battery stepped out of their Fire Direction Center, challenged a person moving toward a nearby gun pit and the intruder answered in Vietnamese. The First Shirt shot him.

I knew that the NVA were after the artillery guns and their Fire Direction Center. If they watched the firebase, the locations of these targets were determined and mapped out for the assault units. I did not like being on the NVA hit list with the possibility that sappers were loose inside the perimeter, so I instructed one of our extra RTOs, Specialist DuVrose, to man a position atop the entrance to the TOC and to protect us from infiltrators. This was a sandbagged position that could cover the approaches through the barb wire. This great young trooper climbed up on top with instructions to challenge and verify everyone that approached. When in doubt, shoot them! The probes of the perimeter continued with increasing noise, spooky shadows from flares, radio chatter and explosions. Shortly after midnight I had one of those thoughts that was out of context, but happened anyhow. I realized that it was now July 22nd, the day that I was to be promoted to captain. At least, if things went bad, I would be buried as a Paratrooper Captain. About 0130 hours we stopped receiving incoming fire of any type and the hill quieted down. Searches at daybreak revealed six NVA bodies, two inside the wire, and numerous blood trails leading back to the surrounding tree line. The good news was DuVrose did not have to shoot anybody.

With my promotion and survival on 22 July, I was now a Captain, O-3, and was paid accordingly. Additionally, I passed four years of service for pay computation, another significant pay raise. With both raises, my pay almost doubled for August. My monthly expenses were next to nothing so I was banking over 90% of my pay into the Soldiers Saving Account that paid 10% annual interest, and a small amount went into my checking account. I realized I would have a lot of money (relative to college student or new Second Lieutenant) when I went home.

AVIATION BREEDS INSANITY
People in a combat zone, including me, often do things that might be considered borderline insane. It's not a matter of losing your sanity, more a matter of being addicted to the adrenaline. Having now survived to a ripe old age, I look back and ask, "What the hell ever possessed me to do this or that?" From my days as a new platoon leader, my first insanity was riding outside of the chopper, standing on the skid during final approach to a combat assault, hoping it was not going to be a hot LZ, but enjoying the thrill. While I was the XO of Cobra Company, taking a day off to fly as a door gunner with 1st/9th Cavalry helicopter gunships from Phan Thiet might not pass a sanity test either.

As Assistant S-3, flying in the OH-6 scout helicopters was a thrill and great fun, but was tempered after seeing the possible consequences when one of the aviators was severely wounded by ground fire. Flying with the 101st Airborne Division's Forward Air Controllers was high adventure when we flew north to the Marine base at Khe Sanh to put in airstrikes. When we ran out of smoke rockets to mark targets for fighters, I threw smoke grenades from the right window of our O-2 aircraft to mark the targets. When we located enemy troops, but had used all our rockets, we attacked with hand grenades in glass jars. That action required a lower and slower O-2 pass at the enemy than did a rocket pass. Both the pass and the grenade attack might not have passed the sanity check on a normal day.

My flying with our 101st FAC over Khe Sanh took a somber note when the wreckage of a C-123 was spotted south east of Khe Sanh airstrip. The visible "WV" tail marking on the wreckage indicated that the C-123 was from Phan Rang airbase, home base camp of the 101st. I found that your heart can jump into your throat when you are dodging

113

a B-52 strike after the location announcement on the common "Guard" radio frequency matched your present location. Three B-52 bomb loads of 750 or 1000-pound bombs falling through your airspace could ruin your afternoon. Nevertheless, this insanity and addiction to flying had become one of my strongest character traits.

13

A Barbarian

August – On a balmy (101 degrees) afternoon I was working as the S-3 duty officer in the TOC when MAJ Duane Cameron, the acting battalion commander, entered,

"Steve, do you want to command a rifle company?"

"Yes, sir" I replied instantly.

"Good, there is an inbound chopper to pick up a replacement for the B Company Commander who is sick. Be on it and you are the new commander of the Barbarians."

"On the way!"

Of course, it would have been nice to have had some advance notice. I scrambled to get my weapon and gear, a basic load of ammo, smoke grenades, food and water, a good set of maps and jam all that into my ruck sack. I met the chopper on time, and off I went.

On board the resupply bird, I carefully followed our flight on my map as we crossed numerous ridgelines. We soon began our approach to a narrow LZ blown amid thick, tall trees on a ridge finger that ran down from a heavily forested mountain. There were several parallel fingers off the mountain top, so I paid attention to exactly where the resupply chopper would land. I wanted to know where I was as I took command. The Huey flared to a stop in midair and slowly hovered down into a forest cut on the ridgeline. The trees towered 60 feet over the sides of the helicopter when it touched down in the only clear spot available. Dust and leaves flew in all directions as a group of three troopers approached my side of the aircraft. I hopped out and shook hands with the gaunt, pale captain as he weakly climbed onto the Huey. I don't know what malady he contracted, but it was kicking his butt. He looked awful: pale, under-nourished and exhausted. I was used to seeing the gaunt, zero body fat grunts, but this was something else and humping the mountains was not going to improve his condition. A week later I heard the doctors sent him all the way to a hospital in Saigon for treatment.

I met my field first sergeant and he led the way twenty-five meters deep into the towering trees to the company CP where my two RTOs, company medic, two engineers and my Forward Observer team were assembled. The platoon leaders were in the process of resupplying their platoons so I instructed my company RTO to ask for all the 6s to report to the CP in twenty minutes. I met my HQ personnel in the next few minutes and was pleased with their time in country and in their current jobs. I met the platoon leaders and asked a few questions about their background, experience on the line and platoon size and strengths. Before we broke up the meeting one of the lieutenants asked the question of the day,

"Sir, exactly where are we on the map?"

I pointed out the correct finger on the 1 to 50K maps and they seemed relieved that I could confirm some estimated locations and refute others. Damn, I was glad that I paid close attention to the terrain as I flew in on the re-supply bird. At least I started out looking capable. Then we moved down the ridge about 500 meters and set up defenses for the night. As the command element settled in for evening chow, my lead RTO, "Red", said "You're that captain that got all the medals at the last standdown. You're not a Cherry."

"Cherry" was a derogatory term for a new guy in country who had not been in a fire-fight.

"No, I have served 16 months in the 327th and we will work great as Barbarians."

Being a company commander was not much different from being a platoon leader, just larger sub-units. As time went on, my experience as an XO paid off because I knew how to get supplies and exceptional support from my XO and the battalion rear. I did inherit an excellent XO in 1LT Bill Rogers. Bill served seven months as a platoon leader, and, coupled with an exceptional 1SG, Alton Barker, they stayed ahead of me in administrative and logistical matters. Those duties aside, every day I still packed up and humped the hills with one or more of my

116

platoons, while maintaining contact with and plotting current positions on all my platoons.

In the first week, we saw only one contact with the NVA, and that was two NVA troops who were probably sent to scout out our positions but walked into an ambush by one of our platoons. Score at week one: Bravo Company - 2, NVA - 0. At my next resupply day, we used a dry terraced rice paddy as an LZ and quickly received our ammo resupply, uniform exchange, food and five new troops for the company. I greeted the new privates and gave them the welcome, watch your NCOs and be careful speech. When I finished and sent them to the two smallest platoons, I mentioned to my field first sergeant my observation that these replacements were "Legs," not parachute qualified paratroopers. My "field first", SSGT Graham, reminded me that the 101st was now an Air Assault Division and no longer an Airborne unit requiring paratroopers. I saw the unit name change a month before while working on the firebase, but, since all the troops on the battalion staff were long time members, they were all paratroopers. This was my first contact with "leg" infantrymen. One of my challenges would be to show no prejudice or favoritism in dealing with my enlisted men, paratroopers or "legs."

On that first resupply helicopter came my company First Sergeant, Alton Barker. Nicknamed "First Shirt", "Shirt" or "Top", he was as surprised as I was to see the no-notice change of company commanders and he figured the only way he would get to know his new Barbarian Company Commander was to come out to the boonies and hump with the company for a resupply cycle or two. 1SG Barker had 26 years in the Army, all as a paratrooper. This was his second tour in Vietnam and he came to Bravo Company from a position as First Sergeant of the Golden Knights parachute demonstration team at Ft Bragg, NC. He was a combat veteran of WW II and Korea before coming to Vietnam. The first paratrooper I ever saw with two stars on his Combat Infantryman Badge. The stars symbolized second and third awards as an infantryman. 1ST Barker was a true professional who performed logistical magic for our company and worked hard to train his NCOs, and the Platoon Leaders (and his Company Commander). About day three after that resupply, I was sitting with 1SG Barker discussing the personnel in the company, and, after a pause, he asked: "Sir, when were you born?"

"November 6, 1944."

He thought for a moment and then said: "Sir, I made two combat jumps before you were born."

There was no disrespect in the observation and I thought about how recent WW II was. One paratrooper's career could include the D-Day jump into Normandy and humping the hills of Vietnam. At least twice a month, 1SG Barker came out to the company to hump hills or rice paddies with his troops. I always enjoyed his company and wise counsel.

TYPHOON BESS

It was the first week of September 1968 and Typhoon Bess arrived in South Vietnam. The Barbarians set up on a small knob near a tributary to the river. Battalion Ops called and said to move to higher ground and dig in for a major storm. The nearest higher ground was back up a ridgeline that the company cleared the day before. I generally disliked going back over an area that we previously traveled, because there was too much chance of running into a bad guy ambush or at least trail watchers. We knew that we were often followed by the NVA scouts to keep tabs on our location. But this was our only option. To move around the ridgeline and then climb a side or go even higher and then descend was going to take way too much time. I appreciated the weather warning when one of the battalion RTOs told me this was going to be a "real frog strangler" and it was coming fast. For three days, we rode out the driving wind and pounding rain. Ponchos and poncho liners leaked and the slightest edge exposed to the wind and rain was blown open and wetness prevailed. By day two of the typhoon our hilltop was an island with a roaring river all around us. Unless the NVA employed landing craft, they were not going to bother us, as they were handling their own problems. The forest protected us from much of the wind, but all kind of limbs and crap were falling from the trees.

The rain stopped for a brief period on the morning of day four and I climbed out of the two-man tent that I shared with my lead RTO.

"Damn, everything about me is wet."

"It don't mean nothing, sir!" Red gave me the 101st evaluation of any situation.

"The only dry things I have are one pair of socks in a battery bag and the writing material in my ammo can. The writing paper is so damp from humidity that it is wilted."

I went to check my company perimeter and ensure nobody was under water. As I stepped out into an opening in the trees, I heard a slight rumble overhead and looked up into the first blue sky seen in days. The rain-washed blue sky that follows a major storm is brilliant and clean. Against this fantastic blue sky, directly overhead I made out white undersides of at least four flights of F-4 Phantoms in formation, moving slowly across the sky. I pulled my compass from my left shoulder harness and aligned it with the direction of the F-4s; yep, they were heading north. I thought to myself: "That must be a better way to fight a war." But the thought of surface to air missiles that could follow your aircraft movements or ending up a POW in North Vietnam brought me back to my rain soaked hill. Infantrymen didn't worry about POW status because the NVA we encountered did not take prisoners. Unless the NVA could mount an amphibious assault, Charlie was not going to hit us for a few days. We couldn't go anyplace and I knew that the foot of rain must have played hell with the NVA's lovely bunker systems. At least my paratroopers were on a higher ground level where the rain could run off.

DAILY COMMAND ADVENTURES

On October 29th, two months in as a company commander, I received the scare of my young life. My command element was moving behind Lieutenant Casper's platoon with another platoon behind us. The point element found a creek bottom that was open and rocky with forest on both banks. The lead platoon carefully crossed the creek bottom and entered the trees on the opposite side. I paused for a few seconds as I looked at my map and then signaled the Command Post to spread out, and we started across the stream bed. When we were exactly in the middle of the open creek bed, a fire fight erupted on the far side of the creek and we ate rocks. Sounds of AK-47 fire mixed with explosions, M-16s and M-60s. I could hear bullets cracking overhead and slapping the trees behind us. A cold fear grabbed my chest as I thought "Holy Shit, I am out here in the open and I am going to die!" In a second I recalled a Ft. Benning instructor yelling "Do something, Lieutenant!" Scared, I yelled "Red, Mouse, let's go!" and, crouched over, I ran to the far bank with my RTO, "Red" and my FO, "Mouse" Williams.

We crawled up the low bank and dove behind several of the huge teak trees. I crawled over to Mouse, and, pointing to my map I said, "Get me a fire mission on this point," indicating a small ridge finger about 600 meters in front of the lead platoon.

When I put down my map, my hands were shaking. Red looked at me but didn't say a thing as he listened for a report from the lead platoon leader. Lt Casper and the other platoon leaders knew if I did not hear from them within two minutes after shooting occurred, I had my RTOs pester them. The shooting stopped and in another minute Lt Casper, 1-6, was on the radio telling me his lead squad encountered five or six NVA coming along a small trail toward our creek crossing area. He suffered no casualties, and, although his troopers said they knocked down four of the NVA, no bodies or weapons could be found. LT Casper said they found three Chicom grenades and three blood trails. It seemed like, on this day, Charlie was lousy at security but very good at recovering their weapons and casualties.

Two days later as we closed into the night position I was working on some documents when Red said, "Hey sir, look over there." Between two trees along our hilltop I looked down on a small clearing and saw a single NVA soldier crossing the field carrying two containers on a pole. I called for two shooters from the third platoon and instructed that on my command, they were to take two well-aimed shots at the NVA, now about 400 yards away. "Ready, Aim, Fire" and six rounds were fired. The NVA went down in the tall grass. I thought about sending out a patrol, but it was dusk and I was not sure where that lone NVA soldier was headed or what size NVA unit was nearby. When the NVA was sighted, I called for Mouse to get an artillery fire mission set up. After we fired at the NVA soldier, Mouse executed a fire mission for the back side of the small hill toward which the soldier was moving. Thirty seconds later, six rounds of 105 mm high explosive landed on the back side of the hill.

I requested aerial reconnaissance of the impact area, but it would be too dark by the time anybody could arrive. The battalion arranged for a FAC mission at first light in the morning and just after daylight the next morning, a FAC assigned to the 101st, call sign "Bilk 1-1", arrived overhead. He confirmed the coordinates that we struck with artillery the previous evening and went to look. Soon, Bilk 1-1 replied that there were numerous camouflaged bunkers, trenches and hooches in that area and he was calling for airstrikes. The Barbarians moved out in a different direction and Bilk 1-1 employed 500-pound bombs and napalm from a flight of F-100s and two flights of F-4s against the bunker complex. The F-100s were on call overhead the 101st AO and the F-4s were bad weather diverts from targets to the west on the Ho Chi Minh trail. I was glad we did not send a unit after the lone NVA and have them stumble into a large NVA complex as dark fell.

On the next resupply day, I left the 4th platoon on a small hilltop, 400 meters away from the company perimeter and LZ, planning to swap platoons after the company CP and the first platoon finished their resupply activities. After an hour, I radioed 4-6 that I was dispatching the 2nd platoon to relieve 4-0 for resupply. Then, just as the 2nd platoon was leaving the company perimeter to relieve the 4th platoon, 4-6 called to say that the relief platoon was making a lot of noise on the trail. I informed 4-6 that the relief platoon was still in our company perimeter. The first platoon leader curtly answered, "Stand by!" Within 30 seconds we heard M-16s, M60 machine gun fire and M-79 grenades. The firing lasted less than two minutes. Then 4-6 called to say his platoon engaged an NVA squad walking down the trail from my position toward his. Despite the helicopter activity on a nearby hilltop, the NVA showed no concern moving down a trail, no real security discipline and made too much noise. Score: 4th platoon – 5, NVA – 0.

We worked our way up a mountain southwest of Hue, scouting every ridge and draw for base camps and logistic support or hospital sites in support of the NVA. The mountain top held a collection of summer homes for the wealthy citizens of Hue / Phu Bai. As we neared the mountain top, I planned a movement to see if there were any NVA troops using that community for their own R&Rs. First Sergeant and I discussed the tactical problems involved including possible booby traps left behind, but decided that it was doable. Then two issues arose: first, we lost a helicopter resupply day due to cloud cover up at our level. That meant no resupply for four more days and any movement toward the "resort" on the mountain top had to be done on limited rations. Secondly, the weather crumped with low clouds and drizzle. Infantry could hump up the mountain, but we could not count on resupply or medevac if a fight ensued and we took casualties. After further consideration, I dismissed the push to the mountain resort for another day. If the battalion wanted troops up there, they could wait for better weather (probably next March) and conduct an air assault onto the resort.

We set up astride a small valley a week later covering three forest trails, with 1-0 on the far-left slope, while the Command element and 3-0 positioned in the middle and 2-0 on the right flank slope. About midnight, I saw a trip flare ignite in front of 1-0's position and a short burst of M-60 and M-16 fire followed. I waited for a contact report and after a couple of minutes of quiet I asked Red to give 1-6 a call and find out what was going on. Red reported that 1-6's RTO said LT Smith was unavailable and the RTO sounded winded. I soon found out that a herd of eight elephants came down the trail that 1-0 was covering and all but one elephant missed the trip wire for this flare. Go figure! When the last elephant hit the trip wire, the flare fired, the herd panicked and charged over 1-0's position. Lt Smith and most of his platoon took to trees and the 1-6 RTO ran in front of the elephants until he could find a climbable and unoccupied tree. There were six injuries but none needed a medevac. No, the injured did not qualify for a Purple Heart; we couldn't prove they were NVA elephants.

In early October, our battalion was pulled back to Camp Eagle for a five-day rest. One of the recreational events was a trip to Eagle Beach for a day of picnics, rest and salt water for our jungle rot. Eagle Beach was a secured area on the barrier island east of Hue on the South China Sea. Other than our arrival by Chinook helicopter and the fact that everyone carried a weapon, web gear and a helmet, this could have been any collection of young men on a Spring Break beach. My twin brother Donald Stevenson and his artillery unit also were back at Camp Eagle, so he sniveled a helicopter ride from his unit and  joined me at Eagle Beach. It was great to be back together after months when our communication was limited to FM radio calls and letters that took seven-day transit, although we were in the same division. I always thought the letters went back to San Francisco, were sorted, and then sent back to Vietnam.

As was the custom on battalion standdowns, we held a rowdy party for officers and mixed "New Lieutenant Drinks" for the lieutenants who joined us after the last party. My trusty company XO, Bill Rogers, tried to be super macho, and, before I could stop him, he chugged two drinks. Despite my strong urging, Bill did not go outside the tent and puke. Thirty minutes later, Bill passed out and had to be carried to the battalion aid station for IV fluids. Man, did he hurt the next afternoon.

Things I never thought I'd see in a combat zone: On day two of the standdown, I entered the back of the Orderly Room tent and found it was partitioned off with hanging poncho liners into four smaller rooms. Before I could ask anything, the 1SG said "Sir, I think you have a meeting in the Officers Mess tent." I watched a young lady's bare ass swing around one of the partitions and the First Shirt escorted me out the door of the tent with "I'll explain later." It seems the First Shirt obtained the services of four call girls from Phu Bai, and, after they passed medical exams by the Battalion Surgeon, a brothel was set up in the Orderly Room tent. "Shirt" was right; there are some things the CO does not need to know at the time.

During that October standdown we were treated to a demonstration of the latest artillery asset, Aerial Rocket Artillery (ARA) from helos of the 3/77th Arty. The Battalion Commander, LTC Bartholomew, gave the briefing to all 1/327 platoon leaders and Company Commanders. As we arrived, one of my acting platoon leaders, a very young SGT Harrison, was stopped outside the briefing tent by the Bn CO and said this was for the officers only. I informed the Bn CO that Sgt Harrison was one of my Platoon Leaders, my best qualified NCO to be a PL and I was down to three officers assigned for my four platoons. SGT Harrison was allowed into the demonstration. The ARA helicopters carried a tremendous amount of firepower, and, while they may take more time to arrive than a tube artillery fire mission, once on the scene, ARA brought a "whole lot of hurt" to the enemy. Attending the demonstration was the 101st Division Artillery Commander, Colonel Edward Vogel. COL Vogel "owned" the ARA assets as an artillery unit and not as an aviation asset. All our grunts approved of the new firepower and little did I know that in two months I would have a tragic and unfortunate reunion with LTC Bartholomew and COL Vogel.

In early November, we moved out of the mountains and began to work the flatlands and the occupied villages along QL1 highway. Our first resupply went badly as one platoon suffered three injured and two evacuated due to an accident. The third platoon was separated from the company CP and first platoon by approximately 1500 meters of rice paddies. Third platoon supplies were dropped off by chopper, and, during the cleanup a hand grenade exploded in the trash burn pit. It was our practice to burn our trash before leaving a resupply site (tactical situation permitting) to discourage Vietnamese scavengers and avoid leaving anything of intelligence value for "Charlie." One of the troops had tossed a cardboard tubular grenade canister into the fire, thinking it was empty. It wasn't; that carelessness cost me two good troops wounded.

Working the flatlands in mid-November, my first platoon got to participate in a rare night air assault. Intel said we needed to check this small village that sat in the middle of a thousand yards of rice paddies in every direction. The plan called for a South Vietnamese mechanized infantry company to seal off the nearest road and for the 101st helos to land a platoon to sweep the village. I flew an aerial recon with 1-6, my FO and the lift aircraft commander. The recon flight was offset to the south of the target village and flown at 4000 feet to avoid alerting any bad guys.

An hour after dark, the lift birds picked up the first platoon several miles west of the village, flew a large looping, low level route and put the platoon right on target as our artillery began to illuminate the village with flares. I could only watch from three miles away as the air assault landed and a brief firefight ensued. The guys in 1-0 took no casualties and killed one VC. They captured two weapons, found several blood trails and discovered a cache of medical supplies. Charlie was good at slipping away, but the only night air assault I heard of to date must have been a real surprise. Hooah to the 101st Aviation gang!

I wasn't a great fan of the widely-dispersed platoon operations necessary on the open plains because it required considerable exposed travel to move from one of my platoons to another. Operations in villages along QL1 also gave our troopers a chance to see that all Vietnamese did not live in bamboo huts. Along some of the river banks we found elegant stone houses with teak floors throughout. The educated Vietnamese attended schools set up or modified by the French colonists and it was not unusual to find extensive libraries of classic novels and modern writings, all in French.

Another regretful adventure was the killing of a Vietnamese farmer's ducks by two of my M-79 gunners. These two troops wanted to see what a M79 "shotgun" round could do to a flock of ducks about 40 yards across a farmer's pond. The rounds were very effective, killing seven ducks and earning the gunners an Article 15 and $100 fine each. I also directed they provide funds for the "field first shirt" to pay the civilian owner for the ducks. The total was about $80 in VN piaster, but worth the few dollars to offset the bad feelings that might have resulted. The farmer got above-market price for the ducks, kept the dead ducks and held a large dinner for his neighbors that evening.

COMMUNITY RELATIONS

One afternoon my troops found a Vietnamese farmer's money (800 piaster) hidden at the bottom of a large rice bin. There were no banks out here, so my Vietnamese interpreter / scout said the farmers hid their savings from Charlie (and the Americans). After a brief discussion with the farmer, I was convinced it was not VC money; we returned it.

That afternoon, in a village search we came upon a funeral. It was more like an extended family wake for a recently killed young South Vietnamese soldier. The funeral ceremony appeared to be Catholic with a small cross on the coffin. The entire extended family, wife, farmer, siblings, and kids, were gathered inside the small farmhouse and they were visibly upset. I watched from the outside of the house for a few moments, then called a stop to the search of the farm and stooped to walk into the small dirt floor house. I removed my helmet, knelt on one knee by the coffin, said a short silent prayer, and then reached out to touch the coffin below the soldier's picture. I then stood and did my best attempt at a Vietnamese bow and retreated. The farmer was clearly touched by this respectful action. He scurried out the door after me calling "Dai Uy", Vietnamese for Captain. He was an old man looking 70 but probably 50, short, wiry, with the close-cropped haircut of the locals and lots of gray showing in his black mane. He jabbered in very fast Vietnamese, and, then, with tears, took my hand and touched it to his bowed forehead. He bowed to me and turned to rejoin his family. I just stood there, trying to imagine his family's grief and the imposition of towering, sweaty Americans intruding on his family's grieving time to search his home and farm.

In one of our village sweeps I encountered a darker side of our war to win the hearts and minds of the Vietnamese. Once we secured this particular village, a young American man, about my age, arrived and introduced himself only as "Mike" and said he would be working in the village for two days or so with some South Vietnamese troops as part of the "Phoenix Program." Mike, as it turned out, was an employee of the CIA and his group was conducting a "selective counter-terrorism" program to detect and eliminate Viet Cong sympathizers and supporters within the villages. His Vietnamese troops were part of a special Provisional Reconnaissance Unit (PRU). Their questioning of suspects would today be titled "enhanced interrogation" and his troops also set out nighttime ambushes for any Viet Cong attempting to infiltrate the village. Bluntly stated, they questioned suspects and tortured those that may have had VC information. Some estimates say the Phoenix program "eliminated" almost 26,000 individuals during the war. That was a very different side of the war, with very different rules.

In mid-November, the Barbarians set up four kilometers east of Phu Loc on a large rocky hill that jutted into Dam Cau Hai bay, a large bay 20 miles ESE of Hue. We used this as our base for patrolling for the next week. The huge rock was reasonably secure, with water on three sides and a very steep approach from QL1 on the land side. There were two large knobs on the hilltop. An American 155mm artillery unit occupied the southern peak while the Barbarians provided all-around defensive positions and our CP and helipad were on the northern peak. Logistics for the two units were delivered by helicopter rather than by road. Convoys on the highway drew too much attention, particularly if repeated, and the rocky road up from QL1 was a hazard and challenge to vehicles.

We constructed my company CP with the aid of an artillery unit bulldozer. We dug a trench, eight feet wide and 15 feet long, sandbagged the front that faced downhill and installed a pierced steel planking roof supported by 12"x12" 20-foot wood stringer beams. Three of the huge beams drifted ashore, just below our knoll, and I persuaded our resupply Huey to make three short lifts with one beam each time from the beach to my future CP location. The chopper landed at the bottom of the hill and some of my troops slid a beam into the cabin of the Huey. The pilot launched back up to our hilltop with six feet of 12" by 12" beam sticking out each side of the aircraft. Our Command post bunker was so well built that it would still be there if not looted and scavenged after the war.

When we moved onto our knoll I was issued a heavy .50 caliber machinegun, which I installed on the eastern slope to provide the best defensive fire, and, from there it could reach Highway QL1 if we needed to stop traffic. We did engage one vehicle, travelling without lights on QL1. As soon as we engaged, we received a panicky radio call that the vehicle belonged to a Marine Civil Action Platoon and was moving to another village. My M60 gunner punched numerous holes in the truck and wounded one Vietnamese trooper before we ceased fire. Don't let friendlies drive around without lights after dark without telling local forces in advance.

As we worked along the shoreline, we often saw the US Navy Air Cushion Vehicles (ACVs) operating in Dam Cau Hai. Battalion CP thought it a clever idea for us to use the ACVs to make a high-speed water-borne raid on a suspected VC village on the coast to the southeast. I went down to the beach below our rocky hilltop to coordinate with the Navy commander of the ACV unit. To my amazement, the unit commander was a USNA grad and a 1966 Navy Classmate. Although  we were peers, he was still a LTJG (Navy speak for a 1st LT). I now appreciated that the Army's early promotion policy for surviving Infantry officers held some advantage. I deployed one platoon with the ACVs and, early the next morning, they conducted an assault to surround and search a hamlet that was reported to have VC. The platoon made a cool ride on the ACVs and encountered only light, sporadic small arms fire from the village, which was immediately discouraged by the Navy's .50 caliber machineguns. A search of the surrounded village was conducted but they found no VC or weapons in the village. Charlie was still very good at melting away when he was at a disadvantage.

Finishing several similar operations, the Barbarians were airlifted to the other end of the AO. The threat spectrum was entirely different and provided a scary night in the hills out near the A Shau. We air assaulted into a small valley where we discovered a road running into the A Shau. Not a trail but a real road that had carried vehicle traffic in the recent past. This was serious NVA out here in bad guy territory. We swept our side of the valley and moved well up into the forest to set up a night defensive position. From our company position and an observation post (OP), we could see a long stretch of the valley floor that pointed east toward Hue. After 2300 hours, I was alerted by the OP that they could see hundreds of small lights, like flashlights, coming from Hue and walking westward. The First Shirt and I moved out to the OP for a look and a decision on whether to engage the light carriers with artillery. We heard a large diesel engine roar to life and then the unmistakable sound of "tracks" moving: "tracks" that clanked, as in tank tracks. Almost in a panic, one of the troops on the OP exclaimed,

"Jesus, they have tanks. They are coming after us with tanks."

First Shirt Barker walked over and grabbed the trooper who was visibly shaking.

"One, we are up in the middle of a teak forest and a tank can't even shoot up here; Two, that is a hell of a steep hill from there to here, so a tank can't climb up here even if it wasn't a teak forest. Three, we are about to call the world down on whoever that is."

"Mouse, get busy with fire missions at that end of the valley and forget about the lights for now," I ordered

Within minutes, we pounded the suspect area with 105mm, 155mm and eight-inch artillery. Mouse added,

"Sir, there is a battleship on station just off the coast. Do you want to call on their 16-inch guns?"

"No, this valley is too narrow and steep-sided to be lobbing one-ton shells in over us."

The small lights went out, probably headed back to Hue on the double, and we heard no more tank or diesel sounds. The next morning our 101st FACs located two tracked bulldozers but no tanks. The Air Force dropped 750 pounders on the bulldozers until they were scrap iron. Just another night in the Nam!

I worked for two different battalion commanders as the B Company Commander: first was MAJ Duane Cameron, call sign "Blackhawk," and LTC Raymond Smith was the second. Both had irritating idiosyncrasies. Major Cameron would tap you in the chest and start an order with, "Young man, you should...." I was not a "young man"; I was a paratrooper Company Commander with more time "in country" than he had. LTC Smith was an Armor officer with enough political pull to get command of an Airborne Infantry Battalion. LTC Smith would design large sweeps across the maps, even when the terrain was nearly vertical ridges that the grunts had to climb up and down. In one planning meeting after such a hand sweep across the map, Captain Tom Kinane, now the Cutthroat Company Commander, leaned over to me and whispered, "YGBSM! Has anyone told him he is not in Western Europe anymore, Toto!"

For my time as Assistant S-3, our battalion commander was LTC Elliot Sydnor, who took us to the A Shau Valley and the real mountains of Vietnam. While I was the Barbarian company commander, a real storybook character, LTC Charlie Beckwith, commanded our sister battalion: 2nd Bn 327th Infantry. Both Sydnor and Beckwith became well known in the Special Ops world in years to come. Colonel Sydnor was the ground force commander during the Son Tay raid to release POWs in 1970. Colonel Beckwith led the ground forces in the ill-fated Desert One raid to liberate prisoners in Tehran in 1980. I was in good company working around those two.

I witnessed a great leadership action by a battalion commander while my Barbarians were pulling four days of firebase security for both battalion CPs. One of the companies from 2/327 discovered an NVA weapons cache and airlifted almost 800 SKS rifles up to their battalion CP. The SKS was a semi-automatic rifle, and, as such it was legal to claim as a war trophy. Usually, if a single weapon was turned in to the battalion CP, the assistant Intelligence Officer or some other rear echelon slug made off with the souvenir weapon and the grunt who captured the weapon rarely got to take it home. LTC Beckwith, CO of 2/327, would have none of that BS. Beckwith ordered his S-2 Intelligence Officer, to do a serial number inventory of the captured weapons and the S-1 Personnel Officer, to provide him a list of infantrymen in the 2/327 battalion, starting at the lowest rank. Beckwith then issued SKSs by serial number to his grunts in reverse rank order. They were to be stored by the S-2 in the battalion rear and handed to the grunts as they departed for the United States. In Beckwith's mind those weapons belonged to his infantry grunts and they were not going to some REMF as a war trophy. I loved it and swore any legal war trophy stayed with my company's grunts in like manner.

In mid-November, my tour extension and transfer to the "Green Berets" of 5th Special Forces Group was approved. That was good news, but also bad news, as the Battalion Commander immediately began a search for his next company commander and decided to make the change as soon as possible. On November 20th, I congratulated my replacement as we shook hands alongside a resupply helicopter, not much of a ceremony, and I went to again be an Asst S-3 until I departed the division. At least my replacement enjoyed more than eight minutes notice and was well prepared for the transfer of command of the Barbarians.

On 27 November 1968, the flight lead of an ARA section from the 3rd Bn, 77th ARA was shot down during a rocket run about 12 klicks southwest of our Battalion CP, then located in a railroad yard at Phu Loc. On board the ARA chopper was the ARA Battalion Commander and the Division Artillery Commander. Due to the mountainous terrain and heavily forested tree cover, it was estimated to be four hours before any 1/327 unit could move to an extraction area, be picked up, and be inserted to secure the crash site. The only way to check the crash site soon was to put somebody in there. Soon! I asked the S-3 if I could get two volunteers and rappel into the crash site to check for and treat any survivors. The S-3 thought we were crazy, but, agreed to the attempt if the helo guys agreed. The problem of rappelling down through tall trees was daunting enough, particularly if the NVA decided to check on the crash site, but once on the ground we would have to wait for D Company to arrive (2-4 hours). The volunteers loaded three lines of 150' rope into our logistics helo and lifted off for the crash site. The ARA birds had refueled and rearmed and would mark the approximate spot in the thick canopy forest where the Battalion CO's gunbird went in. I briefed with my two teammates and the helicopter crew, who agreed to troll the treetops to spot the wreckage; but they would rapidly exit if we drew any ground fire.

Airborne, and after an approximate ten-minute search, our Aircraft Commander spotted the wreckage. As the rotor wash parted the teak tree canopy the three volunteers stepped off the skids and slid down the ropes. I was scared as hell when we rappelled in, but adrenalin is good. I had never rappelled from a helicopter before (I didn't tell the S-3 that), but felt comfortable on a rappel line because I was rappelling since my junior year of college. Hopping off the Huey skid, I let the line slide for about 25 feet and then slowed to a stop just above the tree leaves. I was surprised as I swung under the copter and almost collided with one of the other trooper's rappel line, so I let out some more line to stop my oscillation. I timed the next slide of rope to penetrate the tree canopy and I slid to the ground just a bit downhill from the crash site. I released my rappel line and confirmed our status to the helicopter crew, still in a hover overhead.

Our small team carried two radios for three men, double the basic load of ammo, and smoke grenades. We all reached the ground at about the same time, and, as our helicopter moved away, we moved silently across the forest floor to the wreck. The aircraft was lying on its right side with the front nose crushed in and the tail boom crimped at a 30-degree angle to the left. None of the crew was alive, but one of the gunners must have initially survived the crash and crawled or was thrown clear of the helicopter. He was about 25 feet from the wreckage and lying in a prone position. We set up security on two sides of the crash and I went to confirm the identity of LTC Bartholomew and COL Edward Vogel. Finding LTC Bartholomew in the co-pilot's seat and COL Vogel in the cargo bay, I confirmed the two identities by sight, dog tags and uniform markings and made the radio call that there were no survivors and the two commanders were among the casualties. We adjusted security positions a bit and hoped the NVA were not as eager to reach the crash site as we were. Two thoughts ran through my mind as we waited. First, here was a team of three paratroopers defending a crash site when an entire North Vietnamese Army regiment could be descending upon us; any fool should be scared out of his wits, but we weren't. Second, it was less than two months since COL Vogel and LTC Bartholomew demonstrated the firepower of the ARA birds to the officers of 1/327, and now I was standing guard over their bodies. War sucks!

We soon heard helicopter activity down the mountain as elements of Demon Company began to arrive. In a little over two hours, the lead elements of D Company approached up the ridgeline from their insertion point. I turned the site security over to their lead platoon leader. Then my team made our way down to the LZ, being blown for lift birds to bring in the remainder of the company and later to extract the bodies. Killed in the crash were WO1 John W. Brinkmeyer [AC], LTC Roger J. Bartholomew [CP] Battalion CO, SP5 Loren D. Martinsen [CC], SP4 Ernest L. Barber [G], and COL Edward B. Vogel – Division Artillery CO. Our logistic helicopter returned the bodies to the 327th Battalion CP, where our Battalion Surgeon wanted to make a quick visual autopsy to determine cause of death. I was astounded that none of the other troopers at the CP would handle the bodies, so I assisted the Surgeon in the examinations. All the crew appeared to have died in the crash and two, including COL Vogel, showed what appeared to be gunshot wounds in addition to crash injuries. They were most likely hit in the same burst that brought down the gunbird.

The next week was relatively quiet with little contact by the companies and none at the Battalion Command Post. On December 10th, I hopped on a Huey from the Battalion CP to Phu Bai, caught a plane to Cam Ranh Bay for a night, and then on to Bien Hoa where the division rear was now set up and I out-processed from the 101st Airborne Division. The 101st, and, particularly, the 1/327 had been my family for eighteen months and my heart ached to be leaving the battalion and the men with whom I fought and endured the hardships of paratroopers in combat. I was off to the land of the "Big BX" for a couple of weeks, and, when I returned to Vietnam, it would be enroute to 5th Special Forces Group at Nha Trang for training.

Just in case I did not make it back from my next tour, I sat for a formal portrait photo in Arlington while on leave. It was also a touch of vanity because I wanted a photo showing my blue infantry cord and the green tabs on my shoulder epaulets which indicated a unit commander. At least it was something to leave the family.

14

Green Beret - 5th SFG (Airborne)

As part of my tour extension and transfer to Special Forces in country, I was entitled to another extension leave of up to thirty days, which I took beginning December 15th, 1968. My extension leave airliner departed from Bien Hoa AB to Travis AFB CA. After a shuttle bus to San Francisco Airport (SFO) I made my way through the hippies and war protesters to catch a flight to Dallas. To tell the truth, the leave in the States was *boring*! OK, I loved the cool weather and it was great to unwind for a couple of days at the Garrett's house, but Christmas was not a big deal without a family. I went shopping in Dallas a couple of times but there was nobody around that I knew. Listening to all the protest BS on TV was depressing. I soon decided to head out to San Francisco and see Bev Garrett, stationed at Presidio of San Francisco for a while and then book my flight back to Vietnam.

This return trip to Vietnam started with adventure in San Francisco. Captain George Beverly Garrett, "Bev" to his close friends, was serving as the Commanding Officer of the Headquarters & Headquarters Company at Presidio, California. Part of Bev's job was to round up soldiers who went AWOL before or after a Vietnam flight. Tagging along with Bev one afternoon, I was introduced to the glories of Haight Ashbury, the "real" hippies (peaceful and unaggressive war protesters), various call girls, and numerous "Bunnies" from the Playboy Club. However, the characters that Bev rounded up for the Army were not always nice people. Most of the collected AWOLs were tossed in the post stockade until they could be sent to their owning units. On occasion when Bev encountered a particularly belligerent customer, the AWOL was temporarily sent to the US Marine Corps Brig out on Mare Island in San Francisco Bay. On each occasion, this approach straightened them out in two days, and, on my visit with Bev we found a former malcontent standing at attention at the end of a bunk, being most respectful to Bev, under the watchful eye of the USMC "Gunny." Gunny's motto was "Sometimes you just have to get their attention to adjust their attitude."

After keeping up with the fast-paced events of my favorite Headquarters Company Commander for two days, I was weary of sleeping on the floor of Bev's BOQ room and moved on to catch my flight to Vietnam from Travis AFB. Once again, I got to wear jungle fatigues on the flight across the big pond. I knew I was "cool", wearing a Screaming Eagles patch on each shoulder, a CIB and being a Captain among all the cherries.

I flew into Cam Ranh Bay Air Base (again), stayed at the luxurious Hotel 22nd Repo Depot and next day caught a Huey flight up to Nha Trang. I arrived in Headquarters 5th Special Forces Group (Airborne) on December 31, 1968. For two weeks, I received organizational briefings, processed my Top-Secret clearance, underwent language refresher in Vietnamese and introduction to the Montagnard languages of the Rhade, Hre, and Bru. I was issued several sets of "Tiger" fatigues, and another set of regular green "jungies." All my jungies were now sewn with Vietnamese "Dai Uy" or captain buttons on the front center of my jackets, my Vietnamese parachutist badge above my right breast pocket, the Vietnamese SF (LLDB) patch on the left breast pocket, an SF patch on the left shoulder and a 101st Airborne Division patch on the right shoulder, signifying my previous combat tour. I was issued an M-1 Carbine, .30 caliber, US vintage 1943. After a few weeks in 5th Group, I traded the carbine in for an AK-47, Russian, vintage 1965. The SF Group Officer Assignments folks asked if I had any preference about my assignment, and since I had spent so much time in I Corps with the 101st, I said I preferred going to Company C in Da Nang. That settled, I received orders for next-day transport by C-123 to Da Nang.

A Special Forces tour was going to do several things for me, some of them of my own choosing. My area of interest expanded from a battalion or brigade area to the entire military I Corps. I worked to develop civilian health programs, local trades and economies of villages. I interfaced daily with Vietnamese armed forces and learned a lot more about racial prejudice and discrimination in Vietnam. And I would have a "Special Ops" identifier that is a "3" prefix in my records which followed me for the next twenty-three years.

Company C, 5th SFG (A)'s compound was located on the ocean side of Da Nang, right on the edge of China Beach. Our neighbor to the north was Marines' Marble Mountain Airfield, home for Marine Air Group 16 (MAG 16), consisting of helicopters and headquarters of the first Marine OV-10 Bronco squadron in country. To our south, across several rows of barb wire, was another SF unit, Command and Control North (CCN).

Command and Control North compound contained two types of units. The Mike Force reaction unit was a battalion of Vietnamese and Montagnard soldiers who were paid for their service. For the Vietnamese Mike Force members, this met their military service requirement. The other battalions were organized as reconnaissance or direct action teams and they conducted "Black Operation" type missions in the northern portion of South Vietnam and the adjacent countries. These teams occasionally included one or more US Special Forces members on the team but most teams were made up of third country nationals. The mix of different foreign national and different tribes of Montagnards occasionally created some ethnic strife, but the SF guys kept that to a minimum and under control. One exception occurred in May when two tribes of Yards engaged in a small arms firefight between barracks buildings in their compound. The troops of Company C were sitting in our outdoor theater awaiting an evening at the movies when gun fire erupted down the beach in the CCN compound. From our vantage point on a small rise we could see tracers going back and forth between barracks and hear M-16 and AK-47 fire. We received a call from the CCN command post confirming that no VC or NVA were involved and it was a "disagreement" between units of CCN. For the ten to twenty minutes that it took the SF guys to regain control of the situation, we delayed the movie, *The Great Race*, and watched the tracer show just 300 meters down the beach.

Security at both Special Forces compounds was provided by a company of Chinese Nungs. The Nungs were Vietnamese of Chinese descent and for generations were mercenaries for foreigners and Vietnamese organizations. Their proficiency and loyalty were beyond any suspicion and we felt safe from ground intrusion of any type. They recognized only the Special Forces as their superiors and held no respect for allied or American military if they did not wear the Green Beret. While with the SF at Da Nang, I witnessed the Nungs draw down on a U.S. Army Military Police jeep which was in pursuit of a Special Forces jeep full of drunk and disorderly Green Berets. The MPs were only a few hundred yards behind the SF jeep as it made a high-speed entry into the compound, but when the MPs arrived at the gates, they were met by half a dozen armed Nungs and two loaded .50 caliber machine guns pointed at them. The MPs were notified that the SF compound did not come under the jurisdiction of Army MPs and the MPs should leave immediately. They could contact the Company C headquarters in the morning if that was a problem. The Nungs were great and so serious about security that their officers were authorized to summarily shoot any soldier caught asleep on his post.

Company C of 5th Special Forces was responsible for the Special Forces camps in I Corps. We supported nine camps in the AO, numbered from A-101 at Lang Vei (later at Mai Loc) in the north to A-109, Thuong Duc in the south. Most of my duties revolved around supporting programs for supplying the camps, building market economies, establishing health programs, and training our Vietnamese SF counterparts (the LLDB). This was a major cultural education for young SF Captain Stevenson as I worked with the LLDB and the Yards of different tribes at the camps. Whether it was walking down a street holding hands with my counterpart, Dai Uy (Captain) Trahn, or buying rice balls wrapped in palm leaves on the village economy for lunch, I was about to absorb a lot of culture.

In the S-3 shop, we coordinated airlift of all categories of supplies into the camps, transported troops in and out and requested tactical air support when necessary. Camp A-101 at Mai Loc was originally located well west of the Marine base at Khe Sahn, almost on the Laotian border at Lang Vei. As a precursor to the battle of Khe Sahn, the North Vietnamese Army overran the SF compound at Lang Vei, utilizing tanks for the first time in Vietnam. The presence of Russian-made PT-76 tanks in the NVA attack force was an indicator of the escalated battles that were to come. After the battle of Khe Sahn with its tremendous US airpower use, the survivors of the Montagnard units and a new SF team established the "new" A-101 camp Mai Loc on the edge of the coastal plain instead of back in the mountains and valleys.

I went out to the boonies on several recon missions and worked occasionally with the Command and Control, North (CCN) guys in their "black ops" out of country. Only once did I get into a serious firefight and that was when I joined our Mike Force reaction battalion to relieve NVA pressure on camp A-109 at Thuong Duc.

Proving that Da Nang city was never totally secure, on 27 February 1969, some VC sappers decided to attack the supply infrastructure and blew up a barge loaded with ammunition on the Bridge Ramp, west bank of the Tran Thi Ly bridge over the Song Han River (Da Nang River to our "Running Dog Yankee Imperialists"). That only made a small dent in the ammunition supply, but it killed several sailors and closed one of the bridges from the east side of the river to Da Nang city and the airbase. The official report said it was hit by a rocket, but our SF Intel sources said it was sappers. Almost two weeks passed before truck traffic could cross again. Our SF camp was far enough south on China Beach that we used the southern bridge, so not a big deal for us.

One of the rather misdirected rules put into effect by the military (this time the US Marines) was a prohibition on sale of alcohol by the bottle to US Marines. The Marines could buy all they wanted, one drink at a time from the clubs. Bottled booze was rationed in Vietnam and sold based on an allocation on each troop's "ration card." The Marines simply blocked out those items on each Marine's ration card. We hosted Marines in our SF compound for a planning meeting, and, as it wrapped up, a Marine Colonel pulled me aside and asked if I could buy a bottle of Scotch for his staff. Hey, I'm a lowly SF captain and I have to buy scotch for a Marine Colonel because of some Marine regulation? Unbelievable! Since we used our own club on the SF compound, I did not need my ration card, so I bought a good bottle for the Colonel and one for his Operations Officer: both gifts.

Adjacent to our compound, but within our outer perimeter, was a house of ill repute, established by the Agency and 5th SF Group and providing a service both to the transient GIs along highway QL-1 and our compound residents. The house was a positive cash flow for our SF Company C and as such we audited the books of the house. Guess who, as the newest captain, drew that duty? Yep. I went to meet the Madam and she turned out to be a hell of a business woman. She kept good books on every transaction, expenses and health care for her girls. The guys in our compound referred to her as the "Dragon Lady", but, if you were straight forward with her, she was just a damn good manager. That was a task that I have talked about forever. The lone surprise from the Dragon Lady's employees was one morning when I rolled out of bed early to shower and found two of her giggly young ladies coming out of our showers. It seems two of our SF Lieutenants enjoyed company for the night. I wondered what the overnight fee was.

My room was in a one-story building with waist high concrete walls, unlike the canvas or wooden hooches at Camp Eagle, Cam Ranh

137

and Phan Rang. That was significant because Da Nang Air Base and Marble Mountain were subjected to occasional rocket attacks and the concrete walls provided a significant degree of protection from shrapnel if a rocket landed nearby and you were not in the real bunkers. A lot of us developed a cavalier attitude toward the alarm for incoming rockets, saying that we could lie in our bunks until we learned where the first rocket landed before evacuating the building for the bunker. I shared a room with one of our FACs, MAJ Tom Daniels, who before Vietnam called, was a career KC-135 driver. The FAC living across hall was CAPT A. L. Larson, who later became a tenured faculty member at the Air Force Academy. Our Senior FAC for the SF Company was LTC Tom Albright, a great guy who understood Special Forces and unconventional warfare, a rare capability in the Air Force.

Our room was small but quite comfortable compared to the best the 101st offered. It contained a bed, a wall locker, room for a chair and a wall for my Texas flag. The hooch came with geckos (who had a habit of screaming and occasionally falling on your bed from the ceiling) and a Mammasan that could field strip any weapon (M-16, 45 automatic, AK-47, M-1 carbine) and clean it in record time. I often came by the hooch following an afternoon run to view four Mammasans squatting between the hooches with M-16s, Carbines and AK47s stripped and laid out for cleaning. They chattered away while cleaning the weapons, reassembled them and tested the action. I paid $10 a month to have clean, starched fatigues every day and shined boots. When I came back from the field, I dropped all the grungy tiger fatigues and gear on the floor. I cleaned my carbine or AK-47 as soon as I could after a mission, just to be ready if needed. But, Mammasan took that as an insult and took the weapon out of my wall locker the next morning and cleaned it to her standards. Shortly after breakfast, everything taken to the field was cleaned and put up in the correct place in my wall locker.

The SF Company C compound, on the South China Sea, offered a convenient location to take a daily run. I ran north or south on China Beach's hard packed sand at the water's edge until my feet hurt and then I moved into a couple of inches of water to cool off my feet. I worked my way up to a quick three miles every day that I was in the compound. If I felt brave, I moved my run into the deep soft sand. That was like running with 20-pound weights on your legs. A minute of deep sand repeated a couple of times during a run created a great workout.

The Officers Mess and the NCO / Enlisted Mess were run by an SF Master Sergeant and a dozen Vietnamese. I paid $60 per month for all my meals. Even if we were in the field for part of the month, nobody complained about the fees. We were all part owners in the club and the fee was less than the Rations allowance that Uncle Sam paid us for food, so we made a profit. The O Club bar also served sandwiches and bar food for the late eaters. The prettiest bar maid was Co Ha (Miss Ha), a student at the University in Da Nang by day and our bar waitress most nights. She enjoyed practicing her English and teaching Vietnamese to the SF guys. She took no grief from the troops, and, if you laid a hand on her, you were liable to have your testicles handed to you. Co Ha's younger brother also worked in our bar and loved to bait the SF guys about working for the NVA at night. Some mornings, after Da Nang was hit by rockets, he showed up at the club claiming to be dead-ass tired (his words). He would make a statement like "You don't understand how heavy that rocket gets when you have to carry it for miles, just so it can be fired into Da Nang Airbase." A few of the SF guys told him someday they were going to believe him, and shoot his ass.

Few rockets were aimed at the US compounds at Marble Mountain or China Beach; the high value targets were over by Da Nang Airbase. We became rather callous about rocket attacks, lying in bed when the rocket attack sirens went off. The third month I was at Da Nang, a nighttime rocket alarm sounded, and, as usual, Major Tom Daniels and I stayed in bed to see what the threat was. With a roar like a freight train, three rockets passed over our BOQ and landed just to the east of the buildings. Tom and I were face down on the floor in less than a second. No more rockets arrived and the next morning we found that the rockets landed on the beach about 70 meters offshore. Charlie was a rotten gunner! However, a month later rockets were fired at the Marine Air Group 16 next door and one rocket did not go long. The Marines took a dozen casualties at the outdoor movie when the rocket hit the roof top and spread shrapnel over any moviegoers that were not in a bunker. We usually got a minute's warning of "Incoming" when the rockets were fired, but you sure as hell should respond correctly and not just wait and see. After the next couple of weeks of being vigilant and heading for our bunker, I fell back into the bad habit of not respecting the NVA rockets.

One afternoon in April, the S-1 called me and asked me to meet with a reporter that was interviewing soldiers from Texas, particularly those from the Dallas area.  I agreed and the next morning I went up to the S-1 meeting room to meet Wick Fowler, a reporter for the *Dallas Morning News* newspaper. I knew who Wick Fowler was and read his column back in my Dallas days. We talked for a while about Special Forces, but he was doing color articles on Dallas boys at war and was more interested in the story of Don's and my being in Vietnam at the same time and our tales of being wounded at separate times. Mama Garrett mailed a copy of Wick's article when it was published in the *Dallas Morning News* about three weeks later. Wick's published picture of me in my Green Beret turned out to be the only personal picture that I have of my SF tour.

OPERATION BLUBBER DROP

I always appreciate a young fellow officer who can find innovative ways to fight a war. One memorable day, two huge whales beached and died on China Beach, right behind our neighbor Marine Air Group 16. Fortunately for us, the whales were located downwind from the SF compounds. This was not an unusual event as it occasionally happened elsewhere along the Vietnam coast. We knew that soon the odor would be overwhelming. The Marines, who were the closest units, tried several unsuccessful methods to move the dead whales or tow them back to sea. As the problem began to ripen, a young Army captain, aviator type, found the tactical solution. He convinced two Army CH-54 heavy lift helicopter crews to pick up the whales, around which the Marines finally secured ropes and slings. The CH-54 "Sky Cranes" airlifted the decaying whales some 30 - 45 kilometers west of Da Nang to an area known as Antenna Valley. This was a well-used North Vietnamese Army (NVA) infiltration route, and well defended on the ground. There, from an altitude of about 6,000 feet, the CH-54s dropped the whales into known heavy traffic areas. Worst case, this was probably edging around chemical warfare, and best case, we were hoping to make it unpleasant for the bad guys. I have always pictured an NVA company commander sitting down to write a condolence letter to some soldier's next of kin explaining how NVA private Minh was killed by tons of falling blubber.

WATER BUFFALO DRILL

I was working in our underground operations bunker out by China Beach when the SF A-Team commander from Minh Long (site of the Caribou shoot-down in August 1967) called me with a desperate request. It may seem a strange request in the middle of a war, but the only village water buffalo died of infection and he asked if I could manage a replacement. The importance of a water buffalo to a Montagnard or small Vietnamese village cannot be overstated. It was to a village what a tractor was to an American farmer. It plowed rice paddies and pulled logs for construction projects or clearing forest cuts. A replacement was critical to the Yard camp. The team commander asked if there were funds to acquire another buffalo; reluctantly I informed him that was a "No."

My conscience couldn't let me do that to the A Team or their village, so I asked if I could work it for a few days. I immediately pushed the need to Major Walker, our S-3, and he said to get with SFC McGregor and see what could be done. Sergeant Mac and I bent a few rules; not black market, just a little barter-based commerce. In the end, we found and purchased an adequate water buffalo in Quang Ngai. The delivery, however, was to be our responsibility. OK! Through the Marine Air Group on Marble Mountain Airfield next door I contacted an Army Chinook unit that was supporting units near Quang Ngai. In exchange for a small unit contribution, the Chinook guys would sling load the water buffalo out to the SF camp. The going rate for the unauthorized sling mission was a case of Scotch and four captured AK-47s. Done!

Sgt Mac was tight with the US Navy veterinarians in Da Nang so he persuaded a vet technician to come along and tranquilize the buffalo for his airlift. Three days later we caught a ride on the southbound Chinook which dropped our little team outside Quang Ngai, and as the Chinook crew flew their scheduled lift, we tranquilized the water buffalo and rigged it up in a cargo sling. CAUTION: drugged or not, water buffalo do not like to fly. Just after liftoff, the buffalo proceeded to defecate everything in his digestive tract along a 200-meter trail. The sling load was successful and the Hook crew gently lowered the water buffalo into a "corral" at the SF camp. I was at the camp just after the water buffalo was delivered and watched the village chief wipe tears from his eyes when the A Team commander said the water buffalo was theirs, free and clear. Mission completed, I rode back to Da Nang with the Chinook crew, after assuring several villagers that the drugs used on the water buffalo would wear off by tomorrow. No challenge is too great to provide support to the SF troops in the field and maintain great rapport with the indigenous personnel. See, Special Forces is not always "John Wayne" shoot 'em up stuff as seen in Hollywood movies.

27 April 1969 - We were provided another moment of great concern that became entertainment for our SF troops. The Da Nang Airbase bomb storage area began a series of explosions that lasted almost 24 hours. A US Marine detail was burning trash when the fire got out of control in a strong wind. The fire crossed a berm into an area storing 2000-pound bombs. The detonating bombs tossed 2000 pounders into other storage areas and a chain reaction of fires and explosions ensued. Fortunately, the alarm was sounded in time, and evacuation and sheltering was done for Marine, Air Force and Vietnamese in proximity to the west side of Da Nang Airbase. Before all was finally brought under control the next afternoon, over 1000 tons of munitions were destroyed. Bombs and ammunition were tossed across the Marine side of the airbase and even across two runways to the Air Force C-123 and F-4 areas on the east side.

The next two mornings I was the Special Forces representative to the morning III MAF briefing. This portion of Vietnam was under the command of a Marine Lieutenant General at Third Marine Amphibious Force (III MAF). I watched the briefings of Air Force, Army and Marines as they explained what munitions were available and what the restocking plan and timeline was.

When all the fireworks started, I was working in our underground command bunker and suddenly the filter on one of our air conditioning units blew inward and we heard a loud "Whump" sound. The shock wave and sound of the 2000 pounders exploding reached us, six miles from Da Nang main. One of the NCO's hustled in and shouted, "You guys have to come see this. Da Nang has exploded." We scrambled out of the bunker and up the low hill to the front of the headquarters building. There was a huge mushroom cloud rising from the direction of Da Nang airbase and I mumbled, "Jesus, Charlie has a nuke round for a rocket!" The fireworks varied with the munitions detonating. Fuel or napalm made a soft "Whump" sound and sent a fireball high into the sky. Cannon ammo, 20 or 40 mm, was thrown into the air and exploded like a million sparkling fireworks. The large bombs (500/1000/2000 pounders) and artillery rounds went off with a classic explosion and we could feel the concussion at Marble Mountain. With no way to assist, the SF guys brought lawn chairs and cold beverages to watch the entertainment.

During the evening of April 30, 1969, a Seaboard World Airlines DC-8 mistook Marble Mountain airfield for Da Nang Air Base, four miles to the west, and then proceeded to land, and, amazingly, stop on the 4000-foot-long runway (5000 feet shorter than Da Nang Air Base.) With 219 passengers and a crew of 12, the DC-8 used full braking and reverse thrust to stop with his main wheels on the asphalt and his nose wheels about four feet off the overrun in the sand. I heard a loud roar from my hooch but wrote it off to a low-flying Marine A-6 from Da Nang main. Early the next morning, I walked to the front of the headquarters building and was greeted by the front end of the DC-8 some 300 yards from our compound. The passengers were bussed to Da Nang. The Marines brought in a large tow vehicle which pushed the DC-8 straight back up the runway, moving the main wheels back to within three feet of the overrun edge. The DC-8 was defueled to the minimum fuel needed to safely takeoff, turn right and fly to Da Nang AB. The replacement DC-8 pilot pushed the throttles to the max and stood on the brakes until the wheels slid. He released the brakes, and, with almost nothing on board, the DC-8 leapt into the air just past mid-field on the runway. The four J-79 engines were more than enough push to get it off the *short* runway. An unintended consequence was the hurricane speed engine exhaust that tore through the MAG 16 area and wasted several tents.

Special Forces support to the Montagnard camps was not limited to military training, medical assistance and supplies. When we could, the SF teams coordinated advanced medical care for the Yards. In this case, we arranged for the US Navy Clinic's oral and plastic surgeons to work on a five-year-old girl with a cleft palette. The girl also happened to be the daughter of a village chief. On the day when the girl was to fly from her camp to Da Nang, I happened to be on the chopper, returning from a job at another SF camp. We landed the Huey at the girl's mountain village where the SF detachment medic and the village chief escorted the little girl to the running helicopter. She was obviously terrified of leaving her parents, much less getting on that loud, vibrating, metal flying bird with strangers. As Chief, her father could not leave the village, so the young girl was travelling alone for the 35-minute trip to our Da Nang compound. I helped the team medic strap her into her seat next to me as I sat by the door. She was pale and trembling until she saw the Montagnard bracelet I wore on my left wrist. She grabbed my left arm with a two-handed death grip and buried her face in my side. The Huey lifted off, accelerated, and climbed over the last mountain ridge directly toward the South China Sea coast for a safe over-water flight home.

The little girl did not look up until we were level for a few minutes and we were approaching the coast. When she saw all that water her eyes absolutely bulged out. She knew only the streams around her village. So, in very bad Rhade language, mixed with some Vietnamese, I tried to explain that was merely water and the streams fed the giant water. The longer we flew, the more relaxed she became but she never released the two-fisted grip on my arm. I felt my arm and hand going to sleep. Our helicopter pilots must have understood the young girl's plight because they gave us a very gentle straight-in approach and landing at the Da Nang SF pad, where a team medic and one of the girl's tribe members met us. Through the interpreter, they explained she should go with them to see the doctors. Her language or not, it took five minutes to have her release my arm. I gave her my hand to hold as we hopped down from the chopper and walked to a jeep where they departed as I watched and waved. Two weeks later, our Company C surgeon, Captain Gingus, told me the operations were successful and she was healing and back in her mountain village. I realized it is the little wins with the people that help you win the war.

One evening I was dressed up in black for a run out to bad guy territory on a recon mission as our small team headed over to our SF helipad. We were seven of the toughest looking warriors in country: camouflaged and with tons of gear, radios and weapons. On the side of the helipad were six pallets of baby chickens bound for a couple of SF camps the next morning. Our Army chopper made a hot dog approach and landing on the pad and disaster followed. The troop who was handling the pallets was not there, so the pallets were blown over and the three-sided revetment landing area was covered with cheeping, panicked chicks. Our team immediately set about to round them up for return to their crates. Our highly-trained SF guys chased birds, even crawling under the Huey in pursuit. I chuckled as I stood with an armful of chicks and watched the mayhem. "Yeah, these are America's finest troops and best trained 'killers' in the Army, right here."

Supply and demand was a great aid to restoring an economy at our SF Montagnard camps. The Yards needed a source of income to pay for supplies that we take for granted, such as medical supplies, farming tools and more diverse livestock. You have already read about my baby chicks and water buffalo tales. To make things happen, we set up a system of "horse-trading" for the needed goods. We started by having a SF camp population produce "genuine Montagnard crossbows" for trading. Of course, the crossbows were made from the wooden boxes that previously held 105mm artillery shells for the camp's guns, but they

144

were still made by Montagnards! We traded the crossbows to the Navy for steaks - steaks to the Army for scotch - scotch to the Marines for cash and used the cash to buy supplies for our camps. This was Yankee free enterprise at its best.

As an Assistant Operations Officer, I often flew in an Air Force O-1 Birddog from the Marble Mountain airfield next door. Once again, for me, tactical flying was fun with my roommate Major Tom Daniels, Capt Al Larson, or our Senior FAC, Lt Col Albright. We employed tactical fighters for our SF camps and the other US forces in I Corps. We watched B-52 Arc Light strikes from the air as well as the C-123 "Ranch Hands" putting down more Agent Orange. Policy wise, unlike our bombing from the O-2s in the 101st, there was to be no shooting from the O-1. Seems some FAC down in IV Corps shot up his own aircraft tire while firing his M-16 out the side window of the Birddog. It was rumored that the TASS squadron commander randomly dropped by to inspect the O-1s after missions to see if any spent cartridges incriminated the FAC.

Time flew by with operations, visits to the camps, and massive amounts of coordination and paperwork. Before I knew it, I was down to 60 days left on my extension and I wanted to volunteer for another six months, either here or with the 173rd Airborne Brigade in Vietnam. But back in DC, Department of the Army's Infantry Officer Assignments section thought I was "in country" long enough and must return to the United States for my next assignment.

My desire to extend was based on a feeling this war was an infantryman's job and I could not think of anything better to do. At an unconscious level, I was still wrapped up in my Superman Syndrome, believing that I could not be hurt. Charlie tried multiple times and he blew them all. I offered to extend in place with 5th SF Group, thereby saving Uncle Sam a move, but DA disapproved it. I quickly updated my assignment preferences to list instructor duty at Ft Benning's Infantry School, the US Military Academy or an ROTC teaching position.

Two weeks later, I was summoned to the phone in our Da Nang TOC for a call from an officer in Army Officer Assignments and was offered an ROTC instructor position in San Antonio, Texas at Trinity University. I immediately accepted. If I couldn't get an airborne assignment (no chance having already served with the 101st and SF; and the 82nd was partially deployed to Vietnam), then ROTC was a good assignment. Hey! This was back to Texas and a town I enjoyed, San

145

Antonio. This was the assignment that changed my life. If I received orders to a Basic Training job, I would have parted ways with the Army. That's amusing, because, in less than two years, I did leave the Army. Donald was not too long behind me in leaving Vietnam and our home in the 101st Airborne Division, but he drew an assignment to Ft Polk Louisiana, pushing Basic Trainees. In less than a year, Don decided to part ways with the US Army and was off to the Law School of Southern Methodist University.

On June 27, 1969, I signed out of Co C in Da Nang and caught a C-7 Caribou flight to Nha Trang and the SF Group Headquarters. I out-processed from the Group on travel day two. On day three, I caught a helo ride down to Cam Rahn Bay and the 510th Repo Company. I was initially scheduled to depart on July 2nd, but a backlog of passengers pushed my travel date back to July 4th. I'm leaving Vietnam for "the World" on Independence Day! The delay was a good deal because, on June 30, I came down with an FUO (Fever of Unknown Origin) and for two days I suffered through tremendous chills and poured sweat, soaking through my clothes and the bedding on my bunk. There was no way the Air Force types were going to let me on that Freedom Bird in my condition. I was going to self-medicate for another day before I let the medics have a go at me, knowing they would cancel my Freedom Bird and keep me in a ward until I recovered. Timed like a lot of the FUOs that I saw in country, the fever broke on the morning of July 2nd and, after a good breakfast and a shower, I was almost a human being again. The night of July 2nd and 3rd I applied a little alcoholic pesticide to my system to kill germs and I came through in decent shape.

On the morning of The Fourth of July 1969, my name was posted on the manifest for that night's Freedom Bird. I gathered what few belongings I possessed and was ready to go an hour before manifest time. In my kit bag was an old ammo can in which I carried all my personal effects and papers. Because it could be sealed watertight for papers and precious items, I'd humped that ammo can for the past 30 months and it was as much a part of my gear as my uniform. Speaking of uniforms, the policy still allowed troops to wear either khakis or jungle fatigues as far as McCord AFB or Travis AFB, but you were required to wear civilian clothes onward through civilian airports. Fine by me. Jungies for the long ride were a lot more comfortable than khakis.

All the passengers were given a large 24 inches by 20 inches or so manila Army envelope for the sheets of miscellaneous paperwork, pay records and multiple sets of orders sending them home from the war. I added one item to that envelope. Before turning in my kit bag as baggage for the flight, I moved out of sight and extracted from my bag the barrel of an AK-47 and placed it in my envelope. It just fit, corner to corner. I figured the worst that could happen was it would be confiscated at McCord as a piece of unauthorized junk because there were no wooden stock parts nor bolt, magazine or other parts. I mailed those pieces home to Arlington in one package per week over the previous three weeks. The US Post Office was delivering my other AK-47 parts. Hooah!

Our aircraft was a Seaboard World DC-8, going to Japan and then to McCord AFB at Seattle, Washington, another port that I frequented before. Fortunately, there was an Army Major on our manifest so I did not draw the duty of Troop Commander for the flight. About 1800 hours we began the final boarding process and blue Air Force busses, with grenade screens on the windows, drove us across the hot concrete ramp to board that beautiful DC-8. We were sweaty as the plane closed doors, started engines and taxied to the south end of Runway 02 Left. As the aircraft accelerated down the runway, there were many souls urging it onward, upward and I was one of them. When the DC-8 rotated, flew off and the landing gear closed with a "Clunk", the screaming and cat calls from over 200 homeward bound GIs was deafening. More than a few of these combat hardened troops shed tears as we turned east over the sea and set course for Japan and the US of A. I settled in next to the Major troop commander in the front row (more leg room) and tried my best to make that Freedom Bird fly faster. The flight crews and cabin crews may have shared the fear and anxiety of a flight into Vietnam, but I know they enjoyed the ecstasy of 200+ passengers going home.

An hour or so out of Japan, several of the troops in the middle of the aircraft became rather loud and rowdy, courage fed on alcohol they sneaked on board and were still consuming. The stewardesses met with little success in settling them down and when the troop commander went back and requested some cooperation, he was told to fuck off because they were going home. The major walked back to our front row and asked the stewardess to have the Airline Captain request that we be met by the Military Police after landing.

We landed at Yakota, Japan, and taxied up to the passenger terminal, but we were told nobody could disembark until the Military Police arrived. Soon after, the forward door was opened; in came two MP's, one a very young-looking Specialist 4 and the other a hard looking "old Army" Staff Sergeant. The stewardess identified the leader of the

147

rowdy bunch and the young Specialist stopped abeam his row and asked the drunken troop if he would kindly come with him. The drunk swatted the MP's extended hand and told him "Fuck off. I'm not going anywhere with you."

The Staff Sergeant gave the young MP a gentle sideways push and softly said, "Let me handle this." Stepping up to the drunk's row of seats he stared at the troop and the drunk glared back. In an instant, the Sergeant pulled his nightstick and smashed the drunk on the head with a loud crack that was heard throughout the aircraft cabin. In the next second, he holstered the nightstick, unfastened the troop's seat buckle with one hand, grabbed the troop by the shirt front and dragged his unconscious ass into the aisle. The sergeant turned to the neighboring seat occupants and asked loudly, "Does anyone else want to extend their tour in Asia in our jail?" Dead silence. The MP Sergeant dragged the unconscious troop up the aisle and I thought he would drag him down the boarding stairs until his Specialist lifted one arm and they carried him to the back seat of their MP sedan, driving off with lights flashing. Not a word was uttered until a section of busses pulled up at the foot of the stairs and the beautiful voice of a stewardess sweetly said, "You may now deplane and load the busses, but please remain in the passenger terminal. Our ground time will be approximately one hour 45 minutes and those that want to continue to the United States should be ready to board when called." The troop commander and I both chuckled. It could not have been said any better.

We arrived at McCord AFB one hour before we took off from Cam Ranh Bay, due to crossing the International Date Line and getting a day back. That still made it a 23-hour trip from Vietnam. As we started through military customs, I thought "Well, let's see how this goes." My kit bag was the sixth bag out of the plane, so I picked it up and went over to a customs table manned by a young buck sergeant with a 1st Cav patch on his right shoulder and a CIB. "I might have a chance with another Vietnam grunt" was my thought.

"Sir, if you will place your bag on the floor right here, I need to look at it."

I placed my kit bag as directed and he rapidly unzipped it and ran his hands through the contents. Without looking up, he took out my beat-up ammo can, saying,

"Sir, you can't take this ammo can. It is on the prohibited list."

148

"I humped that can for over two tours and we don't even use that caliber of ammo."

He thought for only a few seconds and then said,

"Yes, sir, but it is on the prohibited list and can't be taken any further. I will need to empty the contents here in your kit bag."

Before I could whine any more, he opened the can, dumped my stationery, mail and other stuff, zipped up the bag, picked up his metal detector wand and said, "Sir, if you will raise your arms." I raised my hands over my head holding aloft the big manila envelope that contained my orders, pay records and part of an AK-47. The Sergeant swiftly ran the metal detector across my front, sides and back while I stood with my records envelope high overhead. The sergeant placed the metal detector on the table and smiled

"That's it, Sir. Welcome home. Transportation to Seattle airport can be made down there." He pointed to a booth at the far end of the building.

I checked at the Transportation booth and signed up for a ride to SEATAC International Airport. I lugged my kit bag into the restroom, changed into jeans and a civilian shirt (the only civvies I owned) and took my AK-47 piece from my orders envelope and stuffed it into the middle of my bag. The busses departed McCord AFB approximately 30 minutes after each Freedom Bird off-loaded, so I did not have a long wait. Trivial things I noticed told me I was home, like the bus did not have grenade screens on the windows and there were green trees and no white sand. Thirty minutes later we arrived at the departure area of SEATAC, and, after making my way past a cute hippy girl selling flowers and some of her unwashed male friends, I purchased a seat on the next connection to Dallas. I was finally home and headed for Texas and San Antonio. Hooah! or maybe "Yee Haw!"

15

Return to Texas

If I couldn't instruct at Ft. Benning or West Point, then Trinity University in San Antonio was a great assignment. Besides having this great university, San Antonio claimed to be "Military City, USA."

I soon heard that CPT John Calloway, a San Antonio native and an Infantry peer, was assigned to Central Arkansas State, in a dry county, and no social life. In August, I talked with John while attending Instructor's School and learned that he and his wife were recently divorced. I'm not sure whether the assignment to Arkansas was a factor, but divorces for returning infantrymen were all too common. The wives or girlfriends went through a lot of stress waiting out the husband's or significant other's Vietnam tour. Often the husband/trooper returning home was not the same person who left for the war a year earlier. War caused many young wives to vote with their feet, and, as John Calloway said, "split the sheets."

After three days of decompressing at Mama Garrett's house in Arlington and buying my new Pontiac in Dallas for cash (ordered under a special BX purchase plan from Da Nang), I drove from Arlington to San Antonio with everything I owned in my new Pontiac LeMans. "Everything" was now up to two suits, jeans, sweats and uniform items, plus my stereo gear from Hong Kong. "Everything" easily fit in my new LeMans.

I checked into the Ft Sam Houston BOQ until I could find an apartment somewhere near Trinity University which was only two miles west of Fort Sam. Without much hassle, I found a nicely furnished, upstairs apartment, about one mile west of Trinity. The apartments were built in quadrangles and the swimming pool behind the adjacent complex provided a pool view from my bedroom balcony. The apartment complex was in a very quiet neighborhood right on the edge of Olmos Park and lots of "old money." This was a lot nicer than anyplace I lived since leaving home, and, as a bonus, there were two pretty bachelorettes living next door to my apartment.

Trinity University was a private Presbyterian school known as a "Presbyterian Convent for Girls", and, when a mom didn't want her daughter going to a decadent state university; it was off to Trinity U. Trinity University produced many teachers and liberal arts grads but there were few business or pure science courses taught. Luckily, during this age of protest, the son of Dean Moore, Dean of Student Life, was recently commissioned and therefore Dean Moore was a big supporter of Army ROTC. The Cadet Corps had just over 200 cadets, a drop from several years prior when Army ROTC was mandatory for all male freshmen and sophomores. When I arrived, the corps had a lot of good cadets because they were all "volunteers" and not enrolled because they had to.

My greatest challenge was getting back into the mentality of "civilian" life - not that Trinity University was the average civilian world. This was a collection of academicians who, for the most part, shut out the rest of the world and worked in their Presbyterian "convent." There was so much money in the student body that the administration asked the faculty to park behind the student parking area because the faculty cars were bad for the image of the school. The students' BMWs, Mustangs and Mercedes looked a lot better from the street than the faculty cars.

The Army ROTC cadre at Trinity was a friendly lot. The Professor of Military Science was COL Hubert W. Gillespie, a graduate of Texas A&M '41. COL Gillespie was commissioned into the horse-drawn artillery and practiced at Camp Bullis on the north side of San Antonio. At that time, Camp Bullis was a full day's travel by horse and caisson from Ft Sam Houston. He was on his final Army tour, ending what would be a military career of 31 years. A large, friendly officer, he lost one eye in Korea and was excused from our conflict in Vietnam. LTC John Marmor, Artillery, was the second in command and a graduate of San Antonio's St Mary's University with a broad knowledge of San Antonio's west side. We often went to lunch in places that John swore were safe, but I wouldn't go back after dark on a bet. The other instructors were MAJ Ed Wiseman, SGTMAJ Bell, MAJ Landry and SSGT Andrews in Supply.

Immediately after signing in at Trinity, I was sent TDY to Ft Sill, Oklahoma, and the Army Central Instructor Course for two weeks. I

152

learned how to "tell them what you are going to tell them; tell them; and then tell them what you told them." With that simple approach and a lot of polishing up on lesson plans, training aids and platform instruction mannerisms, I was ready to teach the Freshman and Sophomore cadets (MS Is and IIs). The junior ranking instructor always got tagged with teaching the newest cadets. The only time I interacted with the upper-class cadets was in the hallway, at weekly Thursday drill periods, on the rifle range, during intramural sports or at the ROTC Summer Camp.

On September 6, 1969, Donald finished up his second Vietnam combat tour and arrived back in Texas. Sad news though: Don caught the "black bean" that I avoided and was assigned to be a Basic Training commander. After a week's leave, Don signed in at Ft Polk, Louisiana, on September 15th to be a company commander of a Basic Training Company. Fort Polk was the prototype "Camp Swampy" with only one permanent building on post. The rest of the buildings were leftover World War II or Korean War wooden barracks buildings.

After work at Trinity and on weekends, I decided to take flying lessons to obtain a Private Pilot License. The ticket to my future was bought with flying lessons from Dan Briggs, Colonel, Army aviator, Retired. Dan was my instructor, first in the Kelly AFB Aero Club and then as I used my VA benefits through GenAero, the Cessna dealer and flight school at San Antonio International Airport. Dan led me through my FAA Private, Commercial, Instrument, Multi-Engine and two Instructor ratings. I still fly by Dan's words: "Fly like a professional. If you think you can – don't try. You have to know you can!"

My teaching assignments were not a tremendous load, so in my spare time I coached three separate but often overlapping rifle teams at Trinity: the ROTC team, University Varsity team and the Trinity women's team. Our Trinity Varsity team shot in a conference, often traveling to other universities to compete. On several occasions, I rented a Cessna aircraft and flew the three girls on the Varsity team to a competition and the three guys drove. To some matches I drove an Army van as we travelled together.

Trinity University felt some misgivings about a traveling coed team, so I wound up briefing the Dean of Student Affairs and the Dean of Women about our team rules and hotel accommodations. On the day of departure for an away competition, I was required to go to the Dean of Women's office and sign as the responsible adult for the three girls. By the second year, my three best female competitors became close

153

friends and were sharing a Trinity dorm suite. They were a diverse group with Margo Bordwell, a student from Hong Kong; Wendy Felkner, daughter of a well-off dentist in Houston; and Carolyn Willey, a real-to-life cowgirl from Uvalde, Texas. The girls possessed superb fine motor skills and developed into good shooters, particularly Carolyn Willey. All they needed was to develop more competitive spirit and a "kill instinct" for competition. Remember though: this was 1969 and the concept of highly competitive girls was not widely accepted yet.

Trinity presented many distractions for a young Captain just back from paying the wages of war. I recall one particularly shapely sophomore coed, referred to by the ROTC cadets as "Nasty Patty." She flaunted her new freedom with mini-skirts and flimsy blouses. She often came into my office, tossed one thigh over the edge of my desk and asked some non-relevant question. I heard her out, and then tossed her out. But, my, she enjoyed the game.

After their sophomore year at Trinity, Margo Bordwell offered to take her two roomies to Hong Kong for the summer if they paid the air fare. They would live with the Bordwell family, learn the Chinese language and culture, and have Margo as a full-time guide/interpreter to Hong Kong and the territories. The only time I remember touching one of my shooters was when Wendy said she would have to think about it. I grabbed the collar of her shooting jacket and told her, "There is no thinking about it. Call your Dad and tell him you are going to Hong Kong with Margo for the summer. That is too great an offer to pass up." Wendy made that call and the three girls went!

Meanwhile, Captain Donald Stevenson was having all the fun he could stand over at Fort Polk. He was a company commander for a basic training unit and was seeing the very mixed bag of draftees, a job that all combat veterans dreaded upon return from Vietnam. After he was tagged as Duty Officer for Christmas Day 1969, solely because he was a bachelor, Don filed an IG complaint about discrimination against bachelors. The ironic part of this Christmas adventure was Don would have volunteered for the duty if asked. Fed up with the Army and "Camp Swampy" attitude and having been accepted to the Dedman School of Law at Southern Methodist University in Dallas, Don separated from the US Army on 1 April 1970. He definitely paid his dues as a citizen of this great country. In the fall semester, 1970, Don enrolled in the SMU Law School with Uncle Sam and the GI Bill picking up a lot of the cost and outside expenses.

16

CLAIRE RHODES

Sometime during that 1969 summer, I met one of my cute next door neighbors, Claire Rhodes. She worked as an editor for Fox-Stanley Photo Products, Inc., and it turned out that, like me, she was an Episcopalian, so we began attending church together at St. Luke's in nearby Olmos Park. Since her apartment door was three feet from mine, Claire often appeared at my door in what I later referred to as a "Hubby hunting" jump suit. Made of thin material, it fit her well and she never wore a bra with the jumpsuit. Her request: "Can I borrow a cup of Scotch?" made me like this girl. Soon we were attending theatre together, and, for some forgotten occasion I took her to the classy John Charles Restaurant located miles north of the San Antonio Airport and out in the country. A huge fireplace in the middle of the restaurant set the tone for exceptional service and food. Many evenings we drove out into the country, just to sit on my car's hood and look at the Texas stars.

In the last week of July 1970, I took one of the Aero Club's Cessna 182s and flew Claire and a neighbor couple to Corpus Christi for a weekend with Claire's family. If I didn't impress him, I at least got off to a great start with Claire's dad, Omer "Dusty" Rhodes. He was a fighting Texas Aggie, Class of '33, and a veteran of WW II. We flew home to San Antonio just one day ahead of Hurricane Celia that soon pounded Corpus and pushed us along at almost 300 miles per hour. When December rolled around, I took Claire flying around San Antonio to see the Christmas lights from the air. Friends and acquaintances said that was so romantic. I was too dense to see it that way and just enjoyed the flying time and beautiful scenes.

I did not realize where the relationship with Claire was headed until that second year. While I was off at Ft Sill, Oklahoma, as a Tactical Officer at the ROTC Cadet Summer Camp, I suddenly realized that I missed her so much. Slow on the uptake, I finally knew that I'd met the love of my life. We were married in November 1970 in the chapel of Houston's St. John the Divine Episcopal Church, which Claire attended during her high school  years. It was a great ceremony, of which I remember little except spending time with Don and super close friends Fred Cuny and Mike Warren. The groom's job was to stay out of the way of the bride and mother-in-law, and show up on time. In fact, Don and I were sitting on the steps to the side door of the church, deep in conversation when the priest opened the door, stepped out and announced, "We are about to begin the wedding service. You might want to join us." So, I buttoned up my dress blue uniform, and, accompanied by my Best Man, proceeded to join the ceremony.

Following the ceremony and reception, Claire and I headed for Houston's Andrau Airpark, out Westheimer Road on the far west side of Houston and hopped into a nice Cessna for our honeymoon vehicle. A wonderful gentleman, Mr. C. G. Benham, for whom I flew charter on several occasions, loaned me the use of his Cessna 210 for my honeymoon. Claire and I flew from Houston to Lakeway Resort on Lake Travis, west of Austin, for our honeymoon. That evening I took time to watch the Darrell Royal Show (UT's football coach) on TV and Claire has never let me forget it. The two-day stay was too short and we were both back to work on Monday.

In mid-1970, I was pissed when the Army again told me I could not attend Army flight training. Officer assignments told me to "Reapply for the Senior Officers Aviation Course as a Major." I was years away from meeting a Majors Promotion Board! My first rejection was "needs of the Army", followed by "You are critical as a combat experienced infantryman"; and now it was "You are too senior in grade, reapply later."

I drove out to Randolph AFB, east of San Antonio, and asked some folks in Air Training Command (ATC) Operations who I should see about getting an inter-service transfer for pilot training. I was finally routed to the correct office, where a Major Brown and his secretary in Officer Acquisitions, AFMPC, handled the paper work. The paperwork assistance and friendly customer service that I received from Maj Brown's office were a turning point in my life. I bought his wonderful secretary a large bouquet of flowers about the time the paperwork was wrapped up. I faced a tremendous decision if I was to move to the Air Force. I could fly, but the down side was being cut loose from the paratrooper and Special Forces community. At least I thought so at that time!

I talked several times with COL Gillespie about the inter-service move and how I would be burning Army bridges behind me once I submitted the official paperwork. But, hell, I wanted to fly! Dan Briggs had convinced me that I could be a very good pilot and I loved the freedom and the challenge. Finally, I took a deep breath and submitted the Army and Air Force paperwork. As the paperwork flowed through the Army wickets, I found myself being counseled by the Deputy Commanding General of 4th Army at Ft Sam Houston. Army regulations required that I be counseled by an Army general officer before a decision could be finalized on such a transfer. The general listened to my background and reasons. He then approved the transfer. The Army side was complete.

Despite encouraging words of Maj Brown's office, I still felt uneasy about the process, and was pleasantly surprised when the US Air Force approved my transfer. But, (there is always a "but") the Pilot Training allocation folks needed to find me an April 1971 pilot training class. I was approaching the upper age limit and Columbus AFB's 72-07 was the only available Undergraduate Pilot Training (UPT) class; that meant a PCS move to Columbus. Huh? I had never heard of Columbus! I thought I would go to pilot training at Randolph AFB in San Antonio and that Claire and I would have at least another year of stability. Wrong, Randolph AFB just transitioned from Undergraduate Pilot Training to be the centralized Instructor Pilot School in February '71, so I won a trip to Columbus, Mississippi. When the inter-service transfer occurred, it was effortless. My big move was literally a change of uniforms from green to blue. I received a total transfer of pay, Date of Rank and accrued leave from the Army to the USAF. The biggest pain was the fact that I received no new clothing allowance. Officers could get only one uniform allowance and I used mine in 1966 in the US Army! I bought all my required AF uniforms out of my pocket. Ouch!

With Claire feeling too pregnant to drive to Columbus, (Did I forget to mention that detail?) we sold Claire's Mustang and I took everything I could carry in my LeMans and drove to Columbus in one day. Off we go into the wild blue yonder. On April 13, 1971, I was discharged from the US Army, and, on April 14, 1971, commissioned a Captain in the US Air Force (no ceremony, just a stack of orders), enroute to Undergraduate Pilot Training in Class 72-07 at Columbus AFB, Mississippi.

Was I ready for a whole new life style?

"I've looked at clouds from both sides now"

17

Columbus Air Force Base

So here we go. I don't want to think of the life stress points when this adventure started. I was making a move from a city we loved to a small Mississippi town. I was making the move with a pregnant wife. I was changing from the service that sent me to war to another completely different culture in the US Air Force. I was leaving my easy-going position as an ROTC instructor for a competitive class of students where every exam and flight could impact my future career. Oh, boy, I couldn't wait.

The day after I drove to Columbus, Claire caught a flight on Trans Texas Airways to the Columbus airport, named Lowndes County Regional Airport. She rode backwards in a bulkhead seat through an extremely turbulent flight. With great mental discipline, the lovely and seven months pregnant Claire was one of the few passengers that did not use a barf bag enroute. When Claire walked across the asphalt ramp at Lowndes County, she was glad to be on a solid, non-moving surface. Unaware of her adventure-filled flight, I was just glad to have my wife. The next morning, I signed in at the Columbus AFB Command Post and I began my life as a member of pilot training Class 72-07.

On a very short three-day leave in mid-March, I flew to Columbus to check out the base and found an apartment, two miles north of downtown Columbus and about five miles from the base. Most of the apartment tenants were student pilots and their families. When we arrived one month later, the apartment was ready, but pregnant Claire broke out crying upon seeing the kitchen area. Dumbfounded, I learned it was because there was no dishwasher and she couldn't reach the sink with her extended belly. I quickly went out and bought a roll-around dishwasher at Sears (she has never let me forget that oversight).

Due to the pending birth of our son, Claire functioned as the Class Leader's wife for less than two months and then turned that task over to Liz Williams. Captain Ron Williams was the second ranking student and Liz was an Air Force wife for four years in SAC, so she handled it very well.

18

CHRISTOPHER SEXTON STEVENSON

June 9th, 1971: As I prepared to head off to the T-37 squadron, Claire informed me that she was going into labor and thought she should go to the hospital. We drove to the Base hospital, and she was indeed in labor. After several hours of hard labor, Christopher Sexton Stevenson was thoughtful enough to be born during "work hours." Claire and I possessed absolutely no experience with babies and there was no pre-natal classes or other programs to prepare us for this kid. Our only family, Claire's parents, were hundreds of miles away and unable to help. We learned everything about babies: diapers, feeding, colic, rashes, and baby clothes from our huge, wonderful, Mississippi hired help, Mary Helen. She'd raised a brood of her own and her kindness and wisdom kept us from many a mistake.

Once Chris was born, Claire and I rejoined the many class social functions. At parties, the couples brought their babies, placed them in a bedroom and tag teamed parents to babysit all the kids. A baby in a stroller is a "chick magnet", so a bachelor classmate, Roger Laman, volunteered to take young Chris for strolls on the campus of Mississippi State College for Women. Roger already showed the makings of a great fighter pilot.

Claire's parents, Dusty and Andy Rhodes, came for a visit after Christopher's birth to see their only grandson and our living conditions. We were getting by in our two-bedroom apartment on a young Captain's pay, but things could get tight and there were not many luxuries. Compared to my standard of living as a bachelor, we were almost poor. But compared to most of the folks around Columbus, Mississippi, we were some of "those rich Air Force folks."

Often, Claire took our colicky baby out to the apartment swing set at night so I could get sleep for pilot training. It was probably five months before I realized she was doing that and it was years before I appreciated the sacrifices Claire made to keep me flying at my best. I did learn early in UPT that support of the student pilot by the spouse was critical to completing UPT. Only three months into the program, Claire told me that a certain student pilot would not make it because his wife did not support his flying. He didn't finish UPT.

LEADERSHIP

The Columbus Wing Commander was Col William A. Boutwell and the Deputy Commander for Operations (DCO) was Col Robert B. Tanguy (a great fighter pilot and leader, later a Major General at the Pentagon). The T-37 Pilot Training Squadron Commander was Lt Col Milton Rickman and the Ops Officer was Lt Col "Bear" Snyder, a colorful, huge bear of a man who claimed to be an "Ace" for the enemy because he bailed out of or crashed five different types of US Air Force aircraft. The T-38 squadron was commanded by Lt Col Horace Clarke.

Before UPT class 72-07 got near an aircraft I won the additional duty of student class leader, all because I possessed the earliest date of rank as a captain (I was the rankest). I spent considerable time explaining American customs, Air Force "Be No's" and expectations to our foreign students. My biggest pain, though, was the Bachelor Officers Quarters on base, where several of my class lieutenants enjoyed sleep-over girlfriends, weekend girl friends or significant others. Many of these young ladies were from the campus of Mississippi State College for Women in Columbus, where some girls went through numerous AF lieutenants during their four years at MSCW. While I defended the rights of my officers, it was bad karma to have the maids find women still asleep in bed when they came into a BOQ room on Monday morning. I gave the "Get them out by 0800!" speech at least a dozen times. I clashed with Lt Col Robert C. Ford, the 3650th Student Squadron Commander, over BOQ rules on visits, foreign students cooking on a grill in the middle of their room, and even a major disagreement about racy pictures in our 72-07 class annual. One discussion with Lt Col Ford became so heated that he threatened me and LT Roger Laman with Article 15s and dismissal from UPT for violating AF Regulations. A former Special Forces captain was not intimidated by some aged ATC Lieutenant Colonel; so, I countered,

"What you want is not written in any regulation and you are, instead, imposing your own moral standards. I would be glad to discuss my Article 15 case at your Court Martial."

He backed down, and, threw us out of his office. I held another meeting with the guys living in the BOQ and we never reached the threats-to-flying stage again. Except for required events, Lt Col Ford and I avoided each other for the remaining portion of my year at Columbus.

BRIEF TIME IN T-41s
After spending three weeks of academics on principles of flight, aerodynamics, and weather, we finally moved on to our first flights. Phase 1 of UPT was T-41 flights from the local airport, Lowndes County Airport on the south side of Columbus. Each morning, half the class was bussed to flight training, and, after noon, the section swapped with the other half of the class for more academics. Our flight instructors were civilian contract instructors, most with a military aviation background. The T-41 was a military version of the Cessna 172 with a few changes in weight and radios. I had just finished almost 200 flight hours giving instruction in the Cessna 172 for the Kelly Aero Club and GenAero back in San Antonio, but I was not going to say squat about previous experience. That was a good plan. It didn't work out that way.

On my first ride as a T-41 student, everything went well (slowly) as I flew to the training area south of the airport and my instructor asked for practice aircraft stalls. I did one clearing turn to look for other aircraft and then went smoothly through an approach to landing stall, a takeoff and departure stall and then an accelerated stall, talking the entire time about what I was doing and what I was feeling on the controls. Each stall was rapidly recovered with minimum loss of altitude. My IP told me to "Take us back to the airport for practice landing patterns." I found Lowndes County airport, correctly entered the pattern, made the required radio calls and flew my first Air Force pattern from downwind through base to final. I was slightly high on final approach with the standard half-flap setting, so I lowered full flaps to make a steeper approach, gracefully rounded it out and squeaked it onto the runway. The IP said only "Do it again." Off we went, and, as we entered downwind, he told me: "Student pilots are not allowed to make full flap landings."

Pondering the rationale / stupidity of that Air Force decision while flying the pattern, again I wound up a bit high on final approach.

With a "be no" rule against full flap approaches, I dropped the left wing and stomped the right rudder pedal to the stops, creating a screaming slip toward the end of the runway. The IP did not say a word but I could feel his hand lightly on his control column. At 20 feet altitude, I took out the rudder, leveled the wings and squeaked onto the runway. The IP told me to turn off at the end and taxi back to parking as he picked up the aircraft and training forms. I taxied to the correct parking place, shut the aircraft down, tied it down and finished the mission checklist. I walked over to the IP, standing under the right wing, and awaited his inputs. He did not look up from the forms but said, "You came too close to the training area boundary; you did not do two clearing turns for each stall and flew two unapproved landing patterns. Let me see your wallet, opened to your FAA ticket."

We never discussed whether I possessed any FAA ratings before this flight, but I pulled my wallet from my flight suit pant leg pocket and opened it. He looked at the licenses, then raised his gaze and smirked: "Commercial, single and multi-engine land, instrument and three instructor ratings, I could have guessed." Handing my wallet and grade book to me, he said,

"You need to work on your Air Force procedures but you fly a damn good airplane. That's the good news; the bad news is this flight was your check ride in the T-41. You are through flying the T-41. The purpose of this program is to sort out those that cannot fly from those that can fly, and will be comfortable doing it. We are not going to waste fuel and IP time on you. You fly as well as our instructors. Study the procedures and the program will be easy for you."

Curses, foiled again! For the next three weeks, my classmates flew around south Lowndes County and I sat at the student duty desk awaiting our class promotion to T-37s. So much for low profile in the T-41 program!

T-37 TWEETS
Our class moved back onto Columbus airpatch for real jet flying in the 3650 Pilot Training Squadron. (later the 37th Flying Training Squadron but same patch, then the 41st FTS in T-6 aircraft). 72-07 was again divided into two flights. In T-37s (nicknamed Tweets for the high-pitched sound made while taxiing), I was in "Sabre Flight", where the Flight Commander was Captain Paul O. Dokken. Paul was the ALO / FAC at Song Be, Vietnam, when I was there with 101st Airborne. In

recognition of our close ties, Paul took it upon himself to be my pre-solo Instructor Pilot.

My T-41 instructor was correct: all I needed to do was do it the Air Force way and the program would be easy. The fancy aerobatic maneuvers aside, the Tweet flew like a Cessna 320, the same approach angle and visual image, so there was no problem landing the short-legged Tweet. Five flights into the program, we flew two touch-and-go patterns at Columbus AFB, landed the Tweet and taxied back to the hammerhead area of runway 13R.

"Shut down the right engine, I'm getting out. Go fly and don't make me use my marshmallows." Paul said.

He climbed over the right side of the Tweet's cockpit and I started up the right engine, pondering his last remark. When I looked over at Paul, he pulled a bag of marshmallows from his flying suit's leg pocket and held it up high. Just in case I crashed and burned, he would make good use of the fire. I thought the plane flew better without an IP and there was no crash or fire. I was a jet pilot on July 7, 1971. Over decades, I would encounter Paul several times. Small world!

Our class slugged along through T-37 academics, solos, aerobatics, instrument and initial formation. The 72-07 class suffered our first attritions when several students couldn't solo the Tweet. My only thought was, "God, I love this stuff!"

T-38 WHITE ROCKET
For T-38 training, the class moved next door to the 3651st Pilot Training Squadron (now the 50th Flying Training Squadron) and I was in "Scorpio Flight" led by Captain Jim Egerton. My T-38 IP for pre-solo phase of the "White Rocket" was a great Canadian exchange officer, Captain Rob Macleish. The T-38 was an adrenalin rush and after a couple of afterburner takeoffs and an afterburner high-G loop, I became a speed junkie and knew that I wanted to be a fighter pilot. My first flight in the T-38 (in a G-suit!) was a demonstration ride where we climbed to 35,000 and went supersonic just to say we did it. The White Rocket was fast and sleek. During that first afterburner takeoff, the acceleration surprised me and I was hyperventilating until Rob told me to slow down, just fly and enjoy it. After my T-38 solo flight on November 10th, 1971, I joined the club of high performance jet pilots.

Our pilot training class included four Zoomies, among them 1LTs Tom Menard and John Bailey. ·Our ROTC officers included Roger Laman, Phil Martin, and Dee Graeber. Two former navigators were in the class, Captains Ron Williams and Mike Gould, along with foreign officers from Italy and Iran. Several Italian students brought their families to Columbus, while the others were bachelors. The foreign

students were constantly changing as we received some who washed back from a senior class and several of our original classmates were washed back to retake a portion of pilot training. Of the foreign students that finished with our class, I remember most two Italian students: Guiseppe Cecchini and Ugo Riso. Both brought their wives with them and I think tried real hard to have kids born in the US and treated at Air Force hospitals. They weren't the greatest of pilots and the thought that they were going back to Italy to fly F-104s was a bit scary. The F-104 could be a handful to fly.

We picked up a wash-back Iranian aviation cadet in Kambiz Anet. He was a very outgoing, young cadet and although his command of English (American) was perfect, he did not have the greatest flying "hands" in the class. He received many "extra" rides to stay with the class. In 1980, I worried about Lieutenant Anet and Lieutenant Mohagheghi, not for their flying, but how and if they survived the Iranian Revolution.

Pilot training was a year-long intense competition because the aircraft assignment you ultimately received was based on your final class ranking. At the end of the year, Air Training Command sent down a list of available aircraft assignments for the surviving student pilots and the student ranked number one got his choice of any listed assignment. It was a true order of merit selection process. By the time we reached the latter stages of our T-38 program there was considerable stress over class standing / order of merit selection and every check ride. 1LT John Bailey kept a running database on the top twenty or so students and updated the top 20 class standings after each written academic test or flight checkride.

Every classmate was an individual story because military pilots are exceptional specimens of our population. Everyone survived the challenges of higher education (even counting the Air Force Academy), military training, aptitude tests and the flight physical exam. Classmate Tom Menard was not blessed with innate flying skill, but he could process information faster than even the T-38 could fly, thus staying ahead of the plane by making continuous corrections. Roger Laman was the greatest natural pilot in the bunch, with only his flight orientation experience back during ROTC at Ohio State. He excelled at every phase of flying. Claire once said Roger made her "heart flutter" with his movie star like presence, but she was married with a baby and Roger was otherwise occupied with coeds, either from MSCW or back at his alma mater. As soon as we finished the T-37 formation phase, Roger and I rented Cessna 150s from the Fixed Base Operator at Lowndes County airport and we practiced formation in Cessna 150s. You have to have fun flying!

The competition thinned our class from a starting 74 students to a graduation number of 37 American and five foreign students. Some of those lost were to be good officers in fields other than flying. One classmate, Dan Penny, washed out in the early phase of T-38s after a couple of bad check rides. Dan worked less than diligently on his academics. The combination led to his departure from pilot training, but I later encountered Dan when he was a Colonel in another Air Force career field.

The foreign pilots coming from Italy and Iran added a great cultural experience to the American officers with little previous international exposure. The Italians could cook and party with the best of Americans and our Iranian First Lieutenant "Mo" Mohagheghi was probably the greatest athlete in the class. Mohagheghi was not blessed with good flying skills but made it through initial T-38 phase before he was washed back to the class following ours. The US Air Force bent over backwards to graduate the foreign students, partially due to political sensitivities, and the Columbus squadrons washed back numerous students to allow them more chances.

The importance of foreign students was demonstrated in early 1972 when a Mississippi State Trooper stopped an Iranian student pilot for speeding over near Starkville. The trooper mishandled the student, made abusive remarks about his nationality and handcuffed him. From the Starkville jail, the student called the base foreign student liaison officer, who called Air Training Command, who called US Senator John Stennis' office in DC. Within two hours, the student was released and back in the BOQ. Within three days, the State Trooper involved was reassigned to some forlorn station down on the Mississippi River Delta. Such is the power of politics.

AIRCRAFT ASSIGNMENTS

As the end of pilot training drew near, 72-07 received the assignment block of aircraft with the associated base locations. Our class scheduled a "practice pick meeting" for the next evening. The real pick would be four days later. The practice pick meeting was held in a large academic classroom and attendance was open to wives, girlfriends, etc. The list, by aircraft type and location, was written on the chalkboard and each student, in order of merit standing, came to the board, made his pick by writing his name beside an assignment and lined out the corresponding aircraft. There was a great deal of discussion among students and family members as the fighter assignments went first, followed by transports and ATC instructor slots, and, finally the SAC tankers and B-52s. This was a common sequence for assignments and caused great concern with the SAC leadership and later led to an ATC change in the selection process.

Despite numerous but short delays for intra-student bargaining and family discussions, we wrapped up a very tentative list of Air Force futures by 9:30 PM and scheduled the real deal for three afternoons later. The results of the preliminary pick were seen by all; our class data keepers copied it all down. I hoped there would be few changes of choices over the next few days, but I knew that students were getting input from family, friends, IPs, God and God only knows who else. I did not sweat selection as I claimed the first F-4 Phantom assignment, behind Roger Laman's A-7 selection, and I was not about to change.

The next afternoon, Colonel Bob Tangey, Wing DCO, came down to the T-38 squadron and invited me into one of the offices for a discussion. I had no clue as to what the DCO wanted with me, but it turned out to be a job offer, of sorts. He asked me to stay at Columbus as an Instructor Pilot, and, after instructing through two classes, I would become a Flight Commander. I told Colonel Tangey, "I am flattered, but there is an F-4 with my name on it, waiting for me in Da Nang and I'd like to stick with that assignment."

Colonel Tanguy flew the F-4C at MacDill AFB and 180 combat missions in the F-4 from Da Nang with the "Gun Fighters", so he thoroughly understood my decision. He wanted me as part of his wing at Columbus, yet he had no misgivings about my selection of the F-4 assignment. A year later Colonel Tanguy became the Wing Commander

168

at Columbus, then at Craig AFB, and later retired as a two-star. Great guy!

The "real for sure final pick" was held in the T-38 squadron briefing room, with only the students, three Instructors, and the doors locked. There was to be no command influence or family discussions this time. I again picked the first F-4, to Vietnam via RTU at George AFB, California. The only surprise was a change by Ray Smith, who selected the first C-141 at the practice pick, who now took the fifth, and last, F-4 slot. His change from transport to a fighter bumped a great pilot, Phil Martin, from that F-4 to a T-33 with Air Defense Command. The changes tumbled a dozen following picks before the list resumed as seen at the practice event. There were a few career decisions made on the fly in the next few minutes, but, fortunately, most of the selection changes involved assignment locations rather than aircraft types.

Roger Laman took the A-7, saw combat in Southeast Asia, and when I saw him last, he was flying F-16s as an exchange officer to the Danish Air Force and living with two tall, gorgeous Danish young ladies. Tough duty, but somebody volunteered for it. As the class leader and an FAA instructor pilot, I coordinated with the nearest FAA office for an Examiner to give the FAA Military Competency Exam at Columbus to all our USAF students so they would leave UPT with a civilian FAA Commercial, Multi-engine, and Instrument license. That would come in very handy for my classmates who later pursued a civilian flying career.

As a class gift to the T-38 squadron, we presented an AK-47 mounted on a beautiful walnut plaque to Lt Col Clark. Engraved brass plaques noted the gift was from Class 72-07 to the T-38 squadron and the history of the AK-47 capture near the A Shau valley in Vietnam. Over the next twenty years, the AK-47 "disappeared" from the squadron.

Class graduation was in the base theater on March 25, 1972, when Claire pinned my Air Force pilot wings onto my blue uniform. She was the primary reason I earned those wings. Then it was on to Victorville, California, George Air Force Base and the F-4 Phantom II. Bigger, better, faster.

19

George AFB, CA

Following graduation from UPT, I headed south to attend the Water Survival course for a week at Homestead AFB, Florida, south of Miami, where we floated in the cooling tanks from the Turkey Point Nuclear Generating Station. I'm surprised the students did not glow in the dark by class end. One of my favorite classes was entitled "What You Can Eat and What Can Eat You." Somehow, I was always picked for demonstrations of being dropped into the ocean and towed through waves, all because of my Senior Parachutist badge. All the Survival course instructors were jump qualified and enjoyed using a paratrooper captain as their training aid.

After my week of fun parasailing into water, or floating in a survival raft for extended periods of time, I graduated and returned to Columbus to gather Claire and Christopher, and, taking a break in Texas to see family, started the trek to the high desert of California and Victorville's George AFB. George AFB was on the edge of the Mojave Desert where we would learn to live with the elevated temperatures and unlimited visibility. George AFB was home to the 35th Tactical Fighter Wing (TFW) with three F-4 training squadrons and one mission-ready operational Phantom squadron. This last squadron trained F-4 students but also maintained an operational status as a fighter squadron. We arrived in Victorville and George AFB two days before my class was to start, and, then on May 2, 1972, I reported in to the "real fighter" squadron, the 434th Tactical Fighter Squadron (TFS) "Red Devils." The 434th just graduated a class of foreign F-4 pilots from Israel, Japan and Germany. That must have been real fun. Our class stay in the 434th TFS was cut short in August when the squadron was tasked to prepare for deployment to Thailand as part of the buildup for "Linebacker II", the escalation of the air campaign against North Vietnam. My classmates were reminded that flying fighters was still a combat occupation and could become deadly very rapidly. When the 434th began train-up for deployment in September 1972, our class moved down the

F-4 ramp to the 4452nd Tactical Fighter Training Squadron which also just graduated a class of new USAF F-4 crews. We finished our F-4 transition training with the 4452nd.

The F-4 Phantom II was a hulk of a fighter, a Jack-of-all-trades; the Phantom could waddle out for takeoff at well over 50,000 pounds. Even in a clean configuration, the F-4 carried internal fuel weighing more than the fully loaded T-38 trainer. By comparison, the latest Soviet/North Vietnam Mig-21's max weight was about 19,000 pounds. With a pilot and Weapon Systems Operator, the F-4 could do air-to-air or ground attack. A load of radar and heat-seeking missiles (later "E" models also added an internal 20-millimeter Gatling gun) provided great air-to-air capabilities while the brute strength of the airframe and two J-79 engines allowed almost any load of bombs or other ordnance to be hung. By 1972, the F-4 was carrying the major burden of aerial warfare against North Vietnam and that was where I was headed.

Life at George AFB was enjoyable, even with the hot desert location. The base provided quarters for all the married students and there were nice apartments for the bachelors in Apple Valley as well as on the mountain slopes at Wrightwood. Victorville was almost half way between Los Angeles and Las Vegas, so the O'Club caught some great acts travelling each direction. From comedians to singers to strippers, the O'Club rocked several nights a week.

Claire, Chris and I were assigned a nice two-bedroom unit at 28 South Carolina Avenue. The house was solidly built from concrete blocks with a tile floor and was part of six single-story units that were connected at right angles to adjacent units. We enjoyed a small brick-walled patio on the back side and a community front yard with huge cottonwood trees. The housing possessed no air conditioning, but used, instead, a "swamp cooler" that blew humidified air into the quarters. With an average humidity down around ten percent, the moving moist air did an adequate job of cooling the house. Our next-door neighbor was an F-4 Instructor Pilot, Jimmy Cash, Fighting Texas Aggie, and a great neighbor whom I encountered fifteen years later, when he was Brigadier General Jimmy Cash.

Our F-4 class was composed of 30 pilots and navigators (soon to become Weapon System Operators) who would be 15 formed Phantom II crews. With one major and several captains in the class, most of my classmates were First Lieutenants straight from UPT or Navigator school. Our F-4 RTU was not cutthroat competition or stress of class standing as we experienced in UPT. With our F-4 and an end assignment, we could concentrate on being the best front seater or WSO.

A great surprise at RTU was meeting classmate 2LT Ronnie Casper during a game at the squadron pool table. In discussing my strange military past, I mentioned I was in the 101st Airborne Division in Vietnam. Ronnie asked what unit and I said with Charlie and Bravo companies of the 1st Battalion, 327th Infantry. He asked when I was in Bravo 1/327. I gave him the 1968 dates and he developed a funny look on his face. It turned out his older brother was a platoon leader in B-1/327 in Vietnam. The dates coincided and he suddenly said: "You are "the Old Man!" He produced a picture of his brother and, yes, I was "the Old Man" from Bravo Company and his brother was one of my platoon leaders during my Company Commander tour.

My first crewed student F-4 backseater was Kent Edie, a new 2LT out of Navigator school, up at Mather AFB, California. I assumed my Weapons System Operator (WSO) in the F-4 would be some math or engineer geek to handle all the computers and radar systems. Not so; Kent was a theatre major from Kent State University. I figured we were all trainable, but I better pay attention in the radar classes. I have kept in touch with Kent over the years and he retired as a colonel a few years after my retirement.

One of the social activities for the class was playing intramural sports on the 4452nd squadron team. Intramural football was fun and we were coached by one of our classmates, Ed Epping "Eppo", who was an All-American tackle at the Air Force Academy. Ed was huge, weighing in at over 250 pounds, with a weight waiver from the Air Force Surgeon General who said Eppo would be anemic at 235 pounds. How he fit in the narrow confines of the F-4 front seat was beyond me. I know that he must have turned sideways to close the canopy. His aircraft boarding weight exceeded the recommended maximum weight for our Martin-Baker ejection seats, meaning Ed could not eject from a stationary F-4 on the ramp and get a fully deployed parachute before ground impact. Ed needed a forward speed of 50 knots to get a good zero elevation ejection. Like most huge men, Ed was a gentle bear to his family and squadron mates and Ed's little daughter wrapped that giant around her little finger.

Academics, simulators and flying made the days fly by. Close Air Support of ground troops was my specialty because I knew how much it meant to the "Grunts" on the ground. I engaged in several heated discussions with instructors and our Army Ground Liaison Officer (GLO) as to the effectiveness of napalm and high-drag bombs in close infantry combat. (An argument that I was destined to repeat in my career.) Our GLO was a Vietnam vet, but as an Armor officer who rode in a tank during his tour and never duked it out with Charlie while lying as flat as you could get. On a night sortie, I was a bit over zealous in defending a simulated "Special Forces Camp" in a night attack scenario and went back for a gun attack when my bombs were expended. Night strafe was a "no-no" in training, and, after chewing my butt, the Operations officer warned the other IPs not to get Captain Stevenson wrapped up in any scenario that involved Special Forces. OK, so I was prejudiced and "got into" defending my SF folks!

I flew a day refueling mission, a four ship of students, led by IP Major Marv Purvis, and, upon entering the Tanker refueling track over the Grand Canyon, we saw a huge aircraft coming down the refueling radial. Purvis called for the tanker to start his 180 degree turn and the tanker replied it was turning. The aircraft in front of us did not move, and, closing at 1000 miles per hour, an airliner blew right through our 4-ship of F-4s. The airliner dropped down from its assigned altitude to let the passengers see the Grand Canyon and thus entered our refueling track airspace. I was close enough to see a blonde stewardess serving drinks. Marv changed frequencies and explained his displeasure to the controllers at Los Angeles Center. We finally located our "real" tanker farther east in the track and refueled. We never heard anything through Air Force Safety channels nor saw anything in the newspapers.

In mid-course, my orders for follow-on assignment to Da Nang were changed to Torrejon Air Base, Madrid, Spain, requirements changing as Linebacker II progressed and the needs of the Air War in North Vietnam changed. Other squadron pilots also received changed orders, with Ted Drake going to the 81st TFW in England and Dave "Dogfight" Bina going to the 525 TFS at Bitburg AB, an air-to-air dedicated unit.

A favorite tale was Dick Hoover engaged in a mock air-to-air fight high over Death Valley, who left his F-4 in afterburner on the downhill side of an engagement. His Phantom very rapidly went supersonic, and, with throttles finally at idle and Dick hauling back on the stick, his steed leveled out about 200 feet off the desert at Mach 1.3. That might have been less embarrassing if he didn't bottom out right next to the Stovepipe Wells Ranger station which absorbed the brunt of his supersonic shockwave. While Dick and I flew F-4s together at George

AFB, our wives became friends and the friendships continued at Torrejon AB, Spain. "Hoov" received an assignment delay at George after RTU for the birth of their second baby; he arrived in Spain about three months after my family.

SECRET U-2 BASE
On a sunny weekend, I sought out the nearest military flying club, which was located on the USAF Test Center at Edwards AFB, some 40 desert miles away. Visiting Edwards AFB, I wandered into Base Operations to get information about their weather services, flight support and other general information.

I often saw Air Force U-2 aircraft flying over the Mojave Desert and I casually asked the duty Master Sergeant at Base Operations if Edwards AFB housed many U-2 aircraft. The less-than-friendly Master Sergeant snapped back "Absolutely Not. The U-2 is a highly classified operational aircraft and there are none at Edwards." Jeez, a grouch!

Put in my place, I returned to looking at charts, midnight requisitioning local area maps and checking weather procedures and forecasts. After a few minutes, I again sought out the Aero Club. I approached the Operations desk to ask directions and this time a young two-stripe Airman was manning the desk. In my friendliest and most humble demeanor, I asked,

"Where is the Edwards Aero Club?"

"Sir, the Aero Club is down on South Base. It shares the hangar with the U-2s."

Sure enough, the Aero Club was a couple of rooms and half a dozen Cessnas and a T-34 parked in the west end of the main hangar on South Base. Only a long "Do Not Cross" tape separated the Aero Club from the U-2s that weren't there.

In June, I received word that I won the Daedalian Orville Wright Award as the outstanding pilot graduate for all the ATC bases for the 2Q 1972. The Order of Daedalians is a national fraternal and professional organization for current and previous military pilots. Somebody at ATC thought paratrooper, Green Beret, two combat tours and finishing second in my UPT class was a big deal. The award was made at a Daedalians formal dining out at the Norton AFB O'Club, "down the hill" in San Bernardino, California. On the appointed evening, Claire and I drove down to the Officers Club at Norton and linked up with our 35th TFW Deputy Commander, Colonel Chuck Beaver. Col Beaver flew fighters in WWII, Korea, and the F-4 in Southeast Asia. When I said, "I was with Special Forces in Vietnam and I worked with the 366th TFW "Gunfighters" from Da Nang, Col Beaver began to smile, then launched into a tale of his time as a new 2LT pilot with the "Gunfighters" in England in 1943-45. He and another new pilot had departed on an instrument and familiarization flight in two new P-47s, and, after a while ventured just off the east coast of England. They spotted a small German boat and decided to make a few strafe passes. The "small German boat" turned out to be a "gun boat" and shot both P-47s full of holes. How does a new Lieutenant explain bullet damage to two new P-47s while on an instrument sortie? Immediately, I knew I liked Col Beaver.

My "Thank You" speech was short, praising the F-4 training at George AFB and I sounded almost sober. Claire dazzled everyone present and won an invitation for us and my WSO, Kent Edie and wife, to visit the North American plant in LA where they were beginning the construction on the B-1 bomber. I knew I married a real winner in the way Claire charmed the Daedalians, young and old, Air Force or Navy. I signed up for a Life Membership in the Daedalians, and I already had a life-long marriage to the gem at my side.

Weekends provided opportunities to see many parts of California. We visited Wrightwood and Big Bear up in the mountains and Los Angeles, "down the hill" from our high desert. Claire's sister Suzy and her family lived in Palos Verdes in the L.A. area overlooking the Pacific and we visited there more than once. From Suzy's neighbor's house, you could look down on the Pacific and watch the whales migrate past L.A. The *Fifth Dimension* group played the Hollywood bowl for our entertainment and I made one Los Angeles Rams NFL game in the LA Coliseum. We ventured up to San Francisco to see Claire's cousin at Palo Alto and explored the desert around Victorville. Victorville sported one decent hotel, a Hilton Hotel along the Interstate, but neither Victorville nor Apple Valley moved into the 1970s with a McDonalds. Claire and I never made a trip to Las Vegas but our squadron bachelors took up the slack. Mondays normally brought tales of who did what, who won how much and who was the big loser in Las Vegas.

In August, the 434th TFS was called to deploy to Thailand for Linebacker II. One of the very popular F-4 IPs, RAF Flight Lieutenant Martin K. Widdowson, almost deployed with the squadron. Martin intentionally wore a flight suit with no markings and made it through two mobility processing sessions before somebody finally realized that he was an RAF pilot and not an American. It seemed the USAF did not want to deploy an exchange officer into combat: no sense of squadron unity or humor inside the Pentagon. To our class' advantage, Widdowson moved with the students to the 4452d squadron to continue as one of our IPs.

During our RTU stay at George AFB, Christopher picked up the nickname "Topher" and it stayed with him to the eighth grade. The NCO's family who often babysat Christopher, cared for another child named Christopher. The elder child got the first half of Christopher and our Christopher got the second half or "Topher." He responded well to the name and we thought it was original and cute. So, it stuck. It was almost two decades before we encountered another "Topher." From here on, "Christopher", "Chris" and "Topher" refer to the same person.

We graduated from F-4 RTU on November 13th, and then most of my class was headed for Land Survival School at Fairchild AFB, Washington. The Air Force loaded us on an "antique" T-29 Convair aircraft that George AFB kept for utility flying, and we launched for Fairchild AFB. We were still an F-4 squadron in every way but name and the first "almost squadron" RTU class to enter Survival School as a unit. The instructors soon learned that, if you picked on one blue polka dot scarf, you took on 28 students. Some of the newest UPT graduates, not in fighters, thinking they could give grief to a "navigator", soon found themselves confronted by one or more F-4 pilots (with blue polka dot scarves) who pointed out these were not navigators but F-4 Weapon Systems Operators who knew a hell of a lot more about tactical flying than did any newbie Air Training Command pilot. Within four class days the rules were well understood by those that were not wearing the 4452nd colors.

The school itself was not particularly difficult for me. The Air Force's SERE was a repeat of the Army Ranger committee POW course, but the AF did not physically hurt me. Our class survival trek into the national forest was COLD: -5 degrees F with snow. That could have been tough, but was not too bad if you were properly dressed. But how cold was that? I never trained in weather cold enough to freeze water in a plastic water bag that was *inside* my field jacket.

The first night of the survival trek, I was assigned a 19-year-old female airman as a tent mate because I was an "old captain" and would take care of her. OK! Somebody needed to take care of her. On day three, the instructors paired me with an absolute dud of an airman who would have died in the woods by himself. Despite his ability to get us lost when I let him navigate, we finally straggled into the destination camp just after sunset, the last team in. After graduation, but still chilled, we headed back to warm George AFB.

At George, we loaded up the Toyota station wagon and started the drive across IH-10 to Texas. We caught an ice storm on IH-10 and spent an extra night in Abilene. With dry highway conditions, we moved on and stayed with Don and family in Arlington, Texas. Then it was down to Corpus for Christmas with the Rhodes family who spoiled Chris rotten (a sworn duty of Grandparents). Right after Christmas, we once again saddled up the Toyota wagon and started the drive to Charleston AFB for our charter flight to Torrejon AB, Spain.

We drove to Charleston, turned in the Toyota at the port for boat shipment to Spain and caught the contract DC-8 for Torrejon. The plane took off and flew to McGuire AFB, NJ (Geeeeez!) and we sat on the ground for almost three hours as they serviced the plane and manifested the passengers from McGuire.

Finally, our charter took off to complete a 15-hour trip, and, by the time we reached Spain the plane was packed with a lot of cranky children and family members. At 0800 local time, in the dark, we landed at Torrejon AB Spain and entered the world of USAFE, F-4 operational flying and the 613th Tactical Fighter Squadron, nicknamed the "Squids" because of the figure on their squadron patch.

THE PHANTOM

20

Torrejon AB, Spain

The 613th Tactical Fighter Squadron was my introduction to the "real" Air Force that I'd heard so much about from IPs. After the long charter airline flight from Charleston, South Carolina, to Maguire AFB, New Jersey, and then across the Atlantic, I arrived with wife and 18-month-old son on New Year's Eve 1972. One of the squadron Flight Commanders, Jim Huntsman, and several other squadron members met us at the passenger terminal / base operations when we arrived at Torrejon Airbase (TJ), less than four miles east of Madrid's Barajas International Airport. ILT Stu Kaufman and his lovely wife Denise were our assigned sponsors, but sponsorship for the arrival of a new pilot in a fighter squadron was always a team event involving the sponsor's flight or the entire squadron. We wound up spending several weeks in the Temporary Living Facilities, a room in a separate wing of the three-story base billeting facility next to the Officers Club. My early days at TJ were divided between (1) checking in with 613th and my assigned flight, facilitating my USAFE F-4 checkout and (2) house hunting.

We located a house to rent in Eurovillas, a housing development south of the base, where two other squadron pilots were living. The three-bedroom house was designed to be a summer weekend residence for Madrileños with minimum heating and stone floors. The marble floors echoed noises throughout the house, and, when a giant lizard took up residence in the house, Claire could hear the "monster" scurrying across the floor for days until encouraged with a broom to leave.

The commute from the airbase was along a narrow two-lane country road that passed through the small village of Pozuelo del Rey. With fighter pilot work hours, the few Squids that lived in Eurovillas often flew through Pozuelo del Rey at very early or late hours. Despite our high-speed transits, we always saw an armed, green-cloaked member of the Guardia Civil, with tri-corner patent leather hat, leaning against the wall at the town's intersection watching all that passed through his domain. The Guardia was scary, and, the more we learned, the scarier they became. They were the feet on the ground for a totalitarian state under Generalissimo Franco.

Shortly after moving into Eurovillas, I took a C-130 "hop" to the US Naval Station Rota, near Cadiz, Spain, to pick up our Toyota station wagon, shipped from Charleston. No sooner did I check into the BOQ at Naval Air Station Rota than the Command Post at TJ called and informed me that Christopher was in the hospital at Torrejon, diagnosed with spinal meningitis and in critical condition. "Topher" was running a low-grade fever for several days but we did not think anything of it since he was recovering from strep throat. But this day his temperature spiked to 104 degrees, his eyes crossed and he jerked his head backward. Claire was in a new house, in a foreign country, with no weekday neighbors, with no phone or car. Our nearest American neighbors were a half mile up the road, a squadron mate, Captain "Fil" Filburn and his wife Shirleen. Claire jumped on her new bike and rode up the hill, leaving Topher in his crib, to ask Shirleen for a ride to the base. Luckily Shirleen was home and they rushed back to the toddler. Shirleen was a nurse and when she saw Topher's condition, she scooped him up and said he needed to be in the Emergency Room *now*. She and Claire drove at some ungodly speed and delivered Topher to the Torrejon Hospital Emergency Room.

I picked up the Toyota as soon as the office opened the next morning and set a land speed record driving from Cadiz to Madrid. There are small towns in southern Spain still searching for a red Toyota that blew through their village. My brother-in-law, Dr. Pete Henney, a prestigious thoracic surgeon, was contacted and offered to put together a team of doctors and fly to Madrid. After Pete talked to the USAF Torrejon Hospital staff, he said he was convinced the doctors at TJ were as good as any group of doctors he could muster. All we could do was wait out the treatment. Fighter pilots are control freaks by nature and I felt totally helpless as somebody else treated my son and I could do nothing. Our primary concern was Christopher could die. It does not come a lot simpler than that. After a spinal tap and lots of antibiotics began working, his fever broke and he was no longer curled backward in pain. Then the question was, "Will there be any permanent neurological damage?" Claire prayed consistently that if God let Christopher live, we could handle anything after that. All our prayers were answered. After a month-long hospital stay, Chris made a full recovery, and, within a year, he was as rough and tumble as any two-year-old boy.

The irony with Topher's illness was the loss of the Filburn's baby to SIDS some three years later. Shirleen saved the life of our child, only to lose her own baby to SIDS.

We now owned wheels in the '71 Toyota Corolla Station wagon, bought in Columbus, Mississippi; and being a "rich American," I soon went into Madrid and purchased a second car, a new tiny SEAT 127 hatchback for a roaring $1400. With an inline four-cylinder engine of 1200 ccs, it got great mileage on my runs to and from Torrejon AB. The white hatchback proved handy when playing tourist, and soon sported a 613TFS decal on the rear window. In those days, all US military registered automobiles displayed Spanish license plates with a wide, bold red stripe running vertically on the left edge. The Spaniards could spot a US car from a half mile away, something of concern to the Americans. It was 15 years before terrorism encouraged the US forces in all European countries to adopt inconspicuous vehicle plates. The SEAT would blend in better with the Spaniards. SEAT was a license of FIAT automobiles of Italy, but assembled in Spain and fitted out a bit sparser than the FIAT equivalent model. Anyhow, the little white SEAT carried us on a second honeymoon along the east coast of Spain, to the mountains for skiing, to Zaragoza for a fun TDY, and trips to Toledo or downtown Madrid for bullfights or football (soccer) with the Real Madrid team.

In January 1973, as a newly assigned officer, I met the 401st Wing Commander (CC), Colonel Dick Collins, in his office with ten other new guys, some F-4 jocks and some support officers. The Vice Commander (CV or just "Vice") sat at desk down the long office and after we all told the CC who we were and where we were last stationed or trained, the Vice was introduced as Colonel Charles Donnelly. Chuck Donnelly was one of the great gentlemen of the Air Force and later became the four-star USAFE Commander. The next evening, Claire, Christopher and I were having dinner at the O Club in civvies when Col Donnelly, also in civvies, approached with his wife and introduced her:

"Carolyn, this is Captain Stevenson, who just joined the wing and I forgot which squadron you are assigned to."

"The 613th, sir." I didn't know who this distinguished man was but I was saved by Carolyn when she took Claire's hand and said,

"I'm Carolyn Donnelly, welcome to Torrejon."

Suddenly I remembered who he was and I blurted out to Claire, "Colonel Donnelly is the Wing Vice-Commander. Sir, this is my wife Claire and our son, Christopher."

He smiled, shook Claire's hand and welcomed us to TJ. I was to learn later that Chuck Donnelly was one of those exceptional folks that never forgot a face or the name that went with it. Carolyn was the Lady to compliment Chuck Donnelly and I enjoyed watching his promotions and career movement over the next fifteen years.

Colonel Vernon H. Sandrock was the 401TFW/DO and later Vice Commander between August '73 and August '75. In early 1975, WSO Bill Stroud and I were starting engines when we heard Colonel Sandrock berating his Crew Chief on his F-4's intercom for some mistake. Instead of staying on the intercom, the profanity laced tirade was transmitted over the Ground Control radio frequency for the whole flight line to hear. As the story got around the base, Sandrock quickly lost the respect of all the line jocks and maintenance folks. That raised the interesting question of whether the radio transmission was an electrical glitch in the intercom/radio system, or did Sandrock inadvertently hold down the radio button instead of the intercom button, or did Colonel Sandrock's WSO hold down the radio button so Sandrock's tirade went out to the world? We will never know. Sandrock transferred to Korea in August 1975 and was not greatly missed.

After the hassle of finding a home, finally moving in, (our household goods from George AFB were placed in storage at Barstow, CA, instead of being shipped to TJ), completing my local check out in the F-4 and all the USAFE procedures, life settled into a repetitive three-month cycle for the next 3 ½ years.

The three F-4 squadrons at TJ rotated 30-day deployments to Incirlik AB, Turkey to maintain an American military presence and to sit nuclear alert, hoping we would never launch. Incirlik is near Adana, Turkey, on the Mediterranean coast, next to the Syrian border, 2000 miles "down range" from Madrid. The rotation cycle meant my squadron deployed to Incirlik for one out of every three months. With common added flight weather delays, maintenance problems, hand-over procedures, and C-130 flights home, the F-4 jocks wound up with a schedule averaging 58 days home and then 32 days gone. While the squadron was "home" on those 58-day cycles, we often deployed to Aviano, Italy, for a week to sit nuclear alert there, or participated in some NATO exercise in the Mediterranean - all taking more time away from home and family. The wives bonded and were forced to become very independent because the men of the squadron were gone so often. My first year at TJ (1973), I was gone for 218 days.

February 1973, brought Valentine's Day and I was on the midday flying schedule. I was leaving the squadron as a drama unfolded over the Atlantic involving factory new F-4Es bound for the 401st TFW at Torrejon. The squadron duty desk was monitoring the radios when one of the new F-4s developed a trapped fuel problem. When the fuel could not properly feed to the J-79 engines, the F-4 would not reach its KC-135 tanker. The F-4 crew, with pilot Major Marv Purvis, was facing the real possibility of ejecting into the wintery Atlantic waters. Major Purvis was an instructor at George AFB where many of us trained and he flew two combat tours in the F-4. He was known and well-liked by just about everyone in the F-4 community; the idea of Marv jumping into the Atlantic Ocean hundreds of miles from land concerned all.

The KC-135 aircraft commander left his authorized refueling track west of Portugal and flew to a rendezvous with Major Purvis' flight some 150 miles farther out to sea. When Major Purvis connected to the tanker's refueling boom, the F-4's fuel gauge showed about two minutes of fuel remaining. Refueled in unauthorized airspace, Purvis' flight continued to TJ where they were met on the ramp by over 50 F-4 jocks and transported directly to the O'Club. After several rounds of drinks to celebrate Major Purvis' survival, the KC-135 crew showed up at the bar and they were rewarded with innumerable drinks offered up by the F-4 crowd.

About 10:30 pm and well intoxicated, I set out for our house in Eurovillas. I staggered into our house four hours later than I told Claire I would arrive. Claire had cooked an exquisite Valentine's Day meal, complete with fine wine, and all was now cold. Additionally, since we did not have a home phone to inform her of my partying at the O'Club, she imagined that I'd crashed on my flight that day and she was yet to be informed of her loss. She was mentally preparing to get the house packed up and trying to decide where and how she and Christopher were going to live. My inebriated arrival was not well received, to say the least, and Claire has never again prepared a Valentine's Day dinner for me. We may go out to a fine restaurant, but there has not been another home-cooked celebration of Valentine's Day.

Our housing situation improved after six months when we were offered Air Force base housing in a community named "Royal Oaks." This was a large community of US military housing along the Burgos highway north of Madrid. While not much closer to Torrejon AB than Eurovillas, Royal Oaks brought many Air Force families together in an "American" community, with more amenities. That sense of community and convenience was crucial when the aircrews and maintenance personnel were gone so much. We gladly packed up our house and moved from Eurovillas to Royal Oaks.

This assignment was going to be my introduction to various Air Force leadership styles through Squadron Commanders, Wing staff, and other squadron leaders. It soon became obvious that, much like my experience with NCOs returning from combat to Ft Campbell in the 101st, there were certain individuals that were great combat pilots but faced a challenge making the mental shift to worrying about the day-to-day reality of MEIs, ORIs and Stan Eval check rides. There were several F-4 jocks in the Squids with whom I would gladly go to war as their wingman, but I was not sure if they could develop programs and perform as well in our Squadron training or scheduling environment.

When I signed in, the 613 TFS "Squids" were commanded by Lt Col Harvey Kimsey, who loved to put on formation airshows with our F-4Es. Kimsey's goal in life was to lead the USAF Thunderbirds. With Kimsey's mindset, flight leaders in the squadron included a few moments of "wring- 'em-out" formation work as part of each mission. I considered myself a little better than most new guys at tough formation flying, but on numerous sorties I landed soaked in sweat. Most F-4 jocks in the 613th believed that you must be a good wingman before you could be a good flight lead. My first view of Incirlik Airbase in Turkey was inverted in the F-4E, looking over the top of my canopy bow, while at the top of a barrel roll as #2 in close trail formation during an "arrival airshow."

Our next commander was Michael P. C. Carns. That was an exceptional experience.

21

Incirlik, Turkey

Torrejon Air Base, Spain, may have been our squadron's home but we saw as much of beautiful Incirlik, Turkey as we did Madrid, Spain. Incirlik Air Base, Turkey is a NATO airfield at the eastern end of the Mediterranean Sea, some 10 miles from the town of Adana, Turkey, and only five minutes flying time from Syria. We called it Incirlik Air Base (or "Inky-Dink" or "the Lick") but the Turkish military designated it as Incirlik Common Defense Installation (CDI) probably because of the US presence on the airfield. Incirlik (whatever) had its origin back in the Cold War when spy flights, including Gary F. Powers and his U-2, flew from the runway over parts of Mother Russia.

As part of NATO, Turkey allowed the US to use the base as a training and deployment base, *but* no aircraft could be "permanently" stationed there. USAF rotations were limited to no more than 18 tactical aircraft in Turkish airspace at one time. That suited us fine since the 613 TFS was an 18-aircraft fighter squadron. The 401st Wing diligently complied with the maximum fighter rule to the extent that squadron exchanges required the departing fighters to leave Turkish airspace before the replacements entered. This became a bit complicated when an outbound F-4 developed a maintenance problem and aborted the re-deployment with replacement aircraft already enroute. It also required sending three or four F-4 crews, but no actual fighter aircraft, by transport aircraft (C-130) to create a personnel overlap, as the squadrons swapped nuclear alert crews.

Rotations to Incirlik could be fun or a pain in the ass, depending on your transportation. If you were one of the lucky jocks who flew an F-4 to Turkey it was a six to eight-hour trip. If you traveled by C-130, it was a ten-hour episode of vibrations and noise. Sometimes, the F-4 flyers got a KC-135 tanker for refueling over the Mediterranean. That was always fun as the first F-4 four ship would launch from TJ moments after the tanker took off, catch up with the tanker about the time it coasted out near Valencia and fly on the wings of the tanker until they refueled southeast of Sicily. After we were aerial refueled, we climbed to an altitude above 30,000 feet for the remainder of the trip. The Turkish Air Force and air traffic control did not have radar coverage over the south coast of Turkey or the Med. So, once we radioed in to the Turkish controllers, we set a course direct to Incirlik and reported whatever navigation points they requested, usually when passing abeam the point on our direct route to Incirlik. While this route was contrary to the existing international flight procedures, it reduced flying time, distance and fuel consumption for the trip.

When tankers were unavailable, the flights flew two or three hops to reach Turkish airspace. NAS Sigonella, Italy and Aviano Air Base were good staging locations depending on the weather and winds aloft. If we flew out of Aviano for the leg to Incirlik, we flew southeast along the airspace boundary of Albania, and, at that time Albania was a renegade country even by Russian standards. They tracked our flights on their Surface to Air Missile (SAM) radars, which we could detect on the F-4 Radar Warning Receiver (RWR) system, making us nervous. We always wondered if they were crazy enough to launch SAM missiles at our flights and claim we penetrated their airspace. I directed my TJ crew chief to pull the safety pin on my F-4E's gun when we were planning to fly by Albania. That way, if things went bad, I could arm my 20mm cannon. Most of the guys did the same.

A rotation to Incirlik was great, with extreme boredom when not flying. We usually flew air-to-air for a full week and then flew gunnery

missions to the air-to-ground weapons range near Konya, Turkey. The air-to-air sorties were necessarily short, logging about 0.7 hour per sortie. The weather at Incirlik was better than Phoenix, Arizona, and, in the summer, the daytime temperatures became extremely hot by midday, so the schedule began with dawn takeoffs.

When not on nuke, or "Victor," alert, we enjoyed the best flying of any USAFE unit. There was no restricted airspace over Turkey within our flying range and the weather was fantastic. We shared a weapons range with the Turkish Air Force at Konya, use of our own restricted airspace 20 miles away on the coastline for air-to-air training and low-level routes through the mountains, across the desert, across the Konya plains, or along the Mediterranean coast. For our tactical intelligence entertainment, we were just moments from the Syrian border and the Syrian conflict with the Israelis. We occasionally intercepted Russian transport aircraft overflying Turkey and passing about 100 miles to the west of Incirlik, enroute to God only knows where in Africa.

Major Montgomery Tuck, kindly known as "Monty" or "Mach Tuck," was one of my first Operations Officers in the 613th. During one of our exercises, I was part of a four-ship that was launching to the range. When I shoved up the power to taxi my F-4 onto the runway and turn left to line up for takeoff, my aircraft's nose wheel steering failed completely, and, with a bit of differential braking, I crossed the runway, into the arming area on the east side. Thank goodness, for arming areas and taxiways on both sides of the runway. I got my 54,000 pound unsteerable sled stopped as Monty roared up in his truck, jumped out, and plugged his headset into my ground communication connection.

"Steve, what are you doing?"

"I lost all nose wheel steering"

Then Monty came up with the exercise quote of the day:

"You don't need nose gear steering. You were going to put your landing gear up in a moment anyway."

"Yeah! OK, Monty, I'll let you take this one!" Sometimes it was hard to tell when Monty was serious.

NUKE ALERT
As a deterrent in the Cold War, USAFE maintained four fighters on nuclear fifteen-minute alert at Incirlik. This was the final and personal step in planning and preparing for an event that you prayed would never occur: a nuclear exchange with Russia. The four "alert" F-4s stayed in a fenced, guarded, sensored facility at the northeast end of Runway 05, where the aircrews and crew chiefs lived in quarters within the "cage" and were within 50 yards, easy sprinting distance, of their assigned aircraft. The cage was the crews' quarters during alert tours with the only outside excursions for meals on base or an occasional squadron meeting. Each F-4 was armed with one B-61 nuke ("Silver Bullet") and the explosive yield was set (10 – 300Kt) according to a specific target assigned to that crew in the Soviet Union, although many of our targets were in Georgia or Ukraine. The ability to change nuclear yields was

189

referred to by the crews as "dial-a-bomb." Each aircraft was placed in its own shelter, initially just metal sheds, though, later, new shelters were constructed of concrete and steel in arches called "Tab Vs." For additional security, each of the four nuke alert shelters was guarded by a Security Policeman and the restricted area inside the shelter was delineated by a painted red line at the shelter entrance. The area across the red line was a "no lone zone," meaning a single person could not enter the area and the two authorized persons that entered must maintain visual contact with each other. Security, Security, Security!

Before an F-4 crew could accept the aircraft and the loaded nuclear weapon from the off-going alert crew, the new crew was required to pass written and verbal exams on the target they were being assigned. The two-man crew also briefed in-depth details of alert procedures, launch authentication, route to the target, bomb settings and draw from memory the visual and radar cues guiding them to the target. After passing these exams, the crew did an inspection of their F-4, ensuring the aircraft and the B-61 nuclear weapon was ready to go, if launched. Then the F-4 crew signed for the shelter from the Security troops and the previous alert crew was released from the cage. Since no alcohol consumption was allowed while on nuke alert, the off-going crew usually sent their regards, once outside the barb wire and gate, by firing a champagne cork back into the alert area. I often wondered why we trusted this bunch with nuclear weapons and the defense of the free world. But they were "dead serious" to get the job done if the need arose.

As flight commander, I normally sat nuke alert with my flight members, mostly with Rich "Hands" Bohman as my backseater or later with George Watson. My first few certifications were with Rich and he was a great aid to a new nuke alert front seater. Over the next three and a half years, the certification process became easier as there were only five or six targets to master in the southern Soviet Union for the four crews on alert. So, after certifying once and listening to my flight members certify on the other lines, I had a lot of information stored in my head.

Once we were "up" on alert, it was a lot of boredom punctuated by a few exercises of which we usually received advance warnings. The exercises could be called by the Incirlik command post, the European command center or the US National Military Command Center (NMCC) in Washington DC. An unspoken rule (maybe it was written but we never asked) for nuclear safety and security held that exercise alerts were done only during daylight hours. Any alert started with a claxon sounding in the "cage" and a tone and message being broadcast over all the alert radios. That led to a sprint to the aircraft if we were in the cage. If we were out of the cage and on base somewhere for a meal, it was a mad scramble for our crew truck and drive like maniacs to get back to our aircraft. Alert crews were known to vault over lunch tables at the Officers Club or drive across the active runway to make their response time on nuke alert. Everything on Incirlik, except life safety, took second place during a nuclear alert.

Captain Dick Hoover set an Incirlik record of being caught three times in the shower when the claxon went off. Three of the aircraft were already manned when Dick came plopping past my alert barn headed for his aircraft in his underpants with flight suit in hand and boots flopping wildly. Once he met his backseater, Jerry Straw, they entered the no-lone zone and Dick jumped into his flight suit and boots at the bottom of the F-4 boarding steps while Jerry flipped the power switches and started his checklists. In 30 seconds, soggy Dick was in the front cockpit, on the phone and radio, ready to copy the encoded "release" message. After the second alert episode caught Dick in the shower, we told Dick, "If you're going to shower, the rest of us will start walking toward our aircraft shelters."

Daylight rule notwithstanding, one evening about 9:30 pm, we were watching a movie in the crew area when the claxon went off. We looked at each other and then bolted for our aircraft. What the hell was this? My heart was in my throat and going a hundred miles an hour. This couldn't be the real thing! By the time I strapped in and put my helmet on to listen for the release message, I was sweating. Not only that, my hands were shaking as I opened our authentication packet and started on the alphabet jumble that was coming over our headsets. George Watson and I both copied the letters and then I decoded them. I mumbled "Sunuvabitch!" and handed the decoder over my right shoulder to George in the back seat. George decoded the letters and replied, "I will kill that bastard." For seven minutes, we believed that we were launching to drop nukes on Russia, and Incirlik would probably be a smoking, glowing hole when we returned - if we returned.

It was a practice alert from the NMCC in Washington. Either some dumb SOB forgot what time it was in the Middle East or he activated a worldwide alert rather than a North America only alert. George confirmed my decoding. We acknowledged to the Incirlik Command Post and we dismounted our steed, cold, sweaty, pissed and scared to death. The Sky Cop guarding our shelter knew what almost happened and he also looked like he had seen a ghost, probably his own.

O'CLUB

The officer quarters at Incirlik were four long, parallel concrete buildings behind the O'Club. Each building was two stories with balconies and suite entrances on the north side. The rotational squadron jocks occupied a BOQ building which was divided into eight suites on two floors with three bedrooms and a bathroom for each suite. The end suite on the ground floor surrendered one bedroom to serve as the squadron bar, "The Auger Inn." Between our building and the building for permanent party officers in front of us, we found a huge BBQ grill and large grassy area which served as our sun-bathing and party area.

The center of our squadron social life every evening, after flying was put to bed, was the Incirlik Officers Club bar. Like any world class bar, the bartender can make or break the bar's business. A great Turkish national named "Mike" was the senior bartender and was a bartender there at least since U-2s flew from the base in the early 1960s. Mike knew the standard drink for any of the officers that were regulars and could even call up your drink when you returned from 58 days back at Torrejon. I can't imagine all the great Air Force officers that Mike served and knew. Other than drinking, singing along with John Denver songs was always popular. You should hear 30 drunk and semi-drunk F-4 jocks belting out *"Take Me Home, Country Roads."*

In a quiet moment at the bar, I reminisced, hardly believing that it was only four years ago when I sat at the Da Nang Special Forces O'Club and sang along with The Animals' hit song *"We Gotta Get Out Of This Place, if it's the last thing we ever do.* **Four years – could it be just four years? Four years is a long time; but this four years was just the blink of an eye.**

That one song symbolized the attitude of the GIs in Vietnam. Every band had to play it or get booed, and it was a regular request on Armed Forces Vietnam Network (AFVN) radio. No matter how badly a band played the song, every GI within hearing range joined in belting out the chorus. Both songs remain key to my memories of the various times and places when I joined in the brotherhood chorus.

One evening, a permanent party Air Force nurse left her club card on the bar when she departed, so the squadron charged a whole evening of drinks on the nurse's card. We thought it was funny; she didn't, even though we repaid her the next day. The O'Club breakfast was varied and usually good, but the only decent lunch item was the French Dip sandwich, and dinner varied greatly in quality. There was always Mike and the bar, the best thing about the O'Club.

Most of the F-4 jocks developed relationships with the Air Force nurses from the Incirlik AF Clinic. Some of the relationships were serious (for a TDY troop) and some were just good friends. After a couple of rotations, I became close friends with a First Lieutenant Sandy Barnes, great nurse and a Beach Boys music fan. She owned every song they recorded. In the summer of 1975, the building housing the nurses lost air conditioning, and, due to the age of AC parts or transportation problems, the AC would be out for at least a week. Incirlik is sweltering in the summer, and, after day one without cool air, Sandy approached me in the O'Club on Sunday evening with a proposition. No "Hello", just:

"Steve, can I sleep in your BOQ room?"

"Uh, OK." I was trying not to say anything stupid, but I was blushing.

"It's just until our AC is back running. We work different shifts: I work late nights, getting off work after you have gone to fly. We will not impose on each other's sleep hours."

"Uh, OK."

The arrangement worked out well after the first day when we needed to explain it to the Turkish maid who found a woman asleep in my bed. I was the winner in this arrangement, for, while Sandy enjoyed air-conditioned sleep hours, my bed smelled wonderful for those four or five days.

In September 1973, as part of a USAFE aircraft swap called Creek Realign, the 401st traded our new F-4Es for old (some ten years old and Vietnam veterans) F-4Cs from the 81st TFW at RAF Bentwaters and Woodbridge (BTW). A triple move sent our F-4Es to Bitburg AB Germany, their F-4Ds to Bentwaters and the F-4Cs from BTW to TJ. The Cs were junky compared to the latest block 556 mod F-4Es. The C did have one advantage: it could out accelerate the Ds and Es. On September 12, 1973, I flew my last F-4E sorties on the wing of the 613th Weapons Officer, Jerry Wallace, as we took two F-4Es to Ankara, Turkey to show the F-4s to the Turkish AF. I was crewed with Rich Bowman for several months and we flew those last two sorties together, doing self-set up intercepts against Jerry on the missions up and back to get some training squares checked off during the flights. The Turks were looking to upgrade their Air Force, considering the F-4E, and, ultimately, they did buy F-4Es. The 613th jocks then watched with little enthusiasm as other Torrejon crews flew in the F-4Cs and took out our "new" F-4Es. We stood down for three days of ground school on the F-4Cs systems and then began flying again. For the next three years, as TJ crews passed through Bitburg AB, we recognized a familiar tail number F-4E which we flew. That Incirlik rotation ended on a dramatic note on October 6, 1973 when Egypt and Syria, and, eventually, six more Arab nations, launched what became known as the "Yom Kippur War" against Israel.

YOM KIPPUR WAR

On October 6th, unaware of the war starting just down the Mediterranean coast, the 613th scheduled a full combat load exercise of conventional weapons on our "new" F-4Cs. Overnight, the munitions and maintenance folks labored long and hard as all the Squid F-4s were configured with six 500-pound bombs, AIM-7, AIM-9 missiles, and made ready to be inspected, accepted and taxied but not flown. If the US Intelligence agencies knew what was beginning down the coast in Israel, the information was classified too highly to tell the US fighter squadron located 12 minutes from the fighting. The local agents of various foreign intelligence organizations knew something was going on at Incirlik because it appeared that all our aircraft were being prepared for at least one mass mission launch, instead of spreading sorties across the entire day. My WSO, Rich Bohman, and I did the preflight inspection of our F-4 and examined the six Mark 82 High Drag 500-pound bombs, four AIM-7 Sparrow and four AIM-9 Sidewinder missiles hung underneath our F-4. Later in our tours, we developed such team trust that I inspected the aircraft and Rich did the ordnance.

The shelters for our fighters were located on the southwest end of runway 05, so, with the usual brisk onshore wind, all the 613th fighters taxied two miles to the arming area for takeoff on runway 23. The movement of all 613th 54,000-pound aircraft was appropriately referred to as an "Elephant Walk." This gave the foreign intelligence base watchers an opportunity to see our parade of F-4s loaded with ground attack ordnance. While we knew that our flight operations were watched by observers reporting to Middle Eastern countries and possibly the Soviet Union, we underestimated the speed of their communication. In January 1974, we received an excellent classified briefing from the US Navy Intelligence in the Mediterranean reporting that the Russian Intelligence sources went ape for a few hours over our exercise, which they thought was real war preparation. This was an entire US fighter squadron loaded for war, taxiing for takeoff not 20 minutes from the Arab – Israeli combat arena. Evidently that was cause for great concern in several neighborhoods, but not within our squadron as we carried on in ignorance of the latest world affairs. A little transfer of knowledge from the Intel geeks would have been nice.

As the Yom Kippur War continued, the 613th was ordered by USAFE to re-deploy to Torrejon. Normally a simple unit movement, that re-deployment proved difficult as USAFE lost their scheduled KC-135 tanker support to Israeli aircraft deliveries. The USAF delivered fighters "purchased by the Israelis", but which were pulled from USAF F-4E units. Squids flying F-4s were forced to island hop home across the Med while support personnel and aircrews (including me) hitch-hiked on C-130s headed west as best we could. At one point, after three days of travel, there were 613th personnel and aircraft at seven locations in the Med and northern Europe.

In the first week of October, the 613th Squadron command passed to Lieutenant Colonel Michael P. C. Carns (informally known to the Squids as MPC²). As scheduled, the 613TFS change of command ceremony took place at Torrejon, but Lt Col Carns' crews were spread across the Mediterranean for days as tankers cancelled, airlift was stolen (re-prioritized) and airspace was blocked. Before departing on a C-130, scheduled to hop to NAS Sigonella and then home to TJ, I called MPC² from Incirlik:

"Hi, sir. Welcome to the 613th. I'm Steve Stevenson, one of your flight commanders and I will see you whenever I can get there."

I departed LTAG on 9 October 1973 for an uneventful ride home, arriving after all but one flight of our F-4s, but well before a group of 613th personnel who were stranded in Naples, Italy and then again in Rota, Spain. They finally made it home to Madrid by train from Rota.

22

Back "Home" Again

My next F-4 flight was from TJ on October 17th, with Gary Aston as my WSO on an AGG sortie to Bardenas Reales Range. Gary and I flew together for some time as my crewed backseater Rich Bohman began to fly more often with the new lieutenants coming into the squadron. I would miss Rich as my WSO, although we flew together occasionally. He was my first "hard crewed" WSO and a great guy. Nancy Bohman and Claire stayed very good friends even after Rich and I were separated and re-crewed. Forty years later, we still stay in touch.

Bardenas Reales Gunnery Range was the primary fighter air-to-ground gunnery range for TJ's 401st Wing aircraft and the 406th Training Wing at Zaragoza AB, Spain. The 406th, with no permanently assigned fighter units, hosted the USAFE squadrons to the USAFE Tactics School. The range was located NW of Zaragoza, Spain, in the Ebro River valley. Oriented northwest to southeast paralleling the river, the F-4 run-in line was straight into the sun for early range times. Radar bombs were a good first event in the early morning because I could barely find the range, much less the targets for a low-level bomb drop. Bardenas was memorable because of the predictable (spell that high velocity) winds that blew along the Ebro River. We fought a headwind in summertime and a very strong tail wind in winter. Sometimes the tail wind was so strong that the bomb release point for high angle dive bomb was off the range property. We hoped the wind blew the bomb as planned.

Ranges were the most common location for fighter accidents. I was airborne and headed for the range when a Torrejon F-4 crashed on a low angle bomb pass on Bardenas. Later, that crash was determined to be caused by a briefed low angle bomb pass of 15 degrees vs 10 degrees. Lead briefed the steeper dive angle but did not alter the release altitude. On the first 15-degree pass, leader's F-4 entered a position "from which recovery was impossible." The pilot's ejection seat never fired and he was killed on impact. The WSO recalled that upon an almost wings-level impact with the ground, he saw his instrument panel split in half just as his ejection seat fired. The WSO suffered bruises, cuts, broken right collar bone, shoulder and right arm. He was presented with his ejection seat, and, during his recovery days, he used to sit in the ejection seat as a recliner on the front porch of his family quarters in Royal Oaks. In a touch of black humor, it was alleged that number 3's backseater, after observing his flight lead crash, asked: "I assume that we have to go through dry and not drop?"

Within months, another Torrejon F-4 almost crashed on Bardenas when the FNG pilot, flying on downwind, put his head in the cockpit to check weapons settings, parameters or change switches. The F-4 started into a serious descent from 500 feet and impact seemed certain. The WSO decided to leave and successfully ejected. The FNG pilot tried to recover from the dive, going to full afterburner and pulling past optimum angle of attack. Miraculously, the F-4 bounced off the ground on its two wing tanks and recovered at ZAB, minus the WSO, rear canopy and rear ejection seat. Other than scrapes and bruises, the WSO was recovered in good condition. The pilot was grounded pending remedial training and the WSO was complimented on good judgment.

In 1975, USAF issued a ban on WSO flying below 5000 feet after an F-4 from Zaragoza was lost when a WSO was doing an aileron roll, lost control of the aircraft and the crew ejected. We violated that "be-no" often coming off the range when our WSOs took control of the aircraft as soon as we were rejoined and they flew, often doing close formation aerobatics for the return to TJ. Many of our seasoned WSOs with Southeast Asia experience possessed "good hands" and flew well in close formation. Those same "good hands" helped a few new lieutenant front seaters on their early air refueling sorties.

USAFE TACTICS SCHOOL

I twice attended the USAFE Tactics School at Zaragoza AB (ZAB), just up the road (150 miles) from Madrid. The school was a week of the latest tactics and lessons learned. The normal schedule was a half day of academics and then one or two sorties in the afternoon. The head shed at Torrejon decided that it was not cost effective to send four F-4s to ZAB, so our four crews did not fly during the course as did the crews from the US bases on "the continent." Instead, we attended academics each morning and then adjourned to our five-star hotel in Zaragoza for pool time followed by an evening of tasca hopping and great restaurants. Unlike the guys from the northern bases, the TJ folks drove to ZAB, so we had wheels. It was a fantastic paid vacation! The Squids attending Tactics School brought their wives and every evening was a miniature squadron party. We believed, when a good deal comes along, grab it because there may not be another. Our hotel in Zaragoza was the five-star Corona de Aragon with beautiful rooms, a pool, three tantalizing restaurants and a Maitre'de who spoke at least five languages (we heard him as we waited for our table). Unfortunately, a major fire in 1979 destroyed the hotel and killed 80 people.

I did have one issue with the course taught at the Tactics School and that was with Close Air Support (CAS) and the use of napalm. The course was taught by a Vietnam veteran, Captain John Madden, who downed three North Vietnamese MiGs, but never got down and dirty supporting the grunts on the ground. When he opined,

"Napalm was a very poor weapon for CAS."

I jumped in, "Who says napalm is not effective for troops in contact? Your statistical analysis book? The psychological value of napalm alone makes it worth hauling around on the F-4s."

"Getting blown away is an accepted risk for grunts, but burning to death was not atop anyone's list of ways to go. Napalm may not destroy much property but the incoming napalm will sure make bad guys break contact and back off. You can keep your bombs, rockets and CBUs for vehicles and mounted troops, but napalm is great for ending a close infantry firefight."

When this Air-to-Air guru asked how I knew this to be true, I nailed him! I laid out the dynamics of an infantry firefight, how CAS should work and how often I was on the ground requesting and using napalm, often up close and very personal. The class was fully on my side, so he finally said, "Thank you" and moved on to another weapon system. Air-to-Air jerk was out of his element.

I was behind my Captain peers in total flying time, having spent the first few years of my career on the ground, so I took every opportunity to gain experience and flying time. I flew cross-country as a wingman as soon as I accumulated enough F-4 time and then pushed to be cleared solo cross country in Europe. I flew one weekend into RAF Leuchars with Lt Col Kimsey. RAF Leuchars was across the River Eden from St. Andrews' "Old Course", and, since Kimsey was a golfer, he brought his golf clubs in his F-4 travel pod to play a round on Friday afternoon. We hit a local pub that evening where I bought a round of drinks because I paid for my beer with an English Pound. Local tradition required that at least one pound be from the Royal Bank of Scotland or Clydesdale Bank, *or* you buy the house. After that lesson, I always carried one Scottish Pound along with English, German, French, Danish, Italian, Turkish, and Greek money in my "cross-country or bailout kit" in my G-suit. I even carried the equivalent of $10 in Russian Rubles, just in case.

By 1975, my goal was to land at every NATO airbase in Europe and I came close to visiting them all. Some of my favorites were going into Furstenfeldbruck Airbase, Germany to visit Munich and the beer halls; Bitburg AB because of the excellent hotel rooms in Trier; and Vaerlose Airbase outside of Copenhagen, Denmark. It amazed me that our F-4 crews were treated much better at other NATO airbases than at our own USAF bases. George Watson and I enjoyed a great stay at Zweibrucken AB, Germany, but when we got ready to depart on Sunday, the USAF base ops officer said we could not take off because of a water main break. So, the fire trucks could not reload water after the initial load was used. I asked

"Are the fire trucks full now?

"Yes."

"Then the problem is for the next crew if we crash and burn and the firefighters empty their trucks. We are going to start and launch."

George and I headed for our F-4 and back to TJ. These trips created an adventure almost every weekend that I was not on rotation in Incirlik. God bless Claire for the patience and understanding of what I was doing.

The huge C-5 aircraft often transited our bases and was nicknamed "Fat Albert". Well, Headquarters Air Force sent an all-world message saying that the C-5 "Galaxy" could not be referred to as "Fat Albert" over the radio. That might offend the C-5 crews. Of course, when you tell fighter guys what they can't say, that pretty well cemented "Fat Albert" into our vocabulary. We often taxied behind the C-5s at TJ and we used the term, followed by "Oh, I meant the C-5."

"Sandy" Sanderson, of the 613th, often taxied in after a mission wearing an old WWII leather helmet with earphones in it, but no microphone. The WSO made the radio calls after Sandy replaced his regular helmet in the de-arm area. The ground crews thought it was cool; the 613th leadership stayed mum, hoping the Wing honchos never saw it

FUNCTIONAL CHECK FLIGHTS (FCFs)

As I became more experienced in the F-4, I qualified to become a pilot for FCFs. These were flights to confirm major maintenance work performed on the fighters. Many of the pilots and WSOs avoided FCF duty because most FCFs were flown on weekends. I was eager for the additional flying time and experience, so I leapt at the opportunity. Now, Claire still reminds me often to keep my hand down when anybody asks for volunteers, regardless of purpose, remembering my eagerness for adventures, such as FCFs. Unfortunately, most of the FCFs did take place on weekends to release the aircraft from maintenance for Monday's flying schedule. We spent a lot of time inspecting the aircraft, finding a problem before or after starting engines and then spent more hours awaiting a fix or a cancel for the day. The FCFs cut into the weekend family time, but Claire was more than patient and defined FCFs as "two idiots flying known broken aircraft." FCFs were not exactly as Claire described them, but the full profile FCF offered plenty of opportunities for excitement and advanced aircraft handling.

To say an FCF was business in a hurry does not do it justice; the whole flight took approximately 17 minutes to burn a full fuel load of 12,000 pounds of JP-4. We logged a whopping 0.3 hours of flight time and we could use up all but the slimmest safety margin of fuel (needing to see if the "Fuel Low" warning light illuminated at the correct fuel level). An FCF started with a thorough maintenance records review in anticipation of what might go wrong, emphasizing what was recently "fixed" and why the FCF was necessary. The standard aircraft configuration for an FCF was a "clean" aircraft with no fuel tanks attached and on two occasions no wing armament pylons were attached. My normal FCF WSO, George Watson, and I then meticulously examined the aircraft from end to end, using a much more detailed checklist than that used by operational aircrews. If the plane passed inspection, we strapped in and, after engine start, made the fastest possible taxi, last chance ground inspection and turn onto the runway for a very special flight clearance. Time was fuel and there was none to spare! All the FCF flights used the same "Traps 27" call sign so the tower, radar approach/departure control and Madrid Center knew who we were and what to expect.

The takeoff was truly a carnival ride start to an action packed 10 minutes or so. With canopies down and locked we taxied onto the runway, and, standing on the brakes, checked the engine parameters at 80% power. I then released the brakes, pushed the throttles to mil power, slight pause, then full afterburner (AB), rapidly recording the maximum RPM, exhaust gas temperatures and afterburner nozzles closing for mil power and opening for AB. While all fighter aircraft will produce a rapid acceleration sensation, a clean F-4 in full afterburner was a true kick in the butt. In seconds, you were at flying airspeed and the Phantom leapt off the runway when you rotated the nose. You better be quick to retract the landing gear because your runaway Phantom rapidly exceeded the airspeed limit for landing gear of 250 knots. By keeping the nose down a bit, the F-4 reached 300+ knots nearing the far end of the runway. At 300 knots, you rotated up to 42 degrees pitch to maintain 300 knots and began the FCF profile. Our take-off clearance was: "Climb and maintain at least 10,000 feet by one mile from the departure end of the runway." Yahoo!

Following the afterburner takeoff, the Torrejon FCF profile called for an AB left climbing turn to 15 thousand feet, reducing throttle to mil power while maintaining 300 knots indicated airspeed. In that turn, we checked the fuel dump very briefly, leaving a pretty white vapor trail from each wing for the ground observers. Once level at 15,000 feet, I made a slight throttle reduction to go steady at 300 knots and we performed roll, pitch, and yaw stability augmentation checks, then accelerated to .9 Mach and made a .9 Mach climb to the coldest ISO temperature level (usually between 30 and 35 thousand feet). Then, leveling the aircraft nose, we began an afterburner Mach run, looking for an engine ramp extension to begin at Mach 1.2 and to be fully extended at Mach 1.5. The Mach 1.5 was often tough to reach in warmer temperatures because it took too much fuel (again, none to spare). We were headed away from Torrejon Air Base, and we wanted to complete the other events and still make it back to the airfield. The acceleration through Mach 1.0 was a non-sensation and we spent a few quiet seconds watching the Mach number slowly increase while the fuel gauge rapidly decreased. Next, we pulled the engines out of afterburner and began a mil power zoom climb to check for afterburner lights above 45K, and then coast down to 10,000 feet for angle of attack (AOA) stability checks.

The stability checks were a series of high angle-of-attack (AOA) approach-to-a-stall maneuvers in different configurations to test the correct rigging of the aircraft. Use of that very high AOA was not tactically sound because it created a horrendous airspeed bleed off, which might give you a turning advantage for a second or two, but left the F-4 as a slow speed strafe target afterwards. Remember that speed is life in an air-to-air fight. I always felt the greatest potential hazard on the FCF flight was an approach to a stall with the landing gear and flaps down. This maneuver was performed just above 5,000 feet, approximately 35 miles east of Torrejon, and outside the Madrid Terminal Control Airspace. The maneuver was not tricky but it was done with very low fuel state after the supersonic run and the higher altitude maneuvers were completed. The catch was that at that low altitude and low fuel state, if the gear did not retract after that test, there was less than a 50% chance of making it back to TJ. There were no other airports between that area and TJ; thus, we were looking at a "worst case" option of bailing out of a fuel starved F-4. That "worst case" event never happened, but on a full profile FCF it was enough of a risk that we always sweated it. The 401st Wing and even 16th Air Force Headquarters could not get Madrid Control to let us do that check in the Madrid airspace; so, on every full FCF you just hung it out and hoped the damn landing gear came up.

One FCF involved a single engine ramp failure at 1.45 Mach, which resulted in a violent, head-slapping yaw movement when one side of the F-4 stopped flying as fast as the other side. On another FCF we experienced a Rapid Decompression following afterburner shutdown at 45 thousand feet. The result was a foggy, cold cockpit, ram air pressure breathing for the two F-4 occupants and my best squeaky, soprano radio call to the nearest airfield, Zaragoza Airbase. Snoopy was not keen on the rapid decompression stuff.

Problems were not always the "phantom's phault." On one FCF, as we were almost finished with the flight, I extended the Ram Air Turbine (RAT) to take over the electrical load from the engine driven generators. This was done at the end of the flight, and, often in the landing pattern at TJ. This time I extended the RAT on initial, but in a rush, I shut off my two main generators in the four "G" overhead traffic pattern break *before* RAT electrical power came on line. Result: I totaled the Inertial Navigation System and most other electrical system gyros. RTFCL!

On another FCF, upon touchdown after an uneventful Sunday ride, the nose gear scissor strut pin failed and the two scissor struts separated, dropping on the nose wheel tires, resulting in blowouts of both nose tires. Amazingly, the plane tracked straight down the runway centerline; it just vibrated like it was about to come apart. My FCF WSO was Dick Cathers and I was afraid for a few seconds that Dick might decide to eject. If Dick punched out I would follow in less than two seconds because we earlier selected dual ejection sequence for the FCF flight. I did not know that the severe vibrations broke the mount brackets on the back-seat radar set and the 60-pound radar set was in Dick's lap. If I decided to eject, it would have killed Dick. I remember saying over the intercom: "Dick, stay with me!" We rode the vibrating Phantom to a stop in the middle of the runway. I made a fast radio call to the Tower, shut down the engines and electrical power, and we both went over the left side of the fuselage. In less than 10 seconds we raised canopies, safed our ejection seats, unstrapped and vaulted over the side. Dick and I were sitting in the grass along our slightly down-at-the-nose F-4, discussing what happened when the fire department trucks caught up with us. The vibrations were severe enough to destroy all the aircraft instruments and gauges. There was no such thing as a simple FCF!

By mid-1974 I upgraded to solo cross-country (and used that a lot), two-ship flight lead and then to four-ship flight lead. After making four-ship flight lead, I was made a flight commander with five crews in my unit and a couple of attached staff guys. Most of my work was seeing to the scheduling of my folks, pushing for their qualification upgrades and ensuring all required training was accomplished. When I was lucky I got to lead a four-ship of my own flight members to Incirlik, to the range or in air-to-air missions. Fortunately, when I became a Flight Commander in the 613TFS, my former 434th TFS squadron mate Dick Hoover was assigned to my flight. Hoov was one of the steadiest and most dependable men in the squadron. I could always depend on Hoov, regardless of the task, administrative or tactical in the air.

23

Life in Spain Between Rotations

By summer of 1973, Claire and I were reasonably settled in and decided to take a driving tour of coastal Spain as a second honeymoon. A very nice NCO and his wife stayed at our house to babysit / housesit for us and we loaded up the small white SEAT and took off. To conserve what little funds were available, we packed bread, sandwiches and lots of Spanish red wine for our hilltop or shady tree picnic stops. We ate at few restaurants on this trip, favoring street vendors or purchased groceries. After a few wine breaks and a day's drive, we made our first stop in Alicante, and then over the next five days we worked our way north along the Mediterranean coast to Benidorm and Valencia. In beautiful Alicante, we ate our first dinner from a vendor off Calle Jovellanos near the beach. I ordered a seafood sopa that came with lots of shrimp and clams, but also a floating layer of grease. Claire would not taste it, but I spooned off most of the grease and loved it. Eat like a native when you can has always been my philosophy. We stayed at hotels that were less than at the top of Fodor's Travel Guide but were easy on our budget and still quite nice. In Benidorm, we stayed in a hotel with a great view over buildings to the beach. In Valencia, we sampled the fantastic Spanish coastal cuisine but were caught in a rain shower. Unfazed by the warm rain, we ran and danced across the plaza in the rain and through the streets to an excellent restaurant. Soaked but enjoying the evening, we were treated to an enormous pan of the world's best seafood paella. It is one of our favorite memories. When young, you can afford to be silly.

Our return trip to Madrid included one night in the fantastic Parador de Alarcon. Paradors are a network of over 90 state-run Spanish hotels consisting of restored Castles, Monasteries, Convents, Fortresses, Manor Houses and Palaces. Almost half way between Valencia and Madrid, the town of Alarcon sits atop a ridgeline in a perfect horseshoe loop of the Rio Jucar. The sides of the ridge and opposing river banks are steep, and, for ages, the only road into Alarcon was atop the ridgeline and across the very narrow neck of the horseshoe river bend. Astride this road sat the medieval castle de Alarcon which was the Parador. We were living in a castle for one night. We entered through a courtyard of cobblestones to magnificent soaring ceilings, walls covered with tapestries and elegant classic Spanish furniture. Our small but clean room was down a narrow corridor with a one-window view across the river to the far banks rising vertically for 100 feet from the River Jucar. The narrow halls and small rooms reminded us that this was once a fortress to house troops and officials during times of turbulence as far back as the 13th century. After such a wonderful location for our final honeymoon night, it was tough to get back in the little SEAT, back on the road to Madrid and return to our normal lives. It was back to being an American family and cool F-4 fighter pilot in Franco's Spain.

The 613th kept a busy social schedule when the guys were home. In the cold season, there were ski trips to the nearby snow-covered mountains and Navacerrada ski resort north of Madrid. In the summer, we held high altitude picnics on the same mountains. We held squadron parties at the O'Club on base, at people's apartments or base housing, at the great restaurants in Madrid and our favorite, the Finca parties with "Bull fights." I only ventured into the ring at one Finca party, making a valiant effort to avoid the horns without looking bad before my peers and the wives. That darn bull learned to charge at the feet showing under the cape, not at the cape.

CLAIRE'S PRIVATE PILOT LICENSE

In 1974, Claire decided she could spare the time and we could spare the funds for her to pursue her Private Pilot License; the love of flying was always one of the things we shared. The Torrejon Aero Club charged very inexpensive rates for flying lessons and I was already a Flight Instructor with the aero Club. I had been an FAA Flight Instructor since shortly after returning from Vietnam. Uncle Sam, through the Veterans Administration, and I spent lots of money on my advanced FAA ratings, back when I was a bachelor. I started a formal program of flight instruction for Ms. Claire, and, on 21 May 1974, she slipped the surly bonds of earth and soloed a Cessna 150 at Torrejon Air Base, Spain. The base paper ran a story and picture of me kissing my aero club student pilot after the first solo. The student, of course, was Claire.

Debbie Manso, wife of Flight Surgeon Dr. Gil Manso, was also a pilot flying at the Torrejon Aero Club. Debbie developed the "Manso Principle" for refueling aircraft. A strikingly beautiful girl, Debbie let her long blonde hair and good looks convince others that they should refuel and or tow her small Cessna, so she would not get dirty. I never saw Debbie refuel her Cessna, whether at Spanish airports or at the TJ Aero Club. There was always an awestruck pilot, including Hank the Aero Club's Chief Pilot, or ground crew to help the young lady. Debbie just batted her eyelashes and, "POOF" some guy was there to refuel her airplane. It was told that when Debbie flew into Spanish airfields on cross-country flights that the Spanish ground crews literally fell over themselves to help "la senorita." Spain may have crawled into the 21st century, but in the early 1970s there were fewer than a dozen licensed female pilots in the country. Half of those were Americans.

My squadron deployments, cross country flights, and FCFs made our continuity of flight training less than desirable, so, not long afterwards, Hank Marien, the Chief Flight Instructor at the Aero Club, took over as her primary instructor and I filled in when I was home. She soon passed her check rides and the FAA Designated Flight Examiner for Europe awarded her a Private Pilot License. This was a great accomplishment, especially in Spanish airspace, and, even though most of her landings were on the grass runway paralleling TJ's main runway, she always flew in mixed traffic with F-4s, C-135 tankers, C-5s and God only knows what the Spanish flew in: ME-109s, ME-110s, JU-52s, F-4s or F-86s. Claire said she could recognize my voice from an F-4 while she was in the TJ traffic pattern in her Cessna 150 at the same time. Some of the sharp aviators out there will ask how was that possible. The TJ tower controllers used a repeater system that put the UHF radio traffic out along with their VHF radio so all the little guys knew what the fast movers were doing.

WINTER VACATION
In the Winter of 1975, Claire and I took a trip through central Europe for our first real vacation together in two years. The trip started with a free, space available C-130 hop from TJ to Rhein-Main Airbase, located on the south side of the runways at Frankfurt International Airport, Germany. Then we took a taxi from the passenger terminal into Frankfurt and a found an inexpensive hotel with the aid of an honest Cabbie. The next day we visited the art museums of Frankfurt, then visited Sachsenhausen district's continuous apfelweinfest for dinner. On day three, we took the express train ("Schnelzug") to Munich and we were lucky enough to stay in a modest room in the American Forces

207

Recreation Hotel, just off the Rotkreuzplatz, not too far from downtown Munchen's (Munich's) Marionplatz and Hofbrau Haus. We visited the sights of Munchen and Schwabing. We enjoyed a great German dinner in the Hofbrau Haus restaurant and then moved downstairs for the oompah entertainment and communal singing in the Hofbrau Haus beer hall. Claire finished a full liter of the great Hofbrau Haus beer, a personal best for her.

Next day we took the train to Salzburg, Austria, to see their beautiful castle and Mozart's home. It started to get quite cold and Claire wound up sleeping in the same bed with me for warmth in our little guest room. Tough duty but I certainly didn't mind. Very economical rooms could be found throughout Europe in those days, hawked by little old ladies who approached you in the train station and offered a spare bedroom in their house for much less than a hotel room. The Frau we met in the Salzburg bahnhof gave us bus tickets to her house, instructions on which buses (it involved one bus change) and saw us onto the bus. Then she took off on her bike, and, as we took a somewhat circuitous route to her local bus stop, she pedaled a more direct line and met us when we alighted from the bus. We were her guest for two delightful nights and learned that the Americans had nothing on the Austrian "Bed & Breakfast" business.

Then we were off by train to beautiful Wien (Vienna) Austria and another Austrian B&B. I am sure we were easy to identify as tourists, and, again, when we alighted at the Wien Hauptbahnhof, we were approached by a nice Austrian lady who offered us what turned out to be a room in a beautiful old apartment building, just across the Donau kanal from Town Centre and off the Obere Donaustrasse, with a huge bedroom and 15-foot-high ceilings. I paid an extra $3.00 for hot baths in our spotless antique bathroom.

We saw some of the Viennese sights and purchased tickets at the Staatsoper for *"Tales of Hoffmann.* If you are in Wien, you must attend an opera. We watched ours from a balcony booth on the left side of the beautiful State Opera House on the Opernring. Travel around Wien was easy by public transportation and a little walking. One particularly cold night the wind picked up and we traveled from one gluhwein vendor to the next roasted chestnut vendor to keep warm. Repeating this process, we finally made it to our destination with lots of warm anti-freeze.

From Vienna, we took the train through the Alps, via Klagenfurt and Udine to Pordenone, Italy and the US base at Aviano, Italy. The train station was the scene of exciting experiences in the Spring of 1976, but that is a later story. Our stay at Aviano was short but great fun as we ran into Captain (Dr.) Mike Berry in the Aviano O'Club. Mike was previously our 613ᵗʰ Flight Surgeon at TJ and was now a Flight Surgeon at RAF Lakenheath, England, with an F-111 squadron on weapons training rotation to Aviano. Mike invited us to go with a bunch of his squadron jocks for an evening at Orsini's, the world-famous restaurant in the adjacent village. Since Claire had a major crush on Mike Berry, it took no convincing to get her to agree to dinner with 18 fighter jocks. Mr. Orsini was in rare form that evening and paid special attention to the pretty lady that accompanied the fighter guys in his restaurant. His food was always exceptional and almost everything was laced with alcohol. You didn't feel any pain upon leaving. Claire never felt sorry for my subsequent 613ᵗʰ deployments to Aviano, now that she knew about Mr. Orsini's.

From Aviano, Claire and I headed for home, again via Air Force C-130 space available travel. While the three-hour flight was a bit loud and uncomfortable in the web jump seats of the C-130 cargo bay, the price was right.

In November of 1975, we flew again "Space A" by C-130 to Aviano to meet Claire's parents in Venice for a wonderful couple of days of sightseeing, shopping and fantastic food. When the visit was over, the Rhodes couple left by train for Rome and we returned to Aviano to catch a C-130 back to TJ. But nothing was flying into or from Spain! Generalissimo Francisco Franco died on 20 November and the Spanish borders were closed. That included Spanish airspace, so there was no C-130 trip to TJ. The Spanish government did not know what would happen: unrest, market crash, riots or revolution. So, Spain was closed. We then flew by C-130 to RAF Mildenhall and waited out the opening of Spanish airspace. Claire was beside herself since Topher was with a babysitting family and we had no news of what was happening in Spain. After we spent two nights in the Mildenhall BOQ, Spanish airspace was re-opened and we caught the first C-130 bound for TJ. Fun, fun, fun.

24

Every Day Flying

Refueling was a critical part of moving fighters from one place to another distant location or increasing fighter loiter time in a combat arena. The fighter formation used their excess speed and maneuverability to establish a position 100 feet behind the tanker, slightly below and co-speed with the tanker. The flight lead advanced straight to the refuel position and other flight members moved to positions just off the tanker's left and right wings. The tanker lowered the refueling boon and the fighter pilot opened the refueling door on the fuselage top and slid forward to the nozzle. The refuel receptacle on the F-4 was approximately eight feet behind the rear cockpit on the backbone of the plane so you flew past the boom nozzle into refueling position. A good technique was to be level with the nozzle and fly straight forward, not from below and behind, because then you must make adjustments both up / down and forward.

The KC-135 had two rows of signal lights along the bottom centerline of the tanker fuselage that changed colors to tell you to move forward / backwards or up / down. The middle lights were two white bars, referred to as the Captains bars, and indicated you were centered in the refueling "envelope." The extendable boom also displayed different colored stripes painted on the extendable probe indicating the extension status of the boom with an eight-inch circular ball painted on the middle of the boom indicating the optimum boom extension. The refueling boom was "flown" by the boom operator looking through a window on the aft bottom of the tanker. He moved the boom to a position inches above the open refueling door and then extend the boom until it locked into place and fuel could begin transfer. For some reason, the younger female boom operators enjoyed this procedure.

If a pilot was good, he could fly into the refueling position, center the lights, center the ball on the boom and stay there while the fighter received fuel. Staying perfectly centered on the boom required a great deal of finesse on the flight controls and throttles as the fighter was taking on fuel. The fuel added weight to the fighter and changed the center of gravity, requiring pitch, trim and power changes to stay in place.

The F-4E was one of the trickier balancing acts because there was a 700-pound fuel cell in the far back end of the fuselage that filled last and made a very noticeable change in fore and aft balance. The pilot continuously made minute changes in power and trim. The F-4E finished refueling in a noticeably higher nose position than when refueling started. When I refueled, I flew into refueling position utilizing both engine throttles, stabilized and then made very small adjustments with just one throttle.

Another technique saw most of the pilots and WSOs refueling with just one click of nose down trim. With that "down trim," any movement that was not a conscious input by the F-4 crewmember took the fighter down and away from the tanker, not up into the boom and tanker. To use more than one click down trim required you to maintain constant back pressure on the stick, a tiring option. I don't think refueling came easy to any new fighter pilot, but, like good close formation flying, it took tremendous concentration and the ability to make very fine adjustments and RELAX. Early on in my tour I often came off a tanker with an aching right hand because I was squeezing the control stick so tightly. With practice, refueling became easier, and, by the time I became an F-4 instructor pilot, I could refuel with light fingertips and it seemed second nature.

The KC-135 boom operator was critical to smooth refueling and we were fortunate in the mid-1970s to have many boom operators who spent time in Southeast Asia and accumulated tremendous experience refueling all types of aircraft in varying situations. As my Torrejon tour went on, we saw more new boomers fresh out of tanker school. Now the boomer was a young 19-year-old airman, as new to being a boomer as some F-4 lieutenants were to refueling their fighters. The young boomers went strictly by their checklist, making numerous radio calls as the refueling proceeded. On the days when one of the senior combat-experienced boomers was on a tanker, we could fly up to the pre-refueling position, open our refueling door, the boomer lowered the boom, we moved forward, the boomer plugged our plane, fuel transfer would be completed, the boomer withdrew the nozzle and the fighter moved out to a position off the wing of the tanker. The next member of the flight slid over to the pre-contact position and the process was repeated until all flight members were refueled. Done without a single radio call and zipping along at speeds of 300 to 450 mph.

Homecomings from the Turkey rotations were a great welcoming occasion for the families of those flying the F-4s home. The families gathered at the 613th squadron building, and, when the guys were about 20 miles out, they piled into the squadron bread van to bring champagne to the arriving crews. They could listen to the radio calls and the family could watch as dad's flight came in, broke over the field, circled to land, de-armed and taxied to the chocks. Quite often, they could listen to a radio as the planes arrived and try to recognize the voices of the crew members.

Kisses, Spanish red wine and champagne were the weapons of the day. The families were waiting just to the side of the F-4 parking places as our screaming, 40,000 pound Phantoms rolled to a stop and shut down. Then the van doors opened and wives, children or girlfriends met the guys at the bottom of the boarding ladders with kisses and champagne. It was great! After about two years of this tradition, some Security Force weenie at USAFE or the Pentagon decided this was a security risk and the families could not come on the flight line, but would have to meet the crews in the squadron building. The Air Force struck another blow for over-reacting and ending a morale boosting tradition for the deployed crews. I wonder what those headquarters guys were thinking or drinking. They obviously never deployed on a rotating basis when the homecoming welcome was a great ceremony and a true morale booster.

AVIANO NUKE ALERT ADVENTURES

In between the Incirlik rotations, we were frequently sent as a flight to sit nuclear alert in "the cage" at Aviano. In early 1974, I was crewed with Rich "Hands" Bohman when my flight was deployed to Aviano to bring the nuke line "back up" because a flight from another USAFE F-4 squadron failed the Aviano nuke certification as part of their Operational Readiness Inspection (ORI). As a result, all the Aviano nuke lines were brought down (i.e. decertified), nukes sent to the storage area and the crews were sent home to Germany. My flight was sent from Torrejon to Aviano to study, rehearse Aviano procedures and prepare for a re-inspection. No pressure being watched by scrutinizing personnel from the Pentagon and Headquarters Europe. All my guys earned perfect scores on their certification exams and upload procedures.

After the nuclear alert lines were re-certified, Rich and I were selected to certify on a separate line called a "Selective Release." This was an individual target to attack with a single aircraft and nuke prior to all out nuclear release. Rich dazzled the Aviano commander and his staff with a great briefing, as a half dozen inspectors from USAFE and Headquarters Air Force looked on. The Aviano commander was Colonel John Piotrowski and in 1985 he signed the performance report that most likely got me promoted to Colonel. In those eleven years since my time at Aviano, Piotrowski moved from a support base commander to a three-star general commanding TAC's 9th Air Force at Shaw AFB, South Carolina. He later became a four-star and Air Force Vice Chief of Staff.

On a squadron deployment to Aviano, we were drinking wine at Orsini's when somebody thought "afterburners" or flaming Sambuca drinks were in order. An afterburner was a shot glass of Sambuca, lit with a match. The liquor burned with a blue flame and the challenge: toss the shot down without burning yourself. The trick was to take a deep breath and blow out the flame just as it approached your mouth. I got my afterburner down with no damage. One of my new lieutenants, Rich Gamm, already intoxicated, missed his mouth and napalmed the right side of his face. The squadron roared as his WSO enjoyed slapping the hell out of his lieutenant to extinguish the fire. No real damage done as Gamm received what looked like a sunburn and flew home the next morning in his F-4. His WSO reported that he flew most of the way with his mask off or very loosely attached. Lucky for him the mask attached on the left side and the burn was on his right cheek.

OPERATION FLINTLOCK
Each year the Allied forces in Europe held a field exercise titled "Operation Flintlock" which involved a lot of survival / Escape and Evasion training. I never volunteered for Operation Flintlock (been there, done that ground thing), but in 1975 I was called by the 401st Wing Intel Officer and informed that I was requested by name to participate. It seems the Army needed a current USAFE fighter pilot, parachute qualified, and preferably with a Special Ops background and clearance history. There was only one of those in Europe: Captain Harry C. Stevenson. I was to report to Flint Kaserne in Bad Tölz, Germany. That told me that the 10th SF Group was involved, or rather, I was about to be involved with the 1st Battalion, 10th SF Group. This sounds like a movie script, but it is how we (lucky few) trained.

After several training days, three "volunteers" and one SF trooper were inserted at night "somewhere". We moved clandestinely through hills and mountainous terrain for five days, avoiding military

214

and law enforcement and contacting only a few specific villagers. The "volunteer evaders" were only informed about one travel destination at a time, but I could tell travel was southward. We slept in barns, cellars and a haystack until finally, late in the evening of Day Six, with the help of two local farmers, we hid along the edge of a field until a darkened helicopter approached and rapidly settled at the field's edge. The four travelers scrambled into the helo and it launched, flying very low-level to the west. Our transportation turned out to be an American Jolly Green Giant helicopter.

After one hour, the Jolly suddenly flared and landed on a darkened portion of Aviano Airbase, Italy. A Security Policeman from Aviano approached the aircraft, but he was met by two heavily armed crewmen who informed him that the helo was permitted to land, he had no need to know and they would be gone in two minutes. The cop backed off and an unmarked van arrived to pick up our team as the helicopter lifted and departed. We were transported to the Aviano BOQ and given pre-assigned individual rooms, in which we found our clothes and equipment from Bad Tölz, along with travel orders for return to our home stations the next morning. Just another fun-filled week in Special Ops!

CREEK SCOPE RADAR BOMBING COMPETITION
WSO Bill Stroud was the best radar bomber in the 613th and in 1975 he was selected to represent the squadron in the USAFE "Creek Scope" radar bomb competition. He selected me to be his front-seater and our three 401st crews were given dedicated F-4s for the competition along with dedicated crew chiefs and radar specialists. Prior to the competition, the three chosen crews, one crew from each TJ squadron, flew together for almost a month with priority range times and tankers for refueling. Captain Mark Trapp from the 612th, created a memorable moment when he suffered a system malfunction as we pulled onto the runway at TJ for a practice mission. Mark then requested to clear the runway and taxi back in a radio call to the female tower controller stating his INS was "tits up." This brought moans from all.

Other highlights were practices on the Ramstein RBS site where we met a tanker high overhead. We flew until our range time or fuel dictated a departure and then left the range to other competitors, popping up 16,000 feet to refuel before going back on the range. I think I accomplished 21 aerial refuelings in one month, and, if I wasn't comfortable refueling before the competition, I sure was by the end.

The actual competition was a night bombing mission, so we deployed to the Ramstein Competition Site. Flying from Ramstein, Bill worked his radar magic on the night low-level and two radar scored bomb runs; one USAF site south of Ramstein and the second farther north and operated by the RAF. In our antique F-4C, Bill beat all other USAFE F-4s, two F-111s and was crowned the Best F-4 Radar Bomber in Europe. Only the F-111s with fifteen year newer and specialized radar could out score Bill.

The one time I totally lost my cool was at that Creek Scope competition when my flying gear was tampered with. On day three, Bill and I arrived in the Life Support room and found that somebody cut the 101st Airborne Division patch and the Special Forces patch off my helmet bag. I was the purest form of irate. Bill said I looked mad enough to kill somebody. I was. Not only did somebody tamper with a pilot's flying gear, a criminal offense, but those were symbols of the units I fought with and bled with in combat. I have no idea why somebody stole the patches, other than they were unique and not normally seen in an Air Force environment. If I ever found the SOB that cut off those patches, I would have tried to beat him into oblivion. What I threatened to do to the NCOIC of the Life Support probably should have earned me an Article 15 or more. My ranting frightened Bill so much he questioned if I was safe to fly that sortie. I finally flipped the mental switch and tuned into flying a radar strike mission. Decades later, I still get wound up remembering that cut-patch incident. Years later Bill paid me an exceptional compliment when he said he always liked to fly with me or Mike Risch, because, of all the 613th jocks, we were the ones that truly loved to fly. Risch is still flying as a commercial pilot.

IP CHECK RIDE
Having been certified solo cross country and a Flight Lead in minimum time, the next step was to become an F-4 Instructor Pilot. So, in June of 1975, I completed my Instructor Pilot training and took my IP check with Major Dean Irwin, a Stan Eval pilot who was previously the Operations Officer in the 613th. The IP checkride was a challenge as I was to brief and lead a 12-ship tanker and strike package with a flight of four from another squadron providing chaff in the "target" area.

Overall it went well: I briefed the mission and use of chaff, and, from my backseat IP position, led our 12-ship (four chaff and eight strike F-4s) to our two tankers in a track off the south coast of Spain. Everyone refueled uneventfully and then we dropped down to fly a Low Level to the target, an oil refinery in the center of Spain. The flights split to

216

attack from different directions as the chaff birds began to climb and dispense chaff. The attacks went well and the egress began as the chaff was turned off and the gaggle rejoined. With the "package" mission complete, the aircraft then split up into flights of two or four for additional training and I returned to TJ for a Tacan approach and multiple back-seat IP traffic patterns. Bad news: the chaff flight developed a problem with one chaff pod still dispensing as they brought it home to TJ. The flight came home at 20,000 feet and shot the Tacan approach from 30 miles east of TJ. With a slight easterly wind aloft, the continuously dispensed chaff spread toward Madrid. Almost undetectable by people on the ground, the chaff cloud descended on eastern Madrid, Torrejon airbase and Barajas International. The expanding reflective cloud "knocked out" the approach radars for Barajas / Madrid International and Torrejon AB. The chaff pod finally ran out of chaff on short 2-mile final at TJ, but the damage was already done. Regardless, I passed my IP checkride and all was well.

LT COL MIKE CARNS

During his tenure as 613th squadron commander 1973 – 1974, Carns was adamant that his 613th crews know their crew chiefs and help on the flight line. He tossed F-4 jocks out of the squadron building when they were not on the schedule and told them to go help maintenance. After doing that a couple of times, I felt compelled to enroll in the Air Force Maintenance Officer Extension Course, where I learned about flight line maintenance, parts supply and aircraft phase inspections. The crew chief on my assigned F-4 was Staff Sergeant Don Vosgien, who taught me how to service the F-4 and let me help with maintenance of the Aero Club Cessnas. After a year, I respected Don's work so much I would have accepted an F-4 on his word. I never did (it made the WSO very nervous), but I would have. I still did the walk-around inspections.

Lt Col Carns and I developed a twelve-item checklist for our jocks on how to launch and recover F-4s, acting as a crew chief. Each checklist event was to be demonstrated by the crew member and signed off by a senior maintenance supervisor. Don taught me well and I worked with him numerous times to launch F-4s: changing air hoses, connecting electrical power, buttoning up panels and doing the flight control checks as crew chief. This checkout became mandatory before you could be a cross-country flight lead or WSO in the Squids. I only used the procedures once for real and that was on a bare base in Denmark. I crew-chiefed Number Two and once his F-4 was running and the INS / radar were warming up, his WSO hopped out and served as my crew chief. It worked as planned, but we needed to borrow a screw driver to button up panels. A screw driver was then added to all the Squid cross country aircraft kits.

Working with Lt Col Carns was challenging, as he demanded excellence in everything from flying to paperwork. Asked if he would lead the squadron into combat, Carns replied, "No, I will go on the wing of our squadron Weapons Officer, the best fighter pilot in the squadron." Lt Col Carns was not an egotist but a realist. Some of the officers felt he was too demanding, but I found him easy to work with. See what he wants, do it correctly and well; and he was great to be around. He was selected for Colonel below the zone and gave up the squadron command after about 16 months. He was on his way up!

Major Ed Rasimus, the great fighter pilot, a flight commander and then our Assistant Ops Officer, and I knocked heads a few times because he thought the Red River Valley Fighter Pilots Association (River Rats) were the ultimate warriors. As a former grunt and Green Beret, I held that they were solid citizens, but, in my opinion, they commuted to the war and returned after each mission to a nice warm bed on an Air Base in Thailand or Vietnam. My exact words were, "I have spent more time in one close-up fire fight than you and the River Rats got in ten trips north." That rubbed Ras the wrong way, but we came to a mutual standoff on ranking the hazards of aerial or ground warfare. The difference came down to the old saying that the Air Force mans their equipment, while the Army equips their men. It was a matter of priorities. The fighter communities need guys like Ras to fight wars. But, it is hard to find good jobs for them in peacetime.

Colonel Chuck Donnelly was not one to let regulations interfere with his own judgment. A year after he became "Wing King", I was scheduled to fly on his wing in a three-ship intercept mission; he was to lead and carry a visiting Air Force Academy cadet in his back seat. Colonel Donnelly cancelled when we lost one F-4 for maintenance reasons and gave me the Academy cadet. I would now be the flight lead while the cadet rode in my pit on an orientation flight. The 401st flying regulations required an Instructor Pilot to fly all orientation flights for non-rated visitors. I tactfully reminded the Colonel that I was not yet an IP, but he said he was sure I would give the cadet a good ride and he authorized the schedule change. The squadron Duty Pig looked confused but made the changes on the schedule, gave us our tail numbers and scooted off to tell the Squadron Ops Officer about the changes the Wing Commander just authorized on the schedule.

Lt Col (P) Dick Pascoe joined the 401ˢᵗ TFW as the assistant Wing DCO in June 1975, and I flew a local area checkout and instrument refresher training sortie with him. Pascoe seemed like a good guy and flew the F-4 well for having been out of fighters for eight years. A month later I flew as the IP lead on a 1 v 1 ACT mission against Colonel Pascoe. After the mission, I debriefed Pascoe on the things I thought he did right and those things that he could do better. It was a friendly and objective debrief and he earned a good grade sheet from me. We parted at the duty desk, and, as Lt Col Pascoe left the building, our squadron Assistant Ops Officer asked me how the flight went. I said that Pascoe flew a good F-4 and, for a soon-to-be Colonel, he seemed to do well at Air-to-Air combat. Ed Rasimus smirked and said, "Let me show you something." We walked across the hall to his office and he dug up a book on the history of air operations in Southeast Asia. He opened to a specific page and handed it to me. The photo and caption showed then-Captain Dick Pascoe painting a red star on his F-4 indicating he just downed his second Mig in combat over North Vietnam. Dick Pascoe was part of Robin Olds' fighter wing. I felt like an absolute idiot in telling Dick Pascoe how to fly air-to-air. Humility check – done that! Colonel Pascoe never said a word to me about his past and I knew I liked him after that. Six years later we met again.

509ᵀᴴ AIRBORNE BCT– VICENZA, ITALY

After finishing an alert tour in the Nuke cage at Aviano, I took the train to Vicenza, Italy to make two long awaited parachute jumps with the 509ᵗʰ Airborne Battalion Combat Team (BCT). The 509ᵗʰ was the Quick Reaction Force for Europe and when I met their Air Force Air Liaison Officer (ALO) Captain Kenny Boone (USAFA '66) while drinking at the Aviano O'Club, he was astounded to find an F-4 driver who willingly jumped out of aircraft. We dummied a set of permissive parachute orders and manifested for two helicopter jumps the next morning. I made the jumps and the 509ᵗʰ Sergeant Major stapled my Master Blaster wings to my chest. I needed only those two jumps to reach the minimum requirements for Master Parachutist wings (65 jumps total, but many specific types of jumps which I earlier accomplished with the 101ˢᵗ and 5ᵗʰ Special Forces Group (Airborne)).

We adjourned to the O'Club that evening where Kenny and I got completely smashed while celebrating with the 509ᵗʰ Army paratroopers. Kenny got us into an auto accident on the way back to his apartment. I hit the dashboard hard enough to suffer a minor head injury that resulted in double vision. Treated at the US Army hospital, I was released for train travel back to Aviano. This meant that I could not fly my F-4 back to TJ. I was very fortunate that fellow Squid Captain Stu Kaufman was on duty in the TJ command post the next morning and phoned Claire to pass on this information and my new schedule. The backup crew took my Phantom home with the rest of my flight and I rode a C-130 to TJ by way of Ramstein, Germany. I caught holy hell from Dr. Kirschner on Monday, but was returned to flying status by Wednesday. The 613th guys didn't say much because they knew I was insane. Just before this ugly event, Kenny was selected as the USAFE Junior Officer of the Year, but then lost his driving privileges in Italy. He went to the ceremony on Ramstein AB, Germany and suffered another DUI accident. That probably tubed his career. I lost touch with Kenny when I left TJ.

Kenny left the Air Force in November 1976 and worked in the defense industry as an aeronautical engineer for almost 30 years before retirement. Robert Kenneth "Kenny" Boone died on 9 May 2010.

25

Spatial Disorientation

It was crystal clear night with no moon and few scattered clouds as I entered the holding pattern for an instrument approach to TJ. My WSO, Johnny Wyatt, and I night refueled, flew a low-level route northward across Spain, made a simulated nuclear attack on an unsuspecting Spanish village and climbed to 20,000 feet to recover at Torrejon. Stars above and lights from the ground were of equal count and intensity, while the few clouds present obscured the coastal lights near Valencia. The lights and darkness merged, there was no horizon!

My first 180 degree turn in holding was OK, but I felt uneasy. When it came time to roll out of the second turn, I moved the stick to the right. The instruments showed that I correctly leveled the wings on the outbound leg. But my head told me that I just rolled left to an inverted position. I checked the instruments again. There was no descent or turn; the heading was steady; but I knew I was upside down. The primary attitude indicator still showed the grey sky up and the black ground down.

"Johnny, how is your attitude indicator working?"

"Looks good to me."

I was developing a twitch on the flight controls as my inner ear and eyes battled for control of the aircraft. It was time to confess what was happening. "Johnny, tell me we are not inverted because my head feels like we are inverted."

"No, we are upright and wings level, on the outbound heading. Do you want me to take the aircraft?"

"Not yet, let me work this out." I glanced outside but the blackness below and above did nothing to turn my mind right-side up. I told myself: "Just fly the instruments. You have flown in thick weather before, this is the same thing."

Madrid Center broke the silence: "Duddy 21, you are cleared for the high TACAN runway 23 at Torrejon." I acknowledged the clearance.

"OK, Johnny, follow me through on the approach."

"Roger that. Thirty-degree left bank and maintain 2, 0, 0. Roll out. You are wings level. You are six miles from the fix, call departing."

Travelling at five miles per minute, it was a nervous and shaky sixty seconds before I reduced power, lowered the F-4's nose and made the radio call.

"Madrid, Duddy 21 is departing the fix and out of 2,0,0,"

"On heading, good descent, descent checklist complete," Johnny called.

I quickly ran my descent checklist, without moving my head for fear of making the vertigo worse. I still felt a tremor on the control stick and I was beginning to sweat. As I approached 10,000 feet, Madrid Center called:

"Duddy 21, continue descent to Flight Level 0-5-0 and contact Torrejon Approach, local Channel Five."

"Duddy 21, down to 0-5-0 Channel Five, gracias." Johnny immediately changed the radios to channel five and simply said "You're up."

Out of habit I turned and looked down to my left at the radio display to confirm that I was, in fact, on Channel Five. Damn! Bad move! My head felt like I started a hard roll to the right. I made a sharp left roll input. Before the F-4 could roll 10 degrees I looked at the attitude indicator and aggressively rolled wings level.

"Are you OK, do you want me to take it?" Johnny called out. He was following me on the flight controls since I confessed I had vertigo. A jerky left roll followed by a jerky right roll was testing his patience. He was ready to take control of the plane because, if we went in, Johnny would be the second aviator to the scene of the crash, 39 inches behind me.

Before I could answer, we broke through the bottom cloud layer, and, there, miles in front of us, were the lights of Madrid, forming a horizon. Instantly, my internal gyros turned upright and the vertigo vanished. What I felt now matched what I saw.

"I'm OK now, I've got the airplane."

I called Torrejon Approach for a PAR and the rest of the flight was normal. We were a subdued crew as we landed, ran checklists, taxied in, shut down and processed through maintenance debriefing. In the squadron, we hung up our flying gear and went to debrief the refueling, low level route, radar bomb run, and then *the* return to TJ. I thanked Johnny again. He said that was the first time he was involved with a vertigo incident. "It was muy interesante!"

26

Colonel Muammar Gaddafi

In 1975, the Cold War was going full steam and numerous national leaders were trying to show their muscle and gain international stature in their realm of influence while the major powers faced off with each other. President Gerald Ford was in his second year as President after the resignation of Richard Nixon and trying to maintain the United States as the leader of the Free World and opponent of Communism. The ruler of Libya, Muammar Gaddafi, declared his country's sole right to most of the Gulf of Sidra in the south Mediterranean Sea. This became Gaddafi's "Line of Death", inside of which Libya would attack any unauthorized ships. The United States and other countries took exception and planned a show of naval force by sending the cruiser *USS Little Rock* across the line and possibly up to the internationally recognized 12-mile limit. Since there were no US Navy carriers in the Med at that time, the F-4s from Torrejon, Spain and other USAFE bases provided fighter combat air patrol for the *USS Little Rock*.

The NMCC in the Pentagon placed four 613th TFS fighters and two of the KC-135 refueling tankers at Torrejon, on 30-minute alert and then the crews moved into the base BOQ for the duration. No going home at night to the family. Major Ed Rasimus, was the selected flight lead and I was the alternate flight lead as number three. The tasking order called for a load of four AIM-7s and four AIM-9s on each aircraft in anticipation of an engagement with any Libyan fighters that might threaten the *USS Little Rock*.

On Day Two of alert we received a call from the NMCC that the *Little Rock* was not going to cross the line today, but we were to remain on 30-minute alert. We had received the same No-Go message the previous day and did not launch, so we believed the Pentagon snakes. I ate a light breakfast of toast, juice, and, since we weren't launching this morning, coffee. I was on my second large mug of coffee in the squadron flight planning room when the alert radio went off telling us the *Little*

Rock was going across the line in just over two hours and to launch immediately. Our eight F-4 jocks grabbed flying gear and hopped in the squadron van as the KC-135 tanker guys were also scrambling out of their squadron building across the parking lot.

To get fighters overhead the *USS Little Rock,* our plan was to start and taxi four F-4s; then, if all their systems passed their tests, we would launch three fighters to go to our first KC-135 tanker refueling. If all three F-4s could take fuel from the tanker and the weapons systems were OK, then Ras and the better-qualified pilot (that was me as the alternate flight lead) would continue and the third fighter would return to TJ. The four aircraft checked good in the arming area, so, I waved goodbye to number four as he waited there until the three-ship became airborne and then taxied back to the F-4 ramp. Ras delayed our switch to tower frequency as we watched the first KC-135 roar off Runway 05, opposite to our takeoff direction.

The huge, heavy tanker rattled our F-4s as it passed with 200 feet lateral spacing and 200 feet of altitude. Tankers often launched off Runway 05 to avoid the final approach course to Madrid's Barajas International Airport. On signal from Ras, we closed our canopies in unison, checked in on tower frequency and pulled onto the runway for departure. After engine run-up, everybody's aircraft again checked good, so, we took 10 second spacing, full afterburner, gear and flaps up, out of afterburner at 250 knots, and began a wide climbing right turn to the east for flight rejoin and our first tanker refueling.

As soon as our flight went level at 24,000 feet, we made radar contact with our tanker, call sign Debar 21, the same tanker that roared past us on the ground at TJ. The Spanish were antsy about anyone refueling over their land, so, after crossing the east coast of Majorca, we joined on Debar 21 who had turned back toward our flight. It was a postcard perfect day in the western Mediterranean and from our perch we could see Barcelona, Ibiza, Majorca, Menorca and all the way to Sardinia. If we were a bit farther south, we could have seen the coast of North Africa. It seemed an unusually beautiful day to fly out and shoot at somebody. With our three F-4s on his wings, Debar 21 turned toward the southeast and we cycled through the refueling process to ensure nobody developed a fuel problem and to top off our fuel tanks.

Now, Ras made a very tough decision for a fire-breathing fighter pilot. The radar on Ras' Phantom developed problems enroute to the tanker and he was left with very limited, if any, radar or radar missile capability. Because number two, Mike Risch, and I were fully operational in aircraft and weapons, Ras made the correct call, turning the flight over to me as the alternate flight leader. Mike and I turned toward the briefed location of the *USS Little Rock*; the tanker turned toward Sicily, where it set up an orbit for more fighters covering the *Little Rock*; and Ras turned back toward Torrejon. I did not want to be Ras' WSO on that leg. Either the ranting and raving or the awful silence would have been too much.

As we headed south I felt that momentary flicker of misgiving that I remembered from days as a platoon leader going into a firefight or as a Company Commander riding into an air assault on the skids of a Huey.

"What the hell have I gotten myself into?"

Ras was the most experienced fighter guy in the squadron with a combat tour in F-105 Thuds and another combat tour in F-4s. This should be his fight. But, just as I did as an infantry officer, I asked the classic question "What are you going to do now, Lieutenant?" I started to think of the numerous options that we faced. Mike Risch, our WSOs and I had flown together numerous times and we had discussed and again discussed the tactics and scenarios that we might encounter today. We were as ready as we could be. The apprehension was now gone as I re-checked my missile armament switches and lights. This is what we are here for and why we train so hard. Let's do it!

Still 100 miles away from the ship, our flight checked in on the assigned UHF radio frequency for the *Little Rock* and we were connected to a radar controller in the ship's Combat Information Center. Our controller fed us information on any surface and air traffic for 200+ miles around the *Little Rock*. Our flight was sent into a race track orbit 30 miles south of and between the *USS Little Rock* and the Libyan coast.

As it turned out, Ras did not miss anything. It seemed the weapons of the *Little Rock* and our air cover were enough show of force for the Libyans to not interfere with the *Little Rock*. After 45 minutes on station, talking with the controller, but getting no action from Libya, we were relieved by a flight of F-4s that had launched from Aviano, Italy on the same tasking. Mike and I flew north to a point about 100 miles south of Sicily where we again met our TJ tanker friend, Debar 21, and cycled through the flying gas station to top off our tanks. We returned to orbit, relieving the Aviano fighters so they could duplicate our refueling. The next 40 minutes were as quiet as our first patrol period and we were soon due to be relieved, then refuel and head home. Between the Navy controller and our two F-4s, we radar tracked every aircraft that flew in that part of the Med as well as some visual reconnaissance of surface vessels requested by the *Little Rock*, but that was it for the day.

At this time, I asked the controller about the ship that was staying five miles behind his cruiser. He informed us the trailing ship was a Russian intelligence trawler that was shadowing the *Little Rock*. Oh, this was too good to pass up for a different type of show! Remember, it was during the Cold War. When the Aviano F-4s checked in to relieve us, I asked the controller if we could drop down and do a fly-by of the *Little Rock*. He agreed and cleared us for a low pass on the starboard side. Mike and I closed the formation from our tactical spread and dove for the surface of the Mediterranean. But I did not head directly for the cruiser. We went level at 75 feet off the waves and one mile aft of the Russian trawler. As briefed in the descent, I took the port side and Mike took the starboard side and we passed within 100 feet of the trawler's bridge and hit full afterburner. Damn, the Russians had a lot of antennas on that intelligence ship. Mike quickly joined into a tight fingertip formation and we gave a good-looking fly-by for the waving sailors on the *USS Little Rock*. I was more than happy to show the Navy that the Air Force was there to cover them when needed. We started our climb to the north and the controller gave us a vector to our recovery tanker, Debar 22. The tanker was some 170 miles north and coming our way with another flight of F-4s on his wing.

Our controller also informed us: "Harassing Russian naval vessels is against Navy regulations."

"Oh, well! That's a Navy regulation and we're Air Force."

Topping off from our tanker south of Sicily, we headed home to complete a 7.8-hour mission. The last half hour was pure agony because I really needed to piss. I used the two piddle packs in the aircraft, but those two large mugs of coffee before launch were doing me in. I cursed the Pentagon puke who said we weren't going, and then changed his mind. I squirmed all the way to the overhead pattern at TJ, made a gentle left break in the landing pattern, touched down and rolled quickly to the de-arm area off the end of Runway 23. I egged on the de-arm crew, taxied a bit too fast to the 613th ramp area, and then it was engines off, seat safe, switches safe, and over the side headed for the maintenance debrief bathroom before the crew chief knew what was going on.

Nobody from the Libyan Air Force came up to play with the American F-4s on that day and it wasn't until August of 1981 that some idiot in Libya sent two Fitters to probe a US aircraft carrier inside the "Line of Death." The two Libyan SU-22 Fitters were met by two Navy F-14s and both Fitters went down, one to an AIM-7 and the other to an AIM-9 missile. Obviously, we planned the correct weapons load for our mission.

27

More Incirlik

Konya Range was the squadron's gunnery training site during deployments to Incirlik. We furnished two American pilots to control the range when the F-4s were utilizing the range, so every flight commander drew four or five days of duty as the Range Officer.

One of our indispensable squadron members while at Incirlik was Adel. He was a Captain in the Turkish Army Reserves and loved his job with the Americans. Adel was interpreter and guide for our trips to Konya. He saw his job as interpreter and teacher of Turkish history, culture and customs to all his charges enroute to or at Konya. He also knew all the best places to eat in Konya. The only thing that he asked in return for his additional services was a bottle of Johnny Walker Red scotch to be shared with the crew on each tour.

We loaded up an Air Force truck with range supplies, picked up Adel, and drove six hours up onto the Konya desert plain and to the town of Konya. In Konya, we stayed in a hotel which was sparse by our Air Force standards, but quite nice for traveling Turks. Adel thought the accommodations were better than the Turkish Army BOQ in Konya and appreciated the US Air Force paying for his room. I also learned that the Muslim ban on alcohol only seemed to apply when they were with other Muslims in their home area. Adel did his share of emptying that bottle of Johnny Walker.

As the Range Officer, I cleared F-4 flights onto the range, watched for safety issues and passed bomb scores to the crews by radio. The scores were determined by triangulation from our elevated range tower and a similar tower 3000 feet to the east. With two azimuths to the bomb impact spot, we could calculate the distance and relationship to the target. The azimuths were provided by Turkish soldiers and translated by Adel. One unwritten but understood rule was a pilot never argued with the Range Officer, not about scores or procedures. I only enforced that rule once: Squid Bud Bennett was taking his initial Tactical Check and his Stan Eval check pilot argued about Bud's first bomb score, so I told the check pilot to safe up his switches and hold high over the range, because he was through for the day. Bud could not believe that I threw his check pilot off the range. I then cleared Bud to drop his second bomb, which he needed to pass the check ride. It was also a good bomb score, Bud passed his weapons delivery event and his flight headed back to Incirlik. When I got back to Incirlik on Friday evening, nothing was ever said about tossing the check pilot.

Just driving thirteen miles out to the Konya range each morning was an adventure. Before leaving town, we stopped at a bakery for a loaf of hot bread. For the equivalent of eight cents, the baker pulled freshly baked bread from the oven with a long wooden paddle and flipped it to Dick Hoover, my Range Officer partner. I opened the back door of our six-pack truck and Dick juggled the very hot loaf until he could toss it onto the back seat. The Turkish range crew always provided butter and honey to make this our breakfast with a cup of tea, "Chi." Often, on the range road that ran from the highway across three miles of desolate plains, we encountered huge wolves. They ran from our truck, but it explained why the sheep dogs wore large spiked collars out here on the Konya plains.

When we had down time at Konya, we took in a lot of Turkish history. The gem of Konya is the Mevlana Mausoleum, home of the "Whirling Dervishes." The Mevlana sect was a branch of the Muslim religion that was established in Konya for over 700 years. The "Green Mosque", now the Green Mausoleum or Museum, built in 1274 was home to the religion until 1925 when Turkish President Ataturk banned the religion but allowed the mosque to become a museum. The Whirling Dervishes were the ancient priests of the religion and now remained as performers of a major tourist attraction in Konya. They were allowed to perform for only two weeks each year, and, unfortunately that festival never coincided with any of my range officer tours at Konya. Other historical sites were sections of the "Old Wall" and the walled city gate that dated from 1000 AD. There were also archeological "digs" in and near the city that showed house foundations that were 9000 years old.

Wildlife at Incirlik was a strange experience for many of us. Each spring the airbase was overrun by snails that emerged from the winter soil. There were so many snails you could hear the crunches when you taxied an F-4 or drove a truck on pavement. The F-4 guy sent to mobile control picked hundreds of snails off the sides of the mobile control box before they could climb onto the glass windows.

The snails were food for the three-foot tall white cranes which came next. The cranes walked around the runway and taxiways with little regard for planes or cars. I think the cranes suffered a hearing problem in the frequency range of our jet engines because we could taxi right next to them and the cranes would not react or move an inch. During crane season, we changed tactical formations from wedge to a line as we crossed the Konya plains. If a low-level F-4 screamed across a marshy area it flushed hundreds of cranes, so you wanted your wingman to cross the marsh in line with you, not trailing behind, or even slightly offset to the side. To my knowledge, the squadron suffered only one crane strike in over three seasons and that crane beat up the wing and fuel tank, but was not ingested into an engine. A crane in the engine intake was not a happy scenario for pilot, crane or cleanup crew chief.

KONYA RANGE TOUR 2
Dick Hoover and I were pulling another week's tour as range officers on the Konya range when Adel suggested that we eat lunch at the Turkish Army Officers Mess in downtown Konya. As a captain in the Turkish Army Reserves, he could use the Mess. Thus, we were his guests as we walked up to the officers' mess, located on a hilltop overlooking much of Konya, paid for our meal and entered the dining area. The dining room looked like a church nave, with a high ceiling and rows of stained glass windows that were at least 20 feet tall on each side. Long tables, set for lunch, were on either side of a central aisle, and, at the head of the dining hall was a huge painting of Mustafa Kemal Ataturk, the father of modern Turkey and its first President. All the officers proceeded down the center aisle, stopped, nodded to Ataturk, and then moved to a table to be served lunch. Adel did the same, so Hoover and I followed suite with the respectful gesture. As we ate lunch, Adel pointed out that the NATO Army Corps Commanding General, a Turkish four-star general just entered to eat. He and his staff sat at the head of the dining room under President Ataturk's painting.

We finished a good lunch of lamb kabob, started to leave and reversed the reverence to Ataturk as we departed. I nodded and turned when a Turkish Major bolted from the head table, ran after us and said the General wanted to speak to us and Adel. We walked to the General's table as Adel turned ghostly white.

The General rose and asked: "Who are you, what brought you to "my" officer's mess, and why did you nod to President Ataturk?"

"Sir, we are American F-4 pilots from Incirlik CDI, operating the air to ground gunnery range outside Konya. Captain Adel invited us to eat in this mess and we were showing respect for the Turkish military customs that we observed."

The General looked at Adel, who I thought was on the verge of a massive heart attack, then turned to us,

"Thank you for respecting our customs."

We took that as dismissal, nodded to President Ataturk again and walked slowly out the center aisle. A little respect for other people's customs and culture goes a long way. Half way down the hill, Adel could finally breathe normally.

ADEL'S FAMILY
During this range tour, Hoover and I were invited to visit Adel's father-in-law's place in a small village on the outskirts of Konya. Hoov, Adel and I drove the blue USAF six-passenger pickup truck down a dirt road and finally arrived in a village of some twenty white-washed walled houses, three stores and one coffee house. Upon our arrival, dozens of children flocked around us, even as we slowly drove to the family home. I was fearful of accidently bumping one of the kids because we could feel the kids' excitement as they ran and yelled around the strange USAF truck with two Americans. We parked the vehicle and I asked Adel if we should take turns watching the truck since it was parked outside the family compound on the main street. Adel said it was very safe since we were visitors to a family there. The children admired the huge vehicle but protect it. It was a matter of honor in the village to protect travelers and their property. When we departed, we found only one dusty hand print on a side mirror. Some youngster wanted to admire himself.

From the street, all we could see of the family residence was a wide eight-foot tall white washed adobe wall with a wooden double door. We passed through the big doors and found the property went back almost 100 yards, filled with rows of apple and other fruit trees. The house was built against the wall on our right and used the same rough white plaster on the walls. A very old-looking gentleman, Adel's father-in-law, greeted us warmly and we needed no interpreter for that part. With Adel working as interpreter, we were invited into the house for something to eat. The house entrance opened into the main room, and, although the house had dirt floors, thickly layered rugs covered every floor in every room. When we entered, Hoov and I observed all the family remove their shoes by the front door (save the rugs), so we followed suit.

While the father-in-law ran the family and fruit business, there soon was little doubt that the interior and functions of the home were run by his wife. The matriarchal family included two daughters, a daughter-in-law and a wonderful, inquisitive year-old grandchild. Adel told us later that the mother was very impressed that Hoov and I took time to unlace and remove our clunky flying boots. We sat on huge cushions that surrounded the room as they served us apples and chi and we played with their granddaughter. Adel earned his pay as an interpreter since none of the family spoke English and my Turkish consisted of 20 words, at the max. We spent over an hour seated on the comfortable cushions discussing families, children, where we lived, and how often we moved.

Leaving came too soon and was quite touching as the grandmother and daughters individually said goodbye and they gave us three apples as gifts, acts which Adel said were exceptionally rare in a traditional Turkish family. We were very honored. On our squadron rotation two months later, I learned of the accidental death of Adel's brother-in-law and asked Adel to pass our regrets and condolences to the family. The family was not told directly that the man died, but that he was very seriously ill and the family must gather. When the family assembled, the news of the death was broken to all. In their culture, it was custom over expediency. Adel said the grandmother wept when she heard that the two Americans thought of their family. I felt the sense of loss by the three close-knit Turkish generations we met and by whom we were so warmly welcomed into their home. This cemented my opinion of the great and warm Turkish people, regardless of the conflicts created by politicians from either country.

Our squadron learned of two American college girls being held in the Adana jail for hashish possession. They travelled with a guy from Lebanon (the real-life subject of the movie "Midnight Express") when the hash was discovered by the Turkish authorities in his VW bus. The Squids and the other two 401st squadrons "adopted" the girls and provided supplies while they were in the Adana jail. There were no nice amenities in a Turkish jail unless the prisoner's family provided them. The TJ guys became "their family" as the two girls remained in the deplorable conditions for months before they were transferred to a jail in Ankara and out of reach of their USAF benefactors. The American Embassy picked up the task from that point.

'74 GREEK – TURKISH WAR

I was awakened by the loud boom of hard afterburner lights early on Saturday morning, 20 July 1974. Who the hell is flying early on Saturday morning? It was light, but the summer sun came up very early at Incirlik!

We soon discovered those were F-100s and F-104s; the Turks invaded Cyprus that morning and all their air support was flying out of Incirlik or refueling / rearming here if the sorties were flown from Konya. Turkish airspace was closed to all other aircraft and the Squids would not be flying for some time.

Headquarters US Air Force ordered an immediate stand down of our Nuclear Alert and the priority task was to pull the enabling plugs of the B-61 weapons and ship the plugs out of country. Then the guys on alert downloaded the actual bombs and the "silver bullets" were returned to the nuke storage area.

By Monday we were assembled in the theatre for a briefing by the Turkish Base commander, who said we were still their welcome guests, but we could not fly except to return to Torrejon in the near future. Our only real-world USAF tasking was to watch the takeoffs and landings of Turkish F-5s, RF-84s, F-100s and F-104s. It turned out there were now five Turkish fighter squadrons on Incirlik.

From the former nuke alert area, we had a full view of the takeoff/landing end of Runway 23. Each evening we went to the Detachment Command Post and made a secure phone report with tail numbers and flight counts to the NMCC at the Pentagon. We could tell by the returning numbers if the Turk fighters suffered losses. The Brits shot down one for violating Her Majesty's airspace at RAF Akrotiri on the far south of Cyprus. Due to false intelligence, the Turk fighters attacked and sank one of their own Navy's destroyers. We also learned two of their aircraft were downed by shrapnel when they flew through their own frag patterns.

Finally cleared to fly out to TJ, our F-4s needed to island hop home, with most flights going to NAS Sigonella, Italy. My flight came out a day later and missed the previous day's crappy weather as we landed at "Siggie" to refuel before heading home. The C-130s loaded with Squid gear and troops went home through various locations including Ramstein AB, NAS Sigonella and NAS Rota, Spain. It was roughly a month before the TJ F-4s returned to Incirlik.

PROMOTION AND DEPARTURE
In late 1975, a new Air Force promotion list for Major was released and I was on it. Not only on it, but I was on the Intermediate Schools list. The AF Personnel folks asked me to extend my TJ tour by six months to match my DEROS with the Air Command and Staff College schedule. Hell, yeah!! Make me fly F-4s for six more months before going to school. The down side was I had to pay for a promotion party at Incirlik because the list was released while the 613th was on rotation. I paid again for a Wing Promotion Party when I returned to Torrejon.

When July 1976 approached, we packed up the house at Royal Oaks and made transportation plans to get home. Claire and "Topher" had the option of travelling on civilian airlines, so I drove them to Barajas Airport in Madrid on 2 July to take an Iberia Airlines 747 ride to JFK airport in New York. I then drove back to Torrejon and caught an evening departure military charter plane to Philadelphia. My half-brother Bill Stevenson met Claire, Topher and baggage at JFK and drove them to his home over in NJ. My military charter landed hours later at Philadelphia and I entered the airport customs area with a helmet bag filled with bottles of excellent red and white wine. I told the customs inspector that was all I had to declare; he glanced into the helmet bag and sent me on my way with a cheerful "Welcome home." It was late and there were no flights or trains over to the opposite side of New Jersey, but I finally found a cabbie who would drive me to Bill's place for about sixty dollars: done deal!

I made it in time for a late dinner and we opened a bottle of excellent Spätläse wine, which tasted great even if a little warmer than desired. Two days later, we borrowed one of Bill's cars and headed north for a trip to see West Point, and then over to Boston for the arrival of the "Tall Ships" commemorating the 200th anniversary of our country. We drove up to Hanscom Field to see Captain John Roe, also an Air Force pilot, and his wife Lembi: one of Claire's best friends from her first years after college. John took us out to a lobster restaurant on the Maine coast where we dined on huge and delicious lobsters. The following day, we returned to Bill Stevenson's house and next day caught a flight to Dallas and on to Corpus Christi.

The highlight of the stop in Corpus was the two days we stayed at the beach house in Ingleside-On-The Bay and Topher got to fish with his Granddad. When it was time to leave, we were driven to Houston, picked up our car which arrived by ship from Europe and we began the drive to Maxwell AFB, Air Command and Staff College (ACSC), Auburn University grad school and all the academia I could stand. Hooah!

While I was having all this fun in Europe, over on this side of the Atlantic, twin Don completed SMU Law School in May of 1973, passed the Texas Bar exam in September and entered private law practice in Dallas.

SCHOOL AND STAFF

28

Back To School

Even in the safe confines of Maxwell Air Force Base in near west-side Montgomery, you could still detect the "old South" and the remains of segregation and discrimination. It was a culture shock to a lot of my classmates, and, particularly to some of our foreign exchange officers. In addition, the base possessed an atmosphere all its own due to a cottonseed plant just outside the main gate. When the wind was just right the fumes could be staggering.

I was lucky enough to get on-base housing in a two-bedroom unit on Catalpa Drive, close enough for me to walk to and from classes. The student on-base housing consisted of four blocks of long single-story row buildings on both sides of three streets and was constructed in WW II as aviation cadet barracks. Now each building was divided into three, four or five family units, with a narrow common front lawn that was allegedly just large enough to hold a cadet formation in the barracks days. The ancient windows were a crank open type, a 1950s upgrade. At least the windows opened on cooler days to assist the inadequate air conditioning. The bathroom was barracks-like black and white check tile floors with a kick handle coverless toilet. Interior walls were moved, bathrooms installed and kitchens provided, but you could see the outline of the original floor beams and ceiling posts under the paint. During our 13 month stay in these quarters, we did get one upgrade; contractors punched out the old windows and put in real double-pane windows. It was a noisy and disruptive time for us. As the ACSC and Air War College student's families checked out in 1977, our quarters and those on our block were receiving an upgraded kitchen and bathroom. By 2005 all the cadet barracks / student family housing was demolished and only an open park area remains there inside the base perimeter.

Maxwell, although still having an active runway, was an academic campus. No aircraft were assigned there. The campus was home to the Air Force's Squadron Officers School, ACSC, the Air War

College, the Chaplain School and several smaller Air Force schools and think tanks, all arranged around a huge circle with the library in the center.

Attending ACSC, while simultaneously working on a Master's degree from Auburn University, made being a "student" a full-time job. While at Torrejon, I was warned by a WSO, Major Humberto "Bert" Charneco, that the combination was an endurance test. However, it was the most efficient way to get my Air Force Intermediate Service School out of the way and get my graduate degree. Bert was so right! Our daily schedule for the academic year was ACSC class from 0800 to 1600; try to grab dinner and read; then Grad school from six to 10 pm. Then you went home to study for the next day. Living in very tight quarters and the hours required to complete my school work prompted us to purchase a great recliner and reading lamp for the partitioned corner of our living room that became my study. Claire became used to coming in after 0100 and finding me dead asleep in the recliner with two or three books laid out on my lap. By Thanksgiving break, there was no doubt left in our military minds that the dual course of study was an exhaustive endurance contest.

The ACSC student body of approximately 450 students from all US Services and numerous foreign countries was divided into 24 seminars. The Seminar was the academic and social center of your time at ACSC and the students were shuffled twice to ensure a more cross-cultural experience and to meet more classmates. Friday night was our sole social time and we enjoyed seminar or class gatherings at the O'Club or pot luck dinners with our seminar mates. Saturday was often research for both schools and lots of reading in the Air University Library from 10:00 am to 9:00 pm. For those ACSC students that were dealing with classified information in class or for their Research Paper, the AU Library contained a secure reading area and secure storage facilities up to Top Secret documents. Classified research / writing was to be done in the secure area and the documents remained in your file folder when you departed.

With Chris in day care, Claire started as a volunteer at the Montgomery Museum of Art. After learning of her expertise in the visual arts, she was hired as the Interim Curator of Education. Claire spent a lot of evenings at the museum for openings and other events. It was an education in many ways, such as the fact that the Montgomery Museum just recently began to allow black citizens to come into their city's Museum. It was 1976, people! (Maybe not yet in Montgomery).

To keep flying, I joined the Maxwell AFB Aero Club, primarily because they had a T-34 aircraft in the club. I previously flew the T-34 in the Edwards AFB Aero Club. This was a tandem seat, former Air Force and Navy trainer that could be flown like a fighter. During the school holiday breaks, I flew with a stick in my right hand and throttle in my left hand. For fun, I started a shallow dive at Prattville, Alabama, and redlined the airspeed for the overhead pattern on Runway 15 at Maxwell. After yanking and banking through the patterns on one flight, my lovely passenger, Claire, said I flew like I was "part of the plane." That was a great compliment from my pilot wife.

We experienced quite a scare when Christopher went missing one afternoon, along with Major Ron Hix's son. They could not be found anywhere. We finally called the base Security Police who searched the base. A brief time later as darkness fell, an Alabama farmer drove up with the two boys in his pick-up truck. We discovered that the two boys followed a dog under the base perimeter fence and down to I-65. The farmer picked up the two as they were trying to hitchhike back to base. He figured that was neither a good place nor a great plan for a pair of five-year-old boys. God bless the "good ol' boy" farmers in this world.

For the first semester of ACSC I was assigned to Seminar 14, facilitated by Major Ron Hartwig. Ron ran a superb and challenging seminar and I soon learned you can learn more from your classmates than even a good syllabus. My classmates in Seminar 14 were officers from the Army, Air Force, a DOD Civilian, and one foreign officer from Uganda, Major Mayella Kikella, who brought his French-speaking family to Montgomery. We felt sorry for this huge black officer and his family in Montgomery, Alabama, and helped in as many ways as possible. Claire spoke more French than any other seminar member or wife, so she became translator and cultural advisor to Kikella's family. Following ACSC, Major Kikella went back to be the Chief of Personnel for the Uganda Air Force. In November three of the captains, including me, pinned on our major's leaves.

A true major accomplishment was completing the Auburn Master of Public Administration program. The MPA program was tough but fun because everyone in my Auburn section, save one, was a non-traditional student. We all came with real world experiences and our professors learned as much from the students as we did from the courses. One classmate was a National Security Council briefer, and, besides being exceptionally good at "tap dancing" as a speaker, he laid out a lot of background on national events.

243

In our ACSC classes we mixed Army, Israelis, Saudis and characters like Lieutenant Commander Dick Marcinko, later to start up and command Seal Team 6. Unfortunately, Dick was court martialed for over-exuberance in supplying non-government equipment for Team 6 with government funds. Great military speakers included General officers like Robin Olds and Colonel Charlie Beckwith. Recognizing ACSC student names from the class roster – mine from our time working together in Vietnam – Colonel Beckwith invited me to lunch with a most "unique" cross-spectrum of his former associates. Lunch included operators, shooters, high level spooks and super classified electronic intelligence spooks. In the summer of 1977, I was designated a "DG", only this time it meant "Did Graduate" from ACSC. The real highlight of two graduations was walking the Auburn stage with my orange undergraduate cape (Tennessee orange rather than Texas burnt orange because they could not locate a Texas-colored cape) and trading it for an Orange and Blue Auburn University Master's degree cape.

Finishing ACSC and graduate school, I tried to get a job under then Major General Chuck Donnelly, our former 401st Wing Commander, but there were no jobs available in his Directorate at that time. Chuck Donnelly earned his fourth star and returned to Europe as the CINC/USAFE in August of 1984. We just left USAFE for Shaw AFB at that time and I was sorry I missed him. General Donnelly retired in 1987 and died of cancer on July 3, 1994.

29

Joint Duty

Completing Command and Staff College and my Master Degree program at Auburn University, I was placed in the assignment pool for a staff job somewhere. I politicked for an Air Staff job with General Donnelly in Air Force Plans and Operations (AF/XO). I found a potential job, but suddenly Donnelly moved to another branch of the Air Staff and I lost the slot to somebody else loved by the new boss. So just before graduation I received orders to Headquarters, Tactical Air Command and the Air-Land Applications Agency (ALFA Agency) on Langley AFB in Virginia. I assumed that somebody looked at my previous life in the Army and thought I was a great match for a joint job. ALFA Agency consisted of Army and Air Force officers, while the Director position alternated annually between an Army colonel and an Air Force colonel. Our offices were on the first floor of the former base jail house on the east end of the base. We still had bars on all the windows! My first Director was Army Colonel Bob Zargan, a great artillery colonel who came from TRADOC headquarters and lived in on-post housing at nearby Ft. Monroe. A year later he was succeeded by AF Colonel Bill Porter, and, in my last year at ALFA, Army Colonel Sid Britt. Each of the Directors was a different personality, but all understood the concept of "Jointness" between the services.

As we moved from tiny base quarters at Maxwell, we were eagerly looking to buy our first house on the civilian economy. Hampton was an OK city, but my new Langley peers seemed to prefer the rural atmosphere and great schools of York County to the north of Langley, much of it on the western shore of Chesapeake Bay. Major Marlin "Kitch" Kitchens and his wonderful bride, Mary, were our sponsors at ALFA and they eased the transition into Langley, the TAC Staff and house hunting. We stayed with the Kitchens at their house for our first three days at Langley, while we worked our way up the waiting list to get into the Temporary Living Quarters (TLQ) on base.

After the move into the TLQ, we began house hunting in earnest, visiting some of Hampton / Newport News, but concentrating on the York County market. We eventually bought our first house at 505 Yorkville Rd, in Grafton, Virginia, an eighteen-minute commute to base for me. Claire held no doubts after we viewed the house: "I have a good feeling about this place. This is the one." The house was an extremely well-constructed brick house of 1600 square feet on a corner lot. The small street loop that ran beside our house went to the water's edge, a block away, and experienced little automobile traffic. Christopher was enrolled into the first grade in a great elementary school in the York County school district and we soon loved the neighborhood, including the eclectic group of neighbors (Army, Navy, Air Force, NASA, Corporate pilot, physicians and blue-collar workers).

This was to be an amazingly stable Air Force tour with regular hours that allowed me to be involved in soccer with Chris and even work as a flight instructor with a Boy Scout Air Explorer post at the local airport. Claire was pleased to be out of the hustle as Museum Curator in Montgomery and was soon into tennis, and, before long, enrolled in Graduate School at the College of William and Mary. Heaven knows she carried the load while I was pounding out grad school in Alabama, so now it was her turn to be a grad student. The College of William and Mary is a great and demanding school and Claire knuckled down to the courses and an internship in her study of Museum Education.

The two commands assigning officers to ALFA, the US Army Training and Doctrine Command (TRADOC) and the Tactical Air Command (TAC), were commanded by two gruff and demanding generals. General Robert Dixon at TAC and General William DePuy at TRADOC earned reputations for chewing up and spitting out briefers and staff members. Having to brief either general was usually an unpleasant task. However, when the two generals met together for joint matters (ALFA's specialty) I was amazed how civil they were to the two staffs. I think they didn't want to embarrass the other service or show favoritism about whose butt they chewed. General Dixon was followed a year later by General Wilber L. Creech, a breath of fresh air. General DePuy was soon succeeded by General Donn Starry, a tank commander to the bone and not at all impressed with the protocols of formal staff work. General Starry didn't care how you got a task done; just get it done. Most of the time the TAC and TRADOC staffs worked well together and rarely did real parochialism rear its ugly head. ALFA's "real" day-to-day bosses were Major General Fred Haeffner at TAC Plans and the Deputy Chief of Staff for Combat Development and

Doctrine at TRADOC, MG Jack Woodmansee. Maj Gen Haeffner was a hard-core fighter pilot and handled "Jointness" with a kind of benign neglect, letting ALFA do its own thing. MG Woodmansee was a bit more involved. As an Army aviator and probably one of the most knowledgeable gunship pilots in the Army, he displayed an exceptional grasp of combined Air Force and Army aerial weapons integration, and worked the "Joint" aspect well. Ten years later during of my tour as TAC Director of Joint Matters (XPJ), DCSDoc was BG Rudy Ostovich. General Ostovich enjoyed a close and personal relationship with the TAC XP, Maj Gen Mike Ryan because Ostovich's son was attending the Air Force Academy while Ryan's son was attending West Point. Jointness!

In addition to my regular duties, I enrolled in the National War College extension courses and in July 1978, I graduated from the National Defense University's National Security Management Course. It seemed like I was studying forever and now I wondered what I should be reading after dinner each evening. But we adjust to the many changes in a military life.

JAWS or JAAT
Other than a few "all other duties as assigned" tasks, most of my work at ALFA revolved around three projects, First, the final development and publishing of the tactics and procedures for the Joint Air Attack Team (JAAT), an integrated and closely synchronized employment of A-10s or other Close Air Support assets, artillery, and attack helicopters. This was MG Woodmansee's baby from inception. The original name of these tactics was Joint Attack Weapons Systems (JAWS). I thought that was a more accurate description of the concept; *but* a certain Hollywood corporation threatened major law suits if we used the JAWS title. Hollywood jerks! Little did I know at that time, I was to participate in the most realistic JAAT ever held, later in Europe.

Second, the White House Office of Management and Budget (OMB) issued a directive (A-109) that required a quantitative analysis in support of all existing and future weapons systems. That started an absolute panic to provide supporting analyses for TAC and TRADOC systems. Maj Gen Haeffner was then succeeded as XP by Maj Gen Larry Welch, an amazing intellectual survivor of a tour in the Pentagon's office of Studies and Analysis: the perfect man for this task. To support these studies, I was sent to the Army's Operations Research / System Analysis (ORSA) course and in short order I became a number-crunching ORSA puke. Our first big joint study was Joint Defense Suppression, often called Suppression of Enemy Air Defenses (SEAD), led by Col James Jones, the Vice Commander of the 35th TFW at George AFB and a former WSO in "Wild Weasels." This was a true Joint effort with weapons systems experts providing inputs on their weapons and all that being fed into a mathematical logic tree that calculated the effectiveness of the systems. This analysis would lead to a relative ranking of weapons effectiveness on the battlefield and drive the budget support for those systems.

TAC found a lieutenant colonel in the Tidewater, with a PhD in math, and he became the creator of the joint statistical analysis model. The Lt Col was an analysis genius but sometimes he got a bit wrapped up in his work. During one heated discussion in front of General Creech and most of the study participants, our numbers hero decided to add a branch to the logic tree for additional weapons analysis. The logic tree was being projected on the wall in General Creech's main briefing room, but our Lt Col whipped out a felt tip marker and proceeded to expand the graphic onto the TAC/CC's wall, explaining the logic tree changes. You could hear the study players take a collective deep breath and hold it. No explosion! General Creech waited until the explanation was completed and calmly said "Colonel Jones, may I see you in my office after this meeting?" When the projector was turned off, there were the added logic limbs and associated weights, still on the General's white wall. All traces were gone the next morning, and, fortunately Colonel Jones and our PhD brain kept their jobs.

After the team loaded all the variables into our equations, we rented the best computers in the country, the Los Alamos nuclear research systems, to simulate a major confrontation and to condense 7-day, 14-day and 30-day wars into win / loss / cost effectiveness data. Armed with the initial analysis, Colonel Jones' team briefed the TAC/CC where we received a shock. The Air Force EF-111 electronic warfare aircraft did not do well in the big picture analysis and would most likely suffer budget cuts to their fleet. General Creech said that was unacceptable and directed us to *"Go back and change the numbers!"* to keep the EF-111s viable in the budget. The team did as directed and General Creech's belief in the effectiveness of airborne radar jamming proved correct when the EF-111s became a vital part in air attacks against high threat targets during Desert Storm in 1991. Ask me about CNN's Bernie Shaw, the "FAC of Bagdad", and EF-111s.

For my third project, I was the coordinating officer and scribe for the meetings of the TAC Commander and the TRADOC Commanding General. This was referred to as the "8-star meeting." The process was much like herding cats! It required coordinating the two four-star general's schedules and dealing with the pettiness of the senior staff members on both sides: The staffers that did not want their boss to hold any meeting that they could not attend or offer an opinion regardless of how little the Deputy Chief of Staff (DCS) knew about joint operations.

We put on a lot of traveling "dog and pony briefings" as part of ALFA's "spread the Joint concept." Fellow ALFA member Army LTC Tom Undercoffer and I travelled to the DC beltway to brief the DARPA (Defense Advanced Research Projects Agency) staff on a concept developed by TAC and TRADOC titled "Air Defense in the Forward Area." We were doing an alternating briefer show to the DARPA commander, Army Major General Julius W. Becton, Jr. After my first part of the presentation, MG Becton never took his stare off me, even when Tom was briefing. He was boring a hole in my Air Force pilot wings, CIB and master parachutist badge. At the completion of the presentation I asked if the audience had any questions. MG Becton asked:

"Major, where do I know you from?"

"I don't think our paths have crossed before, Sir."

After a few questions from the peanut gallery, MG Becton thanked us and the show was over. On our drive back to Langley, Tom asked "What the hell was that all about?"

"I have no clue, Tom. I'm sure I have never met an Army General Becton."

A week later I was talking to twin brother Don and when I mentioned the DARPA episode, Don blurted, "That was Julie Becton, the lieutenant colonel I served with in Vietnam. Becton was my Battalion Commander when our C&C chopper was shot down, forcing Becton, me and others to spend a night in a dry rice paddy awaiting rescue."

Seems General Becton thought I was Captain Don Stevenson, his Fire Support Officer in the 2nd/17th Cavalry. My Air Force blue uniform, pilot wings and CIB totally confused him. Don asked for Becton's address and later sent him a congratulatory note and explanation about the "weird" briefer. Julie Becton retired as a Lieutenant General and from 1989 – 1994, served as the fifth president of his alma mater, Prairie View A&M University. School history records indicate the Becton was the first Prairie View A&M graduate to become a flag rank officer.

On several occasions, the 8-star meeting between TAC and TRADOC escalated and I became the Secretary to "20 Star" meetings. That meant the addition of four-star players from CINCLANT, FORCECOM and the Deputy Commandant of the Marine Corps. Those expanded meetings took place at TRADOC's Fort Monroe, VA; Commander In Chief Atlantic (CINCLANT) Norfolk, VA headquarters; and the FBI Academy in Quantico, Virginia. I had fantastic secretarial support in documenting the Eight Star or Twenty Star meetings in our ALFA civilian, Ms. Roz Forrest, who came to us from Army resources. Roz could take dictation in shorthand, interpret my scratchy notes and have the typed meeting minutes on the street at an amazing speed.

Seafood was a staple in the Tidewater area and an absolute must for visitors. Colonel David Forgan was the Torrejon 401st Wing Vice-Commander in Spain under Colonel Chuck Donnelly, and, since David and his wife Shirley were recently assigned to the TAC staff, we asked them out to our house for a casual dinner. Shirley travelled to Paris on the same Torrejon Officers Wives trip that we took and we'll never forget Shirley's reaction while walking the Place Pigalle with us and revealing her naiveté of such things as "working girls."

As I came home that evening, I was alerted by Claire's screams from the kitchen. She purchased a large bucket of live crabs to prepare for dinner but somehow knocked over the bucket and the large crabs were scrambling across the kitchen floor. Claire was yelling from her escape position atop the kitchen counter. She was most unappreciative of my laughter as I rounded up crabs so she could continue preparation for the Forgan's dinner. She took immense pleasure dropping the former escapees into a pot of boiling water. Claire and Shirley Forgan, a fun animated personality, were closer friends than I was with Dave (a rank thing).

T-39 FLYING

At this point in my career, I was well behind my peers in Air Force flying experience, (my 1000+ hours of civilian flying time did not count) so in 1978, TAC rated assignment folks said I could fly the T-39 Sabreliner as an attached pilot to the Military Airlift Command (MAC) detachment at Langley. The T-39s were antiques compared to the then current civilian VIP transport, Lears, Falcons, or Bombardiers. Most of our T-39 aircraft were 1960 something vintage, no autopilot, no thrust reversers nor antiskid brakes. This was a leap backward from some of the factory-fresh F-4Es I flew at TJ. My T-39 time started with a Sabreliner checkout in St Louis at Flight Safety International for systems / flight simulator training. That was followed by five days at Scott AFB, Illinois, to fly the T-39; and then it was back to Langley as a new T-39 copilot. The flying was much like modern corporate jet flying, for me mostly on weekends to support high ranking government officials. Usually starting the day by flying up to Andrews AFB, we made pick-ups and deliveries of VIPs at major civilian airports such as Atlanta, New Orleans, Dallas Love, Kansas City, Boston Logan, to name a few. Typical of the corporate world, the civilian Fixed Base Operators (FBOs) offered us steaks, shrimp, lobsters, use of cars, steak dinners, or fruit baskets to refuel the T-39 at their facility. Think we ever accepted the offers? I flew as a copilot for almost a year and then upgraded to Aircraft Commander (AC), so I could have more say in operating my aircraft.

An AC checkout was a written exam, a local training flight to fly every conceivable emergency approach and landing, and then a one or two-day passenger-carrying line mission. After passing all phases of my check ride and blessed as an Aircraft Commander, I launched out to carry VIPs. A month later I was notified my AC check ride was invalidated. Get this: The Flight Examiner (FE) at Headquarters MAC was overdue a check ride when he gave a checkride to our FE at Langley. That invalidated the Langley FEs status as an FE and invalidated any check rides given at Langley, including my AC check. So, the Langley T-39 detachment brought in an FE from Andrews AFB and my check was done again. Fun, Fun, Fun. I was soon approved to fly generals and senators again.

I admit that I needed to explain my actions to Mother MAC at the Scott AFB Airlift Center on a few occasions. One "Call MAC to explain" flight was a trip to carry five high ranking DOD civilians from Eglin AFB, Florida, to Andrews AFB. From there we were to hop down to Langley and close out the day. Waiting in the Eglin passenger lounge for the DVs, I met a young captain F-15 Eagle Driver who was trying to get a hop back to his squadron, 27 TFS, at Langley. I was headed that way, but with a full load for the T-39. When the DV party arrived, there were only four passengers. One of the scheduled passengers stayed behind for another meeting. We started the right engine when I asked the senior passenger if we could take a stand-by on the trip to Andrews and then on to Langley. He said he had no problem with that, so I told my co-pilot to start the left engine and I dashed up the red VIP carpet to the passenger terminal.

I found my F-15 pilot in the lobby and told him to grab his bag and come with me. I trotted past the Passenger Service counter and told the NCO to add this Captain to my manifest. The NCO sputtered about MAC procedures as the captain and I headed for my Sabreliner. The Eagle Driver took the vacant seat in the far rear, I closed the steps and door as I came in and my copilot started to taxi as I strapped into my seat. We were gone! By the time we got home to Langley, Mother MAC had already called with a complaint about bypassing passenger procedures, so I explained to our T-39 Ops Officer and then some Major at MAC about critical decision making, not wasting time, and, maximizing seat utilization. I never heard about it again.

A side benefit to flying the Sabreliner was taking part in an Air Force pilot's program called "Volant Spouse" in which pilots could take their wives (at Langley we were still an all-male T-39 Detachment) along on a local training flight. For the wives of the attached TAC staff pilots who had flown only fighters, "Volant Spouse" let wives see what flying a jet, even a Sabreliner, was like. Claire, being a pilot and a lover of flying, jumped at the opportunity. We flew over Virginia, then up the Shenandoah Valley, to DC and to the Chesapeake Bay in a 1962 model Sabreliner – not exactly state of the art in 1979, but still doing the job.

Climbing out of Eglin AFB, in the T-39 on a hot, cloudy summer evening, we began to see Saint Elmo's fire forming on our aircraft's nose. Saint Elmo's fire is static electricity that becomes visible as a pale blue or white wiggly line across a surface. Sailors saw it aloft on their sails and rigging but it is rare in aircraft. Our blue electric line slowly wiggled up the aircraft nose, up the windscreen divider and then into the cockpit. It spread across the top of the windscreen and moved rearward across the overhead panel. Visible static electricity moving across my circuit breaker panel did not seem to be a promising idea. I reached up to the circuit breaker panel with a gloved hand to touch the electric charge. It was a momentary very slight tickle. When our T-39 climbed through the clouds and broke into clear skies, the St. Elmo's fire began to retreat and soon dissipated. Spooky!

One of the civilian pilots I came to know was a close neighbor in Yorktown and the chief pilot for East Coast Tenneco flight operations. In the Spring of 1980, he offered me a corporate Falcon flying job; just two days after the Air Force offered me an A-10 flying slot to Europe. I immediately accepted the A-10 slot to England (after consulting my wife, of course). Timing is everything.

A-10 WARTHOG

30

Back To The Cockpit

In 1980, I was in the pool for a fighter assignment but the F-4 was a dying weapon system, so I tried to snivel my way into the F-16, F-15 or A-10 (the newer fighters). The A-10 was the winner for Major Stevenson and I was off to training. One of the few smart training moves TAC instituted was the short course conversion to a new fighter aircraft for previously qualified fighter jocks. My A-10 qualification course was a conversion rather than a full-up training program in a fighter. The conversion assumed that the pilot could recall basics of bombing, tactical formations, refueling, etc. Fortunately, I fell in that conversion category, so I went through the *"Readers Digest"* version of A-10 training and avoided being treated like a FNG in the cockpit.

HOLLOMAN AFB - RECURRENCY
I started at Holloman AFB, in the White Sands of New Mexico, north-east of El Paso, Texas. TAC conducted Lead-In Fighter Training (LIFT) program for brand new fighter-pilots-to-be and recurrency for "old" fighter pilots at Holloman. I was required to get one jet recurrency flight before reporting to A-10 training at DM. The recurrency flight was part of the standard "pipeline" for pilots coming from staff jobs or schools who had not flown a fighter type aircraft in over a year. Flying the T-39 Sabreliner did not count since the T-39 was a transport (executive jet) as far as TAC was concerned. This recurrency stop at Holloman turned out to be an enjoyable mini-vacation. At Holloman, I encountered numerous pilots and WSOs that I knew in F-4s, either at George AFB or in Europe. One of my former flight members from TJ, Don "Sweet Pea" Rupert, AKA "Rupee", was an IP in the Recurrency Program, and, upon seeing my name on the inbound student list he called me at Langley and offered to be my IP for the two days of academics, simulator and the one required T-38 flight. I gladly accepted. Don left TJ for a remote tour to Korea in the F-4 and was back at Holloman as an IP for just over a year, accompanied by his wife Linda and their two daughters.

On Sunday, April 7th, I loaded up two months of clothes and flying gear and made the bag drag from Norfolk to El Paso by airliner. At El Paso, I found a little Piper six-seat "airliner" for the hop up to Holloman. I helped with baggage loading on the ramp at El Paso in exchange for a right seat co-pilot flight to the Alamogordo, NM airport. This was a *small* airline! At Holloman, I checked into the BOQ and started to explore the base. The temperature was very pleasant and the dry desert air felt great after the humidity of the Virginia Tidewater.

On Monday morning, I met Don at the 434th Squadron. This was a flashback: my F-4 RTU squadron at George AFB was the 434th Tac Fighter Squadron and now I was a two-day student in the 434th FTS at Holloman. The F-4 434th was deactivated in the post-Vietnam drawdown and then reactivated at Holloman when the lead-in program was started. The 434th TFS thus became the 434th FTS (Flight Training Squadron), and, as of 2017, was assigned to Laughlin AFB, Texas. Monday, Don guided me through academics and T-38 simulator training and on Tuesday morning we set out on my real recurrency flight. The sole requirement to make me a "legal" pilot for the A-10 short course was to make one satisfactory landing in a high-performance jet aircraft. After flying in shirtsleeves in the large two-place cockpit of the Sabreliner, I felt a bit strange strapped into the small cockpit of the T-38 wearing a helmet and oxygen mask again. But I loved the control stick in my right hand and throttles in my left, versus the Sabreliner's control wheel in my left hand and the throttles in my right hand.

Despite hazy memories of the T-38 from eight years prior at UPT and with Don's coaching from the back seat, by the time I taxied a mile to the end-of-runway check area for Runway 25, it was coming back to me. For an F-4 and T-39 pilot the visibility from the front seat of the T-38 was amazing. I forgot how great the visibility was in the T-38, compared to the F-4. I enjoyed a glass canopy all around without large metal canopy rails and windscreen bows. And, I did not have a huge instrument panel and HUD in front of me. I could see again! We launched out (Hey, two afterburners!) into the training airspace over the White Sands area to do some airwork and I could get the feel of the plane. God, it felt good to fly an airplane again, to bend it around corners pulling 4 – 5 Gs, and to just do loops and aileron rolls because I could. Returning to Holloman, Don let me make two touch & go landings and the final full stop landing. I finished the TAC recurrency syllabus by late Tuesday morning. I did not have to sign in at DM until the following Monday, so I could either go to DM early and sit on my butt, **or,** I could stay at Holloman for the rest of this week and "sandbag" flights in the

IP upgrade squadron. That was a no brainer for a fighter pilot; I extended my BOQ reservation through Friday night and got five more flights over the next three days.

Wednesday through Friday, I flew as "dumb student" in the 434th FTS (in the squadron's additional role of IP training squadron for T-38 IPs). I got to fly with Don and Karl Henderson, a former F-4 pilot and assistant weapons officer I knew from Incirlik, Turkey. My Thursday morning sortie with Karl and Don turned rather memorable. I flew front seat, with Don as IP in my back seat, and we were doing basic fighter maneuvers against Karl and an upgrading IP in his back seat.

The first engagement was a fairly vanilla follow-the-leader exercise. The second engagement, however, became serious; the student IP set us up as a 90-degree beam encounter, and, after visual acquisition, Karl and I both aggressively turned in to pass head-on. I continued to turn opposite Karl in a climbing, circling 1v1, trying to get a height advantage, that evolved into a maneuver called a vertical rolling scissors. Pig-headed, neither of the two former F-4 jocks would give in as we corkscrewed our way upward, now in full afterburner, on opposite sides of the circle, canopy to canopy, getting closer, both of us running out of airspeed and ideas. We were now about 400 feet apart, noses up, and climbing through 43,000 feet with less than 80 knots indicated airspeed. I was about to break off the fight when it abruptly ended with Karl's double engine compressor stall.

I was looking up and over my left shoulder at Karl when his two J-85 turbojet engines decided they needed more air flow than they were getting through the compressors. Karl's T-38 was a sunlit, brilliant, white rocket in front of a royal blue sky. At this altitude, there was no pollution and the sky was unbelievably clear and beautiful. Karl's white T-38 seemed to shudder and belched a white smoke ring from the front and rear of each engine. Despite Karl's problems, I was mesmerized by the beauty of the white aircraft emitting small grey smoke rings, in the bright sunshine against the blue sky. I gently applied slight pressure on my left rudder pedal, while ensuring I didn't move the throttles or control stick. Passing 50 knots airspeed, the nose of my aircraft slowly sliced left toward the horizon, while, from the back seat Don's only comment was a quiet: "Gently!" Karl radioed "Devil Flight Knock It Off, Knock It Off!", dropped the nose of his aircraft and started the checklist for "Restart - engine failure in flight". Being a fighter pilot first and never willing to give up a good fight, I slid behind his steeply gliding aircraft, lined him up in my gun sight and radioed "Guns, Guns on the gliding T-38. Devil Two copies Knock It Off."

Down below 20,000 feet, Karl got both engines restarted, and, because of possible engine damage due to high internal temperatures in the stall / restart process, we returned to Holloman for Karl's precautionary landing. Rupee and I flew chase on Karl's T-38 to his landing and then used our extra fuel to fly one GCA pattern and two VFR patterns. When we gathered back in the squadron for mission debrief, Karl was sorry the mission ended the way it did. We discussed the differences between fighting against a new lieutenant and an experienced F-4 air-to-air puke. I was going to learn that lesson from the other end in two years when I flew the A-10 against two experienced fighter pilots after training only new First Lieutenant Hog Drivers for a while. Karl didn't even mention my "guns" call after he flamed out because he knew in real combat that would happen. Don and I did not stay for Karl's debrief of his student IP, but I knew that it was going to be detailed and hard-nosed with lots of hand gestures.

I sniveled another Thursday flight and one last T-38 ride on Friday morning. Friday evening, I dined at the O'Club with Don and Linda Rupert and did drinks at the bar as we renewed our friendship. Saturday morning, Don and Linda drove me to the Alamogordo airport for the six-place Piper aircraft that started me on the trip to DM. Again, I loaded my own baggage, and, this time I got to fly from the co-pilot's seat across the desert to El Paso International Airport to connect with my "big" airline flight to Tucson.

DAVIS-MONTHAN AFB AND "HOG HOLLOW"
I signed into Davis-Monthan AFB and the student BOQ known as "Hog Hollow." On the end of the BOQ facing the flight line was painted a three-story high mural of two A-10s attacking an armor unit. The A-10 was a single seat aircraft, so IPs taught and evaluated from a chase plane flying formation off the "student". I was assigned to the 333rd TFS "Lancers" and my primary IP was Captain Jack Guris, with whom I flew 12 of the 19 A-10 transition sorties. Our class in the 333rd was 14 pilots and we were all experienced fighter pilots (10 majors), mostly from F-4s. The new pilots straight from UPT went through a 10-ride syllabus at Holloman for the Fighter Lead-In Program, unlike my one required flight. At DM, the new fighter pilots' syllabus was at least twice the time as the experienced fighter pilots program. I recognized several of my classmates as peers from the TAC Staff and a couple from the Pentagon.

The days at DM were filled with A-10 academics and flights. If we went to academics in the morning, we flew in the afternoon or vice versa. Tucson in the late Spring was already *hot*. This was before the days of covered aircraft parking and the Hogs sat out on the concrete ramp and baked in the sun. We wore gloves to look but not touch the metal on the A-10 while doing our pre-flight inspections. Even the cushion on your ejection was uncomfortably hot unless a smart crew chief covered the seat with a towel until the pilot climbed into the cockpit. We left the aircraft's canopies up during taxi, arming and even onto the runway because the air conditioning in the Hog couldn't effectively cool the cockpit until you reached high engine RPM and airflow into the aircraft AC system. We closed the canopies just before engine run-up and takeoff to avoid the rapid temperature rise and sweat bath that ensued.

I became a certified "Hog Driver" on April 24, 1980, when I flew my first A-10 transition sortie with Jack Guris as my chase pilot. The Hog was a dream to fly, kinda like a 35,000 pound Cessna 210. But, I still had a lot to learn about this aircraft. On a refueling sortie I forgot to flip the A/C switch to "On" before takeoff and within 30 seconds I knew something was wrong. Jeez, it was hot! I looked at the left panel and saw the A/C switch in "Off." I flipped it outboard to "On", and, with a loud "whump" sound, the cooler air flow started and the temperature dropped. This was just a case of "Read The Friggin Check List", often referred to by pilots as "RTFCL."

Compared to the T-38, the Hog presented even greater visibility from the cockpit. In the F-4, the canopy rail was about even with the top of my shoulders. In the A-10, the canopy wrapped around a raised ejection seat and the canopy rails were down even with the top of your hips. You can turn far enough to see over 180 degrees to the rear. You could turn left to see the right vertical tail and vice versa. The Hog provided great visibility in all directions, important in low level combat or in air-to-air fights.

As training progressed, we flew Low Altitude Tactical Navigation (LATN) across the desert to find obscure turn points. One of the IPs favorite turn points was a dilapidated white Volkswagen car shell next to a dirt road junction stuck in the middle of nowhere. Weapons delivery training progressed from controlled gunnery ranges to tactical targets in the desert. I took a while to get back in the bombing groove, but I immediately fell in love with the 30 millimeter GAU-8 Gatling gun on the A-10. I developed a good feel for direct fire and was always either number one or two in Squadron Strafe competitions.

An interesting change for an F-4 driver was the air refueling of an A-10. The air refueling receptacle on the F-4 was located on the aircraft spine behind the cockpits; the tanker's boom operator plugged in his boom to pump gas, but the pilot could not actually see the procedure. The refuel receptacle on the A-10 was mere inches in front of the pilot's windscreen. Any slight movement by the A-10 or boom operator sent the nozzle waving around just in front of the canopy glass and the pilot. My first A-10 Tanker mission was a bit unnerving, watching the boom nozzle in front of my windscreen. Another surprise was the free window wash from fuel spray upon disconnect. When the boom disconnected from the receptacle immediately in front of my windscreen, the residual fuel in the boom escaped and covered the canopy. For a second I was blind, much like trying to drive in a torrential rain storm. Only I was flying just a few feet from the boom and not far below the tanker. That part of A-10 refueling took a bit of getting used to. A-10 drivers learned to refuel with a bit of nose down trim on the aircraft: Like the F-4, just one click down to ensure separation from the boom and tanker at disconnect. Most tanker boomers made a very quick and significant boom retraction after disconnecting to get away from the blind A-10 pilot.

DESERT ONE REPERCUSSIONS
In the last week of April, my Hog Driver class was receiving our weekly intelligence briefing from a skinny Intelligence major, when he announced that there was an attempted US raid in Iran to free the American hostages in Tehran. The raid went badly with loss of aircraft and lives in an accident on the ground. The ground troops involved were Army Special Forces and more details would be forthcoming. Well, Major Stevenson raised his hand and asked, "Was the Special Forces commander a Colonel Sydnor or a Colonel Beckwith?"

Looking surprised and suddenly nervous, the major replied, "I can't say," and completed his briefing. Thirty minutes later, the same Intelligence major returned to our classroom with two Security Policemen and asked: "Major Stevenson, will you come with us? We need to talk."

We moved into the Intel office; the Sky Cops guarded the door and, inside, the major wanted to know: "How did you know the name of the SF mission commander when that information is very highly classified?"

I briefly went through my history with those two officers, my Special Forces tour, and explained the Special Operations world was small. I stated I kept in touch with and even lunched with Colonel Beckwith at ACSC at Maxwell. I further explained the logic of my thoughts: in my opinion, there were only three likely SF commanders for an operation of that size and type, and I knew where one of the three was at that time. The major grumbled a bit, called his boss to explain the situation and then told me: "Do not to discuss the raid. Period!"

And, yes, the ground commander was Colonel Charlie Beckwith.

Academics, check rides, gunnery missions, refueling rides, and formation flights all passed too rapidly, and soon I was blessed as a qualified Hog Driver. My final sortie at DM was with Jack on May 29th and then I out processed to catch a flight the next morning back to Virginia. I still needed to finish up at Langley and make the move to jolly old England. On June 4th, I flew a T-39 co-pilot mission from Langley, just to be current in two aircraft at the same time – an Air Force rarity. Then I out-processed, packed and was off to East Anglia and an A-10 tour.

The family housing situation at RAF Bentwaters was so critical that incoming personnel could not bring their family until they could show a written rental agreement proving they found adequate quarters on the local economy. This was taking almost 90 days on average. So, Claire stayed in our Grafton, Virginia, house as I departed for England. I turned in my Honda Civic on the shipping dock in Norfolk, Virginia, hoping it would be in England shortly after I arrived so I would have wheels for the housing search. Claire, the great military wife, mom, and graduate student was challenged to put the house up for rent, keep everybody sane, and, when I found a house in England, pack up the Virginia household for shipment. She then made air travel arrangements to London, all the while dragging along a very reluctant eight-year-old son.

31

RAF Bentwaters, England

Upon signing in at 81st TFW headquarters on RAF Bentwaters, I was assigned to the 91st TFS (the Blue Streaks) over at nearby RAF Woodridge. Bentwaters and Woodbridge were two separate airfields divided by two miles of Rendlesham Forest and farm lands. The major support facilities for Americans were located on RAF Bentwaters, along with four A-10 squadrons (92nd, 509th, 510th, 511th). Woodbridge was primarily operational home for two A-10 squadrons (78th and 91st), a Rescue HH-53 helicopter squadron, two enlisted airman dormitories and half of the available Air Force family housing units. "Woody" turned out to be the better place to fly because it was away from the 81st Wing staff and we enjoyed less aircraft traffic compared to Bentwaters with transient traffic and four A-10 squadrons.

I signed into the 81st as one of five new Majors to the A-10. The other four were Jock Patterson, Al Rutyna, Jim "Bear" Evans, and Bill Knutson. The five "new guy" Majors were assigned to different squadrons and each became an Assistant Operations Officer in our respective squadrons. Not only were we new to the A-10 community, but we all had relatively similar dates of rank and were awaiting the outcome of the pending Air Force Lieutenant Colonel Selection board.

For the five Majors and a dozen newly assigned pilots, our temporary housing was at the Bell Hotel in Saxmundham, about 12 miles northeast of Woodbridge and Bentwaters. The Bentwaters complex had no temporary quarters for newly assigned officers so all were assigned to contracted hotels such as the Bell Hotel. Retired RAF Squadron Leader Geoffrey Richter was the Bell Hotel owner and barkeep extraordinaire.

The cool damp weather came as a surprise to all the new folks and I soon sent home for heavy sweaters, needed in "summer" in East Anglia. Geoffrey's bar in the Bell Hotel displayed three-foot tall framed scrolls, each with the emblem of the original three squadrons of the 81st TFW (the 78th, 91st, and 92nd). The pilots who lived in the Bell Hotel or frequented the bar, all signed under their squadron patch. The names went back to the 1950s and read like a list of the great fighter pilots of the Vietnam War and many generals afterwards (i.e. Robin Olds and Chappie James). I felt honored to join that list, signing under the 91st Blue Streaks.

My room on the second and a half floor was a dormer room and the ceiling was so low on the dormer side that I could not stand erect within four feet of the window. My view was out the rear of the Bell to the old stables, now car parking. I avoided my room as much as possible because it depressed me: not so much the actual room but the loneliness. The bar of the Bell was the center of social activity and it rocked most nights except Sunday. Late each evening, Geoffrey called "Closing, last call" and then locked the hotel doors, but inside, we could keep the bar open as long as we liked or until Geoffrey became tired.

The bar was rather small, a room of about twenty feet in length, with only six tables along the opposite wall. Over the fireplace at one end was an illustration of a Spitfire cockpit done by an excellent local illustrator, Geoff Pleasance. I bought one of his artworks before I left the 81st. Geoffrey Richter flew Spitfires in the Battle of Britain, throughout WWII, and was on the RAF's Red Arrows Aerobatic Team. He was a great part of the fighter community.

Geoffrey's wife was known as "Lady Bird" and she fussed over all her Hog drivers. She was a tiny woman, barely five feet tall and flitted from table to table or task to task. It was easy to see why Geoffrey nicknamed her "Lady Bird." Dinners were served family style in the small dining room just inside the entrance to the hotel because we were her family. We always showed up for dinner when she made her famous curry; I'm a good Texas boy with lots of hot spice experience, but Lady Bird's spicy curry brought tears to my eyes. If we let her know we were going to be late for dinner, she held a plate for us. Lady Bird also cooked "bar food" for those that were visiting the bar and were not hotel guests. Geoffrey successfully manned the hotel bar every evening while belting down (appropriately named) Bell's Blended Scotch Whiskey doubles with us. We learned not to try to match drinks with that man!

On pleasant Sunday afternoons, Geoffrey would load four of his tenant Hog Drivers in his Jaguar and set off on a pub crawl. Known by every pub owner in East Anglia, Geoffrey brought "his boys" to great and small pubs with names like the "Checkered Horse" and the "Smugglers Pub." Some pubs were so small that somebody needed to leave before Geoffrey's "boys" could get in. Some were large with huge ten by four foot roaring fireplaces. We were always welcome as Geoffrey's boys and we returned to many of these establishments for years to come, often with squadron mates. These were "real" English pubs with low ceilings (tall Jock Patterson had a problem there), darts competitions, and frequented by the locals. Welcome to England, Steve.

After many searches over six weeks, I found a house in the village of Haughley, 25 miles northwest of RAF Bentwaters and just off the A14 highway north of Stowmarket. This small house was two stories with a total of 800 square feet, 20 by 20 feet on each floor. How we were going to fit the furniture from Virginia into this tiny space was going to be a challenge. My suitemate from DM, Captain Bill McGuire, found a similar house for his family on the next street over in the village, so the Yanks invaded Haughley. Our house was owned by an RAF Squadron Leader posted to RAF Gutersloh in Germany and was managed by a neighbor, William Freeman. "Bill" Freeman was employed as an F-4 simulator instructor at nearby RAF Wattisham and was a retired RAF Squadron Leader. He flew with the RAF demonstration team, the Red Arrows, and he displayed an exceptional ability to consume great quantities of Courvoisier brandy. The English taxes on Courvoisier put it well out of the purchasing power of most Brits, but since we Yanks could buy it tax free on our base, I gladly kept Bill's glass supplied with Courvoisier each time he came to visit.

While our house hunting and A-10 flying check outs were taking place at BTW, the Air Force Central promotion board for Lieutenant Colonel took place at the Personnel Center, Randolph AFB in San Antonio. I was so tied up in the pressing two main events that the promotion board slipped my mind. If others were anxiously awaiting the outcome of the board, I was too busy to give it more than an occasional passing thought. With a housing rental contract in hand, I received permission to bring my family to England and my unbelievably wonderful wife loaded up the household furniture, rented out our Grafton house, sold her Toyota station wagon, made travel arrangements, got new passports, literally dragged an uncooperative son along and caught a flight to London Gatwick Airport.

On the morning of 12 September, I hopped in my 1977 Honda Civic and drove the two hours toward London and Gatwick Airport on the south side of town. I made it to Gatwick for the 7:30 AM arrival and was joyfully reunited with my family. We loaded baggage into the tiny Honda, and made the drive to our new home in Haughley. After unpacking the bags, seeing a bit of Haughley, we were relaxing in our house when I asked Claire if she felt well enough to drive into RAF Bentwaters for a promotion party at the O'Club. Claire asked, "Whose promotion party?" With a smirk, I replied "It's my promotion party." I had been selected for Lieutenant Colonel. The promotion list was released three days prior and I decided to withhold the announcement from Claire while she handled the staggering task load of preparing to fly to England with Chris.

The promotion of five new pilots in the 81st TFW presented the wing leaders with a problem. What do we do with these future Lieutenant Colonels? Early the following week, the Wing DO called the five selectees into his office for some career counseling. In so many words he told us that, because of the personnel already assigned to the 81st, we had little chance to be Squadron Operations Officers and even less chance at a command slot. We all had the same silent reaction: "So noted; but *ha*! We will take our chances." The next four years proved we made the correct decision.

The 91st TFS shared a building with the 78th TFS ("The Bushmasters") and the 78th mascot: "Barney", a full-grown Rock Python. The lowest ranking lieutenant in the 78th was assigned duties as the snake keeper, which involved feeding baby chicks to Barney, cleaning his cage and taking Barney for a "walk" outside the squadron building. Barney occasionally got out of his cage (usually at night) and then the 78th posted a sign on the front door stating, "Barney is loose in the building". Barney was too lazy to bother a human as the squadron kept him well fed, but some of the admin personnel refused to enter the building until Barney was found and re-caged. Often Barney curled up in a chair pushed up under a desk to await the screaming panicked owner of the desk. When the 78th TFS changed command, there was a parade formation and the Wing Commander conducted the formal change of command with speeches, passed guidon, etc. Following was the unofficial change of command with the passing of Barney to the new commander. Regardless of personal feelings, woe unto the commander who would not accept Barney from the outgoing squadron commander. I was there to watch Lt Col Glenn A. Profitt II, pass the snake to Jock Patterson as Jock assumed command of the 78th in 1982.

One of the best things that happened while in the 91st TFS occurred when Captain Steve Alderman and his wife Joanie joined the squadron. They and their two small children, Jason and Nathan, moved into a house in the town of Ipswich. Finding they had much in common, Joanie and Claire soon became close friends. Joanie was an amazing teacher and her two boys benefitted from her expertise. I did not get to fly much with Steve in the 91st, but I would see him at least twice more in our military careers in some unusual places.

As I began flying with the squadron at Woodbridge, the 91st TFS Blue Streaks commander was Lieutenant Colonel Jim Main; Major Glenn Howerton was the Ops Officer. With the arrival of my group of majors, five of the squadrons faced a similar problem: each squadron had a major acting as the Ops Officer and now they inherited a senior Major, soon to be a Lieutenant Colonel, who was not yet checked out in a European A-10. This is when squadron commanders earn their commander's pay.

All A-10 squadrons rotated a flight to one of four Forward Operating Locations (FOLs), spaced throughout Germany to provide A-10 coverage for the land battle if the DRPCB's attacked westward. The 91st deployed to and flew from Fliegerhorst Ahlhorn, Germany, in Niedersachsen on the North German plains. Since the American presence was concentrated in southern Deutschland, there were no Americans in the Ahlhorn area except for one brigade of 2nd Armored Division sixty miles away in a small casern at Garlstedt, Germany, north of Bremen and some at the port facility in Bremerhaven. The 2nd AD was landlocked in this small casern and training area and did not have the room to conduct large scale exercises or battle drills. To conduct any large unit training, the troops were required to load their equipment on trains or convoy the tanks on carriers to the training area at Grafenwoehr, Germany. Garlstedt did provide the nearest Exchange facilities and American dependent schools in their nearby town of Osterholz-Scharmbeck, where over 1000 units of family housing for GIs was constructed in 1978. On a good day, these facilities were just over an hour drive from Ahlhorn.

USAFE believed in revolving leaders at the wing command level with each commander getting about two years if they "did good." When I arrived at Bentwaters, the 81TFW/CC was Colonel Gordy Williams (known from Incirlik days). His tour was from August 1979 to May 1981. Then came a ghost from my F-4 past when Dick Pascoe commanded the Wing from April 1981 to August 1982. Then another great officer, Colonel Dale Tabor, commanded from August 1982 to March 1984.

On 18 November 1980, I was preparing to fly with the 91st at Woodbridge. I climbed into my A-10, strapped into the ejection seat, power on and was about to start engines when, over the radios, I heard what seemed to be a Search And Rescue operation being conducted. With a few minutes before flight check-in, I delayed engine start to monitor the rescue. The A-10 of an upgrading Bentwaters pilot, Lt Col William Olson, had collided with the A-10 of his Instructor Pilot, Maj Steve Kaatz, near Itteringham, Norfolk. Maj Kaatz successfully ejected immediately, but was dragged by his parachute across a farm field until the parachute became entangled in a fence line. He was recovered with only cuts and bruises by the rescue team. His A-10 impacted in a farm field, resulting in no civilian injuries and minimal property damage. Olson regained control of his A-10, and, despite loss of one engine and damage to the hydraulic systems, made the decision to fly around the East Anglia - North Sea coastline to avoid all populated areas enroute back to Bentwaters. Due to the extensive damage, his A-10 began to lose hydraulic pressure on the remaining system and Lt Col Olson decided to switch from hydraulic flight controls to Manual Reversion mode.

Manual Reversion is an emergency flight control system built only into the A-10, but the transition is best performed under optimal aircraft control situations. The problems, compounded by loss of one engine, damage to the wing and fuselage internal systems, and turbulent weather made this flight control switch impossible. The switchover did not go well and Lt Col Olson ejected when his A10 went out of control. The wind was more than 40 knots on the North Sea at the time of ejection and Olson slammed into the water's surface and was dragged by his inflated parachute through 10-foot seas at 40+ knots.

The alert RAF Sea King helicopter from 202 Rescue Squadron, RAF Coltishall, was already airborne and quickly arrived on scene. An RAF rescue crewman saw that Lt Col Olson was unable to release his parachute and dropped into the water to make the rescue. Unfortunately, during the rescue attempt with both men on the recovery hoist, the parachute filled with water and then partially inflated in the wind, snapping the hoist cable as the two men were being lifted. The RAF Rescue airman refused to leave Lt Col Olson and tried to support the pilot until the beating of wind and seas proved too much and both men drowned. A USAF HH-53 rescue helicopter from the 67th Air Rescue and Recovery Squadron at Woodbridge was also launched and soon deployed two PJs with full SCUBA gear into the water to recover the victims. The PJs recovered both bodies from North Sea at 1035 hours, eighty minutes after the mid-air collision.

The A-10 pilots of the 81st TFW were devastated by the two losses. Lt Col Olson was a well-liked new pilot and officer. However, the gallantry and determination, then loss of the RAF Rescue crewman while trying to save a US pilot seemed to affect us more. Lt Col Olson died doing what he loved to do. That is a fact of life that every fighter pilot accepts as part of the job. The danger inherent in flying A-10s in Europe or anywhere else was always in the minds of the families, even if the pilots shoved it back into a small dark corner of their consciousness. The spouses and many children knew that when Dad went to work, he might not be coming home to hug them again at the end of the day. The sight of an Air Force staff car with two officers in blue uniforms pulling up in front of your quarters is the nightmare of all spouses.

But the loss of the RAF Rescue crewman was crushing. These were the men that put it on the line to come save pilots when very bad things happened and we regarded the Rescue crews as Supermen who could not die. The memorial service for Lt Col Olson, with the traditional A-10 Missing Man formation flyby, was the first I attended in the A-10 community, but not my last. The RAF Coltishall memorial service for Master Air Loadmaster Dave Bullock was well attended by our Wing and Squadron leadership and numerous Hog Drivers. Dave Bullock was posthumously awarded The George Medal by the Queen. The George Medal is the second highest award to citizens of the United Kingdom and Commonwealth for gallant conduct which is not in the face of the enemy.

This rescue operation also brought home to the A-10 pilots a lesson on use of individual call signs. The security geniuses at USAFE headquarters were on a campaign to eliminate the use of personal call signs. We may have gone too far when the flights used the leader's personal call sign for the flight, i.e. Gene Renuart, AKA "Topspin", used "Topspin" for the flight, with "Topspin 1" as his aircraft and his wingman was "Topspin 2" over the radio. Other times, the squadron call sign was used with sequential numbers, i.e. "Skull" or "Streak" 01, 05 etc. USAFE decided this gave the evil empire Russians too much information, so the edict came down to use only random number computer-assigned call signs or the NATO tasking code. In my humble opinion, "Alfa Whiskey 125 Bravo" does not tell me much about who is flying the aircraft or their qualifications.

The first A-10 flight to arrive on scene to the Kaatz-Olson mid-air and ejection was "Iron" Mike Burski and his wingman from the 91st TFS. "Iron" became the on-scene commander and immediately sent his wingman, "Tree" Schwindemann, to be the high-altitude radio relay to the 81st TFW command post at Bentwaters. As A-10 flights checked in to assist, Mike dispensed with the computer call sign and evaluated their experience based on their personal call sign. Soon, "Swede" the Assistant Wing DO check in, and, based on Swede's extensive Southeast Asia rescue experience, he became the on-scene commander while "Iron" and his wingman were replaced as they ran low on fuel. This experience did little to sell our Hog Drivers on the USAFE approach to eliminate personal call signs, but instead, convinced many that the USAFE staff was composed of inexperienced idiots. A year later, a similar discussion arose at a squadron meeting. The Weapons School graduate, Captain Dean "Eager" Dotson, stated, "I don't care if the Commies know that "Eager" is coming. I expect them to run and hide because they know "Eager" is bringing death and destruction!" A bit strongly stated, but most of the A-10 pilots felt the same about the USAFE-generated garbage call signs.

Life in Haughley had its up and downs, downs such as the Haughley "Motor Cycle Gang." They were "cool" except they possessed only one motor bike among the "Gang" members and most were too young to even get a learners permit to drive. Often, other school boys harassed Chris, the "Yank," when he got off the school bus on the corner of the main street, but Christopher popped into the news agent shop for safety until Claire or I could walk down to meet him. On the other hand, there were great folks like John who owned the Railway Pub about a half mile east of Haughley on Station Road. John welcomed all the Yanks from the villages around and we repaid him by flying our Hogs low down the railroad tracks next to his pub and giving Jon and his patrons a wing-rock or two. John knew that if we came into his pub that evening with a smirk, we were the guilty fliers.

ENGLISH SCHOOLS FOR CHRIS
On the recommendation of Claire's Grad school advisors, we placed Chris in the local state middle school, located just up the road from Haughley at Bacton. He seemed reasonably happy there, but, around Thanksgiving time we were playing darts and when it came to adding score points, we discovered Chris no longer knew his basic math. He could name types of grain and livestock in East Anglia, but recalled little of math or composition. That set off a search for an English prep school

for Chris. The task was to find the school that was a "fit" for him and for the school. We applied to several of the finer schools around Suffolk and none fit him or he them. After an interview and testing at Ipswich School, the Headmaster informed us that Chris was very smart but "he just has not been taught" adequately. So, Chris was enrolled as a "Day Boy" in Ipswich School, meaning he did not reside at the school as a boarding student but commuted from the local area daily. Ipswich School was established in 1399 and enjoyed a reputation for providing excellent students to Oxford and Cambridge Universities. The school was a classic English boys-only prep school with five and a half days of intense classes in math, science, literature, and social sciences. The school prepared boys for the best universities for over 500 years and I think they had the process down. The school was on Henley Road and across the street from the large Christchurch Park in downtown Ipswich. Their associated all-girls school was on the opposite side of the park.

The Ipswich student body was half "day boys," the rest, boarding students. A few students were referred to as "Sundowners" because their parents were in the British Armed Forces and stationed abroad. The term "Sundowner" evolved because the sun never went down on the far flung British Empire and its armed forces. The school also matriculated a sizeable number of Chinese students from Her Majesty's colony in Hong Kong.

Students were required to take advancement examinations every two years to be promoted to the next grade or "Form." We were concerned that Chris would not do well, but, after much tutoring in math, he scored in the middle of his form and moved upward. Several of his classmates did not perform well and were excused from the school. We found it surprising that the sole "Yank", with only a year and half at Ipswich, beat out several students who was there for four years.

"FOOTBALL" REFEREE FOR THE "FA"
Prior to leaving Virginia, I contacted the British Football Association (the FA) about refereeing while I was "posted" in England. RAF Bentwaters was in Suffolk County, so I was put in contact with the Suffolk County secretary. Upon "ringing him up" shortly after we moved into Haughley, he "straight away" gave me a list of my immediate referee assignments. This was a learning experience for me as the lone American referee in adult "football" clubs across Suffolk. I was known as "The Yank" referee and over the next two years I worked my way up the assignment ladder to work the line on several local "Cup" matches

and finally ran the sideline for an Ipswich Town Reserves match in Portman Road Stadium. Ipswich Town was a leader in the Premier League and recently won the European UEFA championship. At the local level, I remember refereeing a match in Stowmarket on the Phillips Inc. pitch which was covered with four inches of snow. We used an orange ball and the company plowed just the marked lines of the pitch. That was fun for a Texas boy but not uncommon in Europe.

HOG CRASH AT DONNA NOOK
In January 1981, with Colonel Jack Pine from RAF Upper Heyford as Board President, and an Aircraft Investigation Team, I was appointed as the Investigating Officer for an A-10 crash (77-0258) on the gunnery range at Donna Nook on the east coast of England where the River Humber emptied into the North Sea at the Spurnhead Light. On 9 January 1981, an experienced A-10 driver from the 81st TFW was on the range, called turning "base" in the low angle bombing pattern and then went "Splash!" There were no signs of trouble and no radio call. The investigation brought in experts to examine every minute part of the aircraft and its maintenance records.

We examined every portion of the pilot's personal life, training and currency in the A-10. The tremendous rip tides along the shore scattered the wreckage for miles and made recovery for examination difficult. Therefore, no real cause was found, due to lack of hard evidence. Was it a control jam in the Sterile Area of the A-10? Did the pilot go "heads down" to check switches or sight settings? The RAF range officer did not actually see the accident as he looked away after seeing the Hog start his turn to base at an altitude of 500 feet. We could find no civilian witnesses among the local population. Further complicating the interviews with the fishermen in the area was their heavy accent -- so much so we needed to contract a local secretary to act as an interpreter.

When the investigation was completed, the team members were scheduled to brief the accident investigation results to the USAFE DO Staff, the DO, and then the USAFE Commander. The briefings were finally scheduled at USAFE headquarters at Ramstein AB, Germany. The dates fell during one of my scheduled rotations with a 91st squadron flight to Ahlhorn, so I flew an A-10 from Ahlhorn to Ramstein. The weather at Ramstein was deteriorating, and, as I talked with Ramstein approach radar, they sent me on an extended downwind leg to the west. I was now down at a relatively low altitude of 4000 feet where my fuel consumption was higher and I was being vectored toward France. I could hear some of the Ramstein based F-4s given priority to land before me and I was rapidly reaching a fuel state requiring diversion to Bitburg AB. When I told the radar controller that I was approaching divert fuel, he asked if I was declaring "Minimum or Emergency Fuel." I again stated that I needed to land soon or I would have to divert to Bitburg. He was unimpressed until I told him, "I have a briefing to the USAFE DO and CINC, starting in three hours, and if you keep delaying my landing until I have to divert and miss the briefings, you will get to explain why to the USAFE Commander!" With that information, I was given priority vectors back to Ramstein and landed with 100 pounds of fuel above my required divert fuel. Ass!

HOGS INVADE AUSTRIA

I was working on the joint 78th / 91st Duty Desk when a 78th flight, under flight leader, Sam Bass, put four A-10s into Innsbruck, Austria. Sam's flight departed Woodbridge with a flight plan to fly around the corner of Switzerland and land at the NATO base at Aviano, Italy. Enroute, the weather in Italy crumped, to the point that none of Sam's alternate airports in Italy were above landing weather minimums. Running out of daylight, Sam weighed all options and declared an emergency to cross Austria to southern Germany and Furstenfeldbruck airfield, the nearest NATO airfield with landing weather. Half way across the Alps, number four said he did not have the fuel to make it to "Fursty." Clearly seeing the rotating beacon at Innsbruck airport, Sam Bass made a command decision to divert again and the four ship soon landed at Innsbruck, Austria (a neutral country). Thinking this could be an international incident, Sam was prepared for the worst. However, they received a friendly Austrian reception and were welcomed as pilots in distress, not as NATO invaders. The airfield security chief asked the Hog drivers to change from their uniforms into civilian clothes and that was the only requirement.

The American Embassy in Vienna was not as nice. The USAF Colonel Air Attaché was an absolute jerk. He demanded that Sam's flight refuel and take off immediately, but a very pleasant Austrian who ran the Air Traffic Control system at Innsbruck refused to allow a night takeoff because the A-10s could not fly the ADF instrument departure. He curtly told the Colonel at the US Embassy to call back after sunrise. Click! Sam still needed to refuel all the A-10s and the airport's ESSO fuel folks did not accept the NATO fuel card that we used throughout NATO. When asked if they could charge four fuel loads on Sam's Exxon card, the fuel man took it without blinking. Sam bought 40,000 pounds of Jet-A fuel on his personal Exxon credit card and wondered if he would get reimbursed by Uncle Sam.

The following day, as the sunlight crossed the Alps and illuminated the far mountain tops on a beautiful clear morning, Sam and his four A-10s were sitting on the taxiway, ready to make a first dawn takeoff on Runway 08 and a climbing left turn toward Germany and Furstenfeldbruck Airbase (less than 100 miles away). Sam made no attempt to phone the jerk at the Embassy, and, when the ATC guy said they were legal to takeoff, they were on the runway and gone. The powers at USAFE were not pleased, but the result was four safe A-10s without an international incident. As a lesson, Sam and his flight were required to brief fuel management and weather check procedures to every fighter squadron in England. In 1999, there was still an A-10 decal stuck to one of the sliding glass doors at the main entrance hall.

In April 1981, I was selected to become the Ops Officer for 92nd TFS, a great squadron with a fighter history that went back to WW II. Previous Squadron Commanders included (later 4-star general) Chappie James, and, more recently Colonel Gene Juve. The latter led the 92 TFS in the conversion to the A-10 Hogs and opened the wing's Forward Operating Location at Leipheim. Gene Juve always hid the soft spot in his heart for the 92nd when it was compared to the other five A-10 squadrons in the 81st Wing. The four other new Lieutenant Colonels who joined the 81st Wing with me also became Operations Officers in four of the other Hog squadrons.

On 24 April 1981, Colonel DICK PASCOE assumed command of the 81st TFW with the appropriate pomp and ceremony for a passing of command of the largest fighter wing in the Air Force (six full A-10 squadrons spread across two bases and four FOLs in Germany) plus the support organizations. I was ecstatic to see Dick Pascoe become the CC because I knew he brought level-headed, common sense leadership to the widespread wing. At the reception following the ceremony, Col Pascoe remembered me by name from our F-4 days and congratulated me on soon becoming a squadron Operations Officer. Wing Commander Pascoe already knew who was in which leadership positions in "his" wing.

32

The 92nd TFS Skulls

In May 1981, I transferred across Rendlesham Forest to RAF Bentwaters and became Lt Col Jim Mathers' Operations Officer in the 92nd TFS (The Skulls). I soon found out the Wing Commander required either the Squadron Commander or the Operations Officer live in base housing. Jim made it clear that he did not want to move on base from his exquisite country manor, so my family moved into quarters 1427B on RAF Woodbridge.

Our quarters were the left side of a duplex with little front yard but a rather spacious back yard with chain link fencing, as were our neighbors' yards. The house contained a "Master" bedroom, two smaller bedrooms, two bathrooms and a relatively well-equipped kitchen. The living and dining rooms were open but adequate for entertaining. It was a monster-sized house compared to our Haughley house. Like all the Air Force family quarters, we found a loud speaker in the living room to broadcast all alerts or announcements from the 81st TFW Command Post.

Jim Mathers had good reason to stay on the local economy because he, wife Linda and their two daughters lived in a large gatehouse named the "Bailiff's Cottage" on an English manor in Tuddenham, Suffolk. They had the use of the manor tennis courts and grounds, making them de facto landed gentry. It would have been difficult for the Mathers family to give up their large house and estate grounds to occupy small, three-bedroom government quarters. Let Stevenson move onto base! That was a break for us because we were cramped in our 800-square foot house with a long, often scary, commute on narrow back-country English roads. Moving onto RAF Woodbridge, eliminated my long commute and made life a lot simpler for the 92nd TFS Ops Officer and for Claire.

At my first squadron meeting, Jim introduced me to the squadron and added that, in reviewing my records, he felt the squadron was getting "some type of John Wayne" as the new Ops Officer. I didn't think anybody ever went back to look at past decorations and the citations behind them. Very early in our relationship, Jim made it clear that he would run the squadron personnel issues, command relationship with Wing, finances, supply and that I was responsible for flying operations for 28 pilots and all the associated training issues. *I loved it!* Jim was also a good all-around jock, having played baseball in college and he sniveled a few TDYs to participate in the USAFE downhill skiing and tennis championships. I ran the squadron in his absence!

On 4 May 1981, I deployed with a 92nd flight to their FOL at Leipheim, Germany. Acting as an attached pilot, I flew as a wingman to become familiar with the pilots, the area and Leipheim operations. After five fun-filled days, we returned to Bentwaters on Friday, 8 May 81. I was scheduled to officially become the Ops Officer when I returned to the squadron. As my flight approached East Anglia and we changed over to a local radio frequency, I heard Search and Rescue (SAR) chatter on the UHF radio. I didn't know what happened except that an A-10 went down. After landing, I found that a 92nd TFS lieutenant, Eric Gagne, ejected on Wainfleet Range, impacted the mud still in his ejection seat, and was killed. The ensuing investigation placed a lot of blame on the outgoing 92TFS Ops Officer for poor training, documentation and evaluation of the pilot. Fortunately for the former Ops officer, he received a good performance report just days before and was soon to PCS back to the States for Command and Staff College. Going to the funeral of a squadron pilot is a hell of a way to start your Ops Officer tenure.

When LT Gagne was killed, his wife wanted only to go home to the States as soon as possible. At the time, the Air Force possessed almost no support procedures for instances such as Gagne's. The squadron was the surrogate family of its members in overseas assignments, and the officers' wives often filled the holes from babysitting, to cooking, to providing moral support. The squadron and base personnel quickly got LT Gagne's family on a flight home via London, but the task of packing up the Gagne household goods for shipment fell to Claire and other 92nd leadership wives. Preparing, arranging packing and shipping of another family's personal effects, particularly in this situation, can take an emotional toll on the wives. It was years before the US military services began to recognize the essential part that families played in support of our country's military mission. Then it took more time to establish appropriate family support facilities, education and programs.

I had a great bunch of guys in the 92nd when I became the Ops Officer: the boss, Jim Mathers was "Hobo"; my assistant weapons officer was "Eager"; one of the better lieutenants was Max "Bam Bam" Dawson; an assistant Ops Officer was Bob "Kiss" Mass; a flight commander was "Top Spin" (later 4-star) Gene Renuart; Lt Ecker was "X"; a bad luck Lieutenant was "Curse"; a Texas A&M pilot was, of course, "Aggie"; and Lt Stewart was "Shaggy". My call sign was "Cowboy", which we can discuss over a beer. All the call signs were earned by some tall tale, appearance, attitude, or a single incident.

In the Fall 1981, Claire did not feel well for a couple of weeks, and, suspecting a case of the flu, went in to see our designated 92nd TFS Flight Surgeon, Captain (later Major) "Doc" Howie Gillis, who soon called and told Claire of her pregnancy over the phone: "I have good news and good news. The good news is that you do not have the flu. The second good news is the rabbit died." To this day, Claire believes Howie did not have the guts to tell her in person of this second surprise. So, Lt Col Stevenson, 92nd TFS Ops Officer, had a pregnant wife. We could now relate well to the Lieutenants' and Captains also expecting a baby; obviously, this was meant to be.

Claire's OB doctor for this delivery was a civilian contract doctor, Dr. John Alexander Chalmers, in Ipswich. A fantastic doctor and gentleman, he, like most physicians, was referred to by the local Brits as "Mister Chalmers" and not Doctor. He kept a close watch on my wonderful bride for the coming months.

One of my highpoints while in the 92nd was an 81st Wing Dining-In and the guest speaker was Sir Douglas Bader of WW II fame. He lost both legs below the knees in an aircraft crash but recovered to fly in the Battle of Britain and into late 1941, when he was shot down over France and finished the war as a POW. Lt Col Jock Patterson (Ops Officer 78th TFS) and I were his designated escorts and we ensured Sir Douglas' every need was met. As might happen at a Dining-In, the Hog Drivers got rowdy, so Jock and I assigned a lieutenant from both the 78th TFS and the 91st TFS to play goalie in front of Sir Douglas, ensuring that our guest did not get hit by the traditional flying dinner rolls. The Wing King was mortified, but placated when Sir Douglas stated that he enjoyed an excellent evening and "the fighter lads showed good spirit." Jock and I got to keep our jobs as Ops Officers.

277

Instead of the 91st rotations to Ahlhorn in northern Germany, the 92nd rotated in and out of the Luftwaffe base at Leipheim AB in Bavaria. There I met Lt Col Gene Juve, the Detachment Commander and Major Briggs Duguid, the Operations Officer. Lt Col Juve, with whom I worked well, was soon promoted to Colonel, moved to Bentwaters and became the DO for the 81st TFW. I saw him again when he became the Commander of the 507th TAIRCW at Shaw AFB, SC. Flying aside, rotations to Leipheim offered up opportunities for great ski trips to the Alps, the Garmish Armed Forces Recreation Center, and easy access to Augsburg and Munchen for culture, beer and shopping.

My scariest day at Leipheim occurred when thunderstorms, imbedded in winter snow showers, were roaring through Bavaria. Gene Renuart and I were both on the ground and one two-ship was left in the air. Just as the two-ship was arriving back in the vicinity of Leipheim, a snow shower came across the field and visibility dropped to much less than one mile; you couldn't see the middle of the runway from our Detachment building on the east end of the field. Gene was the acting Supervisor of Flying and immediately began to check for an alternate air field in the area for our two Hog Drivers. None were available as Bavarian airfields such as Lechfeld, my old favorite Erding, civilian airports and all other German bases were having the same problem; the weather already deteriorated below landing minimums at their fields. The flight lead, Dean "Eager" Dodson, was forced to shoot the radar precision approach to below published weather minimums for Runway 27 with a new A-10 pilot on his wing. The wingman, Lieutenant Ecker (call sign "X"), though new, was a pretty good pilot and that helped, a bit. As they began their approach, a stressed Gene Renuart came into the operations office, tore the patch with name and wings off his uniform (they were attached by Velcro) threw his wings on the duty desk and stated, "This could be the end of my career." I concurred with that opinion and tossed my wings onto the desktop.

We listened to the radar approach on the radio at the Ops counter, and, when the radar approach indicated Eager and X were inside one mile from touchdown, we stepped out into the pelting snow, hopefully, to see the landing. First, we heard the acceleration of TF-34 engines and then two landing lights appeared from the white wall snow. Eager led Lieutenant Ecker's A-10 to within ten feet of the runway surface and then slightly accelerated to land farther down the runway. Separation is a good thing when you can't see squat. The two Hogs landed, successfully braked, turned off at the end of the runway, de-armed and very carefully taxied back to their shelters. I retrieved our wings from the Ops counter and handed Gene's back to him. Note: I'm glad we did not end Gene's career in a snowstorm at Leipheim as he became a four-star general. I could not think of another flight lead better in that situation than Eager. Gene and I drove out to their parking slots as they shut down, handed each Hog Driver a cold beer and I told both, "That was a great piece of flying."

On 24 Nov '81, back at Bentwaters, I led a 2-ship with Kevin Barley that involved refueling from a KC-135 tanker off the coast of Scotland, making two Electronic Warfare (EW) passes at the Spadeadam EW range, and then performing a most unusual CAS w/FAC and uphill strafe at Otterburn Range, Cumbria on the Scottish border, just above Hadrian's Wall. The targets were on the north side of a valley about ¾ up the side of the hill. With a very low pass into the valley and then a slight pull-up maneuver, you were strafing uphill at the targets. When you released 60 rounds of 30 MM cannon fire at the target, the laser spot tracker, aircraft velocity vector and gun cross were all above the artificial horizon line on the HUD. The squadron's Hog Drivers double-checked their HUD TV tape when going to Otterburn Range, just to capture that phenomenon.

After our Otterburn range time, Kevin and I turned south and low-leveled down toward "the Wash", where we made our Donna Nook Range time for Low Angle Bomb, Long Range and Two-Target strafe, then back to Bentwaters with a total mission time of 2.9 hours. A fantastic mission, after turning off the runway at BTW, I opened the canopy and screamed, "I can't believe Uncle Sam pays me to have this much fun." Of course, only God could hear me over the whining engines, but He knew. Incidentally, I was flying A-10 tail #80-0207 which was one of our new Inertial Navigation System (INS) equipped aircraft. The INS could be your helpful friend or bite you in the butt depending on how well you programmed it, whether you believed it too much, and, particularly how you cross referenced the steering information against the real world outside your cockpit. We were ever seeing technology increases in the cockpit.

Christmas shopping in Augsburg. Each year winter came with a frigid blast to Bavaria as proven by Eager's flight and our constant worries about snow storms and runway traction conditions. In Mid–December '81, I was again deployed with one of my squadron's flights to Leipheim and we took a mid-rotation break, loaded up in two vehicles and drove into Augsburg to shop in their famous Christkindlmarkt on the huge Rathausplatz in the center of Augsburg. The Rathausplatz, the plaza in front of the city hall, was packed with what seemed like hundreds of stalls for vendors to sell every imaginable Christmas decoration, toy or delicious snack. Walking among the throng of shoppers, your senses were overwhelmed by the scents of hot roasted chestnuts, gluhwein, pastries and sandwiches. Against the bitter cold, we worked from one gluhwein stall to another, shopping some but drinking a lot of gluhwein. By 10:00 PM, we gathered up our crew and headed back to Leipheim with great memories of the market, friendly Germans, sparkling lights in the light snow and more gluhwein. We could have stayed and misbehaved but flying started early the next morning, and that was why Uncle Sam spent a lot of money to get us to Leipheim.

Unbriefed air-to-air challenges were a common occurrence among fighter pilots in Europe, USAFE and Air Force Regulations notwithstanding. Another nation's fighter aircraft was an instant theoretical target, despite USAFE prohibitions that made these engagements a "Be No." If another fighter turned into you or your flight, the fight was on. Most of these engagements lasted for only seconds as the attacker got off an imaginary shot or the defenders make a move to negate the attack and everyone went his merry way. The A-10s normally stayed very low, as in 500 feet or below our usual training altitude, and turned to negate an attack. If the attacker stayed to pursue the fight, then the turn rate of the A-10 usually placed the attacker in the gun sight of the A-10 after a few rotations of "circle the Hogs." Every fighter squadron knew a stream of 30 mm rounds from the business end of our GAU-8 cannon could dissolve a fighter and was to be avoided. Official air-to-air (Air Combat Tactics or ACT) sorties were rare and were normally coordinated between the pilots well in advance.

On one occasion, the 92nd Hog Drivers were provided great ACT with an F-15 "Eagle" from Bitburg AB, Germany, acting as the aggressor for dissimilar combat. The F-15 pilot phone briefed with an A-10 flight and then flew over from Bitburg and met an A-10 flight in the training area overhead the English "Wash" for several canned scenarios. Then the F-15 and A-10s landed at Bentwaters and the two-man F-15 crew debriefed in the 92nd TFS. The F-15 planned to fly a second sortie from Bentwaters, land, de-brief, brief a third flight, and, after the last engagement (their third) return directly to Bitburg AB for a phone debrief.

After a lunch break on this day, the F-15 pilots briefed with me and Max "Bam Bam" Dawson to fly a 2 v 1 mission. There were two F-

15 pilots involved because this was an F-15B model with two seats and one of the pilots was getting an ACT Instructor Pilot check ride from the 36th TFW Stan-Eval pilot. During our engagements, the Eagle never got a good shot at us as Bam Bam and I countered every attack and often one of us called a "30 mil snap shot on the F-15." The Eagle could always escape by going up in the vertical but we made the low altitude environment very uncomfortable for them, if not unhealthy. In the debrief session I heard the F-15 video tape quote: "Jeez, the old Lt Col has his act together today." You have to take the good news when you can get it.

Training on new systems in the A-10 was fun but you can't get carried away with technology and forget the basics of Hog low-level navigation. I was an IP chasing a new lieutenant who was using an INS system and we were rooting our way north toward Donna Nook Range on the east coast of England. The Humber River flows west to east and dumps into the North Sea, so all the New Guy needed to do was turn right at the Humber and follow it to the sea and Donna Nook range. Well, lieutenant "dumb smack" reached the river and turned west! I gave him about a minute and then called for a 180 turn and told him to follow the river. The rest of the mission went reasonably well and in the debrief session I asked, "Why did you make that turn west?"

"The INS needle pointed that direction to Donna Nook."

"Well, that was 'Garbage In, Garbage Out' (GIGO) and it is now time for back to the basics of land navigation."

One thing the 92nd Squadron could do well was have a great sing-along. Led by Marc Frith (Seaman), Dean Dotson (Eager), Mike Warren (Grumpy) and Jeff Watterburg (Burger), we could do justice to every dirty fighter pilot song known to our Air Force. We held beer call / song fests in the squadron on Friday afternoons. Burger was killed in an A-10 mid-air collision while he was a Squadron Commander at England AFB, Alexandria, Louisiana. We would miss his voice at squadron reunions

Another 92nd jock, Maj Gary Sakuma, lived on the street behind us in base housing on Woodbridge. The houses shared relatively large back yards and a chain link fence running down the block. While many civilian neighborhoods built privacy fences, our open back yards provided a common scene for gossip swapping and flying tales. This close neighborly communication avenue was often the source of impromptu parties, and, on one occasion, a lobster boil party. Gary went back "across the pond" to the States to pick up a new A-10 for delivery to the 81st Wing. His flight of four A-10s staged out of Pease AFB, NH, north of Boston on the Atlantic coast to make the air refueling, non-stop flight to Bentwaters. One of the lobster dealers there developed shaped, plastic lobster containers to fit any Air Force aircraft deploying from Pease AFB to Europe. Everyone in Gary's four-ship of new Hogs was up for fresh lobsters. So, Gary ordered two A-10 packages with eight iced lobsters each that fit behind the ejection seat in the A-10. Packaged at the last minute and delivered to the flight line, the ice kept the lobsters dormant during the flight to England and provide live fresh Maine lobsters to the Bentwaters folks at the other end of the trip.

The flight started and taxied for takeoff behind their KC-135 tanker, but the tanker developed a minor problem and returned to its parking slot to get a "fast" repair. Now, Gary's flight was left in the arming area, waiting for their tanker with no air conditioning running. A portion of the ice began to melt while on the ground and thus about half way across Atlantic, Gary owned some wide-awake and active lobsters. Gary radioed another flight member to close up and check his ice pack, seeing if the lobsters were loose. The Hog driver reported that they weren't loose but very active. Gary said he could hear scratching sounds immediately behind his head, even over the engine and system noises. He just knew they would cut their way out of the plastic and attack him. The 92nd duty officer called Gary's wife when his flight was one hour out, and she called neighbors to gather pots and side dishes. Gary landed, taxied into the 92nd area and set a world record for the quickest shut-down and dismount of an A-10. The crew chief retrieved the squirming lobsters and the critters finally made it to our neighborhood lobster boil. Sakuma's call sign was "Samurai" but the squadron considered changing it to "Lobster."

Just after I moved up to Stan/Eval, Jim Mathers left the 92nd when he was selected for promotion to Colonel. I saw him later at Shaw AFB when he was the Vice Commander of the 363rd TFW. He then moved back to USAFE where he held several command positions and was promoted to Brigadier General. Jim retired in 1996 and has been one of my real heroes.

33

A Black Hat

My name did not come out on the first 1982 USAFE squadron command list, so Col Pascoe (Wing CC) and Col Juve (Wing DO) decided to move me to another high visibility job for another shot at the secondary USAFE Command List. I reluctantly left the 92nd and became the Chief of the Standardization and Evaluation Section for the entire 81st Wing. Titled Chief of Stan / Eval, I was the chief check pilot for 206 A-10 pilots at Bentwaters and Woodridge. I supervised seven Stan / Eval Flight Examiners (SEFEs) and they were the cream of the crop from the squadron IPs. In an upgrading wing like the 81st, it was a case of the rich getting richer in flying time as we almost rode the SEFEs into the ground.

A squadron jock got three flights a week and a squadron IP maybe got five or six. It was not uncommon for my SEFEs to get eight or nine check rides per week and they pleaded for a day off from flying to catch up on check ride paperwork. I tried to limit my check rides to Instructor Pilot check rides. An example of SEFE workload was two weeks in May of '82 when I flew 13 times and 11 of those were check rides. I lived with my flying gear in the trunk of my car, because I never knew whether the next checkride was at Bentwaters or over at Woodbridge. I was attached to the 511th TFS, newly commanded by John Gay, and it was often many days before the very patient 511th Life Support section saw, or could inspect my flying gear. Despite the frequent commute, I could cheerfully say: Darn the luck of having to fly a fighter daily!

When I moved to Stan Eval, I couldn't stay with the 92nd TFS, even as an attached pilot, so I was attached to the 511th TFS for flying administration and social activities. The only time I saw the guys from the 91st or 92nd was when I was giving check rides. It was part of the Air Force policy that, if you were moving up to a higher position, you never moved up in your squadron but moved laterally to another unit. Five of the six Operations Officers that got command slots (that includes me) shuffled across squadrons at Woodbridge or Bentwaters so they did not get command of the squadron where they served as Operations Officer. The sixth Ops Officer, Jim "Bear" Evans, went to Torrejon AB, Spain to be the Commander of the 613th TFS "Squids" and to lead their transition from F-4s to F-16s.

My SEFEs were all "Good Guys" and didn't wear black hats (although our SEFE scarves were black and white checks). The end of the week was always a pain as the squadrons wanted to schedule check rides for Friday afternoons. Hey, they were cutting into our Happy Hour at the O'Club!

I gave a 91st Hog Driver, John Yanaros, one of the most thorough IP check rides ever. It took us two sorties and we covered the most demanding events. He briefed and we flew low level to Donna Nook Range. I used my VHF radio on Donna Nook to call the Range Officer (Yanaros could not hear that VHF frequency) to set up my strafe of a wrong target. Would John would catch it? He did and called me off. I was good at playing the Devil's advocate in my "Black Hat" role. After a full range period, with three bombing and two strafe events, we popped up to refuel on a KC-135 tanker over the North Sea and then back down to low level home.

On the second sortie for ACT and more formation work, I almost screwed up the formation takeoff on John's wing when I drifted in too close, got caught in the vortex from John's A-10 wingtip and nearly was drawn into a collision with Lead. After the flight, I debriefed John for being late to see his wingman sliding toward Lead. But in truth, that was just to cover my ass because the incident scared the hell out of me and I hoped that John could not tell I still felt the shakes when thinking about the takeoff. This was another reminder that Stan Eval pukes were far from perfect fighter jocks. John did a decent job of briefing and then leading some events and critiquing my lead of other events. The job of a single seat fighter IP is a great challenge because it requires a chase of the checkee from another fighter. After a lot of IP time and check rides, a good SEFE could almost tell what the other pilot was going to do, right or wrong, before he did it.

While working as the Chief of Stan Eval, I received a "brotherhood" warning message from one of my former 92nd "Skulls", Captain Robin Stoddard, who flew with me often before I went to Stan/Eval. "Stodds" moved on to DM as an IP and felt compelled to send a message to me and Col Juve about a Bentwaters-bound A-10 student (a Captain Juhl) that they could not wash out. "Stodds" said the Wing leadership at DM exhibited a "don't make waves" mentality and gave this student corrective flights until he reached the absolute minimum level of proficiency in the Hog. Stodds thought the DM guys should have washed him out of fighters and let Air Force Rated Assignments at Randolph re-assign him as a copilot in a big airplane to gain some safe experience. Jeez, when I saw the student's training records from DM, there were more red pages (failed rides) in his grade book than passes. Stodds' warned: "Watch this guy. He will crash an A-10" and he did. A $10 million-dollar aircraft chalked up to "Don't make waves."

ALL IP FLIGHT?

Sometimes a flight can be fun and be a wake-up call at the same time. I flew one such ride in June 1982, with Bill McGuire and another IP. I was Chief of Stan/Eval and scheduled as flight lead. Bill as #2 and our #3 were both IPs in the 509th TFS. This must be a scheduling mistake! The IPs were usually kept busy training new pilots and an occasional Flight Lead or new IP upgrade. Very seldom did the IPs have an opportunity to lead a good flight or to fly wing on an experienced flight lead. The best thing about flying as an IP in the A-10 was the fact that you got to do just that: fly. There are no two-place A-10s so the IP flew his own jet in a chase formation. You did not get stuck in a backseat hole like being an F-4 IP. You got to fly the jet and keep your mechanical skills up, again unlike the F-4 IP whose "hands" could become rusty by letting the upgrading pilots get all the stick time.

Scheduling must have been drinking stale ale to make a mistake like this, or the squadron was desperate for flying time to schedule three IPs in a flight with no new guys. We went out to do basic Air Combat Maneuvers that evolved into decent aerial fights. After a couple of turns and maneuvers, I suddenly realized that what worked against the new lieutenants I normally flew with would not hack it against a very experienced fighter pilot. In the debrief all three of us reached the same conclusion. Because we were flying against the new guys so often, we let our own level of expectation decline. On the way back to BTW, we all got a chance to fly tight formation on a "real" flight lead, rather than on a new flight lead or chase on a new lieutenant. It was a pleasure to keep the wingtip aligned on the ejection symbol and perfectly align the leading edge of the rudders as a smooth flight lead went through climbs, turns and maneuvers. When we had that down, we moved in and forward to align the trailing edges of the engine nacelles. This put our wingtips in very close proximity to each other, but we took pride in holding the tighter formation that we rarely got to fly. Then, we switched flight leads and did some more. I'm sure we were a beautiful sight from the ground.

Bill McGuire was one of those pilots that you sure wanted to fly with in combat, but he was often a pain-in-the-ass and "high maintenance" personality in a peacetime squadron. Bill and I shared adjoining BOQ rooms during A-10 transition at Davis-Monthan AFB and, despite his often-obnoxious behavior, especially toward women, he was still a friend. In 1983, Bill was selected for promotion to Major and was about to pin on his new rank. His promotion presented a problem within the 81st, because, as a Major, he should become an Assistant Operations Officer. None of the squadrons wanted Bill in an Assistant Ops Officer position. He was a great IP and flight commander, but unwelcome in a leadership position to impact a whole squadron. The issue became moot when Air Force Rated Assignments offered Bill an assignment to the Air Force Intelligence Center in San Antonio, Texas. He was to use his A-10 and Wild Weasel expertise as a staff officer. Bill accepted the position which curtailed his Bentwaters tour and took the pressure off the Bentwaters 81st Wing leadership and the six A-10 squadron commanders. I wondered if Air Force Rated assignments knew of the dilemma.

Proving that "Murphy" from Murphy's Law loved A-10s, in March 1982, 1Lt Jim "Blade" Preston ejected near Hereford, Germany after a double engine flameout and consequent engine fires. Blade stalled the engines during high angle of attack maneuvers at high altitude, and, with both engines now quiet, Blade started his emergency procedures, shut off both stalled engines, and set up a glide toward a forested area through a thin cloud layer. Unknown to Blade, the real problem developed because both throttles were incorrectly rigged, so when the throttles were cut off, fuel to the engines was never completely shut off. The trickles of JP-4 caused residual internal fires and left no re-start capability on either TF-34 engine. Aiming for an unpopulated area and passing 4,000 feet, Blade's last thoughts before ejection were: "Damn, I just made a whole new set of maps," which, of course, were going down with the aircraft. His ejection and recovery went smoothly and the Hog impacted in a wooded area with no civilian injuries. The Air Force accident board's investigation discovered the throttle rigging problem and Blade was cleared of any pilot error.

34

TREVOR RHODES STEVENSON

As the arrival of Trevor neared, we moved Chris into a temporary boarding status at Ipswich School and he remained there until the end of the term.

On 5 June 1982, Claire went into labor and I drove her to the Heath Road Wing, Deben Ward, Ipswich Hospital, for the delivery by Mister (Dr.) Chalmers. An impressive ten-story modern hospital, this was to be a completely different and far more pleasant experience compared to the military hospitals at Fort Sam Houston and Columbus AFB, Mississippi and a young captain's wife's first child. The English staff really cared for the mother and baby. After the delivery, Claire was instructed to rest and recover for at least two days, whereas the US military wanted new mothers up and out of the hospital as soon as possible. Claire and I participated in Lamaze classes and were ready to work as a team, paced breathing and focusing on an object. We practiced the procedures as Claire's contractions narrowed in time and she dilated. After an exam by Mr. Chalmers, who arrived from his son's day-long cricket match, Claire was moved to the Delivery Room and I remained in the hallway outside the room. Trevor Rhodes Stevenson, a strong name according to Mr. Chalmers, entered the world at 6:50 PM.

Within minutes, a nurse emerged, stated "There were a few issues and we are going to be rather busy. Here, talk to your son." With that she handed me a large package of blankets, and, at one end was a small scrunched-up face wearing a knitted cap to keep him warm. Trevor did not make a sound other than breathing rapidly and I wrapped him in my arms. For almost 20 minutes, I sat in the hall, talking to Trevor about how lucky he was and all the things he would get to see. At one point, Trevor yawned and then his face became my late father's face, with wrinkles, little hair, and the same familiar shape. For a second I was totally spooked, and then my father was gone and I held Trevor again. Back in the Mother's single room, Claire began the rather painful recovery, extra staples and stitches that I will leave to her stories. On that first day, Claire saw Trevor only to feed and hold him for bonding, then he was taken back to the Nursery and Claire was instructed to rest. I could visit for the feeding period and to again hold my son. Then I was instructed to come back after the mother's rest time. For the next three days, the baby stayed in the room with Claire, again a pleasant change from Christopher's birthing experience. Four days after Trevor's birth, we carefully and slowly loaded Claire and Trevor into our Volvo wagon and drove back to our quarters on RAF Woodbridge.

RAF Bentwaters and the 81st TFW hospital was fortunate to have a superb group of doctors, including (and later commanded by) Col John P. Tindall, the assigned Flight Surgeon for 91st squadron at BTW. Col Tindall's son possessed dual citizenship, since his mother was an English citizen, and he chose to attend the Royal Military Academy Sandhurst, the British equivalent of West Point. Upon graduation, young Tindall was commissioned a Second Lieutenant in the Corps of Royal Engineers. Prior to joining the US Air Force at a late age, Doc Tindall was an esteemed dermatologist, the Chief of Dermatology at the Duke University Medical School and met his British wife during a doctor exchange to a British hospital many years before. Based on his exceptional medical experience and his willingness to be stationed overseas (in his case, England) Doc Tindall was direct commissioned as a Lt Col and made Colonel on the next medical promotion cycle. With his promotion came increased responsibility and he later became the Bentwaters Hospital Commander. His rapid promotion is what we called a "fast burner."

One month after Trevor's birth, I received a rather "no-notice posting" to Germany as the Ahlhorn A-10 Commander. We assessed the school situation for Christopher in Germany, then made a tough decision and changed his enrollment to a boarding student for the coming school year. He, too, became a Sundowner but the only Yank in the school. I think Chris was too young to understand and resented being left behind because of the new baby. It was thirty years before he recognized the decision was extremely difficult for us but in his best interests.

On every school break Chris took the ferry to the continent and spent the holidays with us in Germany. In those days, a passport was required, so he "used up" his passport by the time we came back to the

288

States. His travels also included trips around the UK as I found out when I telephoned on a weekend and was told "Stevenson has gone to Scotland with the Cricket Side." All things considered over the coming years, the excellent education from Ipswich School served Chris well through college.

35

Ahlhorn, Germany

Getting a command at Squadron level is a challenge for any officer, but commanding a geographically separated unit is an exceptional challenge. This proved to be the toughest two years of my career for the family. We were 60 miles from the nearest US school or medical facility. Trevor was six weeks old when I was offered the command of the 81st Detachment 3 in Ahlhorn and just over three months old when he made his first international trip, from England to Germany. We saw Chris on the rare visits back to RAF Bentwaters, or on holidays when he caught the train – ferry – train to arrive in Northern Germany. Claire was assuming the mother hen role of Commander's Wife, while caring for a newborn son.

The A-10 Forward Operating Locations (FOLs) in Germany were extensions of the 81st TFW at RAF Bentwaters / Woodbridge. Three FOLs were located on Luftwaffe airbases at Leipheim, Norvenich, and Ahlhorn, Germany; one FOL was on the American base at Sembach Air Base. The FOLs were to accept deployed A-10s from the 81st TFW in England and maintain a forward close air support presence for NATO nearer the German border. A normal rotation from the 81st Wing squadrons was a two-week TDY of six to eight A-10s and their first line maintenance personnel. The Luftwaffe provided billets for the TDY troops along with a Detachment headquarters and maintenance, fuel, and munitions storage.

Prevailing Air Force wisdom says, when offered a command, you never say no. I was offered command of Detachment 3, 81st Tactical Fighter Wing, the northernmost of the FOLs and a tenant on the German Fliegerhorst Ahlhorn. The airbase was "owned" by the Luftwaffe's HubsrauberTransportGeswader 64 (HTG 64), or 64th Helicopter Transport Wing in English. They provided Search and Rescue, as well as helicopter ambulance service, across northern Germany and the near North Sea.

Ahlhorn was a small town of approximately 3500 residents located on the flat North German plains 40 miles southwest of Bremen and 50 miles from the Dutch border. The town does not show on many maps and maintained a small-town atmosphere. On base at Ahlhorn, the Americans could access the HTG 64 Officers, NCO and enlisted clubs. Space was found in a building on the opposite side of the airbase for a small recreation center and BX, run by our dependent wives and children. MSGT Glenn Nowling and his wife, Pam, were the stalwarts that carried the load of managing the two functions. Pam proved adept at working within both the German economy and the US Exchange system to keep the permanent party and many of the TDY troops supplied with necessities, and a few "luxury" items.

One of the best things about the Ahlhorn command was working with the Luftwaffe Commander of HTG 64, Oberst Werner Geissinger and his amazing wife, Renate. Oberst Geissinger spent more time in the United States during his career than I did in mine. He went through pilot and instructor school in the US, attended the Air War College at Maxwell AFB and then stayed as an instructor for two years. He served as the junior Air Attaché in the German Embassy in D.C. before taking command at Ahlhorn. He liked Americans, and, as we attempted to learn the German culture and language, he helped me and my unit in many ways. However, when I attended my first HTG 64 staff meeting, the Oberst told me his staff meetings would be in English for one month. Then, all meetings would be in German. No pressure to learn German there! His wife Renate was the most gracious hostess I encountered in my career. She could hold a party and every guest felt like the guest of honor. She came by her friendliness naturally and was well trained during their embassy tour.

The Vice Commander was Oberstleutnant Peter Tegeder, a stereotypical Prussian officer who was standoffish with me as the American Commander until Claire and I held a lengthy conversation in Spanish with his girlfriend about her travels in Spain. Peter spoke no Spanish and I think he then came to see me as less of an "Ugly American." As my German improved and I did a few favors for HTG 64, Oberstleutnant Tegeder became a friend, although I rarely saw him smile. After all, he was a Prussian officer!

On my USAF side, upon taking command I inherited only three officers among my permanent personnel in Detachment 3: the Operations officer was Captain Mike Spurlock (call sign "Spike"),

Maintenance Officer 1LT and later Captain Dean Grimes and my Army Ground Liaison Officer (GLO) Captain Bob Landry, US Army Cavalry.

As mentioned, I was not on the first 1982 USAFE Squadron Commanders list, and, was then moved to be Chief of Stan Eval. My Squadron Commander, and the 81st Wing Commander appealed to USAFE to correct the omission. Col Gene Juve later told me Col Pascoe informed the 3rd AF Commander and USAFE DO that I was going to be given a command, so they should adjust the commanders list before that happened or they could explain it, after the fact, to the USAFE 4-star Commander.

In June 1982, an amended Commanders List was released by USAFE, and, amazingly, Steve Stevenson was on this list. The formal Change of Command Ceremony for Detachment 3 at Ahlhorn, Germany was held on August 10, 1982 (Claire's birthday). Rather than drag our seven-week-old newborn across the Channel, we arranged for Trevor to stay with a babysitter as Claire and I rode over for the ceremony in a C-130, then the day after rode in a C-130 back to BTW. I returned to Ahlhorn by A-10 the next Monday and Claire began the process of getting a passport for Trevor and moving our house hold goods from Woodbridge to the home designated for the US commander on the edge of Fliegerhorst Ahlhorn. Chris missed the ceremony, but commuted from Ipswich School to Ahlhorn for vacations.

My "assigned" house was a one-story brick house, built by or for the British forces that occupied northern Germany for many years after WWII, set in a neighborhood that compared favorably to a wooded officers housing area on an American base. It was a well-insulated three bedroom, two bath house with a room for a servant or nanny. There were huge trees in our small front yard, almost a forest on the back half of the lot and a white picket fence along the street and the driveway. Different, though, was the makeup of our fellow neighbors, including an active duty Luftwaffe lieutenant, a German government employee and the widow of a German Army Lieutenant Colonel (Oberst Leutnant).

The houses were administered by the German administrative agency, their equivalent to the US Government Services Agency (GSA). It was known by the acronym "STOV." I cannot begin to remember the lengthy German word from which that was derived. There were many reasons a German could qualify for the STOV housing and I never did understand it all. The regional STOV office was just across the fence from my Commander's house, in a huge and elaborate building which served as the aerodrome's Officers Club in WW I and WW II.

Within a month of my transfer, Claire finished the paperwork to get a passport for baby Trevor and we were ready to move the household goods. Trevor's birth certificate is British and we reported his birth through the Air Force and obtained a document entitled "Consular Report of a Birth Abroad of a Citizen of the United States of America" (Form FS-240). That massively titled form could then be used to obtain a passport. Passport in hand, with a picture of one month old baby Trevor sleeping, we were ready for the household move to Ahlhorn. In early September, I returned to make the move and we directed movers with loading furniture, packed everything possible, including baby and dog, into the Volvo wagon and made a ferry crossing to the continent. In a side note: The quarters for departing families were left over WW II Quonset huts with drip-fuel potbellied stoves for heat. It does get cold at night in late September in East Anglia. The next day we caught the ferry from Felixstowe to Zeebrugge and drove the four hours to Ahlhorn. Our household goods arrived in Ahlhorn the same day we did and we slept in our own bed on our first night in our new quarters.

The nearest American installations to Ahlhorn were a small nuclear storage unit at Sögel, Germany, 40 miles away, or the support units for US Army at Garlstedt, 50 miles away. The only Army tactical unit was the 2nd Armored Division (Forward), based at a new military facility near the village of Garlstedt just north of Bremen. The facilities there cost nearly $140 million to construct, half of which was paid for by the Federal Republic of Germany. The brigade held approximately 3,500 soldiers and 2,500 family dependents and civilian employees. The German government constructed family housing for the GIs in nearby Osterholz-Scharmbeck. In addition to troop barracks, motor pools, an indoor firing range, repair and logistics facilities, and a local small training area, facilities at Garlstedt included a troop medical clinic, Post Exchange, library, a movie theater, a combined officer/non-commissioned officer/enlisted club and the regional DODDS high school.

The 2nd AD (Fwd) facilities were nice, but the German government gave up only a small, almost postage stamp sized maneuver area adjacent to the kaserne (post). That placed a significant restriction on any armor unit and they had to transport everything to one of the southern Germany maneuver areas to get any realistic training or to fire their tank main guns. The largest major American support units were in the US port facilities at Bremerhaven, Germany, 75 miles away. After purchasing my Porsche 911, it was a fun one-hour drive at over 100 MPH on the autobahn, from my office door to Bremerhaven for the Army CG's monthly staff meetings.

While living in the Woodbridge base quarters, we used a young English lady from Ipswich, Debby, as a nanny, and, when the short notice move came we asked Debby if she would come with us. We offered to pay for her passport, a rarity for most Brits, and she accepted the offer. She was of great assistance in setting up our quarters and minding Trevor. But, alas, the lack of social life or peers in the tiny German community was more than she could take. By Thanksgiving, Debby resigned and caught the train and ferry back to Ipswich.

Claire's mother died quite suddenly on Thanksgiving Day back in Corpus Christi, Texas. As commander, I was unable to take leave until Christmas, so we split the family for a while. Claire was the one with major life stress points this time: new baby, new house, new community, new language, her Mom's death and the long exhausting flights. It takes a strong military wife to handle all that. Claire and Trevor caught flights for Corpus starting in Bremen, Germany, and I could join them three days before Christmas. Claire and her sister Suzy were tending to the myriad of details involved in the estate settlement before I arrived home. I could best lend moral support and babysit Trevor while the two women worked the details. We returned to Ahlhorn in the first week of January 1983.

Being an A-10 unit on a Luftwaffe base made us something of an oddity for the Luftwaffe. Our maintenance troops, as well as a pilot, were often called upon to create a static display of the A-10. This was usually held in the closest shelter to the Luftwaffe ramp and wing headquarters. Being on the receiving end of my first request for a static display by the Base Commander Oberst Werner Geissinger taught me a lot about German directness. The Germans have a different concept of tact in a discussion and they state a fact with no tactfulness attached.

"Steve, can you do a static display this Friday for a Luftwaffe general and his staff?"

"Yes sir, I will have it set up and ready in shelter 12 by 1000 hours."

"Nein! That is unsatisfactory."

295

After recovering, and thinking for a moment, I replied, "We can have it set up by 0900 hours if you would like."

"That will be good. Thank you for your help."

The German approach just took some getting used to and required maybe a thicker skin.

The only time I ever saw Oberst Geissinger flustered involved an A-10 static display for Luftwaffe officers. The Oberst's aide called and asked for a static display in a shelter for a group of new doctors that were in their flight surgeon course. Upon completing their course, they became Luftwaffe Flight Surgeons and were assigned to different bases. Since there were both A-10s and Luftwaffe Hueys stationed at Ahlhorn, the new doctors had the opportunity to see both types of aircraft.

At the appointed day and time, the group arrived at the shelter for the A-10 static display, escorted by Oberstleutnant Nichols of the HTG. The class all wore new, standard Luftwaffe grey cotton flight suits with Hauptman (Captain) rank on their sleeves. As we walked around the Warthog, I noticed a strikingly pretty, blue-eyed blonde Hauptman in the group. Not only did her flight suit complement her figure, but she was wearing patent leather flats, a peach color tee-shirt and a string of pearls. I tried not to gawk at the uniform violation but, then, it was their Luftwaffe. As we were finishing the static display, Oberst Geissinger drove up to meet the doctors. The Oberst wanted to shake hands and welcome all the visitors, but, when he stepped up to the gorgeous blonde Hauptman, he was at a loss for words. Oberstleutnant Nichols and I exchanged glances and tried not to smirk. Oberst Geissinger said on several occasions that there were no female officers in the Luftwaffe, and, "We will have no women officers in the Luftwaffe!" OK. But if he wanted to toss this young Hauptman out of the Luftwaffe, she could be my Flight Surgeon.

A-10 LOCAL HOLIDAY FLYING
On long weekends or holidays such as Turkey Day and the Christmas holidays, I asked the 81st Wing to leave one A-10 at Ahlhorn when the rotational personnel and Hogs returned to Woodbridge. There were enough permanent party maintenance personnel to launch and recover one A-10, twice a day if we had an airframe. Mike Spurlock, my Operations Officer, and I alternated as pilot or Supervisor of Flying (SOF). If I flew, "Spike" was the SOF; if Mike was flying, then I pulled duty as SOF. The Christmas holidays were normally quiet times with

very limited flying. Many of the Luftwaffe fighter bases had only one day of flying and that was an informal "Fly-In" for other fighter wings and squadrons to send a representative aircraft and pilot / crew to have some cake and punch and be seen on the airfield. Depending on which aircraft arrived at the host airfield at the same time, the opportunity presented itself for some very interesting dissimilar air-to-air engagements, often directly over the host airfield.

In June 1983, Ahlhorn hosted a deployment of 47th TFS A-10s and the 100 accompanying airmen, from the Air Force Reserve's 917th Tactical Fighter Group from Barksdale, Louisiana. Since Ahlhorn was not equipped to support two full squadrons of A-10s, the logistical work with USAFE, the HTG 64 and our local community was enormous. From rental cars, to supplies, to portable bathrooms, it was crazy in this tiny community but we made it happen. Credit here must be given to my 1st Sgt Kornegay, who solved numerous problems and made answers appear before I knew there was a problem. Leave it to the Senior NCOs to make things work. When the 47th TFS brought a female captain as their Public Information Officer (PIO), the Luftwaffe was astounded. They saw female enlisted personnel with the American A-10 units but they never encountered a female officer. The fact that the PIO was a beautiful TV reporter in her civilian job was also mind boggling to the Luftwaffe.

When all the 47th and their supporters finally arrived at Ahlhorn, HTG 64 threw a major party in one of their hangars to welcome the "Ragin Cajuns." Sometime in the drinking of toasts to everyone's unit and their governments, the pretty PIO drifted off with a Luftwaffe pilot and then came back wearing the Luftwaffe Hauptman's flying suit, while the HTG Hauptman was wearing her flying suit. Let's have a loud cheer for improved international military relations, please.

By about 2100 hours, most everyone was drunk and my communications center sent me a message from USAFE headquarters directing all available A-10s to be loaded with a Standard Configuration Load (SCL) as part of a no-notice command wide exercise. That could have been a disaster for our two units, *except*, we terminated flying at noon and then had all the two unit's aircraft loaded with that specific SCL as part of a self-generated local exercise. When we called "complete load-out" to the 81st Wing Command Post after only 15 minutes, they called the USAFE Command Post and our two Ahlhorn units were exempted from the exercise. I'd still rather be lucky than good.

A-10 CRASH AND AFTERMATH

On 28 July 1983, one of the 91st A-10s (79-0222) flying from Ahlhorn, departed controlled flight at low level and crashed. The Flight Lead was Captain Steve Anderson (one of the Air Force Academy's Anderson twins) with Captain Ron Juhl as the crashee. Condensed version: he was not in the computed safe envelope for ejection yet he walked away from the scene. Of course, this happened on my second day of leave and Claire, Trevor and I were staying in a hotel on Lake Chiemsee in Bavaria. After the phone call came about the accident, I packed up the family, checked out of the hotel and drove straight through to Ahlhorn: 7 hours on autobahns.

The Air Force is unforgiving of aircraft losses. The next day I talked with Colonel Dale Tabor, offering to be the scapegoat since it happened on a flight from my Airbase. We both felt that the Air Force would hang somebody for the accident. This was the same A-10 pilot about whom Captain Robin Stoddard, the A-10 IP at Davis-Monthan, sent the strong warning to me and Colonel Juve. He was bad as a Hog Driver, but was not washed out of Hogs at DM. The first thing I did, when I got a chance was to look at my flying log book to see if I gave a Check Ride to Captain Juhl. I did not want to be the Stan/Eval check pilot who passed this slug. Whew! I never flew with him.

When I went to Bentwaters for the initial accident investigation briefing, I sat in Colonel Tabor's office and again offered to take the hit for the accident. Tabor said I was not directly involved in the training of Captain Juhl and thanked me for the offer. He then said quietly, "I don't know if I will have a job tomorrow." In the aftermath of the crash, the 91st Squadron Commander, Lt Col Bill Knutson, was relieved; Captain Juhl was grounded and Colonel Tabor kept his job (later to make Major General). The USAFE four-star general fired off some blistering messages to the TAC Deputy for Operations and the Davis-Monthan Wing Commander. Captain Juhl met a Flight Evaluation Board (FEB) and was taken off status as an Air Force pilot. Captain Juhl filed a congressional complaint, which turned into litigation; but the FEB findings held up and Juhl went back to his previous career field of being a Security Police Officer.

The A-10 crash highlighted the occurrences of unplanned air-to-air engagements with another country's fighters. Since the Hogs normally rooted around at or below 500 feet, many of our fights took place at very low altitudes. Hog drivers became experts on aggressor tactics and how to negate their attacks especially on the north German plains, where we were always ready for a fight with the "Baron's Boys" from Wittmundhaven AB. With a lineage going back to "The Baron" Manfred Von Richthofen, the Luftwaffe's Jagdgeschwader 71 was the most experienced, and, in my humble opinion, the best air-to-air fighter squadron in Europe. The Baron's boys and Dutch F-16s were always looking to pounce on A-10s at low altitude. The reaction to such an aerial attack was a major contributing factor in Captain Juhl's loss of control and subsequent crash. You needed to be good to hassle and survive below 400 feet. We now knew Juhl wasn't.

A few days after the accident, Spike and I were at the O'Club discussing the ejection over a couple of good German beers. Commenting that Juhl should not have survived that ejection and that the farmer plowed the field that morning was an act of God, I started scribbling notes. We put together a humorous short story and I sent it to the USAFE Flying Safety shop to see if it was worth publishing. I heard nothing from USAFE for a month, so I sent it to TAC for their *TAC ATTACK* safety magazine. Within three weeks TAC sent me a letter saying they wanted to publish the story in the November *TAC ATTACK* edition. In late October, USAFE Safety finally responded, saying they were interested in the story. I told USAFE that they were too late because TAC was going to publish it in two weeks. Upon its release, I was astounded to see that the TAC story was illustrated by Stan Hardison. I worked with Stan while I was on the TAC staff and Stan was famous Air Force-wide for his cartoon strip "Fleagle" and many great illustrations. I was truly flattered to have Hardison illustrate the story and I felt like a famous author, thanks to Stan Hardison.

GUN MISSION FOR BRITISH ROYALTY

On 11 August 1983, I flew (81-0224) a great "CAS with FAC" mission with LT Bill Grimstead from the 91st on my wing. Cowboy flight was scheduled on a challenging laser-spot FAC-directed gun and bomb range event (On Time and On Target, we were) on the Bergen-Hohne live fire range complex, southwest of Munster, Germany. Munster was the headquarters of numerous British armor regiments, ever since their occupation in WW II. We bombed and shot up everything "Lingo Jack the FAC" could designate with his laser. "Lingo Jack the FAC" was the Brit FAC assigned to the British armored units at Munster. Some attacks I led and some "Two" led. As our range time was up, Lingo Jack asked us to cover for a flight of British Harriers due next at the firepower demonstration. The Harriers were a "no-show" due to the foul weather at Gutersloh AB (some 70 miles south of Ahlhorn) and low ceilings on the range. Our two Hogs flew in under the low ceiling weather, while the

Harriers took off IFR from Gutersloh and then could not "get down" to find the range. To cover our range time and the Harriers' time, I knew that I would expend more ordnance than was scheduled, but this was too good to pass up, and "Lingo Jack the FAC" seemed in a bind. To paraphrase Willie Nelson: "If you have the money, honey; I've got the time and ordnance!"

LT Grimstead and I eventually each used over 1,000 rounds of 30mm gun ammo, 12 bombs, and surprised our weapons troops upon return to Ahlhorn after expending every piece of ordnance we carried. The load crews did a quick GAU-8 cannon ammo and bomb up-load for the afternoon sorties, which were also scheduled to go to a range, albeit a different range. Our FAC from the morning, "Lingo Jack", called early evening to thank me for covering the two range periods because an observer was "a member of the Royal Family with military connections." That could have only been Prince Charles, but Lingo Jack could say no more. The Brits enjoyed a great deal of freedom of movement in Northern Germany and sometimes we contacted Lingo Jack operating from a helicopter and other times in a jeep; either way he always used a great laser designator to point out targets for us. Occasionally, we visited Lingo Jack on weekends and spent the nights in his modern apartment overlooking a lake in Hamburg. Tough breaks for Her Majesty's Forces.

From Ahlhorn, our Hogs flew low level on over 90% of our missions, to any gunnery range, to NATO Close Air Support taskings, or, just "rooting around" flying from point A to point B, termed Low Altitude Tactical Navigation (LATN). Hugging the earth was our primary defense against air defenses and "enemy" aircraft. The A-10 community developed a comfort level for formation and tactical flying at 500 feet, 200 feet and in specific areas, down to 100 feet AGL. It took practice not only to fly but also to navigate while doing 300 knots at 500 feet or lower.

I thought I was getting darned good at low level stuff until a sortie in September 1983 kept me humble. Cowboy, with a new 91st TFS lieutenant on my wing, launched out of Ahlhorn in slightly marginal weather, but we were scheduled for a range time on Nordhorn range, about 60 miles southwest of Ahlhorn, and getting there should not be too rough. We picked four or five turn points to hit enroute to the range, part of a zigzag course northwest almost to Papenburg, then south to the Deutsche Bahn (DB) high-speed train test track, and then to Point Xray and the Nordhorn range. It was not by any stretch a straight line to the range. We easily found the first point but the second wasn't found until we were almost on top of it. I thought "Damn, this is getting really tough. I must be losing my touch." We finally made it to the first range holding point (Point Xray) about 12 miles north of the range. (Today, Xray is easy to find with a new autobahn crossing Hauptstrasse just southwest of Meppen.) We changed over to the range frequency and I called Nordhorn range with our call sign and scheduled range time. In his most distinguished English accent the range officer informed me "Not on this range, Sir. We have 1700 meters visibility in smoke and haze and the range is closed!" Well, that explains the very tough LATN. I closed the flight from tactical to loose route formation, climbed to cleaner air at 5000 feet and got a radar pickup by Weser Radar for an IFR recovery to Ahlhorn. That was a case of biting off more than I could chew and not even knowing it. I am not sure if the newbie Hog Driver on my wing knew how many times his leader was "almost" lost.

In mid-1983 I was coming down with "Porsche Fever", a result of being blown off the road by Porsches on the autobahn. I wanted a 911 model, particularly after Captain John Utsanomea, USAFE A-10 Stan Eval and formerly at Bentwaters, drove his 911 up to Ahlhorn and I drove it around Fliegerhorst Ahlhorn while "Uts" was flying. I loved its handling! A new 911 was pricey, even for an Air Force Lieutenant Colonel with flight pay. So, I decided the next best thing was the recently released Porsche 944. Our nearest Porsche dealer was just up the road at Oldenburg, so I drove up there and made inquiries about purchasing a 944. It turned out that the 944 was so popular there was a 15-month backlog to acquire one. I told the friendly salesman, Herr Schneider, that I would be back in the US by then, so I had to pass on a purchase. Two days later Herr Schneider telephoned to say I could get the second American specification 1984 model 911 Targa off the line, *if* I wanted a 911. Herr Schneider knew the Porsche family well and worked with Ferry Porsche in the past. After discussing it with my bank and the Canadian Exchange System's car buying service, I was hesitant to spend that kind of money. But Claire had inherited some money and asked me,

"If you could buy any car, what do you want?"

A Porsche 911."

"We can do that. Go buy the 911!"

The deal was done and I soon was receiving bi-weekly reports on *my* Porsche's progress down the production line, with an open invitation to visit my Porsche at any time as it matured.

Finally, my Porsche was ready. On Thanksgiving Day 1983, Herr Schneider picked me up in his demonstration 911, at 5:30 in the morning blackness and we literally launched for the factory at Zuffenhausen near Stuttgart. Herr Schneider let me drive to get the feel of the newer 911 and we made the trip in less than four hours, driving at normal autobahn speeds (around or over 100 mph). Upon arrival, we toured the production area, ate lunch in the Porsche Executive Lunchroom, and, then, since Herr Schneider had other business, he left me to take a buyer's guided tour of the Porsche Museum and get a two-hour inspection of my metallic blue Porsche 911 Targa with my personal mechanic. The mechanic seemed a bit miffed that this was my first Porsche, but he finally turned over the keys and warned me to stay under 4000 RPM for the first 1000 kilometers. Hell, 4000 RPM in fifth gear is well past 100 MPH! My beautiful baby Porsche 911 Targa flew back to Ahlhorn, has been

with me through seven family moves, and is still exciting to drive.

LIVING HISTORY IN NIEDERSACHSEN
There is an abundance of WW II history in Northern Germany, but you must ask a German the specific question. Where were you, and, what did you do in WWII? I regretted that the Germans were losing their few veterans, as we were in the US. One lunch break at Ahlhorn, I was talking about Luftwaffe pilots and history with some of the Hog Drivers, when my German secretary offered. "I worked at Oldenburg AB for the Wing Commander and he was a WW II pilot. Maybe you have heard of him? He was Oberst Erich Hartmann."

Hartmann was the world's leading ace of WW II with 352 kills. Astounded, we listened to her tales of working for Oberst Hartmann and how he led his Fighter Wing (JagdGeswade 71). If a jock didn't know of Erich Hartman, he shouldn't be in fighters.

I was sitting in a static display A-10 for Ahlhorn's FLUGTAG celebration when an elderly gentleman climbed up the stairs and looked inside the Hog's cockpit. I thought it a bit unusual that he was being escorted by one of the Luftwaffe squadron commanders: Oberstleutnant Hans Nichols, my peer and friend. In German, I asked the gentleman, introduced as Herr Schmidt, if he was a pilot and would he like to climb into the seat. Most definitely! I moved to sit on the far cockpit rail and Herr Schmitt climbed in, sat down and looked at the cockpit displays. Still in German he said, "There are too many instruments. When I started flying there was only barometer, oil temperature, and engine revolution gauges."

"Herr Schmidt means a propeller RPM." Oberstleutnant Nichols interjected in English.

"Nein, the propeller was attached to the engine and the whole engine rotated. It was a Wankel engine"

"Your English is sehr gut, Herr Schmidt," I replied.

"If you had spent time in an English POW camp after both wars, you would learn English also!"

He was an observation and fighter pilot in WW I and WW II. He also had the misfortune (or maybe good fortune) to be shot down and captured late in each war. With his hearing failing, he became a sailplane pilot and held several of the highest awards for sailplane pilots. I got to know Herr Schmitt better at social events over the next year as he was a rather famous person in Niedersachsen. I was amazed, but maybe not, when I saw him on the local German TV station, serving as a judge for a dance contest among very scantily clad go-go dancers. Even at 88 years old he was still a thrill-seeking fighter pilot at heart.

While attending a New Year's party in 1983 at the Officers Club on Oldenburg AB, consuming my share of schnapps and great German wine, I was cornered by three local civilian gentlemen and the conversation turned to flying. It turned out that one of the very nice gentlemen, Herr Jan Späte, was the father of Oldenburg AB's Hauptman Späte whom I met and flew with. Herr Späte's son was flying Alpha Jets in the Wing at Oldenburg and just returned from three years as an IP in the NATO Pilot Training course at Sheppard AFB, Texas. I thought it amusing that Hauptman Späte now spoke English with a Texas accent. Between our combined knowledge of English and German, I learned Herr Späte first flew Messerschmitt Bf-109s on the Eastern front in WW II and then flew the ME-163 rocket fighter from Oldenburg and neighboring airfields. Oldenburg sits under a straight line from East Anglia, England to Berlin, so he had a "target rich environment" and a total of 13 kills including three B-17s near Oldenburg and Bremen. His tales of hypergolic rocket fuel, screaming climbs and high-speed gliding head-on gun attacks of B-17s and B-24s were heart stopping. Herr Späte was never shot down but was grounded when the Allied bombers destroyed all their aircraft, parts and petroleum. Before he could be forced into becoming an infantryman, the Brits crossed the north German plains and he was taken prisoner for a year.

When the other two German gentlemen found I flew the Thunderbolt II, they said they owed their lives to the Thunderbolts in WW II. That seemed rather odd for a German to claim, so I asked "Why?" In the German culture, you must ask a German the direct question. Both gentlemen were 15-year-old conscripts in 1945, loaded with others on a troop train bound from Oldenburg to the Eastern front (almost to Berlin by then). Not far out of Oldenburg, the train was discovered by three P-47 Thunderbolts who "shot the hell out of the engine and the Army guard's car." All the teenagers hopped off the wrecked train and went home to quietly await the arrival of the Allies three months later. The American Thunderbolt pilots never could have guessed that by shooting up that train they saved the lives of many young Germans.

TANKERS AND REFUELING

As with the Bentwaters' flyers, we were scheduled for night tankers out over the chilly North Sea. Because of the very early sunset in winter, we could take off in late afternoon, press out into the North Sea, rendezvous with an Air Force tanker in an assigned track, normally called Aerial Refueling Area 6 or ARA 6, take our allotted fuel in the dark and then sprint back to Ahlhorn for the 5 o'clock Happy Hour at the O'Club.

Air refueling missions were not always successful events for Hog Drivers. We relied almost completely on the radar controllers to get us together because the Hog lacked a radar or any excess airspeed, often used to make up for crappy controllers. On 13 October 1983, I (80-0171)

304

was leading Spike on a refueling and low-level mission to central Germany and the Heidi Refueling Track. There were multiple layers of clouds, with lots of breaks, in the refueling track. The controller must have been on meds (or not, or something else) because he ran one rejoin and we never saw the tanker. Remember, with no Hog radar, we depended on a ground radar controller to get us to visual contact with our tanker. Spike and I grumbled on our squadron FM frequency while this controller set us up for another attempt at finding the tanker. As the controller called our tanker at our 10 o'clock position, we saw the tanker over at 2 o'clock and moving away from us. Spike commented on our internal frequency, "Spike is bingo and that tanker is headed for East Germany."

"Cowboy copies."

On the refueling UHF radio I announced:

"Cowboy is Bingo fuel and departing out the bottom of the refueling track. And you might want to turn that tanker before he enters the No-Fly Zone and East Germany! Cowboy, button 6."

"Two!"

We checked in on our squadron UHF while we dropped from Flight Level 200 to 500 feet AGL and started our low-level home with no kind thoughts for the controller. The 81st Wing would have to schedule another tanker mission.

On 23 November 1983, Spike and I finally filled our semiannual air refueling requirements on one day as Spike led me to a successful day refueling with a tanker, call sign "Dobby 51", in the Heidi track. Obviously, we had a different controller and better weather. We returned to crappy weather at Ahlhorn, but turned the aircraft for another go. After a short break and a very short update briefing, I led the successful night air refueling mission out to ARA 6 over the North Sea with Dobby 52 as our tanker. Both tankers flew from the tanker task force at RAF Mildenhall, England. These were "good Dobbys", long before Harry Potter arrived.

GERMAN POLICE?
Back when we were still worrying about the godless communist hordes attacking to the west, I learned you can't take titles at face value. My A-10 Forward Operating Location (FOL) in Germany was responsible

for air support across the famous north German plains and we often went forward to recon the potential main battle area, from the border fence with East Germany backward toward the Corps rear areas.

Under NATO's General Defensive Plan (GDP) for a possible Russian invasion, the center of our area was the ground responsibility of the Dutch army. The Dutch kept only a very small force in place in Germany and planned to reinforce with their heavier forces directly from the Netherlands if tensions escalated. Due to internal NATO politics, the actual forces that walked the friendly side of the border were German national police, known as the Bundesgruenschutz. These were the guys in green jackets that you saw at the border crossings and at the airports in Germany.

The terrain in northern Germany is quite different from the hills of Bavaria or the Fulda Gap. The land is generally flat and quite soft with numerous rivers; a terrain that is not good for armor approaches except in the dead of winter when things freeze solid. Southeast of Hamburg the border forms a salient that sticks eastward along the Elbe River. The northern side of this arrowhead is the Elbe River, tough to cross, but the southern side offered several high-speed approaches from the East German town of Salzwedel toward Uelzen on our side of the border. This entire salient was cut off at the base by the north-south Elbe-Seitenkanaal, from Hamburg to the canal between Wolfsburg and Braunschweig. The Elbe-Seitenkanaal was wide, built with a sloping eastern bank but a near vertical western bank. It made an effective cliff-like barrier (or tank trap) whose defense could provide delaying time for NATO reinforcements to move forward.

This area was low on the list of viable approaches for the Red armor hordes and low on the list of attention spots by NATO forces. When I learned that the German police were responsible for the "fence," an important tactical delaying responsibility, and, yet, I saw cattle grazing right up to the East German side of the fence, I felt no doubt that this could be a weak link if the war "balloon" ever went up.

I met a Dutch Major, the Dutch Brigade S-3, and he offered a recon by helicopter of our mutual area of responsibility under the GDP. After picking me up at Ahlhorn, we flew right up to the border, looked at the improved roads and railroad sidings on the East German side and scouted out positions to defend with reference points for the A-10s to use in Close Air Support / Air Interdiction. Key was the small hamlet of Bergen, which sits astride the highway about two kilometers from the border, with a dominating view of the approach. Bergen also had water towers and terrain features conducive to identification by the A-10s.

The Dutch S-3 asked if I wanted to visit the border police barracks near Uelzen and I agreed as we turned the helo westward. Uelzen protected the major north-south highway and the intersection of the westbound road from Bergen. A reasonable place to defend, but I still doubted a police force could slow down the large Russian/East German forces. As our helicopter climbed over Uelzen, my first glance of the "police barracks" indicated more than a bunch of border cops. The "barracks" was, in fact, a kaserne with five large multi-story barracks, a headquarters building, PT/training grounds and what appeared to be a large motor pool behind.

We landed at the marked helo pad and were met by a young Hauptman (Captain) wearing fatigues. We were warmly greeted and briefed by the commander, a trim, extremely fit Oberstleutnant (Lieutenant Colonel). This guy was far more Ranger than traffic cop! Following lunch in their immaculate mess hall, the CO escorted us on a tour of the motor pool and his "police cars." His "cars" were well maintained M-113 armored personnel carriers with the latest equipment, including TOW anti-tank missiles. Limited by time that day, we climbed back into our helo for the trip home without an opportunity to further explore the "police" unit and its equipment.

As we departed for the short ride back to Fliegerhorst Ahlhorn, my Dutch host asked if I was impressed by the Bundesgruenschutz. I replied, "I may be a poor A-10 Hog driver, but I know a good Mechanized Infantry battalion when I see it." He just smiled.

HIGHWAY 84

One of the rarest patches from my days flying A-10s was for *HIGHWAY 84*. Only 200 of the patches were made and they were given to the participants who actually landed fighters on a German autobahn (later Autobahn 29) during a 1984 exercise named "Highway '84." Before a new section of the autobahn was opened to autos, the Luftwaffe conducted a three-day exercise to practice operations from an austere autobahn strip located 5 km northwest of Fliegerhorst Ahlhorn.

The Luftwaffe provided the fuel trucks and ground staff, so participating aircraft could launch on a full training mission enroute back to their home base. I led the first two A-10s from nearby Ahlhorn, the first American to land on the autobahn strip. A portable control tower was placed at each end of the runway and communication lines were installed through the local telephone lines to the mobile towers and back to Fliegerhorst Ahlhorn. Hauptman Uli and the Ahlhorn tower controllers worked in the small mobile control tower for all autobahn operations.

Every Northern Europe country in NATO participated. They landed and launched A-10s, F-4s, F-104s, Alpha Jets, Jaguars, Harriers, Viggens, and other fighters. The largest tactical fighters to land were probably the British and German Tornados. In our one incident, a Luftwaffe Oberst taxied off the pavement with resulting minor damage. He then took his wingman's F-104 and flew back to his Bavarian home field, leaving his Hauptman wingman to await repairs.

WILD GEESE

Sounds and sights can create indelible stamps on your memory and heart. On a cold German November night, I stepped out of our house onto the back patio to be amazed by the nighttime quiet of Ahlhorn and bask in the brilliant moonlight of a cloudless sky. Soon the quiet was disturbed by an intermittent and faint honking sound. Closer the faint sounds came until almost overhead. There I saw a perfect "V" formation of at least twenty geese flying south, illuminated by the moon. This formation was followed by two more formations of equal or larger number. I watched in awe of this great night flying show until they disappeared behind the tall trees between our home and the airfield. I believe that *The Sound of Music*'s Maria stated it perfectly, and the "Wild geese that fly with the moon on their wings" will forever be one "of my favorite things."

SOCIAL ODDITIES

Over the years, I noticed some common fighter jock characteristics, whether we were at home base or TDY elsewhere. The first is a drop in military formality when a flight is scheduled. The players become Flight Leader and wingman/wingmen. A Major could fly on the wing of a Captain or a Lieutenant Colonel on the wing of a Captain, becoming just a position number, i.e. Hammer 1, Hammer 2, etc. The radio check-ins sounded like "Cowboy check!" followed in turn with "Two", "Three" and "Four!" In the squadron briefing areas, a Lieutenant did not have to yell for "Colonel Stevenson!" Instead, he called "Cowboy check!" and received a loud "Two", which led him to the correct briefing room. In this case, it was not a Lead/Wingman issue, just trying to get joined up.

The Army didn't quite understand this concept when I was in the 92nd and Captain Gene Renuart, the deployed 92nd Flight Commander, led four A-10s into Feucht Army Air Field with a Lieutenant Colonel as his Number 3. Flight positions were based on experience, not rank, on that flight. We went to a 2nd Armored Cavalry orientation briefing, and, when the Army aviators saw I was a Lieutenant Colonel, their commander, a Major, rushed into the room and said,

"If I knew you were coming, sir, I would have personally given the briefing."

"Why? Is the current briefer, Warrant Officer 3 Howard, telling us lies?"

Incidentally, this Mister Howard could have been a double for the actor / director Ron Howard. Spooky!

In BOQs, individual room doors were used as "social signals" on deployments. This was true at Incirlik, Aviano, Leipheim, or Ahlhorn, along with other locations. Normally the entire squadron / deployment / flight returned to the BOQ at the same time. If it was a rough day due to weather, training, or number of sorties flown, the jocks retreated to their rooms and the room doors would be closed for a while. After some "contemplation time", the F-4 or Hog Drivers emerged and headed off to the O'Club bar or a local restaurant. On a successful day of flying fighters, the jocks did not close their doors and were soon moving freely down the hallway, room to room, telling tall tales and recounting the day's events. The move to the Club happened earlier in this case, with better potential for an interesting evening.

Claire got a different view of the Hog Drivers' life at Ahlhorn when she invited the deployed Hog Drivers over to our Commander's Quarters for dinner. The guys arrived after flying and we ate great steaks and fixings for dinner. Instead of being hard charging and rowdy pilots, several Hog Drivers began to drift off to sleep while sitting on the living room floor after dinner. I explained that it was a long day with multiple sorties flown by all and they normally crash not long after dinner. Despite tales to the contrary, many days on rotation were demanding and exhausting with little time or energy for raising hell. Now, weekends were an exception.

As indicated in the discussion of the A-10 crash near Ahlhorn, time off was hard to come by (and not be disturbed). I did carry on the

309

Christmas ski trips to the Alps with Chris while he was home from Ipswich School. I asked Claire if she wanted to come and ski but she said Chris and I needed some father – son time. So, for the two winters of my Ahlhorn tour, Chris and I travelled to the Garmisch-Partenkirchen Armed Forces Recreation Complex to ski the Alps and the Alpspitze. Chris was like the German kids on the mountain: draw a straight line from top to bottom of each run and then go for it. My approach was a bit less daring and I often stopped at the half-way house for gluhwein to ward off the cold.

OXBOL 1984 - JAAT

In January 1984, the FOL leadership and maintenance troops deployed, with me as the commander, from Ahlhorn to the Danish Air Force Base at Skrydstrup to conduct a coordinated Joint Air Attack Team (JAAT) exercise on the Oksbol Gunnery Range. The Danish peninsula is quite narrow and, in fact, the Skrydstrup GCA pattern for runways 10 or 28, extended from the North Sea in the west to the Baltic on the east. Oksbol was a rather large gunnery range some 20 miles north west of Esbjerg, on the west coast of the Danish peninsula and one of the few ranges that could accept A-10s, artillery and TOW missiles from attack helicopters. The JAAT concept consisted of closely coordinated suppressive Army artillery fire, attack helicopter fires, A-10 attacks, and then suppressive attack helo fires and artillery to cover the A-10s departure. If it worked correctly, the bad guys wound up with 60 seconds of continuous and devastating steel on target.

It was a "Rainbow" deployment to Skrydstrup AB, with the two-ship flights from the 91st and 509th squadrons working under my command at Oksbol. It seems that once word got out to the Bentwaters gang about our planned JAAT training, everyone wanted to play. The US Army artillery was three 8-inch artillery batteries from the 4th Battalion, 3rd Field Artillery of the 2nd Armor Division (Forward) at Garlstadt, Germany. Also from Garlstadt was the battle staff of the 2nd Battalion, 66th armor, who provided the command post exercise inputs to activate the JAAT forces. The Oksbol deployment provided excellent planning and coordination exercises for the Army ground forces since the A-10s were designed and employed to defeat enemy armor for our ground forces, in coordination with attack helos and artillery. The helicopter participants were the attack section and scout helos from the 2nd Armored Cavalry Regiment (2nd ACR) at Feucht Army Airfield, Nuremberg in Bavaria, with whom I worked while in the 92nd TFS. The attack helos worked for the "Battle Captain", CPT Juan Ithier, who spoke with a strong Puerto Rican accent. You did not have to authenticate CPT Ithier on the radio after you heard him speak.

We began with one day of familiarization and then moved to three days of live fire. We started with baby steps, meaning some 90 seconds to complete the attack sequence. Over two days, we cut that in half to a total attack time of 45 seconds. It was fast and furious with artillery starting to suppress the target and then shifting to the flanks as the attack helos popped up and engaged the bad guys with TOW missiles. As the TOW's were launched, the A-10s arrived in a pop-up maneuver to deliver Maverick missiles and 30mm cannon fire. As the A-10s broke off their attack, the helos again attacked. They were closely followed by the artillery shifting from the flanks to the target area. Hooah!

Proving again that it is a small military world, the 4th Bn/3rd Artillery was commanded by LTC Jerry Laws. In 1977, when I arrived in the ALFA Agency we were wrapping up the JAAT concept with tests flown at Hunter Liggett Military Reservation in California. Then Major, Jerry Laws was a project officer for JAAT from the Army TRADOC. I, at that time, was a JAAT project officer at ALFA and for the Tactical Air Command. Now, seven years later, we were commanding two of the awesome firepower components of this JAAT exercise with real world players, seeing what we created in theory become a very successful reality. I enjoyed talking with Jerry on our few meetings. Jerry went on to become a Brigadier General and commanded the Army White Sands Missile Range.

Integrating the eight-inch artillery fires and live TOWS from the helos with A-10s, using the real-world shooters and crews, made this the US forces' best-ever A-10 JAAT training. Every big operation has a few glitches and our tactical glitch came when a young lieutenant A-10 wingman flexed to the wrong side during the target approach and thus came too close to the lateral suppressing artillery fires. We fragged a TF-34 engine with secondary 8-inch artillery shrapnel! I needed to explain that to the 81st DO and Chief of Maintenance. Fortunately, it was a quick fix and the Hog was back in the air the next day. Our entire training was well covered in European *Stars & Stripes* articles on 10 and 11 February 1984; and I even saw my picture in the newspaper. Boy, did I catch grief from my peers over that. I think they were envious of the best JAAT training ever held in Europe and I was the leader of the whole show.

36

Weather and Local Flying

March 13, 1984, Spike and I were going to flip-flop on the flying schedule so that we could each get single ship instrument approaches at several of the Nord Deutschland airfields. I was flying the morning go on this day, so Spike and I checked the weather and I briefed him on my flight plan before filing at the German Base Operations. I would depart Ahlhorn on an IFR flight plan and head north to get a radar surveillance approach from our good buddies at Oldenburg AB and then head northeast VFR. The Luftwaffe Fighter/Bomber wing (JaBoG43) at Oldenburg flew Alpha Jets and an American exchange pilot Captain "Mac" McElveen was assigned. I flew a couple of times with Mac in his Alpha Jet and we often partied with the Oldenburg pilots. They were always welcome at Ahlhorn's O'Club. Even the two Luftwaffe Oberst Wing Commanders were close friends.

I accomplished my preflight, engine start and taxi to the end of the runway in short order. After the "last chance" crew gave my Hog a final inspection in the arming area, they signaled that I was good and my Gau-8 gun was safed up. I saluted the crew chief and thought, "Damn shame none of the ranges were open today or this could be a real fun instrument / gunnery ride." I switched from Ground Control to Ahlhorn Tower with a cheerful "Ahlhorn, Cowboy is ready at the end."

"Cowboy, maintain runway heading, climb and maintain flight level 050, departure on 259.2, Schöen flug, Wiederhoren."

"Cowboy is cleared for takeoff, runway heading, zero-five-zero, departure channel 16. Wiederhoren"

The local towers and departure controllers used "Wiederhoren" instead of the "wiedersehen" often heard among the Germans (and tourists). "Wiederhoren" literally meant "until I hear from you again."

They knew that they would be hearing from me by radio upon my return in a little over an hour.

Strobe lights-on, pitot heat-on, IFF-on and set, instruments-on and set, time-noted, frequency preset, I was ready to go. I closed the canopy thinking, "Man, it actually does get quiet," engaged nose wheel steering, advanced the throttles and turned left to move onto Runway 27. I pulled onto the concrete end of the runway - the middle 6,000 feet of which was porous asphalt with the first 1,000 feet on each end made of concrete. I turned the nose of my Hog on the centerline and put my gun sight cross on the centerline stripe. The aircraft's heading indicator settled on 271 degrees, the correct heading. The ILS needle swung down and centered in the HSI and the steering bar centered in the attitude indicator. At least the plane and the ILS navigation system agreed on where the centerline of the Ahlhorn runway was. That was a valuable help if I came back in marginal weather, although the Ahlhorn GCA unit provided the best PAR controllers I ever encountered. If necessary, they could talk my wheels right onto the centerline.

I pushed the throttles up, checked the fan speed and EGT and released brakes. Off we went. I knew it was a slow flying day in our Niedersachsen airspace because Ahlhorn Departure control handed me off directly to Oldenburg Approach and I did not have to deal with the regional Weser Radar. I asked for and received a Precision Approach Radar (PAR) "talk down" to Runway 28 at Oldenburg and then departed VFR to the northeast for Nordholz AB and an ILS approach to Runway 26. (Nordholz shared a common history with Ahlhorn in that both were zeppelin bases in WW I).

After leaving Nordholz, I leveled off at seven thousand feet, turned northeast when I heard a radar warning (RHAW) chirp in my headset indicating that I was being looked at by somebody in an air-to-air mode. The tone and RHAW symbol on the RHAW scope told me that it was most likely a German Kriegs Marine F-104 from Leck AB, located up the coast almost on the Danish border. My first thought after shoving my throttles to the stops was: "Uh oh, this fight is going to be right over the Elbe River and North Sea, probably within sight of the Hamburg suburbs." Nothing more came of the RHAW chirp, but I kept my head on a swivel for the F-104. Slowing down, I contacted the local Approach Radar and asked for a PAR to Runway 21 at Itzehoe (ITZ, but now identified as EDHF). The radar controller made me confirm that I did not want to land at Itzehoe and that this would be a low approach *only* from the radar approach. Ja!

I lost sight of the ground as I coasted in from the North Sea. The sea was creating a very low-level layer of clouds that looked like the world was covered with snow or thick white cream. I could see one extremely tall communications tower poking its head above the "snow" to the southeast. As I descended and configured my A-10 for the approach I enjoyed unlimited visibility and beautiful clear blue skies above me. The solid layer of clouds began at the Final Approach Fix altitude of 1600 feet, and, as soon as the controller told me to begin descent on the glide slope, the outside world turned gray and I could not even see the wingtips of my A-10.

The PAR went well and I remained in the soup until I reached an altitude of 350 feet, when the brightest landing approach lights in Europe blazed in front of me. White "running rabbit" light, red, green, and blue lights lit up the front of my cockpit. I pushed the throttles up at my 200-foot Decision Height, radioed "Cowboy is missed approach," and, by the time I got the landing gear retracted, the airfield was gone behind me. ITZ was a helicopter and utility airfield. The longest runway (21) was frighteningly short 1800 feet in length. Despite the great approach lighting, the runway was too short for an A-10! That's why the controller earlier confirmed I was going to be a low approach and not to attempt a landing. After climbing up through the gray world to sunshine on top, I was still unable to see anything below, including the Elbe River because of the dense fog. In a kind gesture, ITZ Approach Radar instructed me to maintain 2000 feet to keep me out of Hamburg's Approach Airspace, which was always busy and a pain in the rear (for both of us). Crossing the Elbe, I cancelled my instrument clearance and turned southwest for Ahlhorn.

I contacted Weser Radar a couple of minutes later and was handed off to Ahlhorn Approach, who reported the weather changed and was now 400-foot ceilings with 2 miles visibility at Ahlhorn. "Damn, this is going to be an approach just like Itzehoe, but I have to land out of this one." However, my confidence in the Ahlhorn GCA controllers was unshakeable. I asked Approach Control for a PAR approach with ILS back-up and received an affirmative answer. This allowed me to see the ILS presentation on the A-10 instruments as the GCA controller was giving instructions. At Ahlhorn, the ILS and PAR approaches coincided in space. Many airbases in Europe and even in the US were not that lucky.

Ahlhorn Approach flawlessly vectored me onto a final heading of 271 degrees and I dropped gear, flaps and cracked open the speed brakes. I trimmed up on final – the Hog has no autopilot like big trash hauler aircraft. Hog drivers FLEW every approach. Pitch, heading and power were perfect as the controller told me to begin descent. I reduced power a bit and lowered the nose 2.7 degrees. You don't really think I could read 2.7 degrees, do you? I heard only "On course, on glide path" from the GCA controller, repeatedly. I hadn't touched a thing since I began my final descent. I couldn't believe how perfectly the plane is trimmed for the approach. In the humble voice of a fighter pilot, I mumbled into my oxygen mask: "OK, Lord, you can fly this approach and I will get the next one."

At 100 feet above decision height, both my ILS needles and the Ahlhorn PAR controller were still telling me "On course, on glide path." Cool, but where is the ground? What happened to the 400-foot ceiling? A few seconds later the controller said, "Approaching Decision Height, At Decision Height, on glide path, I will continue the approach." I mentally stuttered and asked myself "Where is the damn ground?" In the second that it took me to start the throttles forward to go missed approach, I saw the running white strobe lights that led to the runway. I retarded the throttles as more of the runway came into view. My landing gear rolled onto the Ahlhorn pavement as my ever-present PAR controller calmly stated, "Wheels should be touching down - now." I continued my roll out to the far end of the runway, thanked the GCA folks (and God) and turned onto the taxiway to contact Ahlhorn Ground Control. I called Uli in the tower:

"Cowboy is clear of the runway; can you have the SOF come up on squadron VHF?"

Shortly, "Cowboy, this is Spike on Victor, over."

"Spike, what the hell is going on? The field is below minimums!"

"Cowboy, you were the only Hog in the air. The weather went down after you started on final and I didn't want to bother you on the approach."

"Damn it, Spike, that scared the hell out of me. You owe me a beer! Or two!"

I could hear Uli and another tower controller laughing in the background as Spike ended with, "See you back in Ops."

DUTCH EVENTS

On occasion, the 81st Wing schedulers at Bentwaters scheduled a flight from Ahlhorn to work on the Dutch island gunnery ranges. This event provided me with a range ride to the gunnery range on the western tip of the Dutch island Terschelling. Straight line, it was about 130 nautical miles northwest of Ahlhorn and involved a great low level across flat terrain. We also worked around the fighter bases at Hopsten, Germany (F-4s) and Leeuwarden, Netherlands (F-16s) where we were fair game to be bounced. When we made it through the "bandits", the range (call sign "Jackpot") was on the sand flats on the west end of the island and our pattern was a run-in of 334 degrees with a left pattern over the passage between the islands of Terschelling and Vlieland. We dropped down as low as was comfortable on base leg and do pop-up for attacks over the beach. Our base leg was along a water passage toward the town of Terschelling and on several occasions, we met sailboats coming out of port as we whistled by at mast-high altitude. At that height, we could also see the gaggles of sea lions lounging on the beach, enjoying the air show. It seemed a bit unusual to be making our base leg on the range yet headed straight for the apartment buildings of the not so distant town of Terschelling. Lengthy but fun missions to the range!

In January 1984, the 91st Flight Commander on rotation at Ahlhorn was pulling SOF duty so that allowed "Spike" and me to take a range ride to Terschelling. It was a bitterly cold but clear European winter day and this should be a fun gun ride. We were low leveling across the Netherlands, skirting Leeuwarden Air Base, when suddenly Spike called "Cowboy, cross!" We both pulled into 4G turns toward each other and crossed to reverse heading. I immediately scanned the skies and expected to engage one or more "bandits", but Spike expanded his information.

"Cowboy, check the town at two o'clock low and the canal. They are actually skating on the canal."

Spike was right! The freeze was deep enough that the townsfolk took to skates on the canal. We had flown into a Hans Christian Andersen fairy tale at 300 knots and 300 feet altitude.

37

Fred Cuny and Departure

In late April 1984, we received a telephone call at home from a young lady in London by the name of "Rita". She informed us that my longtime friend Fred Cuny was going to stop in northern Germany for a brief stay. The call inferred that we knew Fred was coming. In a way, we did, as Fred would show up in any part of the world and we should expect him. I received his inbound flight information for the Hamburg airport and said I would gladly meet Fred and keep him for a few days. I cranked up my Porsche 911 and blazed across the autobahn to meet my long-lost Texas friend.

Fred ambled down the airplane gate like the tall cowboy he was, still in beat up cowboy boots, and squeezed me in one of his famous bear hugs. The big challenge was fitting big lanky Fred and his foot locker into my Porsche. I asked Fred what was in the foot locker and he mumbled something about remains of a refugee that proved Iraqi civilians were being gassed by the Iraqi armed forces. Enough said. We sped back to Ahlhorn where Claire warmly welcomed Fred with his beverage of choice: Dr. Pepper. However, Claire, once learning the contents, refused to let the foot locker and its remains into the house. So, the footlocker remained locked in one of our cars and locked in the garage for the duration of Fred's visit.

Fred made himself at home in our quarters in Ahlhorn. He did not venture out into the town but stayed in our yard, sitting on the back porch or helping Claire in the kitchen, making Fred's famous chili. Fred made a couple of calls to London, and, when asked how long he was staying, he replied that it depended on what "Rita" let him know. Fred was great company and we both enjoyed his stay. I asked why he stopped in Ahlhorn and he said he was keeping a low profile to avoid a subpoena from a US Senate sub-committee. After two days, Fred asked if he could come out to see my A-10 squadron. Fred was a twenty-year pilot of sailplanes and powered aircraft and the sight and sound of the

A-10s overhead made him itch to go fly. The next morning, I took Fred over to the Squadron Ops area. We were waved through by the Luftwaffe guards without a question, but when we entered the flight operations area, I was immediately challenged by my Operations NCO, Master Sergeant Davison.

"Who is the civilian and what is his security clearance to be in this area?"

"Mr. Cuny works for another government agency and I personally vouch for his security clearances. The door sign says no entry without permission of the Detachment Commander. I'm the Det Commander, Mr. Cuny is our guest for a few days and has all the security clearances needed and then some."

Fred never pushed the issue and mostly stayed out of the Operations area. He attended an A-10 flight briefing and then the post flight debrief. I gave Fred a tour of our unit facilities, including our underground operations bunker and we travelled down to a TabVee shelter for a close-up look at an A-10. We did a walk-around of the Hog and then Fred climbed up the ladder and into the pilot's seat as I stood on the boarding ladder. I showed him the cockpit layout and all the weapons switches. When I said the A-10 was just a large Cessna with a gun when it came to flight characteristics, Fred asked "Cool. How do you start this thing?" After a moment of terror wondering how I could explain the awful image in my mind, I said, "Fred, Get out of my airplane!"

Fred laughed half the way back to the Operations building. "You don't think I would try to start and fly the Hog, do you?"

"Fred, I've known you too long to rule out the possibility."

For the next three days, Fred sat outside of our Ops Building in a chair facing the runway, reading, writing and watching A-10 and Luftwaffe flight operations. When he received a call from "Rita" (which must have been some type of "all clear" message), we retraced our route to the Hamburg airport on May 1, 1984. As we traveled in the early morning across Niedersachsen to Hamburg, we saw the bonfires lighting each village as part of a German celebration called "Walpurgisnacht."

Fred's airline ticket was waiting for him; so, Fred and his footlocker corpse were off to London and from there I know not where.

Fred was my brother's and my close high school friend from the neighboring Bryan Adams High School in Dallas. For two summer camps and two school years we bonded, along with Don and Carl Long. Years later, Fred showed up at my wedding to Claire in 1970 in Houston, the first of his unannounced visits that would amuse and endear him to Claire. After our Air Force tour in Spain, Fred made a visit to the Rhodes family in Corpus Christi, another no-notice "Fly-In." We last were blessed by a Fred no-notice arrival at our first San Antonio Christmas Party in 1994. Fred flew down from the Rockwall Airport, east of Dallas. When Fred came in through our front door, and I recovered from the shock of seeing him, I gave him a bear hug. Fred winced and said he was recovering from cracked ribs suffered in a recent truck accident in Turkey.

Acting as one of the world's greatest experts on refugee settlement, Fred travelled through the trouble spots of the world. Fred was murdered in Chechnya in 1995 by the Chechnyan rebels when he was suspected of being a spy for the Russians. Despite courageous and exhaustive searches in that dangerous time and place, Fred Cuny's body was never recovered. His death was a great loss to the world and to me personally. I highly recommend a superb book on Fred entitled: *"The Man Who Tried To Save The World"* by Scott Anderson.

DETACHMENT COMMUNITY EVENTS
Aside from flight operations, being the commander at an FOL meant dealing with family issues ranging from the death of a newborn child at the Army hospital, distraught wives (one diagnosed with acute paranoia), and having to give an Article 15 to one of my finest NCOs, who was caught DUI by the local German politzei. The amount of paperwork that came across my desk was staggering.

Another critical part of my job as commander was supporting the unit chapel activities. Church was important to our small American community. Our inter-denominational church was established by the previous detachment commander and my family and I wholeheartedly supported and attended services. Monthly, we held the service with a circuit-riding Army Chaplain; otherwise, we conducted our own service. The "vestry" of our church was made up of the senior NCOs and families who together prepared everything from music, sermons, and refreshments for attendees, to driving a school bus to pick up families attending the service. As a commander, I believed an ecumenical presence was important to our community, improved morale of our airmen and families alike, and added to the quality of life. Through the strength of this group of 40 or so Americans, many found a spiritual home in this foreign country. An amazing result was the beautiful service at Christmas 1983 when 15 adults and children received a baptism from our visiting Chaplain.

LOSSES

A truly tragic event at Ahlhorn was the suicide of one of our enlisted airman. The airman become involved in an affair with a married woman, and, when the affair was brought to light, he hanged himself, jumping from the second-floor window of an apartment building. The death was shocking to all our Detachment personnel and families. First Sergeant Kornegay took the lead in working with the Army chaplains, securing the deceased's personal effects and arranging shipment back to the States. Kornegay assembled all the enlisted personnel and conducted what is now termed a "Critical Incident Review" to disseminate all the correct information and discuss the events. Senior Master Sergeant Kornegay was indispensable in handling anything that concerned our enlisted personnel. He was indeed the right arm of the commander. We never determined what prompted such an extreme action on the young man's part.

Another family loss was the death of a very young baby to SIDS (Sudden Infant Death Syndrome). Even now, after many years of research, SIDS remains mostly unexplained. The parents, an NCO and his wife, had been trying to have a child for a long time and took the death very hard. The loss was made worse when the family, in their grief, accused the Army hospital of negligence in the child's death. The NCO was completing the second year of his three-year tour and requested an immediate transfer to the States. After discussions with the NCO, First Sergeant Kornegay and the impacted work section personnel, I approved his request and forwarded it. The request was granted by USAFE and the Air Force.

DAS ENDE

On June 15, 1984, I flew my last sortie in the Hog (#82-0656), ending the best four years of flying fighters that I ever knew. The last mission, with Tom Spencer as "Two", was a CAS mission for the British Army, strafe at Nordhorn range and ended with a great (my opinion) airshow back at Ahlhorn. The arrival started with a gear-up 300 knot low pass down Runway 27, then went back around to the south and re-entered for a gear and flaps, low and slow, fly-by of the tower. Spencer was close in tight to my right, as I waved at Uli in the tower, just off my left wingtip. Then we went out and re-entered for a high-speed pass, over the Det 3 area and below the tower level, followed by a beautiful pitch-up to the right-hand traffic pattern. Since my wingie was on my right side, I made an aggressive pull-up and then rolled over the top of "Two", climbing to the 1000-foot-high traffic pattern on the right side of the runway. Spencer flew formation perfectly, rock steady, and then pitched up to follow me. I carefully planted my A-10 on the Luftwaffe runway and taxied back for my last flight ceremony including wet down by my Ahlhorn personnel and the A-10 guys on rotation. Fire trucks, water and champagne. Even Oberst Rappke, the new Luftwaffe Base Commander, came to bid farewell.

The school year at Ipswich School ended just days before my change of command, so Claire, Trevor and I loaded into our Volvo wagon and took the ferry from Hook van Holland to Harwich, England. We drove the now familiar few miles to Ipswich and loaded Chris and his goods into the car and strapped his footlocker onto the roof. We later realized the superb education Chris received in his three plus years at Ipswich made academics easier for him all the way into college. Ipswich School knew how to instruct and develop excellent study habits in students. We retraced our steps back to Harwich and the ferry back to the continent as I was still without follow-on orders and was scheduled to turn the command over to Lt Col Bill Hinton on June 18th. The footlocker on top of the Volvo ruined our gas mileage and we spent some anxious moments in Osnabruck, Germany, trying to find a late-night petrol station to refuel and make our way back to Ahlhorn.

On 18 June 1984, the 81st TFW Commander, Colonel Williams, flew to Ahlhorn to officiate the transfer of Command to Lt Col Bill Hinton, with many local German military and civilian dignitaries present. Attending were three Oberst Wing Commanders and I was very happy to see among them the relatively new HTG 64 Kommodore Jorge Rappke and Oberst Rudi from his Lufttransportgeswader 62 (LTG 62), Fliegerhorst Wunstorf, 65 miles southeast. Other than Oberst Geissinger, I most enjoyed interacting with Oberst Rudi. I won his friendship when I sent an A-10 to stand static display at his base's Flug Tag celebration in late 1982 and we became close associates through our common interests and our frequent social engagements.

My Change of Command ceremony was highlighted by a Luftwaffe gift of a four-ship diamond formation flyby of Alpha Jets from JaboG 43 at Oldenburg AB, one very low, high-speed pass over our unit formation and reviewing stand, then a slower return pass with gear and flaps. Both passes were well done and I sneaked a glance at the JaboG

323

43 Oberst on the reviewing stand who smiled at me, another gift as it was totally out of character for an Oberst at an official function. The local German community was represented by two friends, Gemeindedirektor Herbert Wolff and Grossenkneten's Burgermeister Paul Brinkman, with whom I often coordinated German – American events.

That evening the permanent party folks of Detachment 3 held a joint farewell dinner for me and Mike Spurlock, joint due to the cost of a party at the Luftwaffe O'Club and the limited number of assigned American people at Ahlhorn. Mike arrived at Ahlhorn just two weeks before I took command so we were leaving almost at the same time. The job was a strain, mostly issues not related to flying A-10s, but I was still reluctantly leaving a fantastic job. The German contract moving company that was selected by Bremerhaven Logistics did the best job we ever experienced, packing and shipping our household goods with German efficiency.

We used a commercial company to ship our pet dog, a Sheltie, from Hamburg airport to the States, and, then with the household goods gone, we moved to the wonderful lakeside Gut Moorbeck Hotel near Wildeshausen for our last two nights. On night two, Claire somehow got a moth stuck in her ear; the Germans had no screens on the windows and no air conditioning. The excruciatingly painful noise of the critter beating on her eardrum resulted in a late-night trip to the Emergency Room in the Krankhaus Johanneum Wildeshausen (hospital). The ER doctor used hot water to drown the moth and then extracted it. Claire was wound up mentally for hours and eager to depart Germany the next day. I shipped our two cars to the States; the Volvo by military transportation to Charleston, South Carolina and the Porsche via Volkswagen shipping to Bayonne, New Jersey. With our tour complete in Europe, the four of us took a taxi to the Hamburg airport to begin the trip to South Carolina.

As we left Germany, twin Donald left the Hunt brothers' legal department after six years to enter the court system in the Dallas – Fort Worth area. This was a major leap from corporate law to the judicial side which served him well for the next 30 years plus.

507th TACAIR CONTROL WING

38

Shaw AFB, SC

I remember standing in the garden of our house in Ahlhorn, Germany, on the verge of tears, when I got my orders to the 507th Tactical Air Control Wing at Shaw AFB, South Carolina. I was a fighter pilot, and this was the kiss of death as far as I could tell. Not only was it a non-flying assignment, it was on the "Radar" side of the 507th Wing. The TAC AIR Control Wing consisted of two operational sides. The Radar side was a Tactical Air Control Center (TACC) which provided the planning and air control facilities for a Theater of Operations. It also held four mobile radar squadrons to provide radar coverage for a Theater. The Air Operations side was made up of the deployable Air Support Operations Center (ASOC) which supported the planning, tasking and control of air assets for an Army Corps, a large FAC squadron with aircraft and ground units to support all Army units east of the Mississippi River and a heavy lift helicopter squadron to provide airlift support of all TAC AIR Control Wing units. Of course, the support for these diverse units required a very substantial organization.

Amazingly, in short order we found and purchased a new house on the western side of the city of Sumter, so my commute to the base was only ten minutes. Trevor went into a church pre-school and Chris went to Wilson Hall School, just across the street.

507 TACC
Upon arriving at Shaw AFB and the 507th (also home of 9th Air Force and the 363rd TFW) I went to the DO (Air) and begged to be reassigned to the Flying side of the Wing. "No Can Do" was the reply, so I put on my best face and signed in to my new unit, the 507th Tactical Air Control Center (TACC). I was now an Assistant Director of Operations (ADO) for the TACC and I was the only officer with experience in chemical warfare. Since chemical defense was getting a lot of press in the Middle East at that time, guess what I was going to be doing?

The Squadron Commander and I were the only field grade officers in the TACC who had not been passed over for promotion. Even my boss, Lt Col Don O'Neill, was passed over. Don was great to work for and he gave me total freedom in developing a chemical warfare training program for the squadron. Bringing this huge unit of about 300 troops and a vast amount of equipment up to USAFE chemical warfare standards in just two months was a new and challenging experience for all us. We taught and exercised until it was "Good" but not "Great." Within two months, the TACC deployed for Exercise Desert Eagle to Vandenberg AFB, California. Desert Eagle involved a multi-service exercise reaching over most of the deserts in the far west and the TACC was supporting Air Force Central Command (CENTAF) staff.

Murphy's Law was alive and well in Desert Eagle as an F-4E from Seymour Johnson AFB dropped a 2000# bomb into the California forest from a refueling track located overhead at 24,000 feet. We soon learned it was cockpit switch error! That crew got to ride a C-130 back to Seymour Johnson instead of their F-4E. Fortunately, the National Park Service finally located the unexploded bomb and it was removed. To ensure equal fame for the Army, a Special Forces team put a laser spot on a working civilian mine, located just 200 yards off the Nevada military reservation, and an F-4E dropped a live 2000-pound bomb on that mine instead of the real target. There were no casualties because the civilians were on a shopping run to the nearest, 57 miles away, grocery store. I presume the mine owner, in typical fashion, sued the government, becoming wealthy on Uncle Sam's dollar without digging another ounce of whatever ore he was after.

The TACC communications team deployed our new satellite communications vans for Desert Eagle for the first time. The satellite antenna and the vans were hundreds of yards separated out in the Mojave Desert (a tactical practice) and connected by the "new" fiber-optic cables. After the first four days, we lost connectivity between the antennae and vans every night due to the fiber optic cable being cut. The operators finally discovered that coyotes loved to chew on the coating around the cable; it tasted like candy to them. The crews wrapped the cable with electrical tape and prompted the Air Force to ask the manufacturer to change insulation.

To make deployed life more interesting (and stressful), at one time during the exercise it appeared that an Atlantic hurricane was headed for our homes in South Carolina, while a Pacific hurricane was headed for southern California. I felt totally helpless with one storm bearing down on us and the other storm headed for our families. Both storms eventually turned away from our areas of concern.

682 ASOC

When we returned from Desert Eagle and I attended a few 507th Wing staff meetings, I saw the 682nd ASOC was commanded by Lt Col Bill Alexander. Bill was one of my IPs at Columbus' Pilot Training, some 13 years before. The ASOC supported the Army's 18th Airborne Corps and deployed whenever the 18th Corps headquarters moved from Ft Bragg, North Carolina. Like AFCENT and the TACC, 18th Corps was designated as an element of US CENTCOM, focused on the Middle East. I drove over to the ASOC on the east side of Shaw AFB and said hi to my old IP and we swapped assignment stories. After that meeting, Bill and I regularly lunched at the Golf Clubhouse Grill since it was about half way between our two units. A month later, when Bill came out on the new Colonel's promotion list, I actively sought his squadron command. The 507th DO and Wing Commander took Bill's recommendation and offered me the job; I assumed command of the 682nd ASOC Squadron in March 1985.

I loved being back with paratroopers, and the grunts at XVIII Corps staff meetings were amazed to see an Air Force Lieutenant Colonel with Master Parachutist Wings. They were even more surprised when I showed up at a meeting wearing a Special Forces patch on the right shoulder of my camouflage uniform. Hooah!

Command of the ASOC introduced me to old and new challenges by the score. We ran large convoys of equipment to Ft. Bragg, Camp Pendleton or other exercise sites. I had not conducted a large, long-haul convoy since I was a 2LT at Ft Campbell. Over 100 vehicles and a half dozen pieces of very high-tech communication equipment needed phase maintenance, none of it like aircraft. What did I know about microwave transmissions or the pending upgrade to satellite communications? I had to learn. How do I keep tech controllers in the unit when ATT, Bell Southwest and other companies are offering them pay triple what they are earning, and no deployments? Fortunately, the air asset coordination and aircraft tasking from within the ASOC was part of everything I learned as an Army S-3 (Air), Air Force fighter puke, squadron ops officer, and detachment commander in NATO. Before long, I was off to the Joint Air Operations Staff Course at The Air Ground Operations School (AGOS) at Hurlburt Field, Florida. I needed parts of that week-long course earlier when I was at the TACC, but now it was a paid vacation to Ft. Walton Beach, Florida. Little did I know I would be back to Hurlburt soon.

Training events we instituted in the ASOC were practice set-ups of the entire ASOC complex in a timed race competing with the 18th Corps command elements' set up time. The everyday chores of maintaining almost 100 vehicles, upgrading radio communications, practicing convoys, training convoy leaders, changing our long-haul communications from microwave to SATCOM were challenging and exhausting.

Six months into my command, we received an MEI visit. That is an inspection by TAC of all unit training, certification and management. Overall, we received an "Excellent" rating, but in preparation for the MEI, I disagreed with two of my NCO shop supervisors about their training and record keeping. Even my squadron training supervisor thought the two NCOs were wrong and said so to their faces. Without their making any changes after my direction, I gave them enough rope to hang themselves and when the MEI found major discrepancies in their shops, I fired them. The morning after the MEI, I told them to pack up their personal stuff and be gone. With Chief Master Sergeant "Lucky" Stewart, the 507th Wing's Senior Enlisted Advisor, I was planning possible actions and replacements; we made it happen quickly.

A1C PAULINE PAULE

Over in the ASOC maintenance area, I encountered a very unusual Airman, A1C Pauline Paule. Pauline earned a BA degree in English, but then enlisted in the Air Force and worked in Aerospace Ground Equipment (AGE); that's generators and power equipment. A Pennsylvania farm girl who grew up maintaining tractors, Pauline loved working on our unit's generators and being covered with grease. Unfortunately, on a drive around the base perimeter road in a large 5-ton truck, her truck's mirror clipped the mirror of an opposite direction 2.5-ton truck. My Commander's punishment required her to conduct a briefing on the maximum width of 5-ton and 2.5-ton vehicles and compare the total width (including mirrors) to the width of the perimeter road. It turned out the two vehicles could not simultaneously fit on the pavement; thus, somebody must drop a set of wheels off the pavement to safely pass. I ensured Pauline received briefing preparation assistance from two senior NCOs and two of my better officers. Pauline suffered stage fright at the very idea of giving a briefing to the whole squadron; however, she did it well and there were no more mirror collisions.

A brilliant mechanic, Pauline was terribly informal, just as likely to wave with a cheery "Hi, Sir" as she was to salute. One morning before some VIP visit, the squadron was in Class A blue uniform and I was visiting all the units when I walked into the AGE shop. Nobody pointed out that the collar of my blue blouse was turned up in the back and Pauline decided to fix that for me. With a directive comment of "Don't move, Sir", Pauline moved up against my chest and reached around my neck with both arms to adjust my collar. Since I was taller than Pauline, she pressed rather firmly against me to reach my collar, folded the collar in place and said, "There you go." Master Sergeant Blackwell, the shop NCOIC, looked ready for a major seizure; I was blushing beet red, but Pauline did not move. I lowered my face until I was almost nose-to-nose with Pauline and stammered, "Thank you." She gave me a very perky "You're welcome" and skipped out the door of her work area. Airman First Class Pauline Paule was the Air Force's answer to Gomer Pyle, but no one was better at AGE maintenance. Each time Pauline went home to Pennsylvania she brought back "Shoo Fly Pie" for everyone in her work section and all the supervisors, up to yours truly, the Squadron Commander. I felt quite honored two years later when I was invited to her wedding at the Base Chapel. Pauline was quite an act.

My ASOC work was a long way from jumping out of airplanes or yanking and banking as a fighter pilot. Now, I worried about the quality of Tropo shots through tree tops at Ft Jackson (we fried a squirrel that jumped in front of a microwave antennae), and exercises with various Army units.

In a foreshadowing of events, I took my ASOC battle staff to play the ASOC in an exercise of a fictitious Army Corps fighting a battle in Iraq and southwest Iran. Led by the Deputy Commanding General of US Third Army, Ft McPherson, our fictional unit was the XX Corps. To build team spirit in his new Corps staff, the CG even made shoulder patches for all the players.

We met for a day in Atlanta and then moved into tents simulating a deployed Corps Headquarters, only now we were located on the campus of the AGOS at Hurlburt Field, FL. The exercise went well, due in large part to the great Army Brigadier General playing Corps Commander. Amazing in hindsight, but the battles that we fought in our simulations against Russian forces were on the same terrain that the Allied forces fought Iraqi forces in less than six years. The only significant issue encountered was two days of pounding rain. We proved in the real world our equipment could take hot wet weather. After the exercise, our XX Army Corps Commanding General sent "attaboy" letters to my Wing Commander and the 9th Air Force Commander for our job well done. A general's attaboy from the Deputy Commanding General, Third Army, was good to have in my files later that year.

39

Promotion

After a Friday staff meeting, the 507th Wing Commander, Colonel Dick Rhyne, asked if I was going to be home on Sunday evening. I said we would be home and he said he might drop by after church. I thought nothing of it, since Dick had been to our place several times, and I informed Claire about the possible visit. Come Sunday evening, the doorbell rang and there stand Colonel Rhyne and his wife, Joan, with a bottle of champagne and four glasses. Once seated in the living room, he informed me that I was selected for promotion to Colonel and the Air Force-wide list was to be released in the coming week. He offered a champagne toast to my promotion. I was absolutely overwhelmed by his kindness and his trip out to notify me. When I recovered from my brain freeze and blathering thanks to Dick, I thought "Damn, another move and I will have to find a Colonel's job, probably on a MAJCOM staff somewhere."

Then Dick dropped a bigger bomb: he asked me if I wanted to stay and be the Wing Deputy for Operations, Air. He said mine was the perfect background for the position, but I had to go onto parachute jump status. Throw me in that briar patch!! I did not have to think for a minute and I said, "Yes, I would love to become your DO!" Shaw AFB did well on the colonel's list and I think there were a total of six selectees for Colonel. Within a week, we threw a blast of a promotion party at the O'Club in celebration. At least I was not TDY when the list came out, like I was when selected for Major. I pinned on my Colonel rank on May 1, 1986 after 19 years and 10 months of commissioned service. My small ceremony was held in Colonel Rhyne's briefing room with Colonel Rhyne doing the honors on one shoulder and my beautiful bride pinning my new eagle on the other side.

CLAIRE TO THE COLLEGE OF WILLIAM & MARY
Since my new position seemed to have stable hours, I handed the education baton to Claire in the summer of 1986, when we decided that

she could take a sabbatical for five weeks to finish her Master of Arts degree requirements. For that brief time, Claire shared an apartment in Williamsburg and finished her thesis and other details for her MA degree. William and Mary did not hold graduation ceremonies at the end of the summer, so Claire had to wait until the completion of the Fall Semester to walk the stage and be hooded for her Masters.

In December, the four of us drove up to William & Mary for Claire's graduation ceremony. The Phi Beta Kappa Memorial Hall was packed to the rafters with family and friends of the graduates and we loudly and proudly represented the Stevenson graduate. The graduates traditionally attempted to smuggle champagne bottles into the ceremony and pop the corks during the ceremony. Despite being warned and physically searched prior to entering the hall, several enterprising students succeeded in acquiring champagne bottles on the floor of the hall and corks flew across the crowd. One cork whistled by the head of the featured speaker, the distinguished television commentator Roger Mudd, who did not miss a beat, sniffed the air and commented "Napa Valley 1984, not a bad year" and continued his presentation. The result of challenging work over eight years and four family moves was CLAIRE RHODES STEVENSON, Master of Arts in Museum Education, The College of William and Mary, December 19, 1986.

40

Director of Operations (Air)

As the Deputy Commander for Operations, I was responsible for the ASOC, the 21st TASS, at that time flying FACs in the antique O-2 (shades of Khe Sahn in Vietnam), then later the OT-37 and finally OV-10 aircraft; the ground FACs, parachute operations and deployments with Army units, the 703rd TASS with CH-3 "Jolly Green" helicopters and the ALO detachments at 10 Army units from Ft. Riley, KA to Ft. Drum, NY, to Savannah, GA, to Ft. Polk, LA. Maintaining a regular rotation of visits to my subordinate units kept me on the road a lot (actually in the air). The only Detachment that was within a 150-mile driving range was Det 1 at Fort Bragg, supporting the 82nd Airborne Division, XVIII Airborne Corps and the Army Special Operations Command units. We also were a critical part of the Army's establishment of the Joint Readiness Training Center (JRTC) at Ft Chaffee, Arkansas.

JUMP STATUS RECURRENCY
Even before I was checked out for flying in the O-2 "Duck" with the 21st TASS, Colonel Rhyne wanted me to regain currency as a paratrooper. At 41 years old, I was not in the physical shape that I needed to be a young "ten-foot-tall and bulletproof" trooper, but I hoped to survive on experience instead of brute strength. Our senior paratrooper in the 507th Wing, Master Sergeant Robert "Scotty" Scott made an exception to normal physical fitness testing, and, after some sit-ups and push-ups, I was sent straight to the five-foot platform and the gravel pits to prove proficiency in Parachute Landing Falls (PLFs) and canopy control. AMAZING! I could still do half-ass good PLFs. With a few dozen PLFs, the muscle memory was back and Scotty decreed that I could make a couple of administrative jumps to prove that I was worthy. On February 24, 1986, I jumped out of a CH-3 at McEntire DZ, landed safely and was again a paratrooper. The following week I was off to Florida for my checkout in the O-2, but, upon my return, I made three jumps on the following Friday morning, including one jump with full combat

equipment. Scotty cleared me for all types of jumps. However, he cautioned me not to let my ego overload my capabilities and ass. Hooah! Three months later, I regained my qualification as a Jumpmaster as well.

Along with great Air-to-Air in the F-4 and rooting around very low level and shooting the A-10 GAU-8 cannon, military parachuting was a favorite activity, although it could be scary at times. Over the next seven years I was honored to jump with the Army Rangers, 82nd and 101st Divisions, Special Forces troops, SEALS, Combat Controllers, Canadians and numerous others. We held a Jumpmaster course on the island of Antigua and another at Ft. Benning with the Army Airborne School. I put some 507th Wing personnel on one-day jump status to make a parachute jump as a performance reward (they were already airborne qualified). We flexed schedules to let the Tac Air Control Party jumpers earn advanced parachute ratings, jumped a Deputy Assistant Secretary of the Air Force, entertained visitors and VIP's, and did it all safely. I jumped from Hueys, Blackhawks, Chinooks, CH-3s, C-130s, MC-130s, C-141s, and C-5s, some low and some very high. We found time and resources to conduct parachute accuracy competitions (JumpFests) at Shaw that drew teams from Army paratroopers, Special Forces, our airborne TACPs and Navy personnel. I took a personal interest in the 21st TASS parachute program because the FACs, ALOs, and enlisted personnel that volunteered for the exceptional challenges of being a paratrooper with Army units deserved recognition and reward.

One Friday morning I was participating in a training jump on our home DZ, off the eastern side of the runways at Shaw AFB. Most of the jumpers, myself included, had completed the JMPI and were sitting like beached whales on the ramp awaiting the arrival of our C-130. When the jumper seated next to me struggled to his feet, I noticed his right leg strap was twisted. I yelled, "Staff Sergeant Vaughn, re-check that man's equipment."

The error that could cause injury was immediately corrected.

"Master Sergeant Scott, who did the JMPI on Captain Hamilton?"

"I did, sir!" admitted one of our newer lieutenants serving as assistant JM.

"Scotty, the lieutenant is no longer certified as a jumpmaster in the 507th Wing or the Air Force. See me this afternoon with your plan to retrain him!"

Problem identified and corrected; quick and to the point, thanks to SFC Ernie Holmes some 20 years before. And, it helps to be the boss.

As the DO, I anticipated a broad spectrum of tasks. I had to improve the ASOC interface and work with the 18th Airborne Corps; train airborne and ground Forward Air Controllers for army units; train new pilots straight from pilot training on the demands of tactical aviation as FACs; support and employ the CH-3 helos from the 703rd TASS; and man, train and improve the living conditions of the Tactical Air Control Parties stationed with the Army units: all done within personnel, material and budget constraints.

The first visit to one my earlier military stomping grounds, Ft Campbell, Kentucky, was in an O-2 with COL Rhyne for the change of command at our Detachment 5, which supported the 101st Airborne Division. The outgoing Det Commander, Lt Col Bob Rolfing was going to take over the "FAC-U" training squadron at Patrick AFB. I saw in the ceremony's printed program that the new Det Commander was Lt Col Richard Null, with a home town of Dallas, Texas. At the reception, I asked Lt Col Null where he went to high school in Dallas.

"Woodrow Wilson."

"What year did you graduate from Woodrow"?

"1963"

"I graduated from Woodrow in 1962."

Before I could finish that thought, Null blurted out: "You're one of the twins!"

Fame follows you everywhere and it is indeed a small world in the military.

FLYING AGAIN - IN AN O-2 "DUCK"
As the 507 TAIRCW/ DO, I checked out in the vintage O-2 Skymaster at Patrick AFB, FL. This was a vacation for me because I played assistant FAC in the O-2 in Vietnam, and I flew the Cessna 337 civilian model of the "Duck" in my San Antonio past, and felt comfortable in the "push me

337

– pull you" Cessna. So, in March 1986, not yet having pinned on my colonel's eagles, I headed down to Patrick AFB for some salt air, beach time and flying after two years on ground duty. On my sixth and final transition sortie, March 14th, I won three beers from my 1LT IP in a landing accuracy competition. My IP in the right seat, Captain Trey Stackman, was a good A-10 Hog Driver in the 92nd TFS at Bentwaters, and, despite being an excellent O-2 instructor; he was unprepared for an old Lt Col (Promotable) with a civilian Flight Instructor rating and 1500 hours of civilian light airplane time.

The rules for the competition were simple: on downwind, you could pick your spot to reduce power and start the 180 degree turn to land. You could not touch the power again and the target was the middle of the runway numbers and on the centerline stripe. The approach should land at an airspeed that had the stall warning horn sounding. I rolled all three landings smoothly onto Runway 18, in the middle of the numbers with the stall warning horn beginning to wail. Free beer for the old Lt Col back in the squadron! My flying time in the O-2 back at Shaw was limited since the wing transitioned five months later from the O-2 to the modified T-37 Tweet, now designated the OT-37 Scorpion II.

I had several adventures in the O-2 before they went to that great boneyard at Davis-Monthan AFB. On my first cross country to Ft Benning's Lawson Army Air Field, I taxied in and was greeted by a "Welcome - COL Stevenson" on their VIP Welcome board next to the red carpet in front of the Base Ops building, arranged by our Det 3 Commander, Major Steve Sheffer. You have no idea how fantastic the sight of that sign was for an officer that started out as a dumb-ass infantry second lieutenant. Hooah!! The Ground Controller radioed me as I came off Runway 33 at mid-field:

"Cowboy 6, taxi to the VIP red carpet, drop off your VIP and then follow the guide truck to parking."

"The VIP is the only person on board, so you might as well send me to parking now."

The Ground Controller paused and then replied, "Sir, you may shut down at the red carpet and we will tow the aircraft to VIP parking."

I had a good inspection of Det 3's facilities, dinner with the Sheffers, and, the next morning I took off for Fort Polk, Louisiana. On takeoff, I could not get the O-2's landing gear to retract. I returned to

Ft Benning, landed and called the 507th Command Post. My first indication of increased status in the Wing came when the Command Post said they would send another plane and pilot ASAP and I could continue my trip while the 21st TASS pilot stayed with the broken aircraft until the parts received and the fix made. It suddenly struck me that I was now "Somebody important" if the wing would do that for me, just part of the mental shift required when you become a Colonel in an operational unit. That afternoon in a replacement O-2, I launched for Ft Polk, to conduct a retirement ceremony for one of our 507th officers and a brief inspection of vehicles.

I flew only one gunnery ride in the O-2 and everything else was cross country to my far-flung detachments. I flew my last sorties in the "Duck" on 29 June and 30 June 1986, flying to a Change of Command for Detachment 6 of the 507 TAIRCW at Ft. Polk, Louisiana. It had been a long time since I flew with a 101st Division FAC in the then practically obsolete Cessna O-2 Skymaster, putting in multiple sets of fighters against the North Vietnamese Army during the siege of Khe Sahn.

OT-37 TRANSITION.

June and July saw the 507th transitioning from the old O-2 to the equally ancient T-37 "Tweet." We painted the Tweets green, added an FM / VHF radio and named it the Scorpion II. After academics and seven transition sorties, mostly with CAPT Ken Soileau, I arrived at my OT-

37 Qualification check. My check ride was taken with our Chief of Stan-Eval Lt Col Thomas "TC" Meyers, a long-time Instructor pilot and SEFE from ATC, with more time in the '37 than I had total. The check went well and TC said he could see the gears grinding in my head and eyes as I did "regulation" aerobatics for the check ride. Fighter jocks were used to ham-fisting the aircraft around to arrive at a given point in space. Having to do it to specific parameters for a SEFE was painful. The ride, however, went very well. A little over a year later, however, I was paired with SEFE Bob Sands, former F-111 driver, for an Instrument Check. Stressed at work by other responsibilities, the ride went badly by my standards. I chased airspeeds and parameters for the entire ride. Even the Florence VOR went off the air in the midst of my VOR approach. I was mentally exhausted when we debriefed. Stress, what

stress? I could not remember flying so badly in my life. I think Bob passed me because I was the DO and he wanted to get the checkride off his overdue list. He did say, although it was sloppy, I was never unsafe. In contrast, two weeks later I flew a Tactical Check with Bob. We served as airborne FAC to four A-10s, swapping between low and high threat tactics while working with a TACP on the ground. Then we flew home low level and flew left and right-hand patterns for both of us. Bob gave me an "Exceptional" on the Tac Check and that made up for the piss-poor Instrument Check I flew. Kinda.

An advantage of being the DO was having my name painted on an aircraft, a good crew chief assigned to my aircraft, and I usually got that same airplane when I was going cross country to another base or civilian airfield. My assigned aircraft tail number was 60-0104. That meant the airplane started down the assembly line in 1960. That aircraft was older than the young crew chief that maintained it. My Dedicated Crew Chief, A1C Ron Nearbin, strongly believed 0104 was *his* aircraft and asked me what *I* broke if I had a write-up upon landing: it was never the plane but the pilot that caused problems. Ron spent his own spare time touching up the cockpit, even cleaning floor boards and control knobs to make his plane the best on our flight line. I soon believed it was the best 37 on the flight line and praised him accordingly.

On a low-level sortie from Ft Knox, KY to Knoxville, I noticed a high school, near Oak Ridge, Tennessee, with an ROTC formation in the parking lot by the school's flagpole. I was initially at about 800 feet so I started a right descending 270 degree turn behind the school, out of sight by the formation. After accelerating to max speed, I cleared the rooftop, missed the flagpole and left jet fumes on the ROTC formation. I rocked my wings as I passed and then decided "to hell with it:" I pulled the nose up about 20 degrees and executed a sharp aileron roll to the right. Then it was escape at max speed and get out of sight, on to Knoxville to refuel and home to Shaw AFB. I hope it fostered a cadet's desire to become a military aviator, in any branch of the service.

On another return trip from Fort Knox, I was flying low level for some time when I crossed a large lake in Kentucky (probably Lake Cumberland) and observed a pontoon party boat with two bikini-clad young ladies sunbathing on the roof. From my 500 feet altitude, I started a wide descending left turn to make a low observation pass, just off the side of their boat. I waved at the two girls and they gleefully waved back.

As a flight lead in the 21st TASS, I was utilized by the squadron to teach formation, close trail and tactical formation and tactical approaches to new lieutenants. It gave me an opportunity to see the quality of tactical pilots we were sending on to the fighter force. A memorable OT-37 mission was leading a low-level two-ship with one of the least experienced Lieutenants in the squadron. The mission went reasonably well, and, when we were about ten miles north of Shaw at low level, I rocked my wings to bring my wingman in from the 4-5,000-foot line abreast formation we were flying. My lieutenant came roaring across the airspace and I soon surmised that, despite his steep bank and back pressure on the control stick, he was not going to slow down enough to avoid a collision. In addition to that error in speed, the young tiger increased his angle of bank so sharply that he lost sight of me over the canopy rail. He couldn't have seen me until we collided.

I shoved my throttles to the wall and snatched back stick, climbing enough to see my wingman slide through the space I previously occupied. I took a deep breath and told him to move out 1000 feet and try that rejoin again. The next rejoin was better. After strongly debriefing the mission and almost deadly rejoin with the lieutenant (I did not pound on the desk), I held a stronger discussion with 21st TASS/DO. My wingman was henceforth grounded until he flew two satisfactory formation sorties with the toughest IP in the 21st TASS.

Out of nowhere one day, I received a call in my DO's office with an unusual request from Steve Alderman (of Bentwaters 91st TFS fame). Steve was coming off a non-flying staff job at the Air Force Reserve (AFRES) headquarters and going back to the Hog for a remote tour to Korea. Steve asked if he could get a jet takeoff and landing in one of my OT-37s. This would allow him to skip the TAC recurrency program requirement and he could move straight to a scheduled A-10 requalification course. We weren't in the recurrency business, but this was easy to make happen. I called the 21st TASS and requested they add Steve to a local flight, with an IP and the added training objective of getting Steve up and down in our aerospace vehicle. Steve came up to Shaw on TDY orders, and, after an extensive preflight briefing, he flew; since the IP did not run screaming from the aircraft, I assumed Flying Officer Alderman was now safe. With an official extract of the sortie for his flight records, Steve thanked all and was on his way back to the Warthog. Flexibility is key to making a great Air Force great.

JRTC

Another add-on task came in 1987 as the Army established the Joint Readiness Training Center (JRTC) at Ft Chafee, Arkansas, and the 507th was tasked to establish the TACP in support of this new training center. The JRTC was to become the training and evaluation center for "light" Army infantry units, mirroring the success of the National Training Center (NTC) at Ft Irwin, California. The NTC made major leaps in the training and readiness of mechanized and armor units; the JRTC was expected to do the same for the light infantry units (primarily paratroopers and the 25th Infantry Division). To fill this new TACP requirement, the 507th needed to provide personnel from existing assets until the budget and manpower authorizations could be updated. I recruited volunteers from our detachments to fill the JRTC slots, led by Lt Col Kit Alverson, the current commander of Detachment 5 with the Army's 5th Mechanized Infantry Division at Ft Polk, LA.

Until permanent facilities could be set up at Fort Chaffee, the headquarters of JRTC and the TACP operated from Little Rock AFB and commuted to Ft. Chaffee. Specifically, we set up offices in the former nuclear alert facilities on the east end of Little Rock's Runway 25. The JRTC challenges included developing procedures and all the documentation for the new Detachment TACP troops to act as Observers – Controllers (OCs). Most of my flights to observe and advise my TACPs included a stop at Little Rock AFB and then Fort Smith airport to visit JRTC. At Fort Smith airport, you needed to be very aware of Daisy Air's "Daisy" line girls. The girls wore cheeky short shorts and tiny halter tops, doing their best imitation of "Daisy Duke" from "Dukes of Hazzard" fame. I witnessed a civilian Cessna 182 pilot drop a wheel off the pavement by watching the Daisy instead of the taxi line.

FORT BENNING JUMP SCHOOL (AGAIN)

Whenever I was informed the 507th Wing had an airman or officer enrolled in the Army jump school at Ft. Benning, Georgia, I tried to drop in and make a parachute jump with their class. In November 1986, the first time I asked to join a jump class, I was informed I must get permission from The Infantry School Secretary to be a "guest jumper." I took my records and current 507th Wing jump orders over to Infantry Hall and the School Secretary's office, located across the hall from the Infantry School Commanding General's office complex. As I waited for the Secretary's Executive Officer to see my paperwork and fit me into the Secretary's schedule, I noticed the door plate showed the Infantry School Secretary was a Colonel Ted Chilcote. Damn! When I was a Senior cadet in ROTC, a Ted Chilcote was a 2LT in Law School at the

University of Texas and a frequent visitor to our ROTC activities. I asked if Colonel Chilcote attended The University of Texas and his administrative NCO said "Yes, he did." Suddenly I heard a loud "Colonel Stevenson, get in here!" The short story is we had not seen each other for 22 years, but, after about five minutes of assignment history and playing the name game for these two Longhorns, Ted called out to his Executive Officer: "Colonel Stevenson has my permission to jump with anybody at Ft. Benning!" It was a great reunion and I went back to the 507th Battalion area to be scheduled on the next day's jumps with my Air Force enlisted troops.

The Ft. Benning Airborne departments traced their heritage to the Army's 507th Airborne Infantry Regiment. Since my home unit was the Air Force 507th Tactical Air Control Wing and their Detachment 3 was at Fort Benning, a bit of confusion arose whenever I signed up to jump with the Rangers or the Jump School. I would say I was with Detachment 3, 507th Wing and I was entered as belonging to the 3rd Battalion, 507th Infantry, which was the advanced airborne course at the Jump School. Rather than try to educate every manifest NCO in the airborne world, I just let it ride. 3rd of the 507th was good enough for me.

The next morning, I moved among the jump students in the parachute issue hangar, made small talk, and sought out the Air Force students. These enlisted and junior officers were headed for the 82nd or 101st Divisions as TACP members or even to the PJ's and Combat Controllers. I wanted all the Air Force students to see there were senior paratroopers other than Army.

The Blackhats arranged the jump manifest so I was to jump first pass, first jumper from the C-130, with three Air Force students following me. How cool is that? The JMPI and jump commands were unchanged over the 22 years since I was a jump student.

Airborne and on short final to Fryar Field, the jump school drop zone, the troop doors were raised, platforms placed on the door sill, the JM made his safety checks and I was finally told to "Stand In the door!" I assumed the correct door position and looked down at the Chattahoochee River as we flew northward toward the DZ and a green jump light. The Blackhat Safety NCO kneeling at the trailing edge of the paratroop door, reached up and took a strong grip on my parachute harness' right seat strap. His job was to ensure nobody departed the aircraft before the green jump light came on. Colonel or no Colonel, he was doing his job. The Staff Sergeant was half my age and probably had fewer jumps than I did. He smiled somewhat sheepishly at me, but I smiled back and nodded in recognition of his job performance. The jump light turned green as the south edge of the DZ flashed below me and following a loud "GO!" from the jumpmaster and a smack on the butt, I hopped out of the aircraft, followed by three Air Force paratroopers and the rest of the student load. Hooah! It was another great day in the US Air Force (Airborne).

101ST JUMP

In April 1987, I was lucky enough to make my 101st military parachute jump with the 101st Airborne Division (Air Assault) Long Range Surveillance Unit (LRSU) at Ft. Campbell, Ky. Officially, the visit was to inspect Detachment 4 of the 507th at Ft. Campbell. The Detachment Commander, Lt Col Rich Null, knowing my 101st jump was a special jump, arranged with the only unit on jump status at Ft Campbell to make it happen. When the local cadre in the 101st found out this poaching old Air Force Colonel was a combat veteran of the 101st in Vietnam, the coordination went very smoothly.

The Army set the jump order based upon the jumper's rank, so I was to be the third jumper out, following the Deputy Commanding General of the 101st and then his aide. This was a CH-47 Chinook helicopter jump at Son DZ, usually a great ramp jump, which almost became a disaster. On the first jump pass, a thunderstorm microburst approached the DZ just after the first stick of jumpers, including me, left the CH-47. I hopped off the rear ramp of the Chinook in relatively low surface winds, checked my open canopy and then saw a wall of dust moving at us from the airfield to the northwest. The wind hit my chute; I rocked almost to a horizontal position and I saw one side of my parachute canopy collapse to the middle. I was afraid the whole canopy might collapse and I was psyching myself up for quick reserve chute activation.

The main canopy rapidly recovered to full inflation, but now I was moving over the ground at 35-40 miles per hour. I was well past the DZ as I steered laterally to find an open spot in which to crash. I had just cleared some power lines and a road surface when my feet touched down, going backwards at over 20 mph. Still standing up, I skied backwards down a grassy road embankment and I released the canopy before I began my PLF and roll across a grassy field. The jump was immediately stopped by the DZ Safety Officer, but that first stick of 12 jumpers was already in the air. I landed about three blocks away from the DZ but the last jumpers were spread to the opposite side of Ft

Campbell. A passing Army vehicle stopped and asked if I needed a ride back to the DZ. I took the trooper up on the offer and we waved at other vehicles being dispatched to collect paratroopers across Ft. Campbell. Amazingly, when everybody checked in, there were no serious injuries. Despite his apparent cheerful attitude, I think the general was pissed.

FT BRAGG C-130 LAPES CRASH

July 1, 1987: The official account said *"A USAF C-130E, 68-10945, c/n 4325, crashed during an open house at Fort Bragg, during a display of the low level airdrop technique known as LAPES, (Low Altitude Parachute Extraction System), in which a parachute is used to pull the cargo off the rear door while the plane makes a touch-and-go. Pilot failed to pull-up after deploying M551 Sheridan tank, hit tree line, burned, killing three on board, one soldier on the ground, and injuring two crew."*

Ft Bragg was having a VIP demonstration and open house which included airdrop demos, parachute ops, Army firepower demos and airpower demos for local Army supporters. Because airmen from our Det 1, 507th TAIRCW would be controlling the tactical air strikes, Colonel Gene Juve and I drove up to Ft. Bragg to observe. We were given VIP seats on the front row of the bleachers at the dropzone, sitting with the DO of the Airlift Wing at nearby Pope AFB. His C-130s were doing the parachute drops and the LAPES drop. The parachute drop of an infantry company and their mock combat assault went well and then it was time for the C-130 LAPES drop. The C-130 would make his LAPES extraction on the red dirt assault airstrip, not 100 meters in front of our bleacher seats. Approaching the airstrip at about 500 feet altitude, the C-130 deployed a drogue chute attached to the tank and its pallet. The C-130 then dropped its nose steeply toward the dirt airstrip.

I saw this C-130 was on a very steep approach; within seconds my brain told me that, even if the pilot rotated the aircraft to get the nose up, the vector could not change rapidly enough to avoid ground impact. The nose of the C-130 came up to just above level flight at the last moment, but the vector took the C-130 onto the ground. The C-130 slammed onto the dirt runway! Tires blew! The aft cargo ramp broke loose with the tank still attached! The landing gear doors broke off! The escape hatch on the upper fuselage popped open and deployed a bright yellow raft!

In a cloud of red dust, the aircraft commander applied full power to the four turboprop engines in an attempt to fly out of a bad situation. But his plane was doomed, along with the crew. At impact, I watched

345

the fuselage skin ripple just behind the wings, and, then in slow motion, the vertical stabilizer slowly tilted about twenty degrees to my side of the aircraft. The backbone of the C-130 was broken and the ruined flight controls could never rotate the nose upward. The full power accelerated the C-130 off the dirt runway and into the trees at the edge of the dropzone. In front of hundreds of invited guests and military officials, the C-130 exploded in a fireball, sending smoke skyward. I knew what I had seen and even anticipated. I could play it back in slow motion in my mind, but, at the time, I was having difficulty realizing what had just happened.

The Airlift Wing DO bolted from his seat and was on his radio before he had moved five feet toward his vehicle. Because of the wind pattern and the location of the fire and smoke, within two minutes particles of soot began to fall over us. Col Juve rose and said, "We can't do anything here" as we headed for our nearby vehicle. The civilian spectators were forced to wait for bus transportation to travel to the range for the firepower demonstration, all the while seeing, feeling and breathing the remnants of that C-130.

Col Juve and I drove to the weapons range and explained what we had seen to our paratroopers from Detachment 1. The huge black cloud climbed thousands of feet into the air and was very visible from our range. The civilians and visitors arrived after 45 minutes and the remaining events; including our Air Force employment of laser guided 2000-pound bombs, went well. However, an aura of sadness, shock, and concern among participants and spectators prevailed.

The frustrating part of this incident was the fact the C-130 aircraft commander was warned about overly aggressive LAPES deliveries. The evening before the demonstration, the aircraft commander reportedly told other crews to watch the Open House event the next day because he would put on a hell of a show for the crowd. Sadly, he did.

AIRBORNE TACPs

With obvious prejudice, my favorite TACP was the group of Air Force paratroopers supporting the 1st Battalion, 75th Rangers, on Hunter Army Airfield at Savannah, Georgia. The senior ALO during '85-'88 was a great Ranger, Maj Bill Emsley. I encountered Bill again in 1990 when he was the Commanding Officer of the Alaska ASOC, by then he was a Lieutenant Colonel. One of the excellent ROMADs with the 1/75 Rangers was SSGT Bernie McCabe, a tab-wearing Ranger and the first

Air Force Enlisted Terminal Attack Controllers (ETAC) authorized to employ tactical aircraft weapons without an Air Force officer supervising.

In August 1987, I needed to make an inspection visit to the 1st Ranger TACP and Maj Emsley suggested I bring my combat gear because I might get to jump with the Rangers. I did a quick inspection of the TACP and then rigged up for a jump that turned out to be a full Ranger Regiment jump into Ft. Benning's Fryer Field as part of the Regimental Change of Command for COL Joe Stringham (later BG). I jumped from a lead C-141 and saw 14 aircraft dropping the entire Ranger Regiment behind me. I landed and moved to the northeast wood line, where I was assisting Major Emsley in controlling Close Air Support when COL Joe Stringham, approached, looked over my uniform with AF pilot wings, master jump wings and SF combat patch and asked, "Who are you?"

"I'm Colonel Steve Stevenson from the 507th Wing. Major Emsley and the 1st Battalion TACP report to me."

"Did you just jump in with the First Battalion?"

"Yes, sir. I did. Hooah!"

"Ranger Stevenson, we need to talk later."

He grinned, shook his head slightly and walked on. We did talk later. I was always welcome at Regimental headquarters and we worked well and often to improve the Ranger TACPs' equipment and joint training.

Right behind the Rangers on my favorites list was the TACP at Fort Bragg (Detachment 1, 507th) which served the 82nd Airborne Division, elements of 18th Airborne Corps and the Army Special Operations Command (ARSOC). I also worked with the detachment troopers to provide a small TACP to work with the 5th Special Forces Group (Airborne) at Ft. Campbell, another organization from my past. Numerous troops volunteered from the 507th detachment at Ft. Campbell, but the 5th SFGA required TACP members to be jump qualified, so I was forced to use Ft. Bragg jump qualified personnel.

One of the remarkable Air Force troopers at Ft. Bragg was a young sergeant, Mitch Monroe. He was finishing his college degree and was a quick study at any task. He was my jumpmaster on several occasions at Bragg and Shaw and I was very impressed with his leadership skills. Mitch proved to be a leader and great instructor at our subsequent jumpmaster courses at Ft. Benning and in Antigua.

41

All Other Duties As Assigned

On the morning of October 20, 1987, an Air Force A-7 lost its sole engine, and, while trying to land at Indianapolis International Airport, the pilot ran out of altitude, airspeed and ideas. He ejected safely at 500 feet altitude but the A-7 crashed into the Ramada Hotel, resulting in the deaths of 10 people. Our 507th Vice Commander, Colonel David A. Sawyer, with experience in the A-7, was immediately tagged to be the Accident Investigating Officer, a job of considerable duration. So, for almost four months, I pulled double duty as the DO and the Wing's Vice Commander. I was having way too much fun with budgets, inspections and IG complaints. It was a broadening experience, but I was glad to see Dave finally return for 507th Vice Commander duty. Dave left the 507th in June 1988, to command the 602d Tac Air Control Wing at Davis-Monthan AFB, the 12th Air Force sister unit of the 507th TACW in 9th Air Force. Dave ultimately became a Major General.

ANTIGUA RETURN
Following our Jumpmaster course in Antigua, we headed home in our North Carolina Air National Guard C-130 for an arrival parachute jump onto the Shaw DZ. This was a Hollywood jump (no combat gear) and a ramp jump at that. We stood up at the ten-minute call and went through our usual preparations. As I reached up to connect my static line snap link on the aircraft anchor cable, I began to tremble, almost uncontrollably. What the hell was going on? I jumped six times in the last week and this was a simple tailgate jump back home. I was scared to death! My hand on the static line was shaking so badly I was afraid the loadmaster might think the C-130 was developing an airframe vibration. Thank goodness, the drop light turned green and I followed the three troopers ahead of me off the ramp and into space. As soon as I cleared the ramp and my chute opened, the tremors were gone and I felt fine. I still do not know what the cause was. I followed with another 25 years of parachuting and it never happened again. Was it an accumulation of fear after 21 years as a paratrooper? My only thought

was again the old Ft. Benning phrase: "I don't mind dying, but I don't want to embarrass myself doing it!"

MIKE'S LAST JUMP

The younger Air Force jumpers in the 21st TASS were always working to become Senior and then Master Parachutists. They earned their advanced wings with us at Shaw and with the Army's 82nd Airborne Division, three Ranger units and the Army Special Operations Command. In these operations, there was none of the Air Force Academy's skydiving simulation to count toward their advanced wings. The 21 TASS jump personnel got their requirements with real paratroopers.

On this Friday, we were jumping at McEntire ANG Base, about 20 miles west of Shaw AFB, and Capt Mike Wilmuth, a 21st TASS FAC, needed two final jumps to earn his Master Parachutist Wings. Mike was to depart PCS in three days. Capt Wilmuth had served three years as an ALO on parachute status with the Army's 82d Airborne Division and the 1st Ranger Battalion; he accomplished all his type jumps: day, night, Jumpmaster, mass tactical jumps, etc. and he was deserving of a Master Parachute Badge.

Major Pat Patterson, 703rd TASS Operations Officer, was the Aircraft Commander conducting the day's drops in a 703rd TASS CH-3. After five lifts, but just before Wilmuth's last jump, the CH-3 Jolly developed a minor mechanical problem and was about to return directly to Shaw from McEntire ANGB. If the Jolly could not finish the drops, Wilmuth could not get his Master Parachutist wings. When Pat landed at the DZ to tell us he had to return to Shaw, I stepped up to the CH-3's right window and asked - no, I pleaded with Pat - to do just one more drop mission and he said "No." The CH-3 checklist said only one flight of short duration, no passengers, back for maintenance. Pat could not land back at the DZ after takeoff to pick up his safety gear and drop off a jumpmaster.

Knowing how important this last jump was to Wilmuth, I spent a moment pondering how we could get that last needed jump. I suggested that Capt Wilmuth jumpmaster himself, go as the solo passenger and spot his own jump. Since the CH-3 departed into the wind (from the west) Maj Patterson and his CH-3 could climb to 700 feet altitude heading west and then make a climbing 180 degree turn direct to Shaw, passing over the DZ. By the time they passed over the DZ, they should have 1400 or 1500 feet altitude for a jump; Mike would jump over the DZ and the Jolly could continue directly to Shaw. Pat thought about it for a moment and agreed it was workable. It was a little risky but Captain Wilmuth was qualified in all the needed skills. Mike jumped on board and in short order he stuck his "knees in the breeze" for his last jump.

A short but special ceremony was held that afternoon in the 21st TASS recreation room as Mike was awarded his Master Wings by Master Sergeant Scott, while all the 21st TASS, Maj Patterson and several of the 703rd TASS pilots and I watched. The next Monday morning Capt Wilmuth out-processed from Shaw AFB on his way to F-15 Eagle RTU. I am very sure he was the only Master Parachutist in the F-15 class. I owed Major Patterson big time for helping us make this happen!

RANGER ALO JUMP INJURY:
There was always risk involved for our paratroopers and particularly those ALOs supporting the Army Ranger units. In November 1987, one of our Ranger ALOs from the 21TASS, Captain Mike Schmitt, suffered a broken leg on a Ranger tactical night jump in Utah. Capt Schmitt said all went well until the landing. Mike landed with one foot on his large ruck sack and said as he hit the ground, he heard somebody scream. Then he realized it was his scream. His femur was broken.

Mike was transported to the Air Force Hospital at Hill AFB, Utah, and after three operations, Mike was released for a flight back to Columbia, SC. The pilots from the 21st TASS gathered and a gaggle of about 30 young yahoo pilots and paratroopers (and one aged paratrooper) drove to the Columbia airport to welcome Mike home. Mike was travelling by wheelchair, and, after the plane's arrival at the gate, the airlines provided a porter to wheel Mike out of the plane and into the main terminal. Unfortunately, the porter bumped Mike's injured leg into the wall or a door corner two or three times, causing excruciating pain. The 21TASS/DO reached for the porter and snatched him almost off the ground by the collar with a snarled threat: "If you hurt the Captain again, I'm going to break your leg here and now!"

The porter turned pale. Surrounded by 20 or more agitated paratroopers, he was saved when one of our troops, Capt Jim Hamilton, offered to take over wheelchair duty. The porter offered no objection and quickly disappeared. Once out in the parking lot, the 21st TASS guys loaded Mike into a large squadron van and they celebrated with beer and champagne all the way back to Shaw. Of course, the 507th DO knew nothing about consumption of alcohol in a government vehicle.

The big problem now was whether Capt Schmitt would heal fast enough to make his follow-on assignment to F-16s. Mike was alerted to his great follow-on assignment just before the Ranger deployment. He needed all of the next three months to heal a major leg fracture and be cleared by the Aerospace Medicine mafia for return to high performance fighters. Mike attacked recovery and rehab like a good paratrooper; he did heal and was cleared to make his F-16 class. Hooah!

CANADIAN PARACHUTE SCHOOL
One of the great trips I made as DO was to the Canadian Parachute School at Canadian Forces Base Edmonton, Alberta. I went as a guest jumper, making four jumps from C-130s and using Canadian equipment. The weather was beautiful, but quite cool. I completed the minimum number of jumps and survived the graduation party the night before School Commandant, LTC David Bondurant, pinned on my gold jump wings with a red maple leaf in the center. Fantastic.

JUMPER EXTRACTION
There are two types of paratroopers: static line jumpers and Military Free Fall jumpers or HALO; mixing the two types sometimes produces unusual results. On one of my later jumps at Shaw, I was involved with a mix of static line paratroopers from various units, including the 82nd Airborne, and HALO jumpers, mostly from various Special Operations units. This planned parachute mission was a ramp jump from a C-130 for the static line troopers and then a climb to 10,000 feet for the HALO jumpers. Well, the dumb smack Colonel (not me) acting as primary jumpmaster, delayed the jumpers' exit until the aircraft was well down the drop zone. The delay left one 82d Airborne trooper (about a 19-year-old PFC) in the aircraft when the red light came on to stop the jump. Additionally, the Jumpmaster did a "Follow Me" lead of the jumpers, so he knew nothing of what transpired in the C-130. Twenty-two years earlier, Army SFC Ernie Holmes taught 2LT Stevenson that, even though the JM can go first with a "Follow Me!" attitude, if something went wrong after that, you as the JM did not know what happened in the aircraft. Therefore, a good JM jumps last, after he has accounted for his paratroopers. The C-130 pilot did not know there was still one static line jumper on board as he shoved up the throttles and started a rapid climb toward 10,000 feet for the HALO drop.

With the original JM gone, SSGT Jason Vaughn said he would

function as the Jumpmaster on one more static line pass for our very lonely 82ⁿᵈ paratrooper, still standing on the ramp's edge with his static line hooked up. This was relayed to the pilot. With an aerobatic turn, down we dove from about 6,500 feet toward the static line drop altitude of 1,200 feet. This was all very flexible thinking, <u>except:</u> SSGT Vaughn and all our HALO jumpers armed their parachute Automatic Activation Devices (AADs) as the plane started the initial climb through 3,000 feet. Now, in the rapid descent, when SSGT Vaughn leaned out from the side of the C-130 ramp, into the 150+ knot breeze, to view the drop zone, the "smart computer" in his parachute's AAD thought the parachutist was in trouble i.e. rapidly descending below 2000', at a speed of over 90 knots with no chute open; FIRE! The AAD activated SSGT Vaughn's spring-loaded emergency chute. With a loud "ping" sound, the deployment chute popped out of his backpack onto the C-130 ramp and was snatched off the ramp by the windblast. In the split second needed for his parachute to unpack, SSGT Vaughn looked at the deployed chute and then into the plane with eyes as big as the C-130 propellers. SNATCH! SSGT Vaughn was gone in a flash, in a maneuver resembling the LAPES extraction of a tank from a C-130.

Waving goodbye, Vaughn was now under an open parachute drifting away from the C-130. If that wasn't flaky enough, the Air Force Loadmaster blurted over the intercom to the Aircraft Commander: "Somebody just fell out of the aircraft!" After confirming that SSGT Vaughn was descending under a good parachute, we got the C-130 crew calmed down, made a jump pass with MSgt Scott now serving as Jumpmaster for the visibly shaken young 82ⁿᵈ paratrooper, who had a great tale to tell back at Ft. Bragg.

We climbed again toward 10,000 feet for the HALO jump. During this time, SSGT Vaughn landed about three miles from the drop zone and was expeditiously picked up by a retired US Navy SEAL (already into his six-pack of beer at 8:15 AM) who saw the descending parachute. As I landed and gathered my parachute, the former SEAL returned SSGT Vaughn (plus beer) to the drop zone. Following an extensive debrief to determine what happened, and filing some safety reports to appease the C-130 crew and our Shaw AFB Safety folks, we helped the former SEAL drink more beer and figure out if we could convince folks this happened.

703 TASS CH-3s.
One of my squadrons was the 703ʳᵈ TASS, flying the CH-3 "Jolly Green" helicopters. I jumped from the CH-3s and I thought that if I "owned" a

squadron of helicopters, I at least ought to know how to fly one. I asked the 703rd Commander, their Ops Officer and the 507th Wing Commander if I could get a local checkout in the CH-3. They all agreed and the 703rd Commander said I was the first DO that ever asked to check out in the CH-3. In February 1987, I began a crash course (nice choice of words) in helicopter transition as a Jolly Green co-pilot. I crammed academics and flying as tightly as I could stand. The 703rd scheduled me with an IP on local training flights so they could also conduct flight training with a regular crew, and then swap me into the left seat so I could scare the IP and crew chief. Eventually, not only could I fly the CH-3 safely, but I could do sling loads and paratrooper drops.

REAL HOT SHOT AVIATORS

One of the exceptional images in my visual memory was a CH-3 ride on 18 February 1988, with Pat Patterson as the IP and Aircraft Commander. We were finishing a low-level training ride and were going home. At 50 feet above the water, I flew down Lake Wateree to the small dam at the southeast end. As we hopped over the dam, at our right front (1 o'clock), two huge Bald Eagles sat in the top of a tall, dead tree. The two birds launched off their perch and in a half glide, half flap rhythm set off down the riverbed. I lowered the CH-3s collective a bit and trimmed back on the cyclic so we were co-speed with the two eagles leading us down the river. I was flying the helicopter, but Pat and our crew chief, sitting in the jump seat, were also totally mesmerized by the pair of eagles. After 15 seconds, we felt the eagles knew they were the lead as they crossed the river, switched sides often and flew just inches over the trees. Finally bored of leading the big loud helicopter, the two eagles suddenly broke hard right together, flared and landed in the top of a barren tree. Wow, great flying! Every time I think I am a hot shot aviator, I remember that two-ship of natural, exceptional flyers.

THE "FARM"

In February 1988, I flew as copilot on a CH-3 helicopter mission to Langley AFB with Lt Col George Crecenti. After arrival in the Langley area, we cancelled our flight plan, flew up the York River to meet some special training personnel at the Camp Peary airfield and discussed our support of night and parachute ops at Camp Peary. For the uninformed, Camp Peary (or "the Farm") is the training site for CIA operators. We were needed to assist in their insertion training by helo or parachute. We then made the short hop down to Langley AFB and Headquarters Tactical Air Command, where we were met by a Major from the TAC Intelligence staff. Across the street from the TAC Command building, in the Deputy Chief of Staff for Operations and Intelligence area, we wove our way through doors marked "Secret" and "Top Secret Only" to the Sensitive Compartmented Information Facility (SCIF) vault at TAC/IN to sign an "Official Secrets" document concerning our support of the Camp Peary operations. The Major was a little bent out of shape that we visited Camp Peary before we signed his paperwork.

At our next 507th Wing staff meeting, Col Juve asked George what the mission was and George responded that he couldn't tell him about the missions. Col Juve asked George: "Do you know who you will be flying for?"

"I could tell you, but then I would have to kill you."

For a few seconds, I thought Crecenti had terminated both his and my military careers. Col Juve just smiled and said, "We'll let it go at that." The CH-3s flew numerous missions in support of "other government agencies" and the sorties were reported as "Higher Headquarters Directed – Local", regardless of where they were flown.

CH-3 SUPPORT OF D.E.A. IN THE EVERGLADES

In cooperation with "Other Government Agencies", our CH-3s were tasked in support of the DEA. They provided airlift for an assault team onto a suspected drug-runner site in the swamps of central Florida. Druggie airboats in the central Florida swamps ran under the regular aviation radars, but they could be detected by our tactical radars, if the radar set was elevated on towers or mounds. A radar unit of the 507th, the 728th Tactical Control Flight, deployed their equipment, under cover of darkness, to a man-made radar mound on the USAF Avon Park gunnery range complex in central Florida. The 728th started radar operations in four hours. The next morning, their radar showed 18 tracks on airboats, converging to one location.

The DEA rapidly obtained updated aerial photos and planned a takedown for that night. Already on standby, we launched two CH-3s from Shaw AFB to MacDill AFB, Florida, refueled, and then to Avon Park Gunnery Range, where we on-loaded 16 agents and their necessary firepower. At 3:15 AM, 26 hours after the 728th radar site went operational, we landed two CH-3s in the dark at two LZs and DEA agents assaulted the airboat camp from two sides. Resistance was non-existent after an over-eager CH-3 crew chief in Jolly Two sank an airboat tied alongside the pier with a burst from the helicopter's M-60 door gun.

During the subsequent search of the camp, our senior crew chief, MSGT Boudreaux, found a supply of seven feet-long wooden propellers in the airboat supply shed. Lt Col Crecenti, the Air Mission Commander, asked the DEA Senior Agent In Charge (SAIC) if we could salvage some of the propellers as souvenirs to auction off for our unit funds. The SAIC grinned and said, "I didn't see any propellers", so "poof" the propellers disappeared. The antique propellers were divided between the 703rd and 728th unit funds for auction to support dependent scholarships and recreational activities for the unit families. Today, my $350 beautifully laminated wooden propeller with metal leading edges proudly hangs in my study.

DEMISE OF OUR CH-3 SQUADRON
In TAC's ever-changing organization, the decision was made in early 1988 to eliminate the 703rd TASS and the CH-3 helicopters. On 21 April 1988, the squadron flew the last CH-3 local flight which included a one pass jump on the Shaw AFB drop zone. The winds were marginally high as we set up for the jump run. I was going to jump the door position with full combat equipment, followed by six other Master parachutists, including SSGT Jason Vaughn and MSGT Scott. The DZSO called the winds right at the max limit and the decision was made to go.

We should have aborted the jump, landed and taxied back to the squadron. But, out I hopped into the 70-knot breeze, got a good chute, deployed my equipment and, as anticipated, hit the ground moving sideways in the wind. The full equipment slowed my movement a bit but I was dragged across 30 yards of rough terrain before I could release the canopy. Unknown to me, I peeled layers of skin off my left forearm and hand. Adrenalin and having my sleeves down kept me from seeing the abrasions until after the jump and helicopter ride across the airfield.

Dirty from being dragged in the South Carolina red clay dust, all the jumpers survived the jump. The CH-3 returned to land at our drop zone and picked me up to fly as co-pilot on the last short hop across the airfield to the squadron ramp. Lt Col Crecenti offered that opportunity to me and I jumped at it. It is very seldom that you get to make a parachute jump and then fly the jump aircraft home. I strapped in, pulled pitch and flew across the airfield. While I wanted to make that landing, it was appropriate that George make the last local sortie landing at the home field and he took the controls. Taxiing into the squadron area, we were met by two fire trucks shooting arcs of water over the Jolly Green Giant. Major Pat Patterson and all squadron members met the aircraft with champagne to celebrate the final local flight.

It pained me greatly, but on 1 June 1988, the 703rd TASS was officially deactivated, and, by the time I departed Shaw in August, all the 703rd personnel were reassigned: some to Air Force helicopter units and some of the younger pilots drew choice assignments with US Coast Guard CH-3 rescue units in such spots at Cape Cod, San Francisco, San Diego and Florida. The aircraft were redistributed to an Air Force Rescue and Recovery Wing and to the US Navy.

PAID TO SKI

Lt Col Bobby Whitfield, TACP commander at Ft. Drum, New York, was dating the Marketing Director for the Killington Ski Resort. She offered Bobby a nine-bedroom condo in the last week of January, and, at a much-reduced price, for our TACP organizational meeting. My staff's cost analysis indicated that it would be less expensive to hold the conference at Killington than to require the Det Commanders to gather at Shaw AFB. Travel costs were about the same, but the cost for quarters was less in the condo. Since each commander would have his own room in the condo, Colonel Juve and I pushed for all commanders' wives to participate. For the added price of a wife's airfare, each commander and wife could enjoy a four-day vacation in the snow.

For three days, we held working groups / presentations from 0800 until 1300. Common problems were transition to HMMWVs (Humvees), new communications gear, Army – Air Force relations, work and living facilities and deployment challenges. The Det 1 Commander brought the newest Army field gear and equipment to show how much better the new Army gear was than Air Force issue equipment. Everyone agreed, so I tasked my staff at Shaw to see how to purchase that gear and pay for it with Air Force funds. We broke for each afternoon's skiing on the Killington slopes. On day three, as I finished a budgeting discussion: "Any questions?"

"Is that the last item? The afternoon lift tickets begin in 20 minutes," from Lt Col John Graves, Det Commander at Fort Riley, Kansas, and a former F-4 WSO in the Squids at Torrejon, Spain.

Great snow conditions, but it was *COLD* at the top of the lifts. The wind chill on day two was minus eight degrees up top. When skiing (physical training on the agenda) was complete, everyone retired to the heated swimming pool at our conference center. Fortified with wine, we stood in the warm waters of the outdoor pool while snow fell to form a white snow cap on our heads. Adequately thawed, we dressed and went out for a wonderful team dinner in town. Work, ski, socialize, repeat! Colonel Rhyne once told me he could gauge character of subordinates on the golf course even if they were non-golfers by how they approached the challenge. The same was true on the ski slopes.

REVERSING ROLES FOR A DAY

Every job has its fun moments and one of those at Shaw was a 1988 "Wives Day" when the wives of three of our Colonels, Penny Juve, Claire and Nancy Duane linked up with Mary Jo Horner, wife of the 9th AF Commander, Lt Gen Chuck Horner, to tour the parachute and flight operations of the 21st TASS and the deployable field kitchen and vehicles of the 682nd ASOC. They received briefings on both squadrons, and, then experienced parachute harness and landing training with the paratroopers of the 21st TASS. They later strapped on all the flying gear and took a high-speed taxi ride on the runway as a right seat passenger in OT-37s. See Claire's fighter pilot stare below. Mary Jo Horner tried to egg on the young lieutenant pilot of her aircraft to take off "just a little bit" during a high-speed taxi on the runway at Shaw. Fortunately, the

lieutenant could not be coerced to break the rules, even by the three-star's wife. The wing and squadron leaders knew that if they did take off "just a little bit", that might be passed to General Horner within an evening and we would all be in deep, hot water. Following their OT-37 high-speed taxi rides, the ladies travelled across the field in HUMMVEES. Mary Jo drove and taxed the vehicle's capabilities on side-hill maneuvers. They ate lunch (MREs to eat and canteen cups for coolaid beverages) in the ASOC's deployable dining tent. These were unusual experiences for our wives but demonstrated what we often did daily.

MY LAST FLIGHT AT SHAW AFB

My last flight at Shaw AFB and last in the OT-37, August 25, 1988 was as lead of a 2-ship with Major Hal Lowder, from the 21st TASS as Two. Hal was a very experienced fighter pilot and we worked out the OT-37s with demanding formation work, alternating leads, tactical trail air work, some basic fighter maneuvers and returned to the aerodrome for a great overhead pattern. We did our best Thunderbird imitation of simultaneous canopies up, flaps up and lights off. Then, upon arrival in the chocks and shutdown, the waiting 21 TASS guys and crew chiefs grabbed me and tossed me in a tub of ice water. This was a long-standing final flight tradition borrowed from the fighter community. It was an honor to be dunked by my flying peers, and on a late August afternoon in South Carolina, I needed an ice bath. The cold champagne flowed, but I choked up a bit knowing this was the last Pilot-In-Command flight in my Air Force career.

MY LAST JUMP AT SHAW AFB
My last parachute jump as DO of the 507th, also at the end of August, was a combat equipment jump from a North Carolina ANG C-130 after a low level, with F-16 aggressors in the DZ area. I was jumping the door on the port side with MSGT Scott as the primary JM. Five minutes out of the DZ, I was hooked up, ready, and trying to look out the tiny window in the troop door and figure out where we were in relation to "Fox DZ." Just under two minutes out from the DZ, Scottie threw up the paratroop door, set the paratroop platform on the doorsill, did his checks and looked out for the DZ. Scottie stepped back, and, as the C-130 Crew Chief yelled "One minute", I was told to "Stand in the door." I passed my static line to the safety NCO and stepped onto the platform with a firm grip on both sides of the door.

The plane suddenly climbed 400 feet to jump altitude and then "bunted" the aircraft nose over to go level, making everybody light on their feet. The C-130 rolled first to the right and I was looking at the sky. The plane then rolled into a left bank of 30 degrees. At that bank angle, it felt like I was looking straight down at the ground. I strengthened my death grip on the door. I finally saw the DZ a mile or so out to the left front as an F-16 arced around the left side of the C-130 about four miles away and level. I looked back to the DZ and it moved further toward the rear of our plane. I thought "There is no way in hell that we will make it to the DZ."

The pilot tightened up the turn and the C-130 cranked around in an even steeper bank toward the DZ. I now felt as if I was hanging out into space, I could see the DZ moving around to the nose of the aircraft. Just as the DZ disappeared under the nose of the aircraft, we rolled out of all but 20 degrees of bank. I never saw the green light but Scottie shouted "Go!" and slapped my butt. I hopped out, downward, into the blast of air. The air flow rolled me onto my back and over the toes of my jump boots I saw the retreating C-130 with Scottie waving at me. I still swear I could hear him howling with laughter. Nobody in the aircraft followed me out! It was a set up to hang me out on a "Solo Jump" as my last 507th parachute jump. The rest of the 21st TASS paratroopers and even the C-130 crew were in on it. In seconds, my parachute opened and I maneuvered toward the cluster of vehicles and folks in the center of the DZ. After releasing my combat gear and thundering onto the ground, I was met by Claire, Trevor and numerous 507th Wing and 21st TASS personnel. The C-130 returned for a much more convential pass with the remaining paratroopers making uneventful jumps. With jumps completed, we broke out the champagne and beer to celebrate my last jump. Scottie said he wanted to see if I could handle that on my last jump. Again: "I don't mind dying, but I don't want to embarrass myself doing it."

REPLACEMENT DO

I worked for the past 18 months with a superb officer as my Deputy DO, Lt Col Bob Johnson. I hoped that Bob would come out on the next Colonels promotion list and then replace me as the DO. That was not to be, as the Air Force assigned a Colonel Harrell, from the Air War College, to be my replacement. That assignment turned out to be an embarrassment.

Colonel Harrell arrived two weeks before my departure. At the very least he had a personal insecurity problem. As soon as he was issued his flying gear in the 21st TASS, he decided that his gear should hang right next to the Wing Commander's and Vice Wing Commander's flying gear. On his own volition, he moved the Squadron Commander's and Operations Officer's parachutes and gear down several positions and put his gear on the peg and in the locker which he believed was rightly "his." I learned he wanted to be on parachute jump status, not because he loved jumping or he wanted to support our airborne ALOs, FACs and enlisted folk, but just because he wanted to get enough Jumpmaster jumps to earn his Senior Parachutist badge. I don't know where he had previous parachute experience, but his personality did not strike me as that of a real paratrooper. Colonel Harrell was the same "dumb-smack Jumpmaster" that screwed up the C-130 tailgate jump that had led to SSGT Vaughn's extraction off the aircraft ramp at Shaw, seven days later.

I departed Shaw in late August for TAC Headquarters at Langley and Col Harrell was not making a lot of friends among the young 21st

TASS FACs and enlisted troops. In September, 9th Air Force sent a large staff to Saudi Arabia for a US Central Command exercise and Col Harrell went along, partially for orientation to the area of responsibility and partially for face time with the 9th AF Commander, Lieutenant General Chuck Horner. Sometime in this deployment it was discovered that Colonel Harrell was a cross-dresser and brought a supply of feminine clothing articles along. Very sensitive to Saudi attitudes, and maybe his own, General Horner told Colonel Harrell he had 24 hours to be out of his Theater of Operations and preferably out of his Air Force. Harrell made it to back to Shaw for rapid retirement processing and no retirement ceremony. Being an egotist and a non-team player in any unit will make you stand out; it only takes a little time to get your just rewards.

BACK TO HQ TAC

42

TAC Director of Joint Matters

August 1988 came to Shaw AFB and I found myself with orders back to Langley AFB as the Director of Joint Matters (Office symbol: XPJ). That position was two levels above the ALFA Agency where I served in '77 – '80. ALFA now answered directly to the TAC DCS for Plans (XP), so some progress was being made in elevating TAC's Joint relationships. I later heard that Maj Gen Mike Ryan picked me to lead XPJ based on my official photo and my past tour in ALFA. Mike Ryan looked at my records photo where I wore a CIB and two sets of jump wings, so he figured I knew a lot about the Army, i.e. good "Joint" material.

Claire and I made the very tough decision to have her stay in Sumter with the boys so Chris could finish his fourth and senior year on the Wilson Hall football team. We walked into a home seller's dream situation and quickly sold our Sumter house for cash. That was easy! Claire, Chris and Trevor moved into a two story, three-bedroom apartment on the same side of town as Wilson Hall School. After getting them settled, I launched off to Langley and moved into our old house in Grafton, which came available as our renters were also reassigned, courtesy of Uncle Sam. The 1977 large house of 1500 square feet did not seem so big after 11 years, and now we had a hulking high school senior and a grade-schooler. I worked on the house and garage on week nights, and on Fridays, I skipped out of work about 2:30 and hit the road (I-95) for the 387-mile trip to Sumter and Chris's football games. I was with the family Friday evening to Sunday afternoon, when I made the reverse trek.

Only once did I get caught speeding. It was already getting dark on I-95 just north of Fayetteville NC, when the State Trooper caught me doing 85 in a 70. I mailed the ticket with payment in to the county clerk the next day and I don't think USAA ever got word of it. Lots of I-95 mileage was put on the Porsche that semester.

At the end of the Fall Semester, we *finally* moved the family to the Yorkville Road house and Chris enrolled in Tabb High School for his last semester. Amazingly, Chris found classmates he knew from his 1st through 3rd grade classes at Grafton Bethel Elementary. These classmates remained in the area the whole time, unlike our four family moves in the same timeframe. Chris was adamant that we call him Chris instead of the nickname "Topher" from years past and he introduced himself to all as Chris. However, when a cute blonde classmate remembered him as Topher, he allowed her to call him that. The transfer of high school classes and credits worked out well, except that Chris showed no PE credits. For a while it looked like Chris would have to take PE in summer school to graduate. The Commonwealth of Virginia required at least one semester of PE for every able bodied high school student. We appealed to a great Wilson Hall Vice-Principal, Mr. Fred Moulton, who amended Chris' official transcript to give him credit for a semester of PE based on playing varsity football and soccer for four years. That met the Virginia required credit for PE and Chris graduated with his class in May. Thank God for caring educators like Fred Moulton.

After a year in the small house on Yorkville Road, we were considering a move into a larger house. By luck or providence, we wandered into a small, new development in Yorktown, just off Highway 17 and very near the Yorktown Battlefield – Colonial National Historical Park. The location was nearer our church in old Yorktown and my drive to work was only eight minutes longer. Not only did we find a floor plan that we both loved, but the builder, Bernie Parrish, was great about personalizing it for us. We worked with that developer / builder to construct a beautiful and very efficient house in Yorktown, moving in January 1990.

The day of our scheduled move, a major ice storm hit the Tidewater area; not only could the moving van not make it to our old house, but electrical power was lost to most of the peninsula, including our old house. Faced with a cold dark night, Claire remembered that the new house was heated by natural gas and the immediate Yorktown area did have electricity. So, with no movers, we loaded mattresses, food and bedding into the faithful 1982 blue Volvo wagon and went to camp out in the new house. We had no refrigerator there but solved the storage issue by placing food that needed cold storage into the snow and ice on the back porch. The temperatures did not rise above 40 degrees until we completed the move. Chris missed all this fun as he and I had made the two-day drive to move him into a dormitory in Dallas Texas, where he began his freshman year at Southern Methodist University (SMU) in September.

TAC/XPJ – JOINT MATTERS

My job as Director of Joint Matters at TAC headquarters placed me over four divisions that worked issues in Joint Doctrine, Procedures, or Policy. Each division consisted of five or six action officers, headed by a Lieutenant Colonel, two of whom were eligible for promotion to Colonel in the primary zone on the upcoming Air Force promotion board.

The Air Force officer performance and rating system was nothing if not ever-changing. The system changed (again), and, for the promotion cycle in my second year on the TAC staff I had enough Lieutenant Colonels eligible for promotion that I possessed the decentralized power to ensure promotion of one of them (about 97% surety). Lt Col Mike Fore was the best of my division chiefs and had commanded an F-16 squadron in the Pacific. Mike, however, was waffling about retiring instead of meeting the promotion board. On a quiet Friday afternoon, I walked down the hall to Mike's office, closed the door and bluntly asked him:

"Do you want to stay in and be a Colonel or retire?"

"Stay in"

I gave him the "definitely promote" rating. He was selected by the Colonel board and soon left to be the Deputy of Operations and then Ops Group Commander at Columbus AFB for AETC, the new name for ATC. He was back in the cockpit.

Lt Col Andy Medler, another of my Division chiefs, had previously been passed over for promotion to Colonel, despite having also been an F-16 Squadron Commander. It seemed his rating officer back then included comments about the nasty actions Andy's wife caused during their divorce. I worked with the XP to get that report thrown out of his records since reports should reflect only the performance of the officer. Brig Gen Dick Myers (later General Myers, Chairman of the JCS) rewrote his next OER and as I left TAC in 1991, Andy was selected for promotion to Colonel after that pass over. In the modern Air Force that was almost statistically impossible, but Andy made it, as did our good friend, Steve Alderman, years later. Sometimes there is justice in the screwed-up promotion system.

As in my ALFA tour ten years back, our primary contact with the Army was the TRADOC DCS for Combat Developments at Ft. Monroe, VA, then MG Jack Woodmansee. MG Woodmansee was a career Army aviator, one of the first pilots to fly with Night Vision Goggles (NVGs) and was personally involved in joint concepts, particularly in aviation operations as he was a significant force in the development and use of helicopter gunships. He later became the CG of V Corps in Europe. He was succeeded by MG Rudy Ostovich.

The social bond between MG Ostovich and Maj Gen Ryan paid off in all our joint ventures. I saw both generals years later; MG Ostovich worked in the Corporate Services area of USAA and General Mike Ryan was a member of the USAA Board of Directors. Mike Ryan was a real pleasure to work "with": there was never a "you" or an "I" with Mike Ryan; it was always a "we." I could leave his office with a draft paper or presentation that was virtually dripping red ink from the many corrections, but the interactions were "Maybe *we* could move this to here" or "*We* can say this better this way." I learned this very valuable leadership skill from him.

We promoted the concept of joint operations at every opportunity. Brig Gen Everett Pratt (later Lt Gen), Mike Fore and I lectured twice at The Canadian War College in Toronto. On three occasions, I lectured at the Army War College, Carlisle Barracks, Pennsylvania. The subject was always Joint Operations and Integration of Firepower on the battlefield. The Army students seemed to accept the concept but the Marine students wanted no part of Joint Ops. 'Semper Fi' and leave us alone. Fortunately, that attitude changed during Iraq and Afghanistan conflicts.

ARMY / AIR FORCE A-10 STUDY
One of my interesting projects was as the senior Air Force representative on a TRADOC study for moving the A-10s from the Air Force to the Army. This study was directed by the US Congress at the insistence of several members with an agenda, but no clue. After an objective analysis by the joint panel under the direction of MG Rudy Ostovich, the bottom line reply to Congress was a resounding **NO!** The cost in material, pilot training, attrition, aircraft losses and maintenance of a rapidly aging weapons system was more than the Army wanted to take on. On the doctrinal side of the transfer, the Army commanders all wanted direct control of any A-10s that were in their AO. This was an argument that was settled back in 1942 when the Army Air Forces in North Africa were given theatre control of theatre air assets. It was

"déjà vu all over again" to see the same doctrinal issues arise over 45 years later. New weapon system, but this was the same argument for possession by Army commanders.

A spinoff from the A-10 study was my connection with David Hackworth, a noted military columnist. David was a very outspoken columnist, retired Army Colonel, with a ton of Army decorations from Korea and Vietnam. When he wrote a magazine article proposing the A-10 move to the Army, I responded by sending him an outline of the TRADOC study and the resulting reasons for leaving the Hogs in the Air Force. David and I corresponded for a short while, and, when he saw my background in Close Air Support in the F-4 and A-10, combat experience as a grunt, FAC qualification and ASOC experience, David asked me to be his CAS expert. So, I contributed to his columns as a ghost writer when the subject came around to CAS or joint firepower employment. I continued this collaboration with David until just before his death in 2005.

JSTARS

Another major project during my tenure was the development, testing and deployment of the JSTARS airborne radar system. This may be the only time in recent history when a staff officer saw a system from first prototype to Operational Test and then into combat in a two-year span.

When I was designated the TAC senior officer in the JSTARS operational testing, there was only one JSTARS aircraft available, with a second hand-made prototype on the way. The **Northrop Grumman E-8 Joint Surveillance Target** Attack **Radar** System (Joint STARS) is a battle management and command and control aircraft. It tracks ground vehicles and some aircraft, collects imagery, and relays tactical pictures to ground and air theater commanders.

The aircraft is now operated by both active duty Air Force and Air National Guard units and carries specially trained U.S. Army personnel as additional flight crew. The JSTARS aircraft was retrofitted onto Boeing 707 airliners and the signature characteristic was a digital phased-array radar contained in a long canoe-like attachment mounted under the front half of the fuselage. The system had Moving Target Indicator (MTI) capability or a digital sweep that presented a return so clear and detailed that it resembled a green tint TV picture. The MTI was startlingly accurate as we learned when on a mission from Melbourne, Florida. An operator said he saw numerous targets 70 miles away that were moving at 15 miles per hour but going nowhere. Further investigation revealed that the MTI radar was tracking the metal masts in a Tampa yacht club because the metal masts were blowing back and forth in a 20-knot wind. Cool.

The JSTARS project team spent months training on our sole aircraft and then the Department of Defense thought the JSTARS system should be shown to our NATO allies. As we were planning our Operational Field Deployment (OFD-1), Iraq decided to invade Kuwait in August 1990 and Operation Desert Shield began. To our surprise, despite the buildup of forces in Desert Shield, we were assigned the airlift and commitment for a JSTARS demonstration trip to Europe. In September 1990, we were off to RAF Mildenhall for flights to educate the UK Ministry of Defense.

We received strange reactions from some guests when they saw our mixed civilian-military crew. Officially, the JSTARS aircraft did not belong to the Air Force, but, rather, to a cooperative organization of Northrup-Grumman, Boeing, Cubic Corporation and Raytheon. The military provided the tactical expertise but civilians were still fine-tuning the radar and massive computers on the aircraft. We flew British officials from Mildenhall and then deployed to Geilenkirchen Germany to fly NATO brass from five countries. We then deployed to Ramstein AB, Germany to host USAFE and USAREUR generals.

Included in the flights from Ramstein was General Shalikashvili, the SACEUR or Supreme Allied Commander Europe (Ike's old job). General John Shalikashvili was born in the Soviet Republic of Georgia to nobility. His father was a Georgian Prince and his mother a Countess. They came to the US in 1952 and General Shalikashvili became a US citizen in 1958. General "Shali" became the Chairman of the JCS in 1993. Notable among the flights in Germany was a night mission for LTG Freddy Franks, VII Corps CG. We integrated the JSTARS system into a Corps size exercise, "Exercise Deep Strike" in Germany. Franks was very impressed.

The JSTARS flights above Germany brought up a sensitive subject. Since our radar could see ground objects out to 300 plus miles that meant, while flying in an orbit 100 miles from the German border, we could track or see 200 miles into East Germany. With the fall the Soviet empire and the demolition of the Berlin Wall beginning, NATO did not want to do anything to cause concern to the paranoid Russians or East Germans. NATO therefore directed that we could not point our JSTARS radar toward East Germany in any mode or manner. But

France, Germany (FRG) Low Countries (all NATO) were OK to scan and view.

Related was my discussion on a demonstration flight where I was the briefer for the Luftwaffe three-star commander of their Tactical Air Command (GAFTAC). He was already in negotiations with the East German Air Force about accepting the East German MiGs into the Luftwaffe. A bump in the road was the lousy maintenance of the East German aircraft. The general said it took at least three East German squadrons to make one Luftwaffe squadron of flyable aircraft. I wondered: What was the policy for accepting the East German pilots who recently were the opposition and possibly avowed communists?

After another demonstration in France, the JSTARS airframe was flying straight back to Florida, so our team from TAC and many others flew home via commercial airlines from Charles de Gaulle airport northeast of Paris. It was a rough trip but fighter pilots can hack it. Tales of pub crawls in London, a five-star supper at Englishman Robert Carrier's Hintlesham Hall, night clubbing in the Dutch towns just off the runway end of Geilenkirchen, Amsterdam red light district, schnapps attacks in Germany or touring Place Pigalle in Paris take up more space than I can allow myself. But in exchange for a large Scottish Drambuie-on-the-rocks, I am sure I can remember or make it up.

When Desert Storm seemed imminent, the JSTARS team was of split opinion on whether we would be combat players. Hell, it was a prototype system with civilians in the crew and there existed only one operational JSTARS aircraft. I was sitting in my Langley XPJ office when my admin NCO, SSGT Kim, brought me a message that answered that question.

The Secret message alerted 7th Corps and LTG Franks for deployment to the Middle East. LTG Franks raved to GEN Schwartzkopf about the JSTARS system and demanded its deployment. When I saw the message, I called the JSTARS team and told them to "Pack your bags because LTG Franks said he would never go into an armor conflict without JSTARS." And, he didn't! Civilians and all, JSTARS deployed to Saudi for the conflict and did some splendid work with Army's Delta Force in Scud missile hunting. The JSTAR's Synthetic Aperture Radar (SAR) was so sensitive that we could detect the barb wire fence's spiral image around an Iraqi Scud site.

On the fly, (pun intended), the concept of operations was changed from an intelligence asset to a hunter / killer. The original JSTARS concept, developed by XPJ's Lt Col Steve Anderson, was for JSTARS to detect targets and download the info to ground receiving stations situated with ground units down to Division level. The ground forces would then plan and attack the targets. There were only THREE ground stations produced to date and those went to the Army and Marine commanders, with the third sent to the Joint headquarters in Saudi.

The Joint Headquarters turned out to be beyond transmission range when the JSTARS aircraft was on station over the Iraqi border. Therefore, the "Back End" console operators began to directly task ground attack aircraft sent to JSTARS. We were doing for ground attacks what the AWACS gang did for air-to-air engagements: find the target and then send somebody to kill it. Because our radars could detect most moving armor, the operator could put a cursor on a target two hundred miles away, click it, and then send a very accurate coordinate to strike aircraft, sometimes via digital burst. JSTARS was also one of the first systems to integrate GPS locations with radar target detections. JSTARS was the first source to detect the mass exodus of Iraqis from Kuwait and immediately tasked fighters to attack, creating what was known as the "Street of Death" for escaping Iraqi army troops.

The Air Force ultimately purchased 17 JSTARS aircraft and by 2017 was bidding out for a replacement airframe for JSTARS. The original Boeing 707 airframes were at least 20 years old for Desert Storm and regardless of upgrades to engines and electronics, a new airframe was needed.

DESERT STORM RETURN CEREMONIES

The welcoming ceremony for the 94th TFS return from Desert Storm still stands out in my mind. The first returning 4-ship of F-15s was to be welcomed by the TAC Commander and a lot of the TAC brass. A formal ceremony area was marked off on the Langley AFB ramp and security police set up rope barriers to keep the spectators from crossing onto the ramp where the F-15s would park. Under hot clear skies and the usual high humidity of the Chesapeake Bay, the first flight arrived on time, flew a nice pattern, landed and taxied to a stop in front of over 2,000 cheering spectators. The F-15 four-ship taxied in "Thunderbird style": turned and stopped at the same time, shut down engines, and raised canopies simultaneously. The pilots climbed from their cockpits, and, stood, with their crew chiefs, in front of their aircraft awaiting the welcome from the TAC Commanding General, Robert Russ, and three other generals. The flight lead was the 1st Fighter Wing Commander, #2 was a squadron major, #3 was the 94TFS Squadron Commander and #4 was a lowly 1st Lieutenant.

The reception party spent considerable time talking to the Wing King and then slowly proceeded down the line to talk at length to the major, probably discussing every mission flown in combat. Even I perceived this was going to be a lengthy, hot ceremony. At that moment, I saw movement down the line in front of the number 4 aircraft. Unable to wait any longer, a pretty, young brunette in a very short skirt jumped the rope barrier, sprinted across the ramp before the security police could react and planted a full contact, lengthy kiss on her husband, the 1st LT pilot of number 4. I chuckled and then turned to see the reaction from the TAC 4-star Commander. General Russ looked at the scene for a moment, smiled and then directed the Security Police,

"Take down the rope and let's welcome these folks home."

A flood of family, friends and fighter jocks poured onto the ramp to do just that. After that experience, every returning flight at Langley was welcomed with a *short* ceremony and then released to family and friends. General Russ – he was cool! On May 15, 1991, General "Bob" Russ retired from the United States Air Force with an appropriate retirement ceremony attended by almost every significant Air Force commander, general officer, and the Air Force Chief of Staff.

One of the unforeseen benefits of working Joint Concepts was the assignment to my unit of a Space Officer. I learned more than I thought I'd ever need about geosync / molniya orbits, satellites and space capabilities. As I learned about an infant satellite-based navigation system called Global Positioning System (GPS), my Space Officer loaned me a portable GPS system for use in a C-172. I flew to Fort Bragg and Hunter Army Airfield, using the GPS and asked FAA's Washington Center for clearance direct to Fort Bragg by GPS navigation. "Disapproved!" The FAA controllers did not know what GPS was nor how it could guide me to my destination. Today, most general aviation, military and airline navigation is by GPS.

An Air Force organizational move that TAC/XPJ championed was the move of one Tactical Air Control Party from a heavy armor battalion in an Army Division to that division's Aviation Brigade. The Air Force TACP organization was not keeping up with Army reorganization and the aviation units needed TACPs. All Army divisions were beefing up their aviation assets and the helo guys were going to play a major part in any future conflict. (How true that proved to be in less than two years!) By early 1990, we sold enough Air Force and Army staff leaders on the concept that I was asked to take the concept to the Pacific and brief the Pacific Army Commanding General and then do the same to the AF and Army commanders in Alaska.

Planning and implementing organizational changes are often a long-time process, and, although the TACP change was well accepted, I did not know how long it might require. A war (Desert Storm) within a year expedited the change. Two years later, I met an AF lieutenant at Hurlburt Field who was attending AGOS and then bound for an Army Air Cavalry unit as the ALO. I could have kissed him to see that the change did happen.

Flying into Honolulu, I was greeted at baggage claim by the Senior NCO for PACAF Joint Matters, Chief Master Sergeant Dan Stigge. Dan was a Master Sergeant in my shop when I was the DO at Shaw AFB and now he was a Chief. Hooah! It was great to see him again. Dan arranged for my briefings at PACAF headquarters, and, when we encountered a two-day delay, he took me up the island to visit the 25th Infantry Division's "Light Fighter" school. Knowing how I loved to jump with new units, CMS Dan Stigge even laid on a parachute jump with the Light Fighters, which, unfortunately, was weathered out as clouds enshrouded the mountainside. Instead, the Light Fighter School Commandant, a young Captain, took me on a thorough school tour. Finishing the tour, we were standing in a cloud-covered training area with mist dripping off the bill of our caps. I heard the Captain tell Dan, "I've never seen an Air Force Colonel take a tour and then be willing to stand out in the drizzle to discuss joint training." Dan Stigge replied, "You have never met an Air Force Colonel like Colonel Stevenson, and probably never will again." It was a definite feel good moment for me.

My XPJ staff interacted regularly with a TAC DO's staff unit titled DCS Operations - Ground. That staff unit directed the TACPs and other TAC units, such as the 682nd ASOC, which supported ground or naval units. Their office symbol was TAC/DOG and they were commonly referred to as the "Dog Shop." To my surprise, one afternoon I walked into the Dog Shop to encounter SSGT Mitch Monroe, formerly of my 507th Detachment 1 at Ft. Bragg. He was assigned to TAC/DOG to represent the Air Force ground and airborne TACPs. In due time, I found that Mitch had completed his Bachelor Degree and was applying for Officer Training School (OTS). He asked me for a recommendation to attach to his application paperwork and I was thrilled to do it. I gave him the strongest recommendation letter that I could create, citing his leadership, courage and calmness under stress. I added that I would work anywhere, under any circumstances, with SSGT (or 2LT) Monroe. Application approved, Mitch's assignment to TAC/DOG was cut short in January 1990, and he was off to OTS at Lackland AFB. I wished him the best of luck as an officer and hoped he could get a pilot training slot as well. I loved helping a good guy get ahead in the Air Force.

After working with such tremendous officers as Maj Gen Mike Ryan and Brig Gen Dick Myers, I felt the last TAC/XP that I worked for seemed an ass. A short man with a severe Napoleon complex, he ruled by fear, rather than leadership. Claire took an instant dislike to the man long before I made up my mind. Claire said there was something sleazy about the man and not to trust him. After a couple of encounters with Brig Gen Thomas Griffin, TAC/XP, I made up my mind that he was, in fact, an ass.

At one of his early staff meetings, he had his deputy berate the Directors, all Colonels, to stop lying to the XP. YGBSM! If he was a real leader and somebody lied to him, the offender would be gone. A leader does not accuse an entire unit for the possible actions of one person. The accusation was never further explained, so I have no idea of the initiating incident.

Because Brig Gen Griffin was a West Pointer, I enjoyed screwing with him for the Army – Navy game. At the formal XP Christmas Dinner party in December 1990, held the night before the Army – Navy game, I slid a card under his dinner plate saying "USNA '66 says BEAT ARMY!" Griffin was livid. He suspected me and asked,

"Where were you commissioned?"

That was the wrong question; so, I truthfully answered "The University of Texas ARMY ROTC, Sir!" and I gave a "Hook 'em Horns" sign. He fumed all night about that card. It did my heart good because he gave me grief about jumping and earlier that year said I could not go jump at MSGT Scott's retirement ceremony at Shaw AFB. (I took leave and jumped with Scottie anyhow.) He departed TAC not long afterward, and, in June 1995, while assigned as the 12th AF Commander, Griffin was relieved for adultery and forced to retire by that great TAC/CC and Fightin' Texas Aggie, General Joe Ralston.

After three years at TAC Headquarters, Colonel Assignments handlers asked if I was interested in a tour back to Europe at USAFE or EUCOM. I turned down the tour to Europe, knowing that I would pay dearly for not accepting that assignment. Chris was off to college at SMU, but Trevor was in the third grade and in his third school. I did not want to put Trevor through another move overseas. If I took the Europe assignment, my last job before mandatory retirement, I would be retiring 4,000 miles from our home state of Texas.

Then I received a call to report to the three-star Vice Commander of TAC for a job interview. I had no idea what this was about, but Lt Gen Knight immediately let me know that TAC would soon have a vacancy for the TAC Planner position on the Air Force Special Operations Command (AFSOC) staff at Hurlburt Field, Florida. Not only did I have the Special Ops background, but I could be on jump status. The incumbent TAC officer to AFSOC was tagged for early retirement and I figured that I faced the same fate. My alternative was to give the Air Force 90 days' notice for retirement there at Langley. The position sounded interesting and was better than Europe or retiring on the spot within 90 days. I said "Yes." General Knight was serious, as I received orders in hand three days after accepting the job offer. It was off to the sunny beaches of Fort Walton, Florida. The opportunity to work with Special Ops again and be on jump status with the AGOS guys and Special Ops troops from around the world was tempting enough to make even a short tour at Hurlburt Field, before departing the Air Force, worth the move. Besides, it was closer to Texas.

One of the enormous penalties paid by military families is the monetary loss incurred in selling houses for a PCS move. We were lucky when we departed Langley in 1980 and we could rent out our house until our return assignment. This time was different: rumors abounded that NASA and Langley were going to downsize. The housing market took a nosedive for sellers. Long story short, it took us five months to sell our wonderful home in Yorktown and we took almost $25K in losses. It was a rough consequence of our military lifestyle.

AIR FORCE SPECIAL OPERATIONS

43

AFSOC

In the hustle to get everything done for our move to Florida, we neglected to keep Christopher, now a rising Junior at Southern Methodist University, fully informed. A few days before the move was to occur, Chris called us at home and asked, "You are going to tell me where you are moving, right?" Stress, what stress? After packing up everything, staying in the Langley Temporary Living Facilities (TLF) for a couple of days as I out processed from the base and TAC staff, we, drove to Maxwell AFB for the first night and then on to Fort Walton Beach. My reservation at the Hurlburt TLF was ready, so, we moved in and began house hunting. On day two, the Hurlburt housing officer called me with a house that was to be rented only to a Colonel. It was owned by an Army Colonel who was very picky about to whom he rented. A wonderful huge five-bedroom, four-bath house on a shaded cul-de-sac, 200 yards from the water, in Shalimar, Florida, not too far from the base. We'll take it!

The assignment did offer Claire the opportunity to earn her teacher certification in art at the University of West Florida in Pensacola. Besides the hours of study and student teaching at the inner-city Ft. Walton Beach Junior High School, it meant long commutes across IH-10 for night classes. Claire soon joked that our trusty Volvo could drive to and from the UWF campus by itself.

My small office was across the street from AFSOC headquarters, sharing a suite with the Army Special Forces liaison officer. I was ready to jump into all joint planning, but that was delayed in subject areas where I needed to get additional security clearances for many of the "black" aircraft and projects. Justly so, AFSOC keeps many activities on a tight "Need to Know" basis. It required the Commander of AFSOC grant me clearance to many projects. Some of the deep clearances were for satellite stuff, some for operations around the globe and some that allow the Special Ops troops just to keep their clandestine covers. Some areas were "no need to know", but I sure wanted to know. Too bad!

As I coordinated with many TAC units for air support, I again realized that most of the flying wings did not give a rat's ass about the Army, much less Special Ops. All they wanted to do was fly their supersonic jets and have fun. The A-10 Hog Drivers were the only troops that got the picture. Some of the F-15E aircrews got the picture, but it seemed their wing leadership thought it an inconvenience to support very small operations with their air assets, even if the operations were highly classified and of national importance.

Major General Bruce L. Fister had recently taken command of AFSOC and proved to be a great supporter of TAC asset employment in Special Ops. The AFSOC Vice-Commander was Brigadier General C. Jerome Jones, with whom I traveled several times to partake in planning cells for JSOC in "the cage" at Ft. Bragg and other sites.

On one trip to the Army's JFK Special Warfare Center at Bragg, I did a "Huntley – Brinkley" type briefing with General Jones about AFSOC to the "Charm School" for newly selected Brigadier Generals, or equivalents, from the Army, Navy and Air Force. This was a course to broaden their knowledge about specific (Special) subjects and forces for the soon-to-be general officers. As General Jones and I finished the presentation, Jones asked for any questions and a hand went up near the back row. Standing up was BG (Select) Jack Van Alstyne, Texas A&M, Class of 1966. "Is Colonel Stevenson as screwed up an Air Force Colonel as he was an Army Second Lieutenant?" Jack and I went through Infantry Officer Basic Course and Jump School together at Fort Benning some 25 years earlier. Nice to have old friends in high places!

November 1991. On a chilly day, I found myself standing on the Hurlburt ramp as part of the farewell line for a VIP. The VIP was General M. P. C. Carns, now the Air Force Vice Chief of Staff. His visit was an in-brief on AFSOC operations as part of his new assignment. The briefings were for primary AFSOC staff members only and some portions were too "Black" for even my security clearances. Since I was not at the arrival event or the briefings for General Carns, I decided my chance to say "Hi" was at his departure. As the scheduled departure time approached, I headed over to Base Ops and tagged on to the end of the farewell line that included the 1st SOW Chief of Maintenance, the flight line supervisor, the 1st SOW Senior Enlisted Advisor, and the maintenance flight commander. I simply walked onto the flight line and stepped onto the far end of the line.

We stood at attention alongside the Learjet that would take General Carns back to the Puzzle Palace as two shiny blue Air Force sedans drove up. General Carns and Maj Gen Fister, climbed out of the lead vehicle and started down the receiving line enroute to the awaiting jet. As General Carns was shaking hands with the third person, Maj Gen Fister noticed that his TAC Planner (me) somehow added himself onto the line. He gave me a glare that said he did not approve of my attendance. Just then General Carns looked over and recognized me. Before I could salute, he grasped my hand in a firm handshake.

"Steve, how are you? What are you doing here?"

"I am the TAC air guy for AFSOC and General Fister, Sir."

General Carns put an arm around my shoulders and turned me so we both faced General Fister: "Steve and I go way back in fighters!"

General Fister's glare turned into a rather sheepish grin. We turned back as General Carns asked "How is Claire?"

"She is fine and sends her regards to Victoria and the Carns girls."

"I will tell them. It is great to see you again."

I saluted, and, then with General Fister in tow for a last conversation, General Carns headed for the jet's stairs. The two jet engines wound up as the door closed and General Fister stepped back to salute farewell. As the Lear started to move, I saluted the four white stars on a blue placard in the window holder and then smartly headed for my car behind Base Operations. No use giving·General Fister a target if he was still displeased with my presence at the short ceremony.

I soon found Dr. Jim Daugherty (Lt Col) was the AFSOC Deputy Command Flight Surgeon. A great doc, Jim was the senior flight surgeon while we were stationed at Shaw and we both were on active parachute status there. Jim loved to jump, and, most likely there was a shortage of jump qualified Flight Surgeons in the Air Force. While I was laboring at my TAC staff job, Jim was selected for promotion to Lieutenant Colonel and assigned to the number two Flight Surgeon slot at AFSOC. The Command Flight Surgeon for AFSOC was not a jump slot, so Jim was the senior paratrooper doctor. I always had a jab ready for Doc Daugherty, because, during the "Paratrooper Jump Fest '88" at Shaw AFB, a competition between jump units, Jim was on one of the competing teams and on his third competitive jump broke his arm on the ground. The Doc made a good PLF near the target; but, while rolling over, Jim pinned his left arm under his reserve chute and put his body weight across the arm. SNAP! Jim released his parachute and gear, then stood up, cradled his broken arm and walked to the DZ ambulance to treat himself. One tough Flight Surgeon!

Jim was again our "family doctor" during my AFSOC tour, caring for Claire and Trevor when needed. Since all the Air Force pilots received blood pressure and cholesterol checks as part of their annual flight physical exam, Jim offered to do BP and cholesterol workups on Claire, she received the results back in a sealed letter. Doc Daugherty said her numbers were great and she would outlive us all. After my retirement, we received a Christmas letter in December 1992 in which Jim said all he needed for his Master Blaster wings was five more jumps. Jim Daugherty later was promoted to Colonel and then to Brigadier General in 2005. Jim's official US Air Force retirement photo proudly displayed his Master Parachutist Badge.

Some of my jumps at AFSOC were static line jumps and some were Military Free Fall (MFF) or HALO jumps. On 28 May '92, I made four OV-10 jumps (or slides) at Camp Rudder with the Ranger cadre, including the Ranger Camp Sergeant Major. Hooah! I was allowed to fly with the AFSOC crews, and, on one mission I flew as co-pilot with the MH-60 "Pave Hawk" helicopters from Eglin AFB for a night, open-ocean pick up of some SEALs out in the Gulf of Mexico. The air temperature was 31 degrees, following a rare cold front in Florida, but water temp was 58 degrees – a lot warmer than the air temp. The foot heater on the co-pilot's side was inoperative so the open door in the Blackhawk meant I was freezing my toes. I felt sorry for the SEALS until I realized they were wearing wetsuits in the "warm" water and a lot better off than my feet.

Another night, I was riding as observer in the MC-130 "Combat Talon" aircraft as we refueled AFSOC MH-53s and Army MH-47s from the 160th SOAR from Ft. Campbell. The port side Chinook bobbled a bit (OK, a lot) and whacked the refueling hose line with a main rotor blade. A blinding flash of static electricity and a bit of ignited fuel from the hose followed and the "Hook" made an emergency night landing in a farmer's field in southern Alabama. The event was not over, as the unannounced landing resulted in a minor confrontation with the County Sheriff over access to the aircraft. An unmarked helicopter in a local field and guys in unmarked black flight suits with lots of guns seemed to upset one of the deputies. That was settled as maintenance troops from Ft Campbell flew in to replace a rotor blade and fly the Chinook home. Just another night in Special Ops.

I flew as an observer in the AC-130 "Spectre" gunships on training sorties locally and on two missions for "Operation Patriot Coyote." "Coyote" sorties were in support of the DEA and Customs programs in nighttime tracking of drug runners along the southwest US border. The Spectre sported all the latest sensors and from 9,000 feet we could count bales of marijuana being off-loaded from blacked out aircraft on desert airstrips. We observed and passed the information to national, state and local authorities on the ground, but ground forces usually arrived too late to make a good bust. Our AC-130 Weapons Control Officer wanted to drop a few 40mm rounds on the aircraft and vehicles on the ground. Damn fine idea, but civilian law prohibited that practice. We discovered that the strongest advocates of the 40-mm solution were the state troopers or drug agents that rode with us on all the Coyote missions.

In July 1992, the US Marines/Bell-Boeing team flew the fourth prototype V-22 Osprey tilt-rotor aircraft to Hurlburt Field for AFSOC consideration to replace the MH-53 helicopters. AFSOC lost interest when informed the Osprey's rear ramp could not be lowered in flight. Bell-Boeing said the ramp was an integral part of the empennage strength. This restriction would reduce the number of "fast rope" lines used by Special Operations Forces. The AFSOC Commander said that was unacceptable for SOF purposes and the ramp would have to be opened in flight for fast rope personnel descents. If Bell-Boeing wanted to sell the CV-22 Osprey to AFSOC, the fuselage would have to be strengthened. The Bell-Boeing team promised to look at a design modification.

The V-22 team offered Maj Gen Fister a ride back to the DC area in the Osprey, but General Fister had conflicting obligations. The Osprey (Prototype #4) making that return trip crashed into the Potomac River on approach to Quantico Marine Corps Air Station on 20 July with loss of aircraft and crew.

44

Just Another Night

Brigadier General Jones personally phoned to request my presence in his office. I said "Yes, Sir, on the way" and hustled across the street and up to his office on the top floor of the "head shed." I knocked, entered and he asked if I was available for a short-notice, classified trip. I said "Of course, Sir!" He added "We are going to give the "Huntley – Brinkley" AFSOC briefing again at Ft. Bragg to some congressional staffers, but the trip may be extended, so bring your warm weather field gear, 'no disclosure rules' apply. Tomorrow: 0530 at the 19th SOS."

This was becoming "curiouser and curiouser", but I'd find out in due time. The "no disclosure rules" meant I couldn't tell Claire where I was headed and I truthfully didn't know for how long. That evening I packed everything I should need, not in my travel bag but in my rucksack. If Claire saw me load my rucksack, field gear and helmet into my car, she didn't say a thing. She knew the rules as well.

The next morning, we flew by MC-130 to Pope AFB, NC, and checked into the Ft. Bragg VIP quarters. Use of VIP quarters was an advantage of traveling with a one-star general. That afternoon, we gave our briefing to a group of visiting Congressional staffers from the House and Senate Intelligence Committees and then we checked out of our VIP quarters. General Jones informed me that we were heading for Savannah and Hunter Army Air Field. Hunter AAF was home of the 1st Battalion of the 75th Rangers, so the trip was no longer just a dog and pony show. Hooah!

We landed at Hunter AAF, a former Strategic Air Command bomber dispersal base, now owned by the Army. I was quite familiar with Hunter AAF, having flown there numerous times as the 507th DO to see my Ranger TACP. Instead of going to the Base Operations ramp to park, our aircraft rolled out to the end of Runway 28 and into the old nuclear alert area on the southwest end of the runway. As we unloaded our plane I saw C-5s and C-141s sitting on the old alert bomber parking pads and all were very busy being serviced and loaded. We entered the former alert facility building and an Army major showed us to a couple of bunk beds for the night. Rank doesn't carry much weight here. I flew into Hunter AAF on several occasions when I was at Shaw, always to work with the Rangers or 24th Division TACP at nearby Ft. Stewart, Georgia. But I never ventured into the now-secured alert area on the west end of the field.

Late in the evening, all the C-141s departed with Rangers and returned about 0400 hours. The next morning, General Jones and I were briefed on the operation which was the rescue of a friendly foreign country's Charge D'affair and staff, being held prisoners and threatened with execution in a location half a continent to our south. The Rangers executed a night rehearsal for the night parachute assault and takedown of an airfield in the target area and then returned to Hunter. The plans were fine-tuned and by late morning everyone was ready to go.

The TAC participation in this operation consisted of F-15Es from Seymour-Johnson AFB and the Tactical Air Control Parties with the Ranger units. Air Force Special Tactics controllers were also embedded in other Special Operation units.

The "shooters" were cleaning gear and resting while the planners held a final briefing. I recognized this was a big deal when I walked into the mass briefing with General Jones. The assembled cast of usual suspects included Rangers, Seal Team 6, Delta, the "Night Stalkers" from the 160th SOAR, and crews from the Special Ops Low Level (SOLL) qualified C-130, C-141 and C-5 aircraft. I was walking down the center aisle when I heard a loud "Colonel Stevenson!" Second Lieutenant Mitch Monroe, now a navigator on SOLL C-130s, jumped up from the middle of the C-130 crews and headed my way. We shook hands and hugged, while everyone else wondered how this 2LT navigator warranted a family greeting from the Airborne Ranger Air Force colonel with a Special Forces combat patch on his right shoulder. An instant later, an officer announced "Gentlemen, the Chairman" and everyone popped to attention. In walked General Colin Powell, the Chairman of the JCS and the highest-ranking officer in the US military. High level special operations missions must be approved by the National Command Authority (NCA) which is the President, Vice President or Chairman of the JCS. General Powell drew the duty for this operation.

The briefing went well and General Powell asked just a few very pointed questions. As he summed up the operation, General Powell said, "We are doing this because two countries asked for help and we are the only people in the world that can do this." With that we were "blessed" and ready to go. General Jones and I rode in a C-5 loaded with MH-6 helicopters, "Little Birds", for use in the target areas. Unlike in normal airlift operations, the Little Birds were fully fueled and armed. Late on the ingress, the C-5 flew at low level to avoid radar detection (truly "under the radar") and the flight crew wore NVGs with no external or internal lights turned on. I was rigged to make a parachute jump onto the target airfield if the assaulting Rangers did not clear the runway which was reportedly blocked.

I was emotionally wound up tighter than a banjo, hooked up as number four jumper on the port-side door, when the loadmaster called "Airland!" at the 12 minute-out point. Our jumpers scrambled to get their parachute gear off as Fat Albert began its approach. The Rangers cleared everything off the runway and the parade of landing aircraft began. Seven minutes after we landed, the Little Birds were out on the ramp with rotors turning and assault team members loading on. No further details are releasable, but everything went well; the SEALS got their guys out and Delta retrieved the primary hostage. With everyone recovering to the airfield, a special medical equipped C-130 took the former hostages aboard, launched, and then the aerial armada recovered personnel, equipment and withdrew in good order. The guys were in, job done, and out before sunrise. It was just another day, or, more correctly, just another night in Special Ops, an example of a well-planned and executed mission by the professionals in the Special Operations Forces.

FINAL DAY

With my retirement date set by the Air Force, I was trying to get the most cash from my unused leave sell-back and use the rest of my leave (30 days) as terminal leave. I scrambled to set up my departure and out-processing. Then my main concern was to set up my last *military* parachute jump. Because of aircraft availability, it turned out that my last jumps were on my last active duty day.

The jumps were in support of the airborne ROMAD instructors at the AGOS and the lead jumpmaster for the day was Tech Sergeant Bobby Ercol, who was a ROMAD at Shaw AFB while I was the DO. Bobby had moved to duty as an instructor at the "School House" for ROMADs. There was nobody I would rather have as my jumpmaster on these jumps. I did not advertise these were to be my last jumps or that my retirement was imminent, but this day, to my surprise, Navy SEALs, Army SF troops, two Marines, even a Navy life support tech from Pensacola were manifested, all in addition to our AGOS and Special Tactics troops.

At a decent 0800 hours, the jumpers gathered across the street from Hurlburt Base Ops for roll-call and practice PLFs. All were experienced paratroopers from the AGOS or the 620th Special Tactics Group which furnished combat controllers, ROMADs and medics to the Special Operations units in all US services. We rapidly progressed through the jump procedures and required PLFs. We returned to the aircraft ramp in front of Base Ops where the riggers had delivered our main parachutes and reserve chutes. We drew our equipment and put on the parachutes for the Jumpmaster Personal Inspection. Once again, I went through the helmet to toes, front and back, equipment inspection. Regardless of the parachutist's rank, type of aircraft, location or who was performing as Jumpmaster, the ritual inspection was the same across all services and varied little, even with my jumps from Canada to Vietnam. The JMPI consistency over 26 years was comforting before any jump.

As we finished our inspections, a camouflaged C-130 turned off the runway and taxied toward Base Ops. This was going to be an Engine Running On-load (ERO); so, as the aircraft came to a halt, the rear ramp was lowered, the Loadmaster hopped down, and came over to our circle of jumpers. In 30 seconds, the Loadmaster covered all the required briefing items and asked for questions. No questions from this bunch, so the Loadmaster led the waddling jumpers through the hot engine exhaust and up the rear ramp. In the brief time that we listened to the aircraft brief, TSgt Ercol and the assistant jumpmaster entered the C-130 and inspected its configuration, static line anchors and equipment to ensure a safe jump from the troop doors. We took seats on our appropriate sides of the aircraft, buckled up and the C-130 crew closed the rear ramp and taxied toward the runway for departure and the 15-minute flight to the Drop Zone. The C-130 was on the ground for only nine minutes when it took off.

Ten minutes to the DZ, it was stand up, hook up, check static lines, check equipment, sound off for equipment check, open the paratroop doors and extend wind deflectors; then Bobby checked my door and looked for the DZ. I was honored, due to my rank, to stand in the door and jump first. With my ear plugs and the loud engine noises,

I could barely make out the jump commands. Like the JMPI, the pre-jump hand signals remained constant for three decades and hearing was not required. TSgt Ercol stepped back into the aircraft, pointed at the platform at the bottom of the door and yelled "Stand in the door." I stepped forward so that the toe on my right boot just hung over the platform, crouched slightly and took a firm grip on both sides of the door. Again, there was no fear involved in the grip. Now I was almost out the door, and, if we encountered turbulence, I did not want to fall out of the aircraft. As the great Airborne saying goes: "I don't mind dying, but I don't want to embarrass myself doing it!" Bobby leaned around my left side to confirm the DZ location as I saw the ground change from green pine trees to tan sand. I glanced down at the two jump command lights on the edge of the door and they switched from red to green. Bobby smacked my ass with a loud "GO!" and I sprang out into the 120-mph wind. Good jump; soft landing; turn in equipment; then do it again. Hooah!

It was a 20-minute truck ride back to Hurlburt where we picked up a parachute and reserve for the second jump. We also picked up our field gear and ruck sacks because this was to be a full combat equipment jump. On this jump, my very last, our assistant Jumpmaster commented that my chin strap looked like it served in the Korean War. I blithely remarked that it brought me this far and I can stick with it today. I think the Lord was playing with me, but giving me a warning.

Sure enough, 25 minutes later as I hopped off the rear ramp of the C-130, 1200 feet above the DZ, maintaining a good tight body position in the wind blast, the chin strap snapped and away went my helmet. I didn't even realize the loss until I checked my canopy for full inflation and thought "Man, it's breezy and cooler than the first jump." Then I glanced straight down and noticed my helmet tumbling toward the sandy drop zone. Plunk! Now, with no head protection, I wanted to ensure I did a very tight PLF to avoid smacking my head on the ground. Not to worry: the breeze brought me over the largest sand pit on the DZ. I released my equipment onto the lowering line, and, seconds later I stuck in the soft sand like a lawn dart, with nothing above my knees getting close to the sand.

More importantly, the sand cushioned the landing of the beer and champagne that I had very carefully packed in my rucksack. The undamaged goods were soon liberated and consumed by the great gaggle of paratroopers from four services who celebrated my 26 years as a paratrooper.

45

Checking Out

After cleaning up and changing into a blue uniform, I was driving around the south end of the Hurlburt runway, concentrating on my final out-processing and speeding a bit over the 30-mph limit. A young three-stripe Security Policeman zapped me with a Doppler radar gun, made a sharp 180 degree turn in his truck, flipped on the lights and pulled me over for speeding. He asked why I was speeding and I admitted that I was not paying attention on the almost empty perimeter road. He asked where I was going in a hurry and I said, "I'm on my way to CBPO to out-process from Hurlburt and retire from the US Air Force."

The airman looked at my ID card, handed it back, saluted, and replied, "Thank you for your time in the Air Force. Be careful, sir."

On to CBPO to out-process. Then, after a short ceremony in Major General Fister's office, where General Fister gave me an AFSOC desk set souvenir and the Legion of Merit Medal, I checked into the Temporary Living Quarters.

Claire, Trevor and I moved into the Hurlburt TLQ for three days as our movers packed our household goods, we cleaned the house, and then prepared for the trip home to Texas. We loaded the Volvo wagon and Porsche, and drove for three days to Corpus Christi, stopping in Louisiana and just outside Houston. Two days later, I flew commercial airlines back to Pensacola to get my second car which was parked at the Hurlburt BOQ. Back on Hurlburt, I still needed to say farewells to some folks at AFSOC.

One of the good guys whom I stopped to see was the Vice Commander's Executive Officer, Captain Tom Trask, a great young officer! Tom and I worked on several projects and tasks involving Brig Gen Jones. Tom won a Silver Star as co-pilot of the MH-53 that went to within 30 miles of Bagdad on January 21, 1991 to rescue Navy

Lieutenant Devon Jones, who ejected from an F-14. In July 2014, Tom Trask got his third star for Lieutenant General and became the Vice Commander of U.S. Special Operations Command (USSOCOM).

Tom's parting remarks on our visit at Hurlburt were, "Sir, I hate to see you go. You are one of the good ones. You understand Special Ops."

That meant more to me than the Legion of Merit medal.

As I drove out the main gate of Hurlburt and turned west on US 98, it finally struck me: *My military career is over!* With watery eyes, Snoopy and I headed for Texas.

I looked back on what I accomplished in the past quarter century: defended my country at all costs, managed to get wounded twice doing that, scared myself numerous times, learned a lot about leadership from great leaders (NCOs to Generals), married an unbelievably strong woman, made my family move 18 times, raised two good boys, was formally educated beyond my intelligence level, left every unit or place better than when I arrived, tried to help those who deserved it and never stopped loving to parachute and fly. That pretty well wraps up my career.

"I've looked at life from both sides now"

From the ground up and from above the clouds down, and embraced it all.

Glossary

1 v 1 – fighter engagement of one aircraft versus one aircraft.

ACT – Air Combat Tactics, from simple 1 v 1 to complex multi-aircraft engagements.

Agent Orange – Herbicide used by US forces in Vietnam.

"Agency" – Our friends from the US Central Intelligence Agency; aka "the Company."

AK-47 – Russian assault rifle designed by Mikhail Kalashnikov.

ATC – Air Training Command; owned all AF basic, flight and technical training.

Battalion – Army or Marine organization usually consists of 400 to 800 troops.

Blackhats – Instructors at the US Army Parachutist School at Ft Benning, GA. Also, the nickname for Standardization and Evaluation pilots in the Air Force.

BOQ – Bachelor Officer Quarters.

CAS – Close Air Support. Fighter aircraft supporting ground troops in combat with bad guys. Often VERY close.

CBPO – Consolidated Base Personnel Office

Chaff – a radar countermeasure in which aircraft spread a cloud of small, thin pieces of aluminum, metallized glass fibre or plastic.

"Charlie" – Nickname for Viet Cong by way of the phonetic letters of "Victor Charlie."

Charlie - Charlie – phonetic for the Command and Control (C&C) helo.

CIB – Army award of the Combat Infantryman Badge. Sign of a "Grunt."

Claymore mine – Small explosive device which fires hundreds of pellets.

CO – Commanding Officer at any level up to General Officers, then CG.

Cobra 6 – Call sign of the Company Commander of C Company, 1st Battalion (Airborne), 327th Infantry Regiment of the 1st Brigade, (Separate), 101st Airborne Division.

Cold War – The state of political hostility that existed from 1945 until 1990 between countries led by the Soviet Union and countries led by the United States.

Company - Army or Marine organization usually consists of 160 to 400 troops.

CP - Command Post. CP refers to the location of a unit's command element.

DCO – see DO.

DEROS – Date of Estimated Return from Over Seas.

Diplomat and Warrior – Weekly newsletter of 1st Bde 101st Abn Div in Vietnam.

DM - Davis Monthan AFB, AZ. A-10 schoolhouse.

DO – Often used as DCO, Deputy Commander for Operation, or Operations Officer.

Down Range – In the Middle East.

DRPCB – A-10 pilots term for "Dirty Rotten Pervert Commie Bastards."

DZSO – Drop Zone Safety Officer - Paratrooper to ensure drop zone weather conditions are safe for the conduct of parachute operations of any size.

EW – Electronic Warfare: Detection, avoidance and / or degradation of enemy electronic transmissions by radar or communication emitters.

FAC – Forward Air Controller – In Vietnam, normally a fighter qualified pilot, flying a small, slow, lightly armed observation airplane, to locate and mark targets for the faster jet fighters.

Farm, The – Camp Peary VA, is the Agency's training academy. Located across the Interstate highway from Colonial Williamsburg, Virginia.

FNG – Fucking New Guy: recently assigned personnel, particularly in comparison to troops who have been in a unit for a significant amount of time or number of enemy engagements.

FO – Forward Observer. The FO coordinates/adjusts indirect fire support to infantry units at various levels. See "Redleg."

FOL – Forward Operating Location.

Fox 1, 2, 3, or 4 – type of air-to-air engagement (radar missile, IR missile, guns, collision).

FSB – Fire Support Base.

GCA – Ground Controlled Approach – radar guidance via radio for aircraft, may include altitude as well as heading instructions.

Green Beanies – Semi-derogatory term for US Army Special Forces troops; based on their wear of "Green Berets." Accepted internally, but not for use by non-SF types.

Grunt – An infantryman.

HE – High Explosive.

Hog Driver – A-10 pilot, derived from the A-10 nickname: "Warthog."

Hogs – More than one Warthog.

Hook – Derivative of the proper name for the CH-47 "Chinook" helicopter.

HUD – Heads Up Display: projection of communication, navigation and weapons information onto a glass pane immediately in front of the pilot.

Huey – Nickname for Bell UH-1B/C/D/H utility helicopter: they did it all in Vietnam.

Hump – infantry movement carrying large rucksacks.

In Country – In Vietnam.

IP – Instructor Pilot or Initial Point for a nuclear bomb run.

JCS – Joint Chiefs of Staff.

Jolly Greens – US Air Force CH-3 / HH-3 helicopters used in Search And Rescue (SAR) and Special Operations events.

JM – Jumpmaster for parachute operations.

JMPI – Jump Master Personal Inspection – a detailed, procedural inspection by a JM of a paratrooper and his equipment before he can board an aircraft to jump.

JSOC – Joint Special Operations Command.

JSTARS – The Northrop Grumman E-8 Joint Surveillance Target Attack Radar System (Joint STARS) tracks ground vehicles and some aircraft, relays tactical information to ground and air theater commanders.

KIA – Killed In Action (friendly).

Klick – slang for a kilometer.

Konya - Gunnery Range, airbase and city, in central Turkey.

LBE – Load Bearing Equipment – to attach, canteens, ammo pouches, compass, etc.

L.T. – nickname for a Lieutenant (usually Army type).

LANGLEY AFB, Hampton, Virginia. Home of Air Combat Command, 1st Fighter Wing, and NASA Langley Research Center; the historical name is "Langley Field."

LANGLEY, VIRGINIA – Home of the Agency.

LZ – Landing Zone for one / multiple helicopters used for insertion of combat troops.

MAC – Military Airlift Command, owner of all transport aircraft.

MACV – Military Advisory Command, Vietnam. US headquarters in Vietnam.

Mad Minute – a coordinated concentration of all small arm weapons fire by a unit at one time to test all weapons or to clear an area of suspected enemy.

NCA - National Command Authority - the President, Vice President or Chairman of the JCS.

Medevac – Generic term for helicopters used to evacuate the wounded or killed.

Mister Charles – respectful name for VC or NVA when they are good.

NVA – North Vietnamese Army.

NVG – Night Vision Goggles.

Nuke – a noun or verb regarding a nuclear weapon of varying yields. Also: Silver Bullet.

PAR – Precision Approach Radar – radar approach guidance to landing via radio.

Puff, The Magic Dragon: (AKA "Spooky") – USAF AC-47 gunship with side firing miniguns. Very effective in night close air support of ground troops in contact.

PZ – A Pickup Zone for helicopters used in the extraction of combat troops. See LZ.

QL1 – Vietnam's major north – south paved coastal highway goes from Hanoi to Saigon.

R&R – Rest and Recuperation - three to seven days rest at a secure resort area.

RAF Bentwaters and RAF Woodbridge, Suffolk, England – closed July 1993.

RBS – Radar Bomb Scoring. Computed score of simulated bomb drop.

Redleg – Nickname for US Army artillery personnel and units.

REMF – Rear Echelon Mother F**ker: Non-combat soldier serving in a safe rear area.

Revetment – Three-sided protective walls: metal filled with dirt to protect aircraft or stacked sand bags.

ROMAD – Radio Operator Maintainer And Driver – enlisted member of the TACP. Some trained to be Enlisted Terminal Attack Controllers (ETACs) capable of employing air power without an AF officer's supervision.

RPD - Ruchnoy Pulemyot Degtyaryova, is a very rapid fire 7.62mm light machine gun.

RPG – rocket propelled grenade.

RTFCL - Pilot shorthand for "Read The Fuckin Check List.

RVN – Republic of Vietnam (South Vietnam).

SAR – Search and Rescue operations by various air and ground assets, primarily for downed aircrew members. Later named Combat SAR or "CSAR."

Sapper - an elite combat engineer in the United States Army. In Vietnam usually refers to an NVA/VC carrying explosives to penetrate or destroy defenses and positions.

SEATAC – Seattle – Tacoma International Airport, Washington.

SERE – Survival, Evasion, Resistance, and Escape training.

SERTS - Screaming Eagle Replacement Training School in Vietnam, at Phan Rang.

SF - US Army Special Forces. AKA "Green Berets." US Army component of US Special Operations Forces (SOF). 5th SF Group was the primary SF unit in Vietnam. Experts in unconventional warfare.

SHAW AFB, Sumter, South Carolina.

SLICK – A cargo or troop-carrying Huey / Blackhawk. No offensive armament on board.

Snake – AH-1 Cobra, tandem two-seat attack helo, used by the US Army, then USMC.

Snake and Nape – High-drag 250 or 500 lb bombs (Snake-eyes) and napalm.

SOAR – US Army Special Operations Aviation Regiment, the "Night Stalkers."

T-39 – US military training and executive transport, 1959 – 1981.

T-41 - Military version of a Cessna 172 used in USAF basic pilot training 1964 – 1997.

TAC – Air Force Tactical Air Command at Langley AFB, Virginia. Named later changed to Air Combat Command (ACC) on 1 June 1992.

TACAIR – Attack fixed wing propeller or jet fighters from Air Force, Navy or Marines.

TACP – Tactical Air Control Party. See ALO.

TASS – Tactical Air Support Squadron. home unit for FACs and ALOs.

Thud – F-105 "Thunderchief" fighter – bomber. Designed as a nuclear, supersonic bomber; the Thud was converted to a tactical bomber and anti-SAM attack aircraft.

Tiger Force – a small reconnaissance unit of 1st Bn, 327th Infantry, 101st Airborne Div.

TJ – Torrejon AB, Spain - transferred to the Spanish AF in 1992.

TOC – Tactical Operations Center.

TRADOC – US Army Training and Doctrine Command, Ft Monroe, Virginia.

Tweet – Air Force T-37 basic flying training aircraft. 1957 – 2009.

USAFA – US Air Force Academy at Colorado Springs, CO.

USNA – U.S. Naval Academy at Annapolis, Md.

VC – South Vietnamese communists; Viet Cong; see "Charlie."

Warthog – A-10 nickname.

Wild Weasels – Air Force aircraft tasked to locate and attack enemy SAMs and AAA sites. Large testicles required for F-105, F-4 or F-16 "Weasel" crews.

WSO – Weapons System Operator in an F-4, F-15E or F-111.

WTFO – What The Fuck Over?

XP – Air Force office symbol for the Plans section.

YGBSM – You Gotta Be Shittin' Me.

Zoomie – AF Academy cadet or graduate.

BOTH SIDES NOW
By Ms. Joni Mitchell

Rows and flows of angel hair
And ice cream castles in the air
And feather canyons everywhere,
I've looked at clouds that way.

But now they only block the sun,
They rain and snow on everyone
So many things I would have done,
But clouds got in my way.

I've looked at clouds from both sides now
From up and down and still somehow
It's cloud's illusions I recall
I really don't know clouds at all

Moons and Junes and Ferris wheels,
The dizzy dancing way you feel
As When every fairy tale comes real,
I've looked at love that way.

But now it's just another show,
You leave 'em laughing when you go
And if you care, don't let them know,
Don't give yourself away.

I've looked at love from both sides now
From give and take win and lose and still somehow
It's love's illusions I recall
I really don't know love at all

Tears and fears and feeling proud,
To say "I love you" right out loud
Dreams and schemes and circus crowds,
I've looked at life that way.

But now old friends are they're acting strange,
They shake their heads, they say I've changed
Well something's lost, but something's gained
In living every day.

I've looked at life from both sides now
From win and lose and still somehow
It's life's illusions I recall
I really don't know life at all

I've looked at life from both sides now
From up and down, and still somehow
It's life's illusions I recall
I really don't know life at all

AUTHOR ACKNOWLEGMENTS

Foremost, I want to acknowledge my wonderful bride, Claire, who kept me motivated to complete the book, through the highs and lows of writing and publishing.

My sincerest thanks for the motivation provided by every man and woman who puts on the uniform of the United States armed forces. Part of this book is for you. Special thanks go out to those warriors who leap out of aircraft or hurl their craft "through the great spaces in the sky". I have no words to express my bond with and admiration for those in the Special Operations Forces.

A great thanks to Air Force Colonel (Retired) Steve Alderman, a fellow Hog Driver, who started every greeting with "How's the book coming"?

Thanks also to my primary proof reader, John Boswell, who has eyes as sharp as a hungry eagle, also Dan Foley and Vietnam Brother Ken Pfeiffer.

And a deep "Thank You" goes to my patient editor, Ms. Donna Peacock, who taught me how much I did not know about writing.

Photo credits
Page 14: Fox Ford; Page 42: Hiromichi Mine, United Press International; Page 60: US Army Medical Department Museum; Page 140: Wick Fowler, *Dallas Morning News*; Page 156: Zavell Smith Photographers, San Antonio, Texas; Page 399: Claire R. Stevenson. All other photos are from the Author's collection

ABOUT THE AUTHOR

Photo by Claire Rhodes Stevenson

Born the second of identical twins to a decorated former Army officer, Colonel Steve Stevenson was commissioned a Second Lieutenant, Infantry, in the Regular Army and assigned to the 101st Airborne Division at Fort Campbell and then Vietnam. After combat tours as a "Grunt" and then a Green Beret, he transferred to the Air Force to become an F-4 Phantom pilot, an A-10 Warthog driver and all around "Joint" Special Operations type. He commanded Infantry Platoon and Company, Air Force Squadron and Wing levels. He served as TAC Director of Joint Matters with the Army, Navy and Marine Corps staffs. Steve retired from the Air Force Special Operations Command, flew as Chief Pilot for a Petroleum Corporation, and then joined a national financial management company in San Antonio, Texas. Retired from the corporate world, Steve lives in Bulverde, Texas, and is still married to Claire, his wonderful bride of over 46 years. They have two grown sons.

Made in the USA
Middletown, DE
24 December 2017